# FRANCESCO PETRARCA
## POET AND HUMANIST

"In the time that the morning did strow Roses and Violets in the heavenly floor against the coming of the Sun."

SIR PHILIP SIDNEY, *Arcadia*.

Music
Melozzo da Forli.

# FRANCESCO PETRARCA
POET AND HUMANIST

BY
MAUD F. JERROLD

KENNIKAT PRESS
Port Washington, N. Y./London

FRANCESCO PETRARCA

First published in 1909
Reissued in 1970 by Kennikat Press
Library of Congress Catalog Card No: 78-103195
SBN 8046-0832-6

Manufactured by Taylor Publishing Company     Dallas, Texas

TO MY FRIEND

EVELYN BROWNE

IN MEMORY OF MANY DELIGHTFUL READINGS

# PREFACE

THE central idea of this book has been to present Petrarca in a twofold aspect, as Poet and Humanist, in such a manner that the one should not obscure the other.

For a long time, Petrarca's fame may be said to have rested almost entirely on his vernacular poetry; but as he, perhaps more than any other poet, suffered grievously at the hands of his imitators, who, failing to attain his perfection of form and faultless melody, fell into and exaggerated all his faults of taste, he gradually came to be less highly esteemed. On the other hand, his Latin works, on which he chiefly prided himself, have attracted an increasing amount of attention, so that, in our own time, Petrarca, as scholar and humanist, has again occupied a foremost place, while his claims as a poet are, perhaps, beginning to receive less recognition.

We have, nevertheless, this advantage over Petrarca's students in the past, that we can now read his Italian lyrics in the definite form and shape in which he desired to leave them to the world. The first truly critical edition of the *Rime*, published by Giovanni Mestica in 1896, may, without exaggeration, be said to mark an epoch in this respect. More recently, for the lyrical poems alone, we have had two admirable editions: that of Carducci and Ferrari in 1899, and that of Salvo-Cozzo in 1904; while all that can be accomplished for the text of the *Trionfi* has been done by Carl Appel in 1901.

For Petrarca as a Humanist, I am naturally especially indebted to the works of Voigt (*Die Wiederbelebung des classischen Alterthums*, 2 vols., 1893) and of Koerting (*Petrarkas Leben und Werke*, 1878), and, above all, to the masterly study of M. Pierre de Nolhac (*Pétrarque et l'Humanisme*, 2 vols., 1907, new edition).

Among other writers on Petrarca, under one or other aspect, I have found Alessandro d'Ancona, Carlo Segrè, Bonaventura Zumbini, and M. Henri Cochin particularly helpful and suggestive.

For the text of the *Rime*, I follow Carducci and Ferrari throughout, and have adopted their system of numeration; in the case of the *Trionfi*, I quote from Appel's critical edition. In dealing with the Latin letters, Fracassetti's translation, in spite of its manifest shortcomings, has been of much service; but I have gone direct to the Latin text— my references for the *Epistolæ de Rebus Familiaribus et Variæ* being to his edition of that text (3 vols., 1859-1863), while, in the case of the *Epistolæ de Rebus Senilibus* and the *Epistolæ sine Titulo*, I refer to the edition of the *Opera Omnia*, published at Venice in 1501. I quote the Latin poems from Domenico Rossetti's three-volume edition published in 1829.

I wish to thank my brother, the Reverend Lionel Goodrich, and my friend, Miss Browne, for much kind help and advice; and also to acknowledge my great indebtedness to my friend, Mr. Edmund Gardner, for invaluable assistance in every part of my work.

M. F. J.

*August 4, 1909.*

# CONTENTS

| CHAP. | | PAGE |
|---|---|---|
| I. | INTO BONDAGE | 1 |
| II. | HEIGHTS AND DEPTHS | 25 |
| III. | LAURELS | 47 |
| IV. | THE WORLD OF POLITICS | 70 |
| V. | LA JOYA DE LA VIOLETA | 109 |
| VI. | "IN GRACIOUS TWILIGHTS" | 147 |
| VII. | THE COMPANY OF THE GREAT | 166 |
| VIII. | IN THE FOOTSTEPS OF CICERO | 191 |
| IX. | THE EUGANEAN HILLS | 217 |
| X. | THE CROWN OF VIOLETS | 248 |
| XI. | IN PETRARCA'S SCHOOL | 293 |
| XII. | THE TWOFOLD CORONAL | 324 |
| | BIBLIOGRAPHY | 335 |
| | INDEX | 345 |

# LIST OF ILLUSTRATIONS

Music. By Melozzo da Forlì (*National Gallery*) . . *Frontispiece*

Triumphus Cupidinis.—Fifteenth-century Florentine Engraving . . . . . . . *Facing page* 64

Triumphus Pudicitiæ. Fifteenth-century Florentine Engraving . . . . . . . . ,, 144

Triumphus Mortis. Fifteenth-century Florentine Engraving . . . . . . . . ,, 158

Rhetoric. By Melozzo da Forlì (*National Gallery*) . ,, 190

Triumphus Famæ. Fifteenth-century Florentine Engraving . . . . . . . . ,, 240

Triumphus Temporis. Fifteenth-century Florentine Engraving . . . . . . . . ,, 288

Triumphus Æternitatis. Fifteenth-century Florentine Engraving . . . . . . . . ,, 322

# FRANCESCO PETRARCA
## POET AND HUMANIST

### CHAPTER I

INTO BONDAGE

"The allotted bondman of her palm and wreath."
D. G. ROSSETTI.

IT is strange indeed that Florence, that "fairest and most famous daughter of Rome," should have despoiled herself of glory in exiling her greatest sons. The fateful year 1302 which made Dante, as he proudly said, a citizen of the world (*nos autem cui mundus est patria*) saw also the banishment of his friend and fellow-townsman, Ser Petracco di Parenzo. This man was a notary whose ancestors had borne an honourable name and filled important posts. Petracco himself was chancellor of the *Riformagioni*, and at the time of his exile had just married Eletta Canigiani, whose family had also held public offices.[1] Having, like Dante, attached himself to the party of the White Guelfs, he, in company with about six hundred others, was driven out by the rival faction and, under a false charge of corruption, was forbidden to re-enter the city without the loss of his hand and the payment of a heavy fine.[2] He fled with his wife to Arezzo, and there two years later, on July 20, 1304, a little son, Francesco, was born, at the very moment when the father was taking part in the ill-starred attempt upon Florence, of which Villani, as an eye-witness, has

[1] Cf. G. O. Corazzini, *La Madre di Francesco Petrarca*.
[2] Cf. O. Zenatti, *Dante e Firenze*, Appendice vii. pp. 510-518.

given such a graphic account, showing how every possible mistake of time, and place, and circumstance was made, and pointing the moral to his own satisfaction that " to whom God wills ill, from him He takes all wit and judgment."[1] Certain it is that the expedition spelled failure and the hopes of the party came to an end.

Meanwhile to the little Francesco life began in turmoil; the restlessness which characterised his whole history haunted his cradle also. He was only seven months old when he was taken by his mother to Incisa, where they had a small property, about fourteen miles from Florence, and on the journey he was almost drowned in the Arno.[2] At Incisa other children were born, one who died in infancy, and one son, Gherardo, of whom there is much to be known. There is also a shadowy sister, Selvaggia, whose existence has been called in question, since she certainly did not leave Italy with her parents, and Petrarca nowhere makes the smallest allusion to her. On the other hand, she may have been left to be brought up by relations in Florence, and there is mention of her marriage with Giovanni di Tano di Semifonte in 1324, and that a considerable sum was employed for her dowry.[3]

Neither was Incisa destined to be a permanent resting-place, for when Francesco was only six years old the coming of the emperor, Henry VII., awakened new hopes in the breasts of the Florentine exiles, and Petracco hastened with his family to Pisa to await events. Occupying precisely the same political position as Dante, the same desires being no doubt alive in both, Petracco, also " exul immeritus," looked to Henry to open to him the gates of Florence. It is likely that Dante was at Pisa at this time, and this then would have been the scene of Francesco's one meeting with him which we know from himself did take place. In a letter to Boccaccio, he describes Dante as " a man whom I

[1] G. Villani, lib. viii. cap. 72.     [2] *De Reb. Fam. Præfatio.*
[3] L. Bruni, *Vita del Petrarca;* G. B. Baldelli, *Del Petrarca,* pp. 189-191.

only saw once and that in the first years of my childhood. He was contemporaneous with my grandfather and my father, but was younger than my grandfather and older than my father, with whom on one same day and by the same whirlwind of civic faction he was driven out from his country. And as it often happens in such cases among companions in misfortune that great friendships are contracted, so more particularly it fell out between these two, who, besides a similar lot, had also a great resemblance in their pursuits and in their mental disposition." [1]

The Pisan sojourn was but a short one, occupying probably only a few months, and in 1312 the family moved to Avignon, which, since it had been made the seat of the Papacy, was fast becoming a centre for Italians of every description—exiles, malcontents, and place-hunters. Going by way of Genoa and Marseilles, they made another perilous journey of which Petrarca writes thus:—

"My Tuscan wanderings ended at Pisa. Torn thence again in the seventh year of my age, and conveyed by the sea-journey into France, I suffered shipwreck from the winter storms not far from Marseilles, and narrowly escaped being again called back from the very threshold of youth." [2]

Writing in 1368 to Guido Settimo, then Archbishop of Genoa, Petrarca reminds him of the earliest events of their lives which resulted for them in a lasting friendship:—

" At that age, which is the borderland between infancy and childhood, we were both transplanted at almost the same time into transalpine Gaul.. . . . and, united at once by such a friendship as that age allows (which, however, will endure until death), we entered on the path of life together. . . . The goal of our childhood's journey was Avignon; but, since the town was small for the Roman Pontiff and the Church which with him had but newly wandered thither, poor at that time in houses, and overflowing with inhabitants, our elders determined that the

[1] *De Reb. Fam.* xxi. 15.      [2] *Ibid. Præf.*

women and children should move to a neighbouring spot. We two, then boys, went with the others, but were sent to a different destination, namely, to the schools of Latin. Carpentras was the name of the place, a small city, but the capital of a little province. Do you remember those four years? What happiness we had there, what safety, what peace at home, what liberty abroad, what leisure and what silence in the fields. You, I am certain, feel the same. As for me, I am still grateful to that time; nay, rather, I am grateful to the Author of all times who gave me that so tranquil epoch, that, without any storm of external things, as far as the weakness of my mind allowed, I might suck the tender milk of childish learning and thereby grow strong to take nourishment of more solid food." [1]

Convenevole, the master of the school at Carpentras, is a pathetic figure, and his career, alas! does not stand without a parallel in the history of teaching. A schoolmaster for sixty years, he failed even to make a competence, and died in abject poverty at his native city of Prato, when his fellow-citizens paid him the empty honour of a magnificent funeral, and called upon Petrarca to write his epitaph. How much the illustrious pupil owed to his master it would be difficult to say, but Convenevole was, at any rate, stimulating and appreciative. He was probably more deficient in method than in scholarship; he had a passion for writing, but nothing was ever brought to a conclusion. He wasted his time on introductions, headings, and notes, but left nothing complete except a treatise on the Fourteen Virtues, and a poem addressed to King Robert of Naples, calling on him to redress the woes of Rome. It is possible that Petrarca drew a little inspiration from this; at any rate, it is not wholly unimportant that he should have had a poet for his teacher.[2] Here is his own account of the matter:—

"I had, almost from my infancy, a master who first

[1] *Rer. Sen.* x. 2.
[2] Cf. A. d'Ancona, *Convenevole da Prato* (*Studj sulla Letteratura Italiana*).

taught me to read and afterwards taught me Latin and rhetoric, for he was of such merit as a professor and teacher of both that I have never known his equal—in the theoretical part, I mean, but by no means in the practical, like the whetstone of Horace which can sharpen steel but not cut. He, for full sixty years, as it is reported, kept school, and the number of pupils that in so long a time the generous man had is easier to imagine than to state. Among them were many men distinguished for learning and position; professors of law, to wit, masters of divinity, bishops, abbots, and finally a cardinal to whom I, as a boy, was dear for my father's sake; a man not greater in position and fortune (albeit he was Bishop of Ostia) than in prudence and learning.[1] And among so many great men, that good master of mine, strange to say, loved me the most who was the least of all. This was known to every one, neither did he make any secret of it; and on this account Cardinal Giovanni Colonna of blessed memory used to joke with him; for he delighted in the conversation of this simple old man and excellent grammarian, and would ask him when he came to visit him: 'Tell me, master, among so many great scholars of yours whom I know you love, is there some place for our Francesco?' And he, with his eyes full of tears, either kept silence or went away, or, if he could speak, would solemnly swear that he had never loved any of them all so much as poor wretched me! As long as my father lived he helped him generously, for poverty and old age, importunate and difficult companions, were pressing on him. After my father's death, he placed all his hopes on me. But I, albeit little able, feeling myself nevertheless bound by faith and duty, helped him to the utmost of my resources; so that, when money fell short (as was frequent), I succoured his poverty among my friends by standing

---

[1] This was Niccolò da Prato, whom Benedict XI. sent as legate to Florence to try and establish peace. Cf. Villani, lib. viii. 69, etc. A letter formerly attributed to Dante is addressed to him (*Oxford Dante*, ep. i.).

surety or by prayers, and with the usurers by pledges. Thousands of times he took from me for this purpose books and other things, which he always brought back to me until poverty drove out fidelity. Hampered more than ever, he treacherously took from me two volumes of Cicero, one of which had been my father's, and the other a friend's,[1] and other books, pretending that they were necessary to him for a work of his. For he used daily to be beginning some book, and he would make a magnificent frontispiece and a consummate preface (which although it stands first in the book is wont to be composed last), and then he would transfer his unstable imagination to some other work. But why do I thus prolong the tale? When the delay began to arouse my suspicions (for I had lent him the books for study, not to relieve his indigence), I asked him point-blank what had happened to them, and hearing that they had been put in pawn, I besought him to tell me who it was who had them, that I might redeem them. Tearful and full of shame, he refused to do this, protesting that it would be too disgraceful to him if another should do what was his bounden duty: if I would wait a little longer, he would fulfil his duty quickly. Then I offered him all the money which the transaction required, and this also he refused, begging me to spare him such a disgrace. Though trusting little to his promise, I held my tongue, being unwilling to give sorrow to him whom I loved. In the meanwhile, driven by his poverty, he returned to Tuscany whence he had come, and I, remaining in my transalpine solitude near the source of the Sorgue, as I was wont to do, did not know that he had gone away, until I knew of his death by the request of his fellow-citizens that I would write an epitaph to be placed on the tomb of him whom they had tardily honoured by bearing him to the grave crowned with laurel. Nor afterwards, in spite of every diligence, could I ever find even the least trace of the lost Cicero, for the other

[1] Cf. *Rer. Sen.* xv. 1.

books mattered to me much less, and thus I lost books and master together." [1]

And here we ought to notice Petrarca's precocious admiration for Cicero, of which he gives an account in the present letter:—

"From my earliest childhood," he writes, "when all others desire Prosper or Esop, I brooded over the books of Cicero, either from natural sympathy or because of the encouragement of my father who was a great worshipper of that author, and would himself have mounted high if domestic cares had not distracted his noble mind, and compelled the man who was banished from his country, and burdened by a family, to direct his thoughts to other objects than study. At that time I could understand nothing; but nevertheless the sweetness and the sonorous sound of the words so held me captive that every other book that I read or listened to appeared to me to ring harsh and discordant. For a child, as I was, I must confess this was not a childish judgment; if one can call that a judgment which is not founded upon reason; and certainly it is wonderful that, understanding nothing, I felt then just what I feel now, when, although it may be only a little, I at least understand something. This desire grew in me from day to day, and the kindness of my father, who wondered at it, promoted for a while my immature devotion." [2]

Thus, from the very first, is perceived the poet's fine sense of sound, which he possessed not only as touching the singing quality of words and measures, which was the distinguishing mark of his own poetry and the note of his acute admiration for the work of others; but this was allied

---

[1] *Rer. Sen.* xv. 1. In this letter Petrarca clearly states that the friend was Raimondo Soranzio and the book the *De Gloria* of Cicero. Cf. also A. d'Ancona, *op. cit.* pp. 114, 115. On the other hand, M. de Nolhac demonstrates that no trace of the work existed in the fifteenth century, and that it was most unlikely that the poet had ever possessed it. Cf. *Pétrarque et l'Humanisme*, tom. i. pp. 261-268.

[2] *Rer. Sen.* xv. 1.

in him with an exquisite musical ear and sense of harmony, so that singing to his lute became one of his favourite pastimes. His change of name from Petracco to Petrarca has been attributed to his craving for harmonious sounds, but it was, of course, in accordance with the Latinising taste of his time.

Only one incident of the life at Carpentras has come down to us, and Francesco relates it in the letter already quoted to Guido Settimo, asking him if he does not remember one day among their delightful school-days " when my father and your uncle, being then about the age that we are now, came, as was their wont, to the little town of Carpentras, and a desire, arising I think from the nearness of the place and the newness of it to him, seized your uncle, as a stranger, to see the renowned source of the Sorgue, which, famous of old for its own sake (if it be permissible to boast of a small thing to a friend, that is, to oneself), has become somewhat more famous through my long sojourn there at a later date and through my poems. A childish longing made us anxious to be taken too, and as it was thought that we should not be safe on horseback, there was assigned to each of us a servant to ride the horses and hold us fast on the saddle. Now after having at last obtained leave, with many fears and admonitions from the most affectionate mother in the world (mine by nature and yours also by love), we set out in company with that man whose memory is so dear to me, and whom you, bearing the same name and surname, have surpassed in learning and fame. And when we had reached the source of the Sorgue, I, being impressed by the unwonted beauty of the place (for I remember it as if it were to-day), said among those childish thoughts of mine as well as I could: ' Here is a place most suited to my nature which, if I am able, I shall some day prefer to the most famous city.' This then I silently resolved with myself, and thus later, when I became a man, so far as the world did not envy my leisure,

I made this manifest by clear signs; for here, albeit often interrupted by business summoning me hence, and by the difficulty of my affairs, I passed many years, and in such peace, such sweetness, that I can truly say that, of all the time that I have lived, only what I spent here deserves the name of life, and the rest has been but continual torture." [1]

Petrarca's happy time at Carpentras came to an end in 1319, when he was torn from his beloved Ciceronian studies, and, together with his brother, Gherardo, and Guido Settimo, was sent to acquire law at Montpellier. He gives us himself the reason for this decision:—

"Through the overpowering desire of my making a living, they forced me into the study of civil law that I might learn the law concerning contracts and loans . . . and forget Cicero who describes the most salutary laws of life. It were truer to say that I utterly lost seven years, rather than that I spent them, in that study. And in order that you may hear a thing that will move you to laughter as well as to tears, I will tell you what once happened to me. Surely by a most ungenerous determination, all the books which I had been able to collect of Cicero and of some of the poets, as enemies to lucrative study, were in my very sight dragged out of the secret places in which I (fearing what soon came to pass) had hidden them, and committed to the fire as though they were the works of heretics—which spectacle I lamented as though I myself were being cast into the flames. Then my father, as I remember, seeing me so unhappy, straightway snatched two books, already half-scorched by the fire, and holding Virgil in the right hand and Cicero's Rhetoric in the left, he held out both to me, smiling as I wept. 'Keep this,' he said, 'for an occasional solace to your mind to help you in your legal studies.' And being comforted by these companions, so few but so great, I restrained my tears." [2]

Of these lost years Petrarca speaks again to Guido

[1] *Rer. Sen.* ix. 2.   [2] *Ibid.* xv. 1.

Settimo, reminding him how, after remaining four years at Montpellier, " we went to Bologna, than which I do not believe a freer and more beautiful place could be found in the whole world. You will remember the assembly of scholars, the order that was there, the vigilance of the professors whom one might have believed jurisconsults. . . . And how great then was the abundance of everything, so that already by long-established appellation Bologna was called *pinguis* by all lands." [1]

The reason of Petrarca's transfer from Montpellier to Bologna does not appear, but it was probably on account of the small progress that he made at the former place, and because it was hoped that the greater fame of the Bolognese professors would spur him on to effort. In his dedicatory letter to the friend whom he calls Socrates, he tells us that during the three years which he passed at Bologna he ran through the whole *Corpus juris civilis,* and that great hopes were entertained of his success if he would have persevered in his legal career. And this is the reason he gives for having abandoned it: " It was not because the authority of the laws did not appeal to me, for doubtless it is great, and full of that Roman antiquity in which I delight; but because the practice of them is corrupted by the wickedness of men; therefore I objected to learn what I would not use dishonestly and could scarcely use honestly, and, had I wished to do so, my uprightness would have been attributed to stupidity." [2]

There is a tradition, perpetuated by the Abbé de Sade, that one of Petrarca's masters at Bologna was Cino da Pistoia. This man of equal fame as poet and legist, and famous above all as the friend of Dante (who makes frequent mention of him in the *De Vulgari Eloquio*) and the author of the canzone on Beatrice's death, was intimately connected with Bologna, but was almost certainly not there during the time of Petrarca's studies. Cino, or Guittoncino

[1] *Rer. Sen.* x. 2.  [2] *Epist. ad Post.*

de' Sinibuldi, was born in 1270, at Pistoia. He studied jurisprudence in Bologna, and was afterwards judge in Pistoia, and he lectured at many universities. His greatest work was his *Lectura* on the Codex of Justinian, in which he displayed a liberal spirit and a great independence of thought.[1] It was on the completion of this commentary that he received the *laurea dottorale* at Bologna, in 1314. Professor by turns at Treviso, Siena, and Perugia, there would have been nothing strange in his occupying a chair at Bologna, but the archives of the city contain no record of it. The confirmation of the fact is only to be found in a letter printed by A. F. Doni in his *Prose antiche*, purporting to be from Cino to Petrarca, and dated Bologna, February 20, 1329, in which Cino compliments the poet on his success as a law-student. " Learned Bologna," he writes, " mother of erudition, must hold your prodigious memory in everlasting remembrance, since in less than four years you had learned by heart the whole body of the most intricate civil laws, just as another would have learned the delightful romances of Lancelot and Guinevere." But he goes on to reproach him thus: " Letting yourself be deceived by the vain glory that poor, miserable Poetry promises to her followers, you have abandoned those true and lasting honours which the magnificent science of the law was able to give you." [2]

This is so little in character with anything we know of Cino that it is sufficient to discredit the authenticity of the letter, coupled with the fact that there is a reference in it to Petrarca's sojourn at Lombez, which did not take place until 1330.

But while giving up the relations of master and pupil, there is no doubt that both Petrarca and Boccaccio, like Dante before them, greatly admired Cino as a poet, and the former wrote a sonnet on his death, which begins:—

[1] Cf. Carl Witte, *Cino da Pistoia, Giurista*.
[2] A. F. Doni, *Prose antiche*, p. 78.

> Weep, ladies, Love shall also weep with you;
> And, lovers, weeping go through all the land,
> Since he is dead who well did understand,
> What time he lived, to give you honour due.[1]

Cecco d'Ascoli is another poet who is said to have taught Petrarca.[2] He would seem to have been professor of astrology and philosophy at Bologna from 1322 to 1325, but, as Petrarca had a peculiar hatred of astrology, it is not likely that there was much sympathy between them. Cecco's poem, *L'Acerba*, is in five books and deals with physics, moral philosophy, and religion; it treats at great length of the stars and also of the qualities of gems, but, as there is nothing in the style to recommend it to Petrarca, and the matter was such as to have been extremely distasteful to him, we may regard the legend that he was the author of a sonnet beginning:—

> Tu sei il grand' Ascolan che'l mondo allumi,

as being wholly without foundation.

One celebrated master with whom Petrarca has been credited was Giovanni d'Andrea, called the Archdoctor of the Decretals, but it is now generally agreed that this great professor was absent from Bologna during the time of Francesco's studies, and the friendship, which undoubtedly existed between them, began most likely in 1328, when Giovanni was sent as ambassador to John XXII. by Bertrando del Poggetto, Cardinal-legate at Bologna.[3] The professor of civil law in 1324 was Raniero da Forlì, and under him Petrarca must certainly have studied, so it has been conjectured that the letters (*De Reb. Fam.* lib. iv. 15, 16) which De Sade and others have taken as addressed to Giovanni d'Andrea were really written to Raniero. But, though it is related of him that he was choleric and

---

[1] *Rime*, xcii.
[2] Cf. V. Paoletti, *Cecco d'Ascoli*, Bologna, 1905; G. Castelli, *Cecco d'Ascoli e Dante*, Rome, 1903.
[3] Cf. *De Reb. Fam.* iv. 16, Fracassetti's note, also *ibid.* v. 7, 8, 9.

contentious, there does not seem any evidence that this most famous professor was the victim of the egregious vanity for which his correspondent takes him to task with such amazing outspokenness; though it must also be said that this trait seems equally out of character with what we know of Giovanni d'Andrea. It was in answer to a reproach from one of these masters for having abandoned his legal studies that the poet wrote rather cleverly:—

" To the accusation that you bring against me of having deserted the service to which I had vowed myself because, when I was beginning to make some progress, I abandoned the study of law and Bologna, the answer is ready, albeit I do not think that it will prove acceptable to you who do so singularly adorn that city and those studies. . . . Nothing can succeed that is against nature; she made me a lover of solitude, not of the forum. In fine, be assured of this, that I have either never done anything prudently (as I rather think), or, if anything, this was primarily, I dare not say wisely, but happily done—that I saw Bologna and that I broke away from it." [1]

The primary cause of Petrarca's departure from Bologna was the death of his father, which took place on April 26, 1326, and Petracco's wife probably survived him only a few months: these, however, are much disputed chronological points.[2] The very indifferent epitaph which Francesco composed for his mother establishes the fact that her name was Eletta:—

Electa Dei tam nomine quam re.

---

[1] *De Reb. Fam.* iv. 16. For the question of Petrarca's masters at Bologna, cf. two articles of F. Lo Parco, *Dei Maestri canonisti attribuiti al Petrarca* (Revue des Bibliothèques, Paris, 1906), and *Pietro dei Cerniti Bolognese* (Giornale storico della Letteratura Italiana, vol. lii. Turin, 1908).

[2] Cf. *Epist. ad Post.* Fracassetti's note, pp. 216-222, and G. O. Corazzini, *op. cit.* Another view is that Eletta died about 1320, and that Ser Petracco then married Nicolosa di Vanni Segoli. Cf. F. Lo Parco, *Il Petrarca nel Casentino* (Rivista d'Italia, Aprile, 1906, Roma); as also for the question of the date of Petrarca's return to Avignon.

It also makes it fairly evident that her son was present at her death. With a fine arrogance he promises her immortality with himself:—

> Vivemus pariter, memorabimur ambo.

The affairs of the brothers, Francesco and Gherardo, were in anything but a prosperous condition. The little that their father had left behind was dissipated by the dishonesty of trustees, and Petrarca records that it was to their ignorance, not to their integrity, that he owed the only valuable thing that was left to him—a manuscript of Cicero.

It is difficult to reconcile the slender resources of the two with the manner of life they now affected, of which Francesco has left us more than one account. They both took the tonsure as the first means of opening a path of advancement through the Church, but as it was long before any advantage came to them from this, it is hard to see how they lived at all. Writing to Gherardo long afterwards, his brother reminds him of their habits at that time, when they were obviously trying to make an effect in society:—

"Do you remember that excessive display of most elegant attire which still, I confess, holds me captive, though growing less day by day? That trouble over putting on and putting off, a labour repeated morning and evening; that dread lest when, once arranged, our hair should get loose, or a light breeze should ruffle the elaborate arrangement of our locks; how we fled from advancing or retreating horses, lest our perfumed and brilliant raiment should receive any adventitious dirt. Truly how vain are the cares of men, but especially of youths! For to what purpose that anxiety of mind? That we might please, forsooth, the eyes of others. But whose eyes, prithee? Surely of many who displeased our eyes.... What of our shoes shall I say? See with how grievous and continuous a war they pressed that which they seemed to protect. . . . What shall I say of the curling-irons and the business of our hairdressing? How often did that labour put off our sleep, and then disturb it! What slave-driver would inflict more cruel tortures than we inflicted with our own hands? What nocturnal scars did we see in the morning in our mirror burned across our red foreheads, so that we, who wished to make a show of our hair, were compelled to cover our face." [1]

This is only a laughable picture of the foolishness of very young men, and no doubt Francesco, at any rate, had personal beauty in his favour, for, although he expressly disclaims it, his portrait, as drawn by himself, is a most attractive one. " I do not boast of remarkable beauty, but such as could please in the flower of youth; a bright complexion, between fair and dark, vivacious eyes, and sight that for a long time kept most keen." The characterisation of himself in the same letter is, perhaps, less taking. Of this period he writes: " Then I began to be known and my acquaintance to be sought by great men; but why, I now confess that I know not and wonder; then, forsooth, I did not wonder—for I seemed to myself, as is the fashion of youth, to be most worthy of all honour." [2] In later life Petrarca appears to have shared Browning's theory that " youth with its beauty and grace, would seem bestowed on us . . . to make us partly endurable till we have time for really becoming so of ourselves, without their aid."

It is thus evident that Petrarca was not free either from vanity or frivolity, but he has left a record of other and better inclinations. A life of society and admiration could neither fill nor satisfy a mind of his order; his taste for serious study now and always prevailed, procuring him valuable friendships; and the Italian poems which he had already begun to write were much commented on and

[1] *De Reb. Fam.* x. 3.   [2] *Epist. ad Post.*

praised. His real craving for the higher things of life is nowhere better set forth than in a letter which describes his intercourse with Giovanni da Firenze, a man who had been for fifty years one of the papal *scriptores*, and who yet found time to attain to a high degree of culture. Of him Petrarca writes:—

"In the early years of my youth there was living a venerable, grey-haired, old man, my fellow-citizen, remarkable for the austerity of his character, and more than ordinarily learned in letters, although he belonged to the flock of those who are called the pope's copyists, whom we appreciate more for their laboriousness than for their intellect. He held this office more than fifty years, and fulfilled it with much fidelity and diligence. His name was Giovanni and, because only his country gave him his surname, he was called " Of Florence "; and this, I think, was the origin of his love for me. . . . As often as he saw me, he would spur me on, and with fatherly kindness would incite my young mind to virtue, to knowledge, and, in the first place, to the love of God, without which, he would say, nothing can be done well, nay, assuredly, a man is nothing, however great learning and power he may possess. One day, in a meditative mood, I went by myself to see him, and found him alone and intent as usual on honourable studies; and that gentlest of men rejoiced at my coming. ' And what,' he said to me, ' is the reason that I see you weighed down with care more than is your wont? Am I mistaken, or has something new befallen?' Then I: ' Neither are you mistaken, excellent father, nor has any thing new befallen, but I am troubled and harassed by old things. For you know my labours, you know the cares of my mind, you know with what great zeal I have ever burned to lift myself above the multitude, and, so to speak, with Virgil and Ennius, have essayed that way by which I might raise myself too from the ground, and live victoriously on the lips of men. Nor has zeal or intention ever failed me, nor did ability seem to be lacking, to which, even if all else were absent, had not your testimony abundantly sufficed? How often in the hearing of men have you not given me signal praise for remarkable ability? . . . How often, taking me apart, have you not counselled me in a low voice to exercise such an intellect in good arts, and not to allow so great a gift of God and nature to grow dull by sloth. And I, with such a witness, strove on more confidently and nothing seemed difficult to me; I persevered, and spent all my hours in the pursuit of letters, so that none was wasted; and, not content with what I had done, I aimed assiduously at something new, soothing my labour with the thought that I was not toiling in vain, but I promised myself all that is great and splendid. And lo! without any intermission of study, whilst I thought gradually to attain to the heights, I feel myself sent down to the depths and the wonted fountain of my intellect dried up. Whence this unexpected curse I know not; what then seemed easy now seems impossible; where I ran without hesitating, now, coming to a halt and doubting about everything, I hardly walk. . . . I confess I know nothing . . . and seek counsel from no other but you.' He did not let me go on any longer, in my youthful fashion and not without tears, declaiming these and suchlike things; but: 'Do not,' he said, 'my son, do not, I beseech you, lose that time in complaints which ought to be employed in thanksgiving, for the thing is better than you think. You knew nothing as long as you seemed to yourself to know much; on the day that you grasped your ignorance, believe me, you made inestimable progress. Now, at length, you begin to know something when you believe yourself to know nothing. . . . For whoso ascends a mountain begins to see many things which, when at the foot, he neither saw nor believed worth heeding. Wherefore do you, who (as you say, and as I do not deny) entered on this path with my encouragement, go on with what you have begun, for I not only encourage but urge you to continue in it. God will help you, do not doubt." [1]

Another learned and venerable friend was Raimondo Soranzio, a famous jurist of Avignon. He had a fine library which he was always trying to increase, and he made Petrarca copy many manuscripts for him; in return for which service he placed his books entirely at Francesco's disposal, and not only lent but gave him many valuable works. Petrarca says of him that he was a venerable and excellent old man, who had good right to the name of jurist which is unjustly usurped by so many. He was learned in name and fact, with an admirable freedom and firmness of judgment; and with an invincible mind he upheld his arguments against the Roman Pontiff himself, so that, while many of less note than he were promoted to great honours, he alone had the glory of not mounting higher. Being primarily a great jurist, although he possessed a very rich library, he did not prize any books beside law-books, excepting only Livy. In this he took great delight, but, not being accustomed to read histories, though endowed with much talent, he found it difficult to understand. Petrarca tried to explain it to him, and, pleased with his help, Soranzio began to regard him rather as a son than a friend, and was beyond measure liberal to him. By him the poet's library was enriched with Varro and Cicero, and of the latter in one volume, among other works generally known, were the books *De Oratore* and *De Legibus*, imperfect as they are always found: and, besides these, the *De Gloria*, whose existence has been called in question.[2]

But the most influential friendship that Petrarca contracted at this time was that with Giacomo Colonna, of whom he makes frequent and enthusiastic mention in his letters. Their acquaintance dated from Petrarca's student-days in Bologna, when they seem to have been attracted to each other without making any close friendship. Giacomo

[1] *Rer. Sen.* xvi. 6.   [2] *De Reb. Fam.* xxiv. 1; *Rer. Sen.* xv. 1.

continued his studies for a longer period than the poet, and, being early made a bishop, he returned to Avignon and there met his former companion again, probably with surprise, as Petrarca tells us that at Bologna the intimacy had not progressed far enough for Giacomo to know who he was or whence he came. The strict inquiries which the bishop caused to be made concerning him must have proved satisfactory, as from this time Francesco lived on the most intimate terms with him. Everything he tells us of this man commands our admiration—his gentle and courteous manners, his quick wit combined with great modesty, his wisdom, courage, and firmness, make up an exceedingly attractive character; added to which he had the gift of great personal beauty and such dignity of bearing that merely seeing him in a crowd you would have said he was a prince.[1] Speaking of the Colonna family in the Letter to Posterity, Petrarca says that they lavished every sort of honourable welcome on him, such as he did not deserve, at any rate at that time, nor perhaps at any time. He then relates how Giacomo Colonna, Bishop of Lombez in Gascony, invited him to go thither, and how, in company with him and his friends, he passed a summer in such divine happiness that he cannot recall it to mind without sighs of longing.[2]

That sojourn, however, was not to take place until 1330, and long before that date another incident was to cause the poet to give utterance to " sighs of longing." It was on Good Friday, April 6, 1327, that Petrarca first saw Laura in the Church of Santa Chiara in Avignon. Her identity—indeed her very existence—has been called in question, but it seems most likely that she was Laura de Noves, wife of Hugues de Sade, whom she married in 1325, she being then about eighteen years old.[3] This meeting was destined to

---

[1] *Rev. Sen.* xv. 1.                    [2] *Epist. ad Post.*
[3] That this lady was Petrarca's Laura is better established by the facts about her death than by anything that is known of her life. The poet,

transform the poet's whole after-life; and yet, lovely and romantic as the story is, there is in it an element of disappointment, of shortcoming.

From the image of Petrarca and Laura it is impossible to dissociate the companion-picture of Dante and Beatrice —the greater poet and the diviner woman. All that has ever been revealed of the heights and depths of love, all that human language is capable of conveying, and far more than it ever expressed before, is enshrined in the poetry of Dante and ensphered in the vision of Beatrice. The great lovers of all ages to come will only be able to follow afar off, for that Lover and that Beloved reached such spiritual heights as others can hardly hope to attain, where Beauty was but the veil of the Divinity, and Love the worship of the Divine.

We must descend a very long way from this to reach the level on which Petrarca lived out his life-idyll. The most certain thing we know of Laura is her wonderful beauty, for which the poet felt a passionate, absorbing adoration, which did not permanently change but fluctuated, which accentuated the natural restlessness of his character, and brought him torment, ecstasy, and inspiration. All this we shall study presently in the Italian poems; but it is to be remembered that from this year, 1327, the poet's life is coloured by his love; and his actions, his motives, and decisions cannot be understood apart from it.

It was in the summer of 1330, as has been said,

who entered both the day of his first vision of her (to wit April 6) and the day of her death on the fly-leaf of his Virgil, records also that she was buried on that same day in the year 1348 in the Church of the Friars Minor. In this church is the mortuary chapel of the House of Sade, whose archives record that Laura, wife of Hugues de Sade, who made her will on April 3, 1348, and wrote therein: *Eligo sepulturam corpori meo in Ecclesia Fratrum Minorum Civitatis Avinionis*, died on April 6, and was buried the same day in the Church of the Friars Minor. Cf. *Mémoires pour la Vie de Pétrarque*, par l'Abbé de Sade, vol. ii. pp. 460, 461, and vol. iii. Pièces justificatives, viii.

that Petrarca accompanied Giacomo Colonna to Lombez. Writing an account of this after the lapse of forty-four years, he attributes his invitation partly to the keen interest the Bishop took in vernacular poetry, and says with what promptitude and obedience he entered his service, and that no summer has ever appeared more delightful to him. He also relates how on his return Giacomo presented him to the other members of his family, to Giovanni, the eminent and blameless Cardinal, to all his other brothers, and to Stefano, his father. Stefano Colonna came to Avignon in 1331 to visit his two sons, but soon returned to Rome. Another member of the family who made a longer stay was Giovanni di San Vito, lord of Gensano, brother of Stefano, and uncle of the Cardinal and the Bishop. He had travelled in Persia, Arabia, and Egypt, and was learned in the history and the manners of those countries, but his passion was for Rome and things Roman, and he was subsequently a valuable guide to Petrarca, whom he now began to know and love like a son. To amuse him the poet wrote a comedy called *Filologia;* we can imagine it must have been rather a dreary work, and the author was careful not to preserve it. Questioned about it in later life, he owned to having composed it when he was very young, but says that he made no account of it and did not consider it worthy of attention.[1]

The summer at Lombez was important, among other things, for the formation of two of the greatest friendships of Petrarca's life, and no man ever had more than he the genius for friendship. His friends not only evoked the noblest part of him, but they may be said in some sort to have created it. They called the highest thoughts into being, furnished him with inspiration, set him on new paths. And, with the imagination of the poet, he was independent of their immediate presence, he could associate himself with them at a distance, and absence seemed no

[1] *De Reb. Fam.* ii. 7; vii. 16. Also cf. P. de Nolhac, *op. cit.* i. pp. 189, 190.

obstacle. Through his friends he lived a higher and completer life; they called him up to heights he could not otherwise have reached; his heart, and in great measure his genius, would have been starved without them.

At Lombez, then, Petrarca made the acquaintance of two men who were installed as inmates of the house. One of these was Lodovico di Campinia, a Fleming, from the neighbourhood of Bois-le-duc, whom, on account of his intellect and culture, Francesco elected to call Socrates, and to whom he dedicated his long series of Familiar Letters in a special prefatory epistle. Writing of him after his death, Petrarca states that from the first moment of their meeting they became one, and that never for a moment did this friend's love and faith towards him diminish. He regards this as a wonderful thing in a man who was born in a barbarous country, but says that their long intercourse, their life together, and above all the strength of their mutual love, had so steeped Socrates in Italian ways and tastes that it seemed as though Italy had given him birth since she alone possessed his heart. Francesco adds that he experienced an immense delight on account of this remarkable transmutation of nature and habits, regarding it as an honour to himself, since Socrates had set his affections on him more than on any other human being.[1] And in a letter addressed to him, Petrarca again expatiates on the difference of country which could make no separation between two people who loved each other so much, and concludes: " I gave you a name which should correspond with the seriousness of your habits and the gentleness of your manners . . . and you were called our Socrates." [2]

The other friendship formed at Lombez was with Lello or Lelio, son of Piero di Stefano, a Roman gentleman, whom Petrarca called Lælius after the two men of that name who were friends of Scipio Africanus. After the Bishop's death, Lælius entered the service of Cardinal

[1] *Rer. Sen.* i. 3.  [2] *De Reb. Fam.* ix. 2.

Colonna, and on his decease returned to Rome, but his intimacy with the poet remained unbroken for thirty-four years, when, bewailing his death, Petrarca writes: " He was unique in the world for intellect, eloquence, and virtue." [1]

Of the intimacy which followed on his introduction to Cardinal Colonna, Petrarca says: " I lived under him for many years, not as under a master but under a father—nay, not even that, but as with a most affectionate brother, or indeed as though I had been in my own home."[2]

It would be hard to overrate the advantages which must have accrued from this residence. Member of one of the most illustrious Roman families, held in the highest repute at the papal court, distinguished alike by birth and personal endowments, the Cardinal made his palace the centre of all that was learned, famous, and virtuous. No one of any note passed through the city without visiting it, and thus Petrarca must have become known to an enormous circle, and must have attracted the attention of all those whose interest was worth gaining. The poet's position in the household seems to have been that of a kind of chaplain, and he also concerned himself with the education of Agapito Colonna, a young cousin of his patron, to whom he subsequently wrote of the trouble he had taken to assist and direct his noble intellect to a sublime goal.[3]

In a place of such profuse luxury, the Colonna household must have stood out in noble contrast to its surroundings. Magnificence, no doubt, there was, but without extravagance or ostentation. The Cardinal's first pride was that he was an Italian, and loved all that belonged to Italy; Petrarca's Italian poems were what first won his heart. And following close on his taste for poetry was his devotion to literature of all kinds. His library had his first attention; he was a diligent collector, and had manuscripts carefully copied and collated; he studied much, and would always have a book read aloud to him at dinner. Among

---
[1] *Rer. Sen.* i. 3.   [2] *Epist. ad Post.*   [3] *De Reb. Fam.* xx. 8.

visitors of distinction came Richard de Bury, sent on an embassy by Edward III.; he was called the most learned man in England, and was the author of the famous little work, *Philobiblon*, in which many wise things are said about the love of books—a love which was so alive in Petrarca's soul that the two men have written things on the subject which are almost word for word alike.

" All the glory of the world would be buried in oblivion unless God had provided mortals with the remedy of books." And: " All who are smitten with the love of books think cheaply of the world and wealth." These are some of the gems we may pick out of the *Philobiblon*. Like Petrarca, Richard took a special interest in geography and maps, and the only conversation recorded between the two authors relates to the legendary island of *Ultima Thule*, the poet requesting to be told where it lay. Richard discreetly replied that he could not answer the question without his books, but that he would write—which he never did![1] He is said to have made two visits to Avignon, but the first was very brief, and it is probable that the meeting with Petrarca belongs to his second sojourn in 1333: he died in 1345, and is honourably remembered as a man " who loved books in an age and country when people loved them so little."[2]

This same love of books contributed largely to send Petrarca forth on his first travels.

[1] *De Reb. Fam.* iii. 1.
[2] *Philobiblon*, edited and translated by E. C. Thomas, London, 1888.

## CHAPTER II

### HEIGHTS AND DEPTHS

" I am a wanderer: I remember well
One journey, how I feared the track was missed,
So long the city I desired to reach
Lay hid; when suddenly its spires afar
Flashed through the circling clouds; you may conceive
My transport. Soon the vapours closed again,
But I had seen the city."
R. BROWNING, *Paracelsus*.

LOVE of change, love of books, curiosity to see new places and hear new things, a great feeling for natural beauty, and the dire necessity of distracting his mind from his hopeless passion for Laura—all these causes combined to make Petrarca set out on his journeys, but it was the genius of his own character which made of the fourteenth-century poet a traveller, as it were, of our own day. The love of nature is so much a part of modern life as we understand it, that it requires a great effort of the imagination to cast ourselves back into a time when it counted for very little. In the ancient world the Greeks, " ever treading delicately through brightest air," [1] and imbued with the fullest sense of joy in physical life, were certainly observers of nature, not perhaps as an object of primary importance, but rather as the background to human life which alone was of absorbing interest. Yet we have many examples—pre-eminently in Homer, but also in Sophocles, Euripides, and Pindar—of close observation; in minute descriptions and in the choice of epithets we find such unerring justness as could

[1] Euripides, *Medea*, 830.

only be obtained from long and close consideration, though there is always to be noted a leaning towards the definite and the distinct: clear light, the spaces of the sea and sky, sharp outlines; and on the whole there is an aloofness, an unwillingness to come too close, or to explore dark places. This can be well explained by the Greek religion which peopled the whole of nature, and endued every object with life and mystery. To men to whom the immortals were so near—gods of the sea and the mountain, nymphs of the streams and of the trees—for whom every grove and cave was haunted, nature must have worn an aspect unknown to us. The whole world of flowers for the Greeks was more overcharged with poetry than it has been for any other race. For them the daffodils told of Proserpina, the hyacinths wailed for Adonis, and the narcissus arose but " to die of their own dear loveliness "; and so those who knew they might meet with majestical Pan by hill or river walked the earth with an alert hope and wonder, and yet with an awe which did not choose to venture too near.

The Latins seem to have had a more homely, if also a more intimate, appreciation; they were apt to confound beauty and utility, and hardly to admire one without the other, valuing most the quiet and retirement of the country, the feeling of leisure which it induced, and the sense of ease which comes from being at a distance from the noise and preoccupation of affairs: in this connection Horace will be present to the mind of every one, so that it is superfluous to mention him. But Lucretius plunges us into quite another world; for him nature is the ruler and creator, he gazes into her secrets with the eyes of a seer and bows to her inexorable laws. Virgil, too, who wrote of himself:—

> Me vero primum dulces ante omnia Musæ,
> Quarum sacra fero ingenti percussus amore,
> Accipiant; [1]

---

[1] *Georgics*, ii. 475 ff.

strikes an even loftier note, and it would be difficult anywhere to meet with passages breathing such love and intimate knowledge of nature, and showing such delicate insight, as we find in the second *Georgic*. He has lost something of the swiftness, of the inexhaustible lightheartedness, of the older world, but he has also lost the aloofness and detachment. Not content with sight and sound, he discerns the heart of the mighty mother, he reads man into nature, he is alive to " the tears of things "; it is this sadness, this sense of pity and kinship, which makes him more than any other in his intercourse with nature the forerunner of the moderns.

In Hebrew poetry we get nature under quite another aspect; we hear of " the treasures of the snow," " the everlasting hills," " the clear shining after rain," and one could multiply examples of a most minute observation from almost every book in the Bible; but none of these things is noted for the sake of nature but for the manifestation of God, not even in that wonderful nature-poem, the hundred and third Psalm, which is but the apotheosis of God's Providence. For the Hebrew mind did not progress through nature to the Divinity, but rather went straight to God, seeing Him everywhere immediately present: " The Lord also thundered out of heaven and the Highest gave His thunder: hail-stones and coals of fire "; " Thy way is in the sea and Thy paths in the great waters." And so nature acquired a twofold import: first, that every wonder, and mercy, and terror was the very act of God, and, secondly, that each of these things did but symbolise God's dealings with His people. " As the rain cometh down, and the snow from heaven, and returneth not thither but watereth the earth, and maketh it bring forth and bud . . . so shall my word be." " The earth shall be filled with the knowledge of the Lord as the waters cover the sea."

Again, ignorance of science must have tended to make natural phenomena appear more terrifying, and so men seem to have turned more directly to God as protector and defender. With the moderns it is otherwise; a more intimate knowledge of the laws of the physical world has, to a great extent, driven out awe, and fear, and mystery; there has grown up a sympathy with nature and a belief in her sympathy with man, so that for the whole modern world nature seems to be a link with the divine. We see and love God in His works, and this is yet another instance of the unfailing law of balanced loss and gain: we see Him perhaps more closely and constantly, but at the same time with a less startling directness. Saint John of the Cross, who winged his mystical flight like an arrow straight to the Highest, speaks of the dark night into which the soul perforce must enter to attain to union with God, and he says the road to this union is rightly called *night* for three reasons: first, on account of the point from which the soul sets out, because it has to be despoiled of the desire of all pleasure in all the things of the world by an entire detachment from them, which is as night to the natural longings and senses of man; secondly, from the way by which the soul must go, that is, by faith, which is dark as night to the understanding; thirdly, from the goal to which it tends, which is God, who, as He is incomprehensible and infinite, may be called in this life a dark night to the soul; and through these three nights the soul must pass.[1] And it may be that as most men lack courage to enter into that darkness, the paths of nature, winding and allusive, are vouchsafed to them. The modern poets who have walked in these ways have been tinged with a pantheism which found its utmost development in Shelley. Dante, with his wonderful observation and profound knowledge of nature, has far more kinship with the Hebrew singers than with these; his allusions are never introduced for themselves, but are either illustrations or allegories:—

[1] " Subida del Monte Carmela," cap. ii., San Juan de la Cruz, Madrid, 1853.

> E come gli stornei ne portan l'ali
> Nel freddo tempo, a schiera larga e piena,
> Così quel fiato gli spiriti mali.[1]

or,

> Come l'augello intra l'amate fronde,
> Posato al nido dei suoi dolci nati,
> La notte che le cose ci nasconde,
>
> . . . . .
>
> Previene il tempo in sull' aperta frasca,
> E con ardente affetto il sole aspetta,
> Fiso guardando pur che l'alba nasca;
> Così la Donna mia si stava eretta
> Ed attenta, rivolta inver la plaga
> Sotto la quale il sol mostra men fretta.[2]

Even the famous " riso dell' universo " is but a parable.

Petrarca breaks away from this point of view, and shows himself to us as a modern man in the way he loves and seeks nature, identifying her with all his moods. Professor Zumbini has pointed out that in all poetry there is no woman so constantly surrounded with natural beauty as Laura: her poet establishes an intimate and mysterious relation between her and nature. He notes, too, effects of light, flowers, the music of running waters, and the notes

---

[1] " And as the wings of starlings bear them on
In the cold season in large band and full,
So doth that blast the spirits maledict."
*Inf.* v. 40, Longfellow's translation.

[2] " Even as a bird, 'mid the beloved leaves,
Quiet upon the nest of her sweet brood
Throughout the night that hideth all things from us,

. . . . . . .

Anticipates the time on open spray
And with an ardent longing waits the sun,
Gazing intent as soon as breaks the dawn:
Even thus my Lady standing was, erect
And vigilant turned round towards the zone
Underneath which the sun displays less haste."
*Par.* xxiii. 1-12, *ibid.*

of birds—but for themselves, not to illustrate other music and sweetness and radiance, and in this he has stepped forth from the background of his own age and become the herald of ours. For love of nature, as of all things else, can be of many kinds. There is the love of the artist who seizes an effect and constructs a picture; there is intellectual love which is impressed by brightness, or sombreness, or savageness, by mystery or simplicity, according to the cast of mind; there is the love of association which marks out certain scenes and places from all others, not because of what they are, but for what they suggest and embody; and then there is the spontaneous love of nature for her own self, the only love which is entirely worthy of the name, which is all-embracing, which does not look for sympathy but imparts it, which does not ask to be understood but understands. None of these loves was foreign to the soul of Petrarca, but the last was pre-eminently his, and in this he was a pioneer. Yet, though his eyes were opened to the whole world's beauty, we cannot fail to notice that Italy enraptured him as did no other place; no skies were so clear, no landscapes so alluring as hers. He had made himself master of every detail of her ancient glory, he extolled her present beauty, and believed in her future greatness: she was ever to him " the flower, the lady of lands." And, while all varieties of loveliness appealed to him, that of solitary places, of deep forests, of shaded, silent nooks was what he loved best. He was too restless to be wholly satisfied with retirement, but his unquiet temperament caused him to long for it: hence Avignon necessitated Vaucluse, and Padova Arquà.

Paris, Belgium, Germany, Switzerland, the Rhine, and the Ardennes were the scenes of Francesco's first journey. Paris—*nutrix studiorum*, as he calls her—could not fail to interest him. Learned men, both French and Italian, abounded; Roberto de' Bardi, a Florentine, was Chancellor of Notre Dame and introduced him into the Sorbonne;

while with the Augustinian monk, Dionisio da Borgo San Sepolcro, who was professor of divinity and philosophy at the university, the poet formed a lasting friendship, making him his confessor, and receiving from him a small copy of St. Augustine's *Confessions*, which henceforth he always carried about with him. We have repeated instances of the Padre's influence and of the far-reaching effect of his gift, especially in the *Secretum*, one of Petrarca's most powerful and pathetic writings.

It would seem that his patron, Cardinal Colonna, had strictly charged him to write voluminous accounts of his travels down to the smallest details; we are fortunate in having three of these, of which the first runs thus:—

"AIX-LA-CHAPELLE, *June* 21, 1333.

"I have just been travelling through France, not on any particular business (as you know), but from a love of seeing things and from youthful curiosity. I penetrated as far as Germany and the banks of the Rhine, carefully noticing the customs of the people, and, being greatly delighted with the sight of countries hitherto unknown to me, I went about comparing the things I saw with those at home. And though on all sides I found much to admire, I never regretted having been born an Italian. . . . I visited Paris, the capital of the kingdom, which claims to have been founded by Julius Cæsar . . . and looked well all about me, eager to see and to discover whether the things that I had heard of it were true or false, and in this way I consumed a great deal of time, and when the day was not long enough I employed the night also. . . . Then, without speaking of intermediate places, I visited the town of Ghent, which boasts the same founder, and I saw the people of Flanders and Brabant who are famous for woollen manufactures and weaving. I also visited Liège, renowned for its clergy, and Aix-la-Chapelle, the residence of Charles the Great, where, in a marble church, the tomb of this prince is venerated by the barbarian nations. . . ."[1]

The second letter is from Lyons:—

"*August* 9, 1333.

"Leaving Aix-la-Chapelle, having first bathed in its waters which are warm like those of Baiae, and from which the city is thought to have taken its name, I proceeded to Cologne on the left bank of the Rhine, celebrated for its position, its river, and its inhabitants. Wonderful in a barbarous country is the great civilisation, the beauty of the city, the dignity of the men, and the elegance of the women! It happened to be the Vigil of St. John the Baptist when I arrived, and it was near sunset. According to the wish of some friends of mine (for I have friends here whom my fame rather than my merit has procured for me), I was immediately dragged from the inn to the edge of the river to behold an extraordinary sight, nor was I disappointed. All the river-bank was covered with an immense and splendid concourse of women. I was astonished! Good God! what lovely forms and faces! And what dresses! Whoever had been heart-free must have fallen in love with one of them. I had taken my stand upon a bit of rising ground from which one had a good view of what was going on. The crowd was unbelievable and yet there was no disorder. I saw them all, half-hidden by the sweet-scented grass, joyously turn up their sleeves above the elbow and bathe their hands and white arms in the stream, holding pleasant talk in their foreign tongue. . . . In order to understand something of what I saw, I turned to one of my friends and asked in those words of Virgil:—

Quid vult concursus ad amnem;
Quidve petunt animæ?"[2]

In answer to his inquiry, Petrarca was informed that

[1] *De Reb. Fam.* i. 3.   [2] *Æneid*, vi. 318.

this was a very ancient custom, for it was a common belief, especially among women, that by bathing on this day in the river any calamities that were impending in the coming year would be washed away, and that good fortune would be assured. Consequently this ablution remained in favour and took place with unfailing regularity every year. This explanation caused the poet to congratulate those who live by the Rhine, since neither the Po nor the Tiber has the gift of washing away misfortunes.

He continues: " During the following days I wandered about the city from morning till night with the same escort, enjoying my rambles very much, both on account of the things that I actually saw, and still more for the reminiscences of our ancestors who have left such illustrious monuments of Roman power so far from their own country. . . . I saw, too, the great church in the very centre of the town; it is magnificent, although incomplete, and not without reason do they extol it above all others; and there I venerated with devotion the bodies of the three Magi which came in three stages from the east to the west. . . . On June 30, I left Cologne in so much sun and dust that I longed many times, like Virgil, for the Alpine snows and the fogs of the Rhine. Then I crossed the forest of the Ardennes all alone and (what will astonish you more) in time of war. It was already known to me from books, and is a truly wild and dreadful place, but, as they say, God takes care of the unwary. Without retracing with my pen the long journey which I have just wearily made on horseback, I will only say that, having passed through several countries, I reached Lyon to-day." [1]

Here a great disappointment awaited him, for happening to meet a servant of Cardinal Colonna, in answer to his inquiries for all the family, he was informed that the Bishop of Lombez, whom he was hastening to join, had already set out for Rome. This appeared to Petrarca as a

[1] *De Reb. Fam.* i. 4.

kind of desertion, and the tone of his concluding paragraphs is hurt and reproachful. An expostulatory letter to Giacomo Colonna was enclosed with this, but Petrarca must have recovered from his annoyance when he became acquainted with the circumstances which had necessitated the Bishop's hasty departure. War had again broken out between the ever-turbulent Houses of the Colonna and the Orsini, and the great qualities of Giacomo Colonna had caused his family to summon him to their aid. In spite of all his efforts, however, it was long before any truce was concluded.

In the Letter to Posterity, referring to this tour, the poet says: "Youthful curiosity led me to travel in France and Germany, and other motives were alleged in order to gain the consent of my superiors; in truth, I only wanted to satisfy my mania for seeing new things."[1] And we get other side-lights out of two later letters, of which one was written to Padre Luigi Marsili, an Augustinian friar, and accompanied the gift of St. Augustine's *Confessions*, which the donor begs his friend to make the companion of all his travels.

"I gladly give you the little book for which you asked me, and I should give it you still more gladly if it were now what it was when given to me by that Dionisio of your order, a most excellent professor of sacred letters, and in all respects a remarkable man, and my most indulgent father. But, owing to my natural eagerness and boyish vivacity, I used to make continual journeys, and I always took this book with me on my tours through Italy and Germany, it being delightful as regards the contents, dear for the author's sake, and a most convenient size for the pocket, so that it was my inseparable companion."[2]

From the second letter we glean the following details: "In the journeys that I frequently made because of my desire to know and hear new things, I often saw in the

[1] *Ep. ad Post.*      [2] *Rer. Sen.* xiv. 7.

distance some old monastery, and, immediately turning aside, I would make my way towards it, always hoping to find some of the works for which I was greedily searching. And when I was about twenty-six, travelling hurriedly through Belgium and Switzerland, when I reached Liège, I was told that a great number of books were to be found there. So I stopped, and, having begged my friends to wait for me, I discovered there two orations of Cicero, of which I transcribed one, and the other I got a friend to copy for me, and by means of me Italy has received them both." Petrarca then adds that the copying was performed under difficulties, because, though Liège was a town of some considerable importance, ink was almost impossible to obtain, and what there was was as yellow as saffron.[1]

The next few years were passed by Francesco at Avignon chiefly in the study of poetry, but by no means untouched by contemporary events. The desire of John XXII. to organise a crusade waked a ready echo in the poet's heart, and inspired a sonnet [2] and a fine canzone, *O aspettata in ciel*, which is generally supposed to have been addressed to Giacomo Colonna, Bishop of Lombez; [3] and the accession of Benedict XII. was the occasion of a long poetical epistle with which we shall deal later. Benedict bestowed on Petrarca his first ecclesiastical benefice, a canonry at Lombez, which was conferred on him by a bull of January 25, 1335, in which he is commended for character and knowledge of letters.

In the same year Petrarca won fame for himself in the line which he had abandoned. Rival claimants for the lordship of Parma arrived at the papal court. Martino della Scala, lord of Verona, having ousted Orlando Rossi and possessed himself of Parma, had confided the government of it to his uncle, Guido da Correggio. Desirous of legitimatising the position, Martino despatched Azzo da

---

[1] *Rer. Sen.* xv. 1.     [2] *Rime*, xxvii.
[3] *Rime*, xxviii. Cf. Cochin, *La Chronologie du Canzoniere*, p. 47 and note.

Correggio, brother of Guido, together with Guglielmo Arimondi, to beg the Pope to confirm him in the possession of the conquered city; while at the same time Marsilio Rossi, brother of the defeated Orlando, also came to plead his cause. Azzo, young, brilliantly handsome, so strong that he was nicknamed *Piede di bronzo*, with a cultivated taste and a wonderful memory, soon became a close friend of Petrarca, being of the same age and the same country, and distinguished by the same love of letters; and when Azzo had to defend the cause of the Scaligers before the Pope, it was to Francesco that he turned, confident in his legal knowledge and relying on his eloquence. And Petrarca, for whom legal success had been lavishly prophesied if he would but have persevered in his studies, did not disappoint his friend's expectations, but pleaded his cause with such lucid arguments, such strong and eloquent language, that the Scaligers were confirmed in the lordship of Parma.[1] This, of course, served to strengthen the friendship between Azzo and Petrarca, and was the latter's first alliance with one of the despots of Italy. Henceforth it was said of him that, if he had not willed to be the greatest poet of his age, he might have been its greatest orator.[2]

In the April of the following year, 1336, Petrarca again vindicates his claim to modernity by an action so common in these days that it is difficult to realise that, at that time, it was a strange and unheard-of thing. His usual restlessness inspires him with the desire of ascending a neighbouring mountain, and he writes an exhaustive account of the expedition to Padre Dionisio:—

"To-day I have ascended the highest mountain of this district, which they not undeservedly call *Ventosus*, led by the sole desire of beholding the remarkable height of the place. This expedition had been in my mind for many years. For from my infancy, as you know, I have dwelt

---

[1] Cf. *De Reb. Fam.* iv. 9, Fracassetti's note.
[2] Cf. De Sade, i. p. 274.

in these parts by the will of fate which turns the affairs of men; and this mountain, visible from every quarter, is almost always before my eyes. An impulse at length seized me to do for once what I was daily doing in thought, especially when yesterday, as I was re-reading the history of Rome in Livy, by chance that passage presented itself to me where Philip, King of Macedon, he who waged war with the Roman people, ascended Mount Hæmus in Thessaly. . . . And it seemed to me that what is not blamed in an old king is excusable in a youth in private life. But when I thought about a companion (wonderful to say), scarcely any one of my friends appeared in all respects suitable. So rare, even among dear ones, is that complete concord of character and desires. One seemed too inactive, another too inert; one too slow, another too swift; one seemed too sad, another too cheerful; one was more foolish, another more prudent than I should wish; one's silence, another's forwardness, one's gravity and heaviness, another's leanness and imbecility deterred me; of one the cold indifference, of another the ardent absorption discouraged me. These things, however serious, are tolerated at home, for love beareth all things and friendship refuses no burden, but the same would become too serious on an expedition. . . . And what do you think? At last I turn homeward for aid, and unfold the affair to my only brother, younger than I, whom you know well. He listened with the greatest gladness, being delighted that he should hold with me the place of a friend as well as that of a brother. On the day fixed we set out from home, and came at evening to Malaucène, a place at the foot of the mountain, looking north. Having stayed there one day, we at last ascended the mountain to-day, with a servant apiece, not without much difficulty, for it is a precipitous and almost inaccessible mass of rocky ground. But well was it said by the poet: *Labor omnia vincit improbus.* The long day, the mild air, the strength and dexterity of our bodies, and everything of that kind helped us on; the nature of the place was our only obstacle. We found an old shepherd in a hollow of the mountain, who strove with many words to draw us back from the ascent, saying that he himself fifty years before, in the same impulse of youthful ardour, had climbed to the very top, and had brought back nothing thence save sorrow and labour, and body and clothes torn by the stones and briars; nor ever, either before that time or after, had men heard of any one doing the like. While he shouted out these things, our desire was increased by his prohibition, since the minds of youths disbelieve their admonishers. So the old man, when he perceived that his attempts were to no purpose, going on a little further, showed us with his finger a steep path between the rocks, giving us much advice, and reiterating it after we had turned our backs on him. Having left with him whatever of our garments or aught else might be an impediment, we set ourselves vigorously to the ascent alone, and mounted quickly. But, as usually happens, sudden weariness follows upon a great effort. So at a little distance, on the top of a cliff, we came to a standstill. Starting off again, we pushed on, but much slower. I especially advanced along the steep way at a more moderate pace. My brother, by a direct path up the mountain itself, was making for the height; I, less energetic, was turning downwards, and, when he called me back and showed me the right road, I replied that I hoped to find the ascent easier on the other side, and that I did not mind the way being longer if only I could go more comfortably. Excusing my laziness thus, when the others had already reached a considerable height, I was wandering through the valleys, and, far from presenting any easier access to me elsewhere, the way was longer and the useless labour more fatiguing. Meanwhile, exhausted and disgusted by my confused wandering, I resolved to seek the heights; and when, weary and out of breath, I joined my brother who was waiting and had been refreshed by a long rest, for a time we went on side by side. But we had hardly left that hill when, forgetting my former digression, I took a lower path again. . . . In fact, not without laughter from my brother, and to my own annoyance, within a few hours this happened to me three times or more. . . . Then, my thoughts flying suddenly from material to incorporeal things, I addressed these or such like words to myself: ' That which thou hast experienced to-day so many times in ascending this mountain, thou must know happens to thee and to many who are entering upon the blessed life. . . . The life which we call blessed lies also in a high place; narrow is the way, it is said, that leads to it; many also are the hills that rise between, and we must mount by noble steps from virtue to virtue.' . . . I cannot tell you how much this thought raised up both my mind and my body for what remained of the ascent. . . . The highest peak of all is called by the country-people the *Little Son*, why I do not know. . . . On its top is a little level space on which at last we rested after our fatigues. . . . At first, deeply moved by a certain unwonted quality of the air and the unrestricted view, I was as one stupefied. I looked down; the clouds were under my feet. And now Athos and Olympus were made less incredible to me, whilst I beheld in a mountain of less fame what I had heard and read of them. Then I turned my eyes towards Italy, where my heart inclines most. The Alps themselves, stiff and snow-clad, through which that fierce enemy of the Roman name erst crossed, breaking through the rocks (if we believe the tale) with vinegar, seemed close to me, albeit they are far distant. I sighed, I confess, for the skies of Italy, which were visible to my mind rather than to my eyes, and an immeasurable longing came upon me to see my friend and my native land again. . . . Then a new thought occupied my mind, and translated it from places to times. For I said to myself: ' To-day it is ten years since, having abandoned thy boyish studies, thou didst leave Bologna. O immortal God! O immutable Wisdom! How many and what great changes in thy character has the time seen that has passed since then. I pass over innumerable things; for I am not yet so securely in port that I can calmly recall the storms I have passed through. The time will, perhaps, come when I shall run through them all in the order in which they happened, prefacing them with those words of your Augustine: " I desire to recall my past foulness and the carnal corruptions of my soul; not because I love them, but that I may love Thee, O my God." [1] But in me much remains which is obscure and hurtful. What I used to love I love no longer. . . . I lie: I do love it still, but with shame and with sadness. Now, at last, I have spoken the truth. For so it is: I love, but what I would fain not love, what I long to hate.' . . . These and such like thoughts kept stirring within my breast. I rejoiced at what progress I had made, I wept over my failings, and compassionated the common mutability of human conduct; and I seemed in a measure to forget where I was and why I had come; until, leaving such thoughts, for which another place were more suitable, I gazed round and saw what I had come to see. Warned that the time for departing was near, for already the sun was setting and the shadow of the mountain lengthening, and rousing myself, as it were, I turned round and looked to the west. The Pyrenees are not seen thence . . . but the mountains of the province of Lyon to the right, and the bay of Marseilles to the left, were most clearly visible. . . . The Rhone flowed under our very eyes. Whilst I gazed upon these one by one, now tasting some earthly pleasure, now by the example of the body raising the mind to higher things, it came into my head to look into the book of Augustine's *Confessions* (the gift of your love which I treasure for the sake of both author and donor, and always have in my hand). I opened

[1] St. Augustine, *Confessiones*, lib. ii.

this handy little volume, of very slight bulk but of infinite sweetness, in order to read whatever might meet my eyes. For what could I see save what was tender and devout? But, by chance, it opened at the tenth book of that work. My brother was standing with intent ears, expecting to hear something from Augustine through my mouth. I call God and him to witness that where first I fixed my eyes was written: 'And men go about to admire the heights of mountains, the mighty waves of the sea, the broad courses of rivers, the compass of the ocean, and the revolutions of the stars, but themselves they consider not.'[1] I confess I was astounded, and begging my brother, who wished to hear further, not to importune me, I closed the book, angry with myself because I still wonder at earthly things, who should already have learned, even from the pagan philosophers, that nothing is so wonderful as the human soul with whose greatness nothing can be compared. . . . And this, too, occurred to me while making the descent: 'If I do not grudge so much labour and trouble that my body may be a little nearer heaven, what cross, what prison, what torment, should terrify a soul that is drawing near to God?' . . . Occupied with these thoughts, without noticing the difficulties of the way . . . I arrived after nightfall at the rustic hospice which we had left before dawn; and while the servants have been busy preparing supper, I have gone alone to a retired part of the house to write this to you at once, lest, if I delayed, through change of place my desire might change, and the purpose of writing cool down. See, therefore, most loving father, how I would wish nothing in me to be hidden from your eyes, since I so diligently reveal to you, not only my entire life, but even my individual thoughts. Pray for these, I beseech you, that they, so long wandering and unstable, may some time find rest, and that, tossed about vainly through many things, they may turn themselves to the one good, true, certain, and immutable."[2]

[1] St. Aug. *op. cit.* lib. x.     [2] *De Reb. Fam.* iv. i.

It would seem that the Bishop of Lombez had not ceased to implore Petrarca to join him in Rome, an invitation to the acceptation of which the latter constantly alleged two obstacles, the one that he was pledged to Cardinal Colonna, the other that he was thrall to Laura. The latter excuse brought him a half-bantering letter from the Bishop, doubting the existence of the lady, and identifying her with the poet's laurel, of which Petrarca was even then known to be covetous. This letter is lost, but its tone can be gathered from Francesco's reply:—

"You say that I have invented for myself the beautiful name of Laura, in order that she of whom I love to speak should be one and the same with that which gives others occasion to speak of me, nor is there any other *Laurea* in my heart than that which grows to be the honour of poets; that this living Laura, by whose beauty I confess myself ensnared, is a thing of pure imagination, the verses feigned, and the sighs simulated. In this one thing, indeed, would that your jest were very truth, for then were my love a pretence and not a madness."[1]

It was probably as a means of escape from this "madness" that Petrarca resolved on the Italian journey. Italy, as we have just seen, was the land of his desires. In one of his letters he says: "One should call every one an exile who is condemned to live out of Italy"; and in another place: "I went to Rome, which from my cradle I had most ardently desired to see" . . . "that city who is the lady and queen of the world, eternal Rome, and whoso has not seen her has no right to admire any city how great soever."[2] It was in the last days of 1336 that he set out, by which route is not exactly known, but it is most likely that he went by sea from Marseilles to Città Vecchia, and thence to Capranica, where he stayed some weeks with Conte Orso dell' Anguillara, who had married Agnese, daughter of Stefano Colonna. Capranica was in a picturesque country

[1] *De Reb. Fam.* ii. 9.  [2] *Ibid.* ix. 13; *Ep. ad. Post.*

full of Virgilian associations, and Petrarca seems to have found his visit there delightful. He wrote several descriptive letters to Cardinal Colonna; in the first he says:—

" The spot is of little note in itself, but is surrounded by famous places. Here is Monte Soracte, illustrious as the dwelling of Pope Sylvester, but, ere the time of Sylvester, celebrated in the songs of the poets; yonder is the mountain and lake of Ciminus, which is mentioned in Virgil. . . . Hills without number encircle the country on every side, neither too high nor too hard to climb, and no wise impeding the spaciousness of the view . . . and, below, leafy woods spread on all sides to afford shelter from the heat of the sun . . . and if, by chance, I were to be asked whether I should prefer to go hence, I should not know what to answer, for it seems to me that departure would be profitable and remaining here is agreeable." [1]

Another letter says:—

" In this mountain of goats, which should rather be called a mountain of lions and tigers, lives your Orso, Conte dell' Anguillara, more gentle than a lamb, without fear of war, secure in the midst of strife, but desiring peace. He is as generous a host as any ever was, strong in counsel, showing a mild severity and a noble kindness towards his own people, favourable to the Muses, and famous for prizing and admiring the best intellects. With him . . . is his wife Agnese, your most noble sister, of whom it is better to say nothing than to say little. . . . To these is now added that divine and unique man, your brother, Giacomo Colonna, Bishop of Lombez. With these noble minds I am now living, and I experience so much delight therefrom that it often seems to me that I am no longer on earth; nor do I greatly care now to go on to Rome, but we shall go nevertheless. . . ." [2] And, in fact, they set out within a few days of the Bishop's arrival, and with an escort of two hundred soldiers to protect them from the Orsini.

[1] *De Reb. Fam.* ii. 12.     [2] *Ibid.* ii. 13.

Petrarca's first letter to Cardinal Colonna is proudly dated *In Capitolio;* it is but short:—

"What will you expect me to write you from Rome when I have written you so much from the mountains? ... I remember that you used to dissuade me from coming here because you feared that the sight of these ruins, corresponding ill both with their fame and with the idea I should have conceived of them from books, would diminish my ardour. ... But, wonderful to relate, my respect was not in any respect diminished, but rather altogether increased. Verily Rome was greater and her relics are greater than I imagined. I wonder no longer that the world should have been conquered by such a city, but only that it should have been conquered so late." [1]

The best account that remains to us of Francesco's impressions of the eternal city is in the form of reminiscences in a letter to Giovanni di San Vito, who served as his guide and companion during all his sojourn there. He reminds this friend how they had roamed about the city and the environs. He writes pages of classical allusions, takes note of temples and antiquities, and, coming down to Christian times, gives records of many Christian martyrs. The poet is obviously recalling all these details for the mere pleasure of carrying himself back to the remembrance of all that he had so much enjoyed and appreciated; for why indeed, as he himself asks, should he describe them to one who knew them better than he, not through being a Roman citizen, but because he had ever felt their interest and fascination. And here Petrarca bewails the fact that in his day none was more ignorant of Rome than the Romans; in no place was Rome so little known as in Rome. He bewails this, not so much on account of ignorance, though that is deplorable, as because he doubts not that, if Rome began to know herself, she would immediately rise again. The baths of Diocletian used to be a favourite resting-place

[1] *De Reb. Fam.* ii. 14.

for these two sight-seers, when tired by a long ramble through the city, and they would climb to the top of the vaulted roof to enjoy the splendid air and the wide view, all the while discussing history, in which each seemed to have chosen his own sphere, Giovanni being better informed about modern, and the poet about ancient, times.[1]

Petrarca's love of books did not desert him even here, where he must have had so much to occupy his attention. We find him still on the search for rare manuscripts, but he could only find here two devotional works, which he bought for the beauty of the copies, and on which he duly inscribed *Romæ emptus*. This first visit to Rome lasted but a short time, and the poet's return journey is shrouded in mystery. On the strength of a few ambiguous statements, one in the *Secretum*, and two in the metrical epistles, some commentators have imagined that he coasted Spain and came as far as the shores of England; but his rather vague references to the "*Oceani terminos*" do not necessarily bear this construction, and it would be very extraordinary if Petrarca, with his well-known dread of the sea, and his love of new places and people, should have adventured himself so far without landing on strange shores which could not have failed to attract him. However that may be, he returned to Avignon in the August of 1337, and before the end of the year a son, Giovanni, was born to him. It is strange that the mother's name has never been known, nor have any particulars of an attachment existing at the time come to light, though it is generally supposed that the same woman was the mother of the daughter born in 1343, whose subsequent history is a brighter one than her brother's. The whole story of Giovanni is a record of misery and mistakes. Of his bringing up until he was eight years old, nothing is known; then his father sent him to Verona, and in 1347 procured his legitimation. The boy was moved from school to school, from town to town, never

[1] *De Reb. Fam.* vi. 2.

giving satisfaction to his father, though sometimes to his masters. In 1352, through the influence of Azzo da Correggio, he obtained a canonry at Verona, but was deprived of it two years later when Azzo fell into disgrace. Returning to his father again, fresh causes for displeasure arose, and at length the boy died in 1361 at the age of twenty-four. The event is thus sadly recorded on the flyleaf of the poet's Virgil: " Our Giovanni was born to be a trouble and a grief to me; living he burdened me with heavy and perpetual cares, and dying he has wounded me with a bitter sorrow." [1]

Giovanni's birth in 1337 forms a mournful sequel to the poet's reflections on Mont Ventoux, but Petrarca's own confessions are the best commentary on his temptations and his falls. In the Letter to Posterity he states, with the utmost simplicity and candour, that by nature he was peculiarly susceptible to the influence of the senses, although he always saw and detested the baseness of sensual pleasures; and he counts it as one of the greatest blessings granted to him that he was able, whilst still in the prime of life, to put such things, and even the memory of them, away, and to free himself from so humiliating a slavery. Elsewhere he returns to the same theme, setting forth with equal frankness his weakness, his sins, his repentance, and his victory.[2]

[1] " Joannes noster, homo natus ad laborem ac dolorem meum, et vivens gravibus atque perpetuis me curis exercuit, et acri dolore moriens vulneravit."—*De Reb. Fam.* vii. 15, Fracassetti's note.

[2] *De Reb. Fam.* x. 5; *Rer. Sen.* viii. 1.

## CHAPTER III

### LAURELS

" Have the high gods anything left to give,
Save dust and laurels and gold and sand? "
A. C. SWINBURNE, *The Triumph of Time.*

" HAVING returned from my travels, and being overcome by my innate disgust and dislike of all cities (but above all of that most detestable one), I looked about for some retreat, some harbour, as it were, and I discovered a very small, but lonely and delightful, valley called Vaucluse, where the Sorgues, queen of all streams, takes its rise. Captivated by the beauty of the place, I transplanted thither myself and my books."

So writes Petrarca in the Letter to Posterity, but, simple and direct as the statement is, it contains the history of a momentous change. From this time we see the poet in a new light, or rather in a hundred lights, for his is no simple character, but one of which the complexity often seems to defy our powers of dissection. What, then, were the forces that led him into the desert? Surely of him, too, it may be said, *Libertà va cercando,* and with all the more pathos in that so many years were to elapse before the achievement of the quest. Meanwhile, we must picture him tormented by a love complex as his own nature and which, though not wholly ignoble, was alloyed by unworthy longings and lowered by selfish desires, whose very restlessness marked its imperfection, dividing it sharply from that *Amor Amicitiæ* which is *simpliciter et per se amare,*[1] and which carries its possessor up to those high places where (to recall Goethe's majestic lines) a great calm reigns. Prob-

---
[1] St. Thomas Aquinas, *Summa Theologica,* I. ii. Q. 26, A. 4.

ably we may discern in his denunciations of the luxury and dissipation of the city that these things were not quite indifferent to him; indifference rarely produces such bitterness, which is rather the fruit of a corresponding attraction. Pleasure, comfort, adulation, music, varied and intellectual society, the importance of his increasing reputation—he must have felt these chains fastening on him, and must have found that the higher powers of his soul were being stifled; and so, with a courage to which justice has hardly been done, he broke with his old life and went forth voluntarily to endure hardness. For a man of his kind this might well command our respect even in our day, but at that time such a line of conduct was amazing as well as admirable. None of his friends appear to have understood his motives or approved his choice; it seems to have puzzled, frightened, and repelled them. And what is to be the worth of these quiet years at Vaucluse? It is that in them Petrarca set up his standard of taste and perfected his ideal. There, in that self-elected leisure, he strengthened his judgment by his choices and his decisions, he rejected the second-rate, familiarised himself with perfection, with the right word and the right way, until he had built for himself a kingdom of righteousness into which he delighted to usher the elect. For there is a hunger and thirst after justice in the literary as well as in the religious life, and Petrarca, to whom the vision had been vouchsafed, may well have felt it fading from his eyes in the turmoil of a court life.

Long ago he had recognised the supreme worth of the classics. Taking Virgil and Cicero as his models, collating, copying, and comparing, he had trained himself in the refinements of taste; his delicate ear appreciated all shades of meaning, his artistic mind grasped the significance of form. At the present day he is either extolled as an inspired love-poet, who has suffered cruelly from his imitators, or slightingly referred to as the author of monotonous Latin poetry, and of a voluminous correspondence which hardly repays perusal (a somewhat inadequate estimate of his large services to Latinity); but there is yet another side which is somewhat in danger of being forgotten: he was a judge and a critic; he formed the taste which he inspired.

And, first of all, he was the most completely educated man of his time. His passion for Italy gave him the insight to recognise that one source of her greatness lay in the Latin language that was still her own, and in the Greek influences that she had never wholly forgotten. For him, her history was an inspiration and her monuments a living record; to him, as to Dante, belongs the honour of having seen across the centuries—Italy. Petrarca had long ago laid the foundations of scholarship, and had begun to reap his reward in the sureness of touch for which he was already gaining distinction, but it was in these years of seclusion that the gift came to perfection. To model himself on great examples, to labour, to polish, and to alter, imbued with the " divine discontent " of genius—this was the work he set himself to do, and it can hardly be uninteresting to see in what environment he looked to accomplish it.

Vaucluse is a place apart; its character is as complex as the poet's own, and indications are not wanting that he felt this to be the case.[1] It is situated about fifteen miles from Avignon, from which it is separated by a ridge of hills on which olives and vines flourish. Beyond this ridge lies the village of L'Isle, through which the Sorgues flows, of which J. A. Symonds writes: " Those who expect Petrarca's Sorgues to be some trickling poet's rill emerging from a damp grotto may well be astonished at the rush and roar of this azure river so close upon its fountain-head."[2] If we would trace it to its source, we must go on until we reach the little village of Vaucluse at the very entrance of the valley, which is shut in by limestone rocks, one of which

[1] *Rime*, cxxxv. 84-90, cclix.
[2] *Sketches and Studies in Italy and Greece*, vol. i. p. 72.

rises so tall and sheer at the end of the defile as to appear like the impassable gateway of some giant's prison. Before we have advanced thus far, however, we are in a land of fruit-trees and gardens, through which the river wins its rapid, turbulent way, and, as we learn from Petrarca, often holds its own against the gardeners, destroying in one night the work of months. As we proceed, figs and mulberries, vines and olives, give place to a growth of small shrubs, to the box and the ilex—that wizard-tree which seems to have woven into its branches the immemorial magic of the world. The valley narrows, the aspect becomes more threatening, we have reached the imprisoning barrier whose arching pent-roof seems to frown upon us, and lo! beneath it is the famous *Speco*, the grotto of the fountain of the Sorgues. The water is wonderfully dark in hue; no one seems to satisfy himself in describing its colour; it is not green, or violet, or blue, or black; it seems to be as elusive as the eyes of Laura, and perhaps best corresponds to Shelley's "firmament of purple light"; it wells up pure and still into an untroubled lake, and, when it has reached the brim, it overflows and rushes on its impetuous course. The forbidding sternness of the grotto, the mysterious calm of the rising water, the force and fury of the torrent, the austere hill-side, gradually lending itself to cultivation and dimpling down into the valley, almost a poem in itself, was surely no inadequate setting for a poet's soul.

We have already seen how the place attracted him in his boyhood, when he said that it was a spot he should prefer to any city however famous, and he bought here a little farm and established himself in it with a dog [1] and only two servants—villagers it would seem, for none of his town servants would consent to accompany him. In after years

[1] The dog was a great feature, being a gift from Cardinal Colonna, and he is the hero of one of Petrarca's Latin metrical epistles, in which he is extolled for his agreeable manners and for the way in which, forgetting the princely luxury to which he is accustomed, he adapts himself to his humble surroundings. Cf. *Epist. metr.* lib. iii. ep. 1.

he altered and embellished his dwelling, but at first he lived in it just as it was—a humble, common little farm-house. His bailiff, Raimond Monet, lived in a cottage alongside, and of him and his wife Petrarca has left full accounts, testifying to their excellent qualities. Thus at the age of thirty-three, though accustomed to luxury, to fine clothes, good fare, and a great *train de maison*, we find him electing to turn his back on all these and to live in the most primitive simplicity, and Vaucluse continued to be his place of residence for the best part of fifteen years. Owing to his letters, we are fortunately at no loss for details; one, in particular, to Francesco de' SS. Apostoli, gives a vivid picture of his way of life. He tells how he has been passing the summer at the fountain of the Sorgues, and this in order that he may wage war on his body with the help of Him without whose aid he should be hopelessly vanquished, since all his senses appear to him in the light of cruel enemies, which have been to him the cause of a thousand evils. His eyes, in particular, have ever led him towards a precipice, and so he has shut them in such wise that they can see scarcely anything but the sky, and the mountains, and the streams; neither gold, nor gems, nor ivory, nor purple, nor horses (except two very miserable ones which, in company with one servant, take him round the valleys). Lastly, he cannot look upon the face of any woman whatever, except that of his stewardess, which is like a desert of Libya or Ethiopia, arid, withered, scorched by the heat of the sun, without a blade of grass or a drop of moisture to fertilise it. But since, after this picture of her person, it would not be right to cheat her of the praise she deserves, he must affirm that her soul is as white as her face is black, by which it may be demonstrated how little one can argue about the souls of women from the ugliness of their bodies. It would be impossible to find a woman in the whole world more faithful, more humble, more active than she is. She spends the whole day in the open fields, and in the evening returns lively and contented, without a complaint or a grumble, and, like a young person who is but just out of bed, she will turn the indomitable strength of her small body to domestic cares, providing for the wants of her sons, her husband, the household, and the guests, with a zeal and an activity as incredible as is the little care she takes of herself. Her only bed is a little straw spread upon the ground; her food is dry, hard bread, and she quenches her thirst with vinegar which is called wine, and which is only drinkable on account of the water she mixes with it.

His eyes being thus mortified, Petrarca proceeds to speak of his ears, and tells how they are never now delighted with songs or sweet sounds, harmonies of strings or of lutes, from which he used to derive such acute pleasure. In this place nothing strikes on the ear except the lowing of cattle, the bleating of lambs, the song of the birds, and the murmuring of the waters; while as for his tongue, which so often excited emotions in himself and others, it is now inert and keeps silence from morning till evening, since it finds no one but itself with whom to speak. For his food, the bread which the villagers eat both suffices and pleases him; he dislikes white bread, and gladly leaves it to be eaten by the servants who bring it to him. Already habit is becoming pleasure, and his bailiff, an inflexible but most lovable man, has no other fault to find with him except that he treats himself too harshly, and predicts that his master will not be able to endure it for long. Francesco, on the contrary, thinks that one can bear common, simple food longer than delicate and costly living. Figs, nuts, and almonds are his luxuries; and the little fish with which the stream abounds please him very much, and never more than when they are being caught, because he zealously looks on and is already beginning to take pleasure in handling the fish-hook and nets himself. As for his wearing apparel, everything is changed. " If you were to see me now, you would say that I was a labourer or a shepherd, although I have no lack of better clothes, nor have I changed them for any other reason than that I now despise what once pleased me. . . . And what shall I say of my house? It would seem to you like that of Cato or Fabricius, and here I live with one dog and two servants." Near at hand is the house of his bailiff. He then begins to tell of his chief delight, his two small gardens, which are so admirably adapted to his mind and taste that he fears he shall be too prolix if he begins to describe them, and so will only say that there are none like them in the world; and, at the same time, he confesses to the almost feminine weakness of feeling annoyed that such a spot should exist out of Italy. The garden he calls his Transalpine Helicon is very shady, admirably adapted for study, and sacred to Apollo. It overlooks the fountain of the Sorgues, and behind it are only rocks and cliffs, naked, broken, and inaccessible, except to the wild animals and the birds. The other garden is near the house and lies right in the middle of the rapid and beautiful stream. No place could be more conducive to study, and here he delights to pass the afternoons; his mornings are spent in wandering over the hills, and in the evenings he roams about the meadows or into that wilder garden near the fountain, which nature has made more beautiful than the hand of man can do. In conclusion he says: "I could spend all my life here, were Italy not so far or Avignon so near. . . . I fear nothing so much as returning to cities."[1]

It is evident that, next to his library, which he called his "daughter," Petrarca loved his garden, and this was a taste that he kept all through life, nor did it always cost him so much labour as in his present abode, where he disputed possession with the Naiades of the Sorgues; the winter was always propitious to them, the summer to him. He gives a spirited description of this in his epistles to Cardinal Colonna, saying how there has been great war

[1] *De Reb. Fam.* xiii. 8.

between himself and the nymphs, and how the victory has remained with them.[1] He did not, however, desist from the combat, and eventually made a flourishing garden, whose beauties he is constantly commending to his friends.[2] Once, when Petrarca was absent at San Colombano, Guido Settimo passed a few days in his retreat, and the poet wrote pleasantly saying that Guido's presence would console his books for the long absence of their master, and that the little garden (whose like he has never seen in the world) will no longer resent his remaining at a distance; and he adds a learned little digression on the best time for planting trees.[3] At Vaucluse, no doubt, as everywhere, he planted laurels; this seems to have been his first care in every garden that he made. At Milan they refused to grow, and, after two failures, he makes another venture when Boccaccio is visiting him, in hopes that the presence of his friend may bring luck.[4] He never tires of praising both the place and the climate. "Here," he writes, "the air is mild, the winds soft, the fields open, the springs clear, the streams full of fish, the woods shady . . . here flowery meadows stretch before our eyes, while nothing but the lowing of cattle, the songs of birds, and the murmuring water breaks the silence, and the beautiful valley, shut in on every side, hence derives its name of Vaucluse. . . . I truly believe this to be the place of peace and the house of leisure. . . . There is no place on earth more fitted to inspire noble and lofty ideas . . . here the tired mind finds grateful relaxation and pleasant diversion from its cares; here are silence and liberty, secure joy and joyful security."[5]

From other letters we can gather that Petrarca's choice of a residence found no favour among his friends, for he explains that it is not the hope or need of anything what-

[1] *Epist. metr.* lib. iii. 1 and 4, *Ad Cardinalem J. Columnam.*
[2] *Ibid.* lib. i. 8.
[3] *De Reb. Fam.* xvii. 5.
[4] Cf. P. de Nolhac, *op. cit.* tom. ii. pp. 262-264.
[5] *De Reb. Fam.* xvi. 6; xvii. 5.

ever which attracts him hither, nor any pleasure except that which he takes in dwelling among fields and woods. Nor can it be said that the reason which would be the noblest of all—the love of friends—has concurred in alluring him here; the only reason is the love that he feels for solitude and quiet and nothing else. The ordinary course of his life is as follows: he rises at midnight and leaves the house at the dawn of day, but, as in the house so in the fields, he studies and thinks, reads and writes, with this view before him, to withhold sleep from his eyes, softness from his body, pleasures from his soul, and idleness from his actions. Thus the characteristics of the ascetic and the poet are discernible in his habits. Many a dark night, he says, has found him alone in the fields. He rises at midnight to recite Lauds, and then is tempted to ramble out of doors, especially by moonlight. He has even ventured alone at that hour, with mixed feelings of horror and delight, into that terrible grotto of the fountain, which one does not enter without fear even in broad daylight and with companions. The valley is wholly secluded. No one comes there by chance, and there is nothing to bring any one except the sight of the beautiful fountain, or the longing for a retreat for quiet study; but people with such desires are rare. For himself, he feels that there is no place out of Italy that offers him a more restful abode; it conduces to virtue and contemplation, and enables him to escape from the disturbance of the multitude and satisfy his desire for a solitary life.[1]

But if the poet's former friends only paid him rare and fugitive visits, he was fortunate in finding two men in his immediate neighbourhood who were eminently fitted to afford him companionship. One was Philippe de Cabassole, the young and gifted Bishop of Cavaillon, in which diocese Vaucluse was situated. The town of Cavaillon was about six miles distant, but the bishops possessed a

[1] *De Reb. Fam.* xi. 12; xii. 8; xv. 3; *Rer. Sen.* x. 2.

small chateau, perched upon the rocks above the Sorgues valley, where Cabassole frequently stayed, and where Petrarca was a constant visitor, being from the first attracted by the talents and scholarship of the prelate. He is thus described in the Letter to Posterity: "Philippe, always great in soul, but then bishop of the small diocese of Cavaillon . . . who ever loved me, not like a bishop, as Ambrose loved Augustine, but with the affection of a brother." The poet addressed an immense number of letters to him, the first being a lengthy and conventional letter of condolence on his brother's death; and he also sent him some verses made in his early Vaucluse days when, at the request of Cardinal Colonna, he made an expedition to the grotto of Ste. Beaume, near Marseilles, where St. Mary Magdalen is said to have lived for thirty years. The verses are poor, and the only interest that attaches to this excursion is that Petrarca's brother, Gherardo, was of the party and made his first visit to the Carthusian monastery at Montrieu, in the neighbourhood, which he subsequently entered. This forms the subject of one of the poet's eclogues, in which he introduces his brother and himself as two shepherds, and thus explains the poem: "The two shepherds are our two selves, you, Monicus, and I, Silvius. If you want to know the reason of the names, I call myself Silvius both because the eclogue was composed in the woods, and because from my earliest years I have so loved forests and abhorred cities that many call me Silvius rather than Francesco. . . . The solitary grotto to which Monicus retires is no other than Montrieu . . . where you have professed the monastic life, or else the grotto into which the penitent, St. Mary Magdalen, withdrew, which is close to your monastery."[1] The *De Vita Solitaria*, one of the best fruits of Petrarca's sylvan tastes, was dedicated to Cabassole. The second friend that Cavaillon afforded him was Pons Samson, of whom the poet said that he was as remark-

[1] *De Reb. Fam.* x. 4.

able for prudence, courtesy, and strength of mind as his Hebrew namesake had been for strength of body.

But Francesco could hardly have wished for any more excellent friend than his unique and faithful servant, Raimond Monet, to whom reference has already been made, and of whom we have many amusing and touching details. He is described as "a kind of aquatic animal, bred up among springs and streams," and his master writes that it would be saying little to say that no servant could be more faithful, for he was fidelity itself. Writing of Vaucluse in his old age, Petrarca speaks of it as the place where he had passed the most fruitful years of his life, and gratefully recalls the tranquillity and happiness that he enjoyed there, which, however, did not prevent him from making frequent journeys. He relates how Monet, when he saw him constantly on the move, would rebuke him with gentle freedom, saying, either when he set out or returned: "If I mistake not, you are going to roam about, but, believe me, your purse will suffer for it"; and often he would add up the expenses of the journey with such exactness that he did not make even the smallest mistake, saying on his master's departure: "You will spend so much," or on his return: "You have spent so much," so that one would have said, not that he had stopped at home to cultivate the little farm, but rather that he had been a travelling companion and had written down the list of expenses in every inn. . . . So much for the business capacity of this remarkable man, but he had still more striking characteristics, for, though only a rough labourer, it was not the farm alone that was entrusted to him. All the books were placed under his care, and Petrarca relates that, of the many different volumes that he possessed, when he returned after a long absence he never happened to find even one missing, or changed from its place. For Monet, though illiterate himself, loved letters, and moreover, knowing that the books were most dear to his master, he kept them with the greatest care, and had learned to know their names and to distinguish between them. He would glow with pleasure when Petrarca chanced to place a book in his hands, and would press it to his bosom sighing, and then in a low voice he would ask the author's name, and, strange to say, he esteemed himself more learned and happy merely from seeing and touching books.[1]

The want of books had weighed heavily on the poet during his Italian journey; he complained of his desolation when he found himself without one of the volumes with which he was accustomed to converse, and had to be content with his memory for his only companion;[2] but to Vaucluse he brought every book that he possessed, and added steadily to their number. He wrote to a friend: " If you love me, commission faithful and learned men to search through Tuscany, ransacking the bookshelves of the religious houses, and of the men who are most addicted to study, and find means to discover something that will appease or stimulate my appetite. For the rest, you must know that I have made the same request to friends in England, France, and Spain."[3]

We have already noticed his predilection for Cicero, and he seems very early to have created a taste and incited to the search for Ciceronian manuscripts. His own greatest discovery in this direction was of the letters to Atticus, which he found in Verona and copied himself, and of which he writes that he possesses some of Cicero's letters in a big volume which he copied entirely with his own hand, because the copyists were not sufficiently experienced and did not know enough; and though he had been ill at the time, the great love, the delight, and the burning desire to make them his own property rendered him insensible to the fatigue.[4]

Petrarca seems to have had for that time a remarkably good historical library, for, in his *De Viris Illustribus*, he

[1] *De Reb. Fam.* xvi. 1.     [2] *Ibid.* iii. 1.
[3] *Ibid.* iii. 18.     [4] *Ibid.* xxi. 10.

quotes not only from Livy, with whom (as far as his incomplete edition allowed) [1] he had a most intimate acquaintance, but also from Sallust, Suetonius, Pliny, Valerius Maximus, Orosius, and Cæsar's *Commentaries*. The *Africa* was, of course, the direct outcome of his historical enthusiasm; history was for him no dry record of facts; it fired his imagination; he read it as a poet and an artist, and people and events became alive to him. The *De Viris* is a succession of living portraits, and Scipio his ideal knight. This vivid conception of history made him a collector of coins and medals, and gave him, as was natural, an intense interest in all topographical details; we are told that no present pleased him more than a map, and, in conjunction with King Robert of Naples, he is said to have directed the making of a map of Italy. His poetical library was more unique than his historical one, for, besides Virgil, he seems to have possessed Horace, Ovid, Catullus, and Propertius, the last two being then very little known.[2] By far the greater part of his Italian poetry was written at Vaucluse, and it is evident that he drew special inspiration from the scenery. Of the prodigious amount of work undertaken there, he writes that it would take too long to reckon up what and how many things he did in so many years; but all his works, if not entirely composed, were begun, or at any rate conceived, there. The lonely character of the place inspired him to write his pastoral poems, which were composed in an astonishingly short time, and no small part of his epistles in prose and poetry emanate from Vaucluse. In no other place did he find better leisure and a stronger incentive to write about the illustrious men of every age and place, and, allured by the solitude, he set forth the advantages and the praises of the *Vita solitaria* and of the *Otium religiosorum*. It was, too, while wandering over the

---

[1] P. de Nolhac, *op. cit.* tom. ii. ch. vi.
[2] Cf. P. de Nolhac, *op. cit.* tom. i. ch. iv. Also *Epistolario* di Coluccio Salutati, lib. iii. 13, 20, and 24.

mountains, one Friday in Holy Week, that the thought of writing a poem about Scipio Africanus came into his mind and took such strong possession of it that, in a transport of enthusiasm, he immediately set to work with great impetuosity; but, owing to a thousand distractions, the task was broken off. This was, of course, the *Africa*, of which he writes in another letter that it is pleasant to him to remember that he began it in this place and with such ardour that, in later life, when he set himself to repolish the work, he trembled at the audacity with which he had laid foundations so vast that the poem was destined never to reach completion.[1]

It has been well said that " it was one of the intellectual forces of Italy never to have lost sight of the polar star of Greece,"[2] nor were Greek influences very remote. The Greek tongue was still native to several villages of Sicily, and the hope of the reunion of the Eastern and Western Churches was the cause of constant intercourse. It was this which gave Petrarca his first chance of acquiring the Greek language, but that is only the evidence of the fact that he had fully grasped the significance of Greece. He already possessed a Plato which he had obtained in France; it was an enormous volume containing several of the Dialogues, and had an honoured place in his library at Vaucluse, though he was unable to read it; but he reverenced Plato's philosophy, and, following St. Augustine, he rated him above Aristotle. He recognised Homer as the supreme poet, and felt that Plato occupied the same place as a philosopher. The poet's Greek studies, however, were not extensive; indeed, he seems to have felt that the field would have been too vast a one.

The Basilian monk, Barlaam, a native of Calabria, but Greek by origin, having been sent by the Emperor to treat with the Pope on the subject of the reunion of the Churches,

[1] *Ep. ad Post.; De Reb. Fam.* viii. 3.
[2] Emile Gebhart, *Les Origines de la Renaissance en Italie*, p. 136.

apparently made the poet's acquaintance at Avignon in 1339, and, when he returned on the same mission in 1342, Petrarca chose him for his master in the Greek language. Boccaccio has described him as "*hominem corpore pusillum praegrandem tamen scientia*,"[1] and he was a theologian and a gifted mathematician, but his knowledge of Latin seems to have been of the smallest, and he was in no wise a humanist, so that it seems doubtful if his pupil would have gained much fruit from the lessons, even if Barlaam's speedy departure for a bishopric in Calabria had not put an end to them.[2]

"There were," writes Petrarca, "some very learned Greeks in our time in Calabria, and especially the monk Barlaam, and Leone or Leonzio, who were both very friendly to me and of whom the first was my master."[3] But the fullest light on these Greek studies comes to us in a letter to Niccolò Sigero, who, being a man of influence at the court of Constantinople, was also sent on an embassy to the Pope in 1353. On this occasion he became intimate with the poet, and, like all his friends, was pressed into the search for manuscripts, the result of which was that he sent over a Homer. The arrival of this work was one of the great days in Francesco's life, and, in acknowledgment of it, he wrote as follows:—

"The gift you have sent me is as noble as your mind. You have given me Homer, whom Ambrosius and Macrobius rightly call the source and origin of every divine invention. . . . This, then, my dearest friend, you have given me, mindful of your promise and of my desire, and what doubles the value of the gift is that you have given it to me, not violently wrested into another language, but pure and incorrupt in the original Greek which issued from the

[1] *De Geneal. Deorum*, xv. 6.
[2] On Petrarca's recommendation King Robert of Naples offered Barlaam the bishopric of Gerace in Calabria, which he accepted, and where he died in 1348.
[3] *Rer. Sen.* xi. 9.

divine lips of the poet. . . . But now, what can I do? You, the fortunate possessor of both languages, are a thousand miles away, and our Barlaam has been taken from me by death, though, to speak truly, I took him from myself when, intent on gaining honours for him, I did not think of the harm that would accrue to me, and procured his being raised to the episcopal dignity; and so I lost the master under whose instruction I had no uncertain hope of profit. Great, however, I must confess is the difference between you and him, because you can benefit me greatly, and in nothing can I be of any assistance to you. But he, while trying earnestly to teach me every day, declared that he derived from intercourse with me not less, but indeed perhaps more, advantage than he gave. Whether he said this sincerely or out of courtesy I know not, but he was as poor in the use of Latin as he was rich in Greek, and, though subtle in his wit, he nevertheless found difficulty in expressing his ideas." [1]

The subject is again referred to in a letter to Boccaccio:—

"I longed earnestly to know Greek, and if it had not been for my ill-luck and for the untimely death of my excellent master, perhaps I should to-day have been something more than a beginner." [2] Nevertheless, Petrarca has the glory of being the pioneer in Greek studies—the first humanist to reopen that golden door.

In 1339 Padre Dionisio passed through Avignon on his way to Italy. He had been for many years professor of divinity and philosophy at the University of Paris, but, feeling himself growing old, he was retiring to his native country for rest. This intention, however, was not carried out, as he was very shortly summoned to Naples by King Robert, who made him Bishop of Monopoli; he proved a most congenial friend and adviser to this monarch whom Boccaccio called "the wisest king since Solomon," and of whom Petrarca gave utterance to so many flatteries that

[1] *De Reb. Fam.* xviii. 2.   [2] *Var.* 25.

# LAURELS

selection becomes difficult. Who is there, he asks, who is there, not only in Italy but in all Europe, greater than King Robert? And he extols him as truly glorious and truly a king since he rules and guides, not only his subjects, but himself.[1]

Robert was the grandson of Charles of Anjou, brother of St. Louis, and was the third King of Naples of the House of Anjou; he was also lord of Avignon, being Count of Provence, and was therefore Petrarca's suzerain. He was an excellent ruler, and was really remarkable both for his tastes and attainments. He had studied theology, philosophy, mathematics, astronomy, and medicine; he would always live surrounded with books, and insisted that some one should read aloud to him during meals. It is a surprise to find that this enlightened monarch and Padre Dionisio made a study of astrology, and still more wonderful to find them commended by Petrarca, whose views on the subject differed widely from the prevalent ones, to which he gave full expression in other connections.

The visit of Padre Dionisio to Avignon and his subsequent establishment at Naples are connected with a very picturesque event in the poet's life, and one to which he attached great importance at the moment, though, as time went on, his estimate of its value altered considerably:[2] this event was the ceremony of his coronation with the laurel crown. In after life Petrarca regarded this as a mere

---

[1] *De Reb. Fam.* iv. 2.

[2] " I was young in years when I obtained the laurel, and bitter to me were its leaves. . . . It was nowise profitable to me for learning or for eloquence, but only brought me most bitter envy and deprived me of repose, making me pay the penalty of vainglory and youthful audacity. From that day all tongues and pens were directed to my hurt, and I was obliged to sustain a continual battle, to stand always on the defensive, and, now on the right hand, now on the left, to parry the blows showered upon me by the friends whom envy had converted into enemies. . . . In a word, all I gained from the laurel was to be known and to be abused, and without it I might have had what some consider the best kind of life, namely, to live in peace and obscurity."—*Rer. Sen.* xvi. 2.

vanity, and one whose only effect had been to arouse jealousy. His biographers for the most part share this view, and attach some blame to him, both for harbouring the ambition for the crown, and for the steps that he possibly took to secure it; and it seems certain that the poet cannot have been quite idle in the matter, for his Latin epic, on which he set the most store, was but just begun, nor was his Italian poetry much known; indeed, the greater part of it was not yet written. Still we need hardly imagine him as making strenuous efforts for the coveted honour; his intimacy with the Colonna family would have sufficed to procure him all he wished in Rome without any endeavours on his part; and, while Padre Dionisio mentioned and extolled him in Naples, it is probable that he also sent word of Francesco's attainments and desires to his old colleagues in Paris. On the whole, this seems to be a many-sided question, and has more than one noble aspect. There are, of course, ambitions that are wholly selfish, but no one would contend that the poet's desire for fame is necessarily of this nature. The laurel is a world-old symbol of victory, and, while it was awarded to kings and conquerors, it was no small thing that the conquerors of the kingdom of the soul should have been distinguished in like manner; it is the art, not the man, that is crowned, and in that lies the real triumph. And, in a world that responds so readily to pomp, and noise, and military glory, it is a supreme service to give pause to the multitude, and to make it recognise in one flash of intelligence that it is the scholar, the artist, and the poet who are kings by divine right.[1]

A yet more personal attraction lay for Petrarca in the laurel, of which he has written so much that we are in no uncertainty of the signification that it had for him. To some it may seem a trivial, and even a tiresome, association, but to him it was alive with reality, and there is no

[1] Cf. Dante, *Par.* i. 13-33.

Triumphus Cupidinis.
(Fifteenth Century Florentine Engraving.)

doubt that part of the charm of a ceremony, endeared to him alike by antiquity and tradition, lay in the fact that he was winning another distinction for his lady, and that he felt himself so much the more identified with her as he bound her name about his brows.

Claudian is said to have been the last poet to be crowned in Rome, though this is probably no more than a legend, but the practice had been revived in other cities of Italy, Mussato having been crowned at Padua in 1314,[1] and Convenevole at Prato. It was on September 1, 1340, that Petrarca received two letters offering him the laurel; one was from the Roman Senate, the other from the Chancellor of the University of Paris. Meanwhile, no doubt through the good offices of Padre Dionisio, the poet had been brought into communication with King Robert, who had sent an epitaph of his own composition on his niece, Queen Clémence, widow of Louis Hutin, on which Petrarca naturally wrote a flattering commentary: "Happy the pen," he says, "that can compose such things!" And to the Padre he wrote:—

"You know how I regard the laurel, and, all things considered, I remain firm in my desire not to receive it from any one in the world save from that monarch. If I am of sufficient merit to be invited, well; if not, I shall pretend to have heard something, or, as doubting the sense of the letter which he sent me in his supreme and most kindly condescension towards an unknown man, I shall go into those parts that I may seem to have been invited."[2]

Subsequently, as we have seen, invitations were not wanting, and, hesitating between the two, Petrarca sought advice from Cardinal Colonna, telling him how he had received letters from the Senate, who, with a thousand epithets, beg and conjure him to go to Rome, there to be made poet-laureate; while the same day an envoy arrives

[1] Wicksteed and Gardner, *Dante and Giovanni del Virgilio*, pp. 41-45.
[2] *De Reb. Fam.* iv. 2.

from his illustrious fellow-citizen, Roberto, Chancellor of the University of Paris, bearing a letter with the same invitation. Perplexed and delighted, Petrarca finds himself incapable of forming a sound judgment; exceedingly rejoiced, he is yet undecided as to what he ought to do. On the one hand, the novelty of the experience attracts him, on the other, the reverence for ancient times; on this side, his friend, on that, his country. His mind is tossing on a sea of bewilderment, and he calls to the Cardinal to take the helm and to direct his course.[1]

The counsel of a Colonna could hardly be other than to go to Rome, nor is it likely that Francesco desired any other; but he seems to have felt some shyness, for he could not decide to go thither direct, and resolved to go first to Naples, to visit that "great king and philosopher, Robert, more famous and celebrated for his learning than for the royal crown. He was the only king of our time who was the friend of all knowledge and all virtue." So writes Petrarca in the Letter to Posterity, and continues:—

"I remember now with wonder . . . the honourable welcome and the demonstrations of affection which he courteously made me. . . . And, when we had talked together of a thousand different things, I showed him my poem, the *Africa*, which pleased him so much that he begged me, as a singular favour, to dedicate it to him. I could not but consent to such an honourable request, nor indeed had I any wish to refuse. And for that which was the object of my journey, he fixed a day on which he examined me continuously from mid-day till evening. And because the time was too short for the many matters which arose for discussion, he continued the examination during the two following days; and so, for three days, he put my poor abilities to the proof, and at last pronounced me worthy to receive the laurel. He offered it to me there in Naples, and earnestly besought me to accept it there, but the love

[1] *De Reb. Fam.* iv. 4.

of Rome had more power over my mind than even the august wishes of that great king."[1]

The three days' examination appears to have included dissertations on history, science, geography, and poetry, but of the latter King Robert declared himself to be very ignorant. Petrarca instructed him in this neglected branch of his education, explaining the different kinds and uses of poetry, and did not desist from his lecture until he had altered the king's attitude towards it. Respecting the poet's desire to receive the laurel where Virgil and so many other great ones had been crowned, Robert only regretted that his age prevented his accompanying him, but he invested Petrarca with his own royal robe, charging him to wear it at his coronation, and sent Giovanni Barrili as his representative. The envoy, however, was waylaid by robbers, and did not arrive in time, neither was Giacomo Colonna, Bishop of Lombez, able to be present, to Francesco's great regret.[2] The ceremony took place on the Capitol, on Easter Day, April 8, 1341, being the last day of the senatorship of Orso, Conte dell' Anguillara, who said that no one but himself should have the honour of crowning the poet. Monaldesco has written a vivid little account of it. " There were twelve youths of fifteen arrayed in scarlet, and all sons of gentlemen and citizens . . . and then came six others dressed in green cloth . . . and they

[1] *Ep. ad Post.*
[2] The Bishop was then in Gascony, and, a short while before, Petrarca had thus written to him: " You must know that I am going to receive the Delphic laurel, as I have ardently desired. Once the object of the fervent vows of emperors and of poets, to-day spurned and ignored, to me it has been the cause of many sleepless nights. . . . But you will say: ' So much labour, so much fatigue, so much trouble, and for what? Do you think, perchance, that you will become better or more learned on account of the laurel? Will you not rather only become more notorious and be the more exposed to envy? What is the use of this pomp of leaves? ' What do you expect me to answer? Nothing but the saying of the wisest of the Hebrews: *Vanitas vanitatum et omnia vanitas.* Such is human nature! "—*De Reb. Fam.* iv. 6.

each carried a garland of divers flowers. After these appeared the Senator in the midst of a multitude of citizens, wearing on his head a crown of laurel, and he sat upon the throne prepared for him, and the aforesaid Messer Francesco Petrarca was summoned to the sound of trumpets and fifes; and he presented himself arrayed in a flowing robe, and cried three times: Long live the Roman People, long live the Senators, and God preserve them in liberty. And then he knelt before the Senator, who said: *The crown is the reward of merit;* and lifted the garland from his own head, placing it on the head of Messer Francesco, who recited a fine sonnet in honour of the valour of the ancient Romans. And this ceremony was concluded with much praise of the poet, for all the people shouted: Long live the Capitol and the Poet." [1]

Besides the sonnet, of which no trace now remains, Petrarca delivered an oration. Taking for his text a passage from the third *Georgic*, he began thus:—

" Sed me Parnassi deserta per ardua dulcis
    Raptat amor.

To-day, magnificent and venerable men, I must proceed in poetic fashion, and therefore I have chosen my text not elsewhere than from the writings of the poets. Moreover,

---

[1] Annali di Ludovico Monaldesco, *Rer. It. Script.* xii. col. 540.

There is another account of Petrarca's coronation, purporting to be by his friend and contemporary, the poet Sennuccio del Bene, but it was only published in 1549, and is most certainly a fable, which does not prevent its being very amusing reading, the whole pageant being treated as a public show, and the hero thereof made into a mere mountebank. In particular the author informs us that " they could not put our poet on the back of a lion, or a tiger, or of any other wonderful wild beast . . . because there was not at that time in Rome any strange animal, for, if there had been any, without doubt he would have been placed upon it." (*Il Petrarca con narrazione del suo coronamento di Sennuccio del Bene*, London, 1796.) This narrative certainly seems to emanate from a later period than Petrarca's, and is more characteristic of that time when, as Burckhardt tells us, " cities and princes were alike eager to keep live lions and to buy the largest animals."

and for the same reason, having for the present set aside those subtle distinctions which one is wont to use in theological discourses, and having invoked the favour of the Divine Name, I think that, in order that I may deserve to obtain this, the salutation of the glorious Virgin must not be passed over in this brief discourse, which, for the rest, I will make as short as possible." He then recited the *Ave Maria*, and, continuing the oration, related his hesitation between Paris and Rome, but says that he was guided by Virgil's verse saying: *Vicit amor patriæ*. He then speaks of the difficulty of the poetic art—arduous above all others, beset with obstacles, and arousing on the whole little interest and enthusiasm, and, if they would inquire whence came to him the courage to adventure himself on such a steep road, the only answer would be: *per amorem*. Having spoken of the labour, he must also speak of the reward, and here, of course, he has a word to say of the laurel: it is the ornament of temples, the honour of emperors, of heroes, and of poets, possessing and conferring immortality.[1]

After the ceremony, Petrarca was conducted with great rejoicings to St. Peter's, where, after giving thanks to God, he deposited his crown as an offering to be hung up in the church.

And so ended this triumph, which, among other distinctions, conferred upon the poet one which he specially prized: he was made a Roman citizen. At his present age, with his present thoughts and ambitions, no prouder title could have been bestowed upon him; but in the years to come we shall see him returning for another celebration, and with the nobler ambition of fitting himself to be a citizen—

Di quella Roma onde Cristo è Romano.

---

[1] Attilio Hortis, *Scritti inediti di Francesco Petrarca*, pp. 25-37, 311-328.

## CHAPTER IV

### THE WORLD OF POLITICS

" An ignorance of means may minister
To greatness, but an ignorance of aims
Makes it impossible to be great at all."
E. B. BROWNING, *Casa Guidi Windows*.

LEAVING Rome—not without peril, for he fell among thieves, and had to flee back to the city and start again with a suitable escort—Petrarca went first to Pisa, from whence he wrote an account of the ceremony on the Capitol to King Robert,[1] and then to Parma, where he arrived on April 21, the very day on which his old friend, Azzo da Correggio, with his three brothers, took possession of the town. We have already told the history of their acquaintance, and it seems to have been renewed in 1339, when Azzo came to Avignon to treat again with the Pope, and it is likely that he went to Naples with Petrarca, who must, in that case, have been aware of his designs.

The career of Azzo is an expression of the time. The Scaligers, whom he dispossessed, were his relations and benefactors, but it would seem that the atrocity of their government induced the Correggesi to conspire against them and take Parma for themselves. In order to compass this, they entered into negotiations with Robert of Naples, with the republic of Florence, with Luigi Gonzaga, lord of Mantua, whose daughter Azzo had married, and with Luchino Visconti, who gave them substantial help and to whom they promised to cede Parma at the end of four years.[2] At first, at any rate, the result seemed to

---
[1] *De Reb. Fam.* iv. 7.
[2] M. Villani, xi. 126. Cf. Corio, *Storia di Milano*, iii. 5.

justify the means; the revolution was acclaimed by the populace, and the new lords of the city gave promise of a righteous government; it is, therefore, not incongruous to see the poet making one of their company and celebrating their triumph. He writes thus of the event to Cardinal Colonna:—

"I entered Parma under the auspices and the escort of your friends, the lords of Correggio. . . . This very day, the adherents of the tyrant having been expelled, they re-entered the city now restored to them, to which, with a sudden revulsion of things, and amidst the incredible joy of the free people, one sees that liberty and justice have returned. Here then, giving way in all things to their prayers and hopes, I propose to pass the summer, not doubting that you will be willing to give me your permission. For they swear that they greatly need my presence, which I am sure comes from their courtesy, rather than from any necessity. And of what use could I be in this state of affairs? I, who delight, not in noisy citizens, but in the silence of forests; I, who am born, not for the cares of arms or of administration, but for solitude and leisure. But these lords, who know my desires, promise me that I shall be able to live here in quiet, when the outburst and ardour of popular joy has cooled down. However that may be, I must accede to their gracious entreaties. We shall see each other at the beginning of the winter."[1]

It was some time during this winter that the dramatic incident of the blind man of Pontremoli occurred, which bore remarkable testimony to the poet's widespread fame. He relates the story in one of his letters:—

"You have heard of the visit of that Perugian, an old blind man who kept a grammar school at Pontremoli, and who, with good reason, I shall call poet, if a great love of letters and an ardent enthusiasm suffice for that to be said of one. For hardly had he heard that I had gone to present

[1] *De Reb. Fam.* iv. 9.

myself before the King of Naples than he went to that city, leaning upon a youth, his only son, urged by the desire of making my acquaintance. Tidings having reached the king of the motive of his coming, he had him summoned into his presence . . . and having seen and contemplated the face of this man, which was like a bronze statue, and having heard from him what he wanted: 'You must make haste,' he said to him, 'if you want to find the man you are looking for in Italy; if you delay even a little longer, you will be obliged to go to France for him.' 'And I,' replied the poor man, 'if my life were not failing, would go in search of him even to the Indies.' Astonished and moved to compassion by this, the king wished that the expenses of his journey should be given to him, and the man tracked me as far as Rome, whence, not having found me, he returned to Pontremoli. But having heard that I was at Parma, in the heart of the winter he crossed the Apennines white with snow, and having sent me beforehand some not bad verses, came there to present himself to me. . . . Oh, how many times, raised in the arms of his son and of one of his pupils, who was like another son to him and served him as a guide, did he kiss this brow which had thought, and this hand which had written, the things in which he said he had taken ineffable delight. . . . For three days he never left my side, and the whole city, having heard who he was and why he had come, was filled with wonder. . . . One day he said: 'I should be grieved to be troublesome to you, but I cannot have enough of you whom I came to see from so far, and with so much fatigue'; which word *see* having moved the bystanders to laughter, he, being aware of it and understanding the reason, turned to me much more excitedly, and said: 'You yourself whom I kiss and none other, I call you to witness that I see you far better and more distinctly than do these who have eyes.' At which speech they were all amazed and held their tongue."[1]

*Rer. Sen.* xvi. 7.

Of Petrarca's life in Parma we get a glimpse in his Letter to Posterity:—

" Leaving Rome, I went to Parma, and there I remained for some time with the lords of Correggio, who were always most liberal of every favour to me, and excellent in every way, but unfortunately they did not agree together. At that time they set up an incredibly good government in that city, such as had never been seen before, nor will there probably be any to equal it in the future. Mindful of the honour that had just been conferred upon me, and anxious to show that I was not wholly unworthy of it, while I was strolling one day, I took the road to the mountains and found myself on the banks of the Enza, in the territory of Reggio, at the entrance of Selvapiana. On looking at these places I felt the thought of my interrupted poem on *Africa* re-awaken in my mind, and, inspired by my re-kindled enthusiasm, I wrote a great many verses that day. Afterwards, when I returned to Parma, to that quiet and retired dwelling which I bought later, I set to work upon it with such good will that I soon completed it, and with such celerity that I have never ceased to wonder at it." [1]

It is probable that Petrarca did not buy the house until his second sojourn in Parma, in 1343; it had a big garden and was situated near the Church of San Stefano: it still stands, and bears the inscription:—

FRANCESCO PETRARCA
POSSEDETTE ED ABITÒ QUESTA CASA.[2]

From another source we learn that the poet had a little house in the village of Ciano, in a very old and delicious forest on the right bank of the Enza, and here he was accustomed to go in the autumn.[3] So is Selvapiana the companion-picture to Vaucluse.

This first sojourn at Parma was embittered to the

[1] *Epist. ad Post.*   [2] *De Reb. Fam.* iv. 9, Fracassetti's note.
[3] G. M. Allodi, *Serie cronologica dei Vescovi di Parma*, i. pp. 635, 636.

poet by three grievous losses. The first was that of his earliest friend and patron, Giacomo Colonna, Bishop of Lombez. This friend had been begging him for another visit, and Petrarca had promised it in the coming spring; but, in the meantime, news reached him of the dangerous illness of the Bishop, and one night he had a remarkable dream, which he relates in one of his letters. He dreamed he was walking in his own garden at Parma, and suddenly he saw the Bishop alone and about to cross the stream that watered the place. Petrarca ran to meet him, asking him one question after another; whence he came, whither he was going, why he was in such a hurry, why all alone. Making no answer to these inquiries, the Bishop looked as if he were going to smile, and said: " Do you remember how wearisome the storms of the Pyrenees were to you when you stayed with me beyond the Garonne? Well, I am weary of them now, and am going to Rome, never to return to Lombez any more." Francesco begged to be allowed to accompany him, but was gently repulsed once or twice, after which the Bishop's aspect and the sound of his voice changed all at once: " Have done," he cried; " I do not want your companionship now." Then Francesco, fixing his eyes upon him and perceiving his bloodless pallor, saw that he was dead. Overcome with grief and fear, he cried aloud, and, waking at the same moment, heard the last sound of the cry. He took down a record in writing of the event and of the day, and told it to those present, and wrote an account of it to his absent friends. And lo! twenty-five days later, he received the news of the Bishop's death, and comparing the time, he found that, that same day on which he had seen the apparition, Giacomo Colonna was really dead.[1]

Petrarca's second grief was the death of Tommaso da Caloria, with whom he had studied at Bologna, and they had remained fast friends ever since. He was a poet of

[1] *De Reb. Fam.* v. 7.

some note, and receives honourable mention in the *Trionfi*.[1] In January, 1342, Padre Dionisio died at Naples—an irreparable loss to Francesco, to whom he had been friend, confessor, and adviser.

It was during this first visit to Parma, and inspired no doubt by that government "*non come signori ma come padri,*" that the poet wrote his canzone, *Quel c' ha nostra natura in se più degno*, which he afterwards excluded from his collection, probably not as deeming it inferior in merit, but because its radiant prophecies had been falsified by the disasters that befell Azzo. There is, indeed, a note of moderation and of self-repression in it, sadly at variance with the subsequent conduct of Parma's rulers.

> O Liberty, sweet and desirèd good,
> Ill known of him who ne'er thy loss has known,
> How welcome to the noble must thou be.
> Through thee has life in leaf and blossom blown;
> By thee is gendered such a happy mood
> As to the high gods doth resemble me.
> I would not wish for honours without thee,
> Or wealth, or all the things that men desire.
> A lowly roof with thee contents the mind.
> O grievous weight unkind
> Which for so long a journey doth but tire!
> Her first shall we not find
> Who shall relieve our shoulders of this load?
> So tiring is the road
> By which one needs must climb to virtue's height
> That men are fearful only at the sight.[2]

---

[1] *Triumphus Cupidinis*, iii. 59, 60.

[2] "Libertà, dolce e desiato bene,
  Mal conosciuto a chi tal or no 'l perde,
  Quanto gradita a 'l buon mondo esser dèi!
  Da te la vita vien fiorita e verde:
  Par te stato gioioso si mantene
  Ch' ir mi fa somigliante a gli alti dei:
  Senza te lungamente non vorrei.

In the spring of 1342 Petrarca returned to Avignon, for which step various reasons have been adduced. It is extremely probable that he was recalled by Cardinal Colonna; it has also been stated that, as he was now a Roman citizen, he was deputed to go as an envoy to the new Pope; or it may be that the death of Benedict XII. and the accession of Clement VI. was in itself a sufficient reason for him to hasten his return. At any rate, he addressed a letter to Clement, as he had done to his predecessors, and the pontiff, though disregarding his appeal, awarded him a priorate at Migliarino in the diocese of Pisa. One great consolation awaited Francesco in Avignon; he found that his two friends, Socrates and Lælius, were now established in Cardinal Colonna's household. They all became more intimate than ever, Socrates, in particular, being so devoted to the poet, that he even followed him into the solitude of Vaucluse.

Whether or not we may consider Petrarca to have been a Roman envoy, it is certain that another messenger of very different importance was despatched a few months later. Disturbances had been rife in Rome; the Senate had been overthrown and the rule of the thirteen *buoni uomini* reinstated, the Pope being still considered the nominal head of the city. The man chosen was a young notary, Cola di Rienzo, already noted for his surprising knowledge of antiquity, his eloquence, and his personal

---

   Ricchezze, onor e ciò ch'uom più desia;
   Ma teco ogni tugurio acqueta l'alma.
   Ahi grave e crudel salma
   Che n'avei stanchi per sì lunga via!
   Come non giunse in pria
   Chi ti levasse da le nostre spalle?
   Sì faticoso è 'l calle
   Per cui gran fama di vertù s' acquista
   Ch' egli spaventa altrui sol de la vista."
    *Rime di Francesco Petrarca sopra argomenti storici
     morali e diversi*, G. Carducci, Livorno, 1876.

beauty; he was also known as the determined foe of the nobles, by whom his brother had been murdered; and the friend of the poor and the oppressed, whose cause he made it his business to champion. This embassy to Avignon was his first political venture, and the fearless sincerity with which he depicted the unhappy condition of the city owing to the tyranny of the great houses, warmly appealed to Clement. Rienzi was further deputed to implore the Pope's return, and to ask that the Jubilee might be held at shorter intervals. This latter request had also been pressed on the Pope by Petrarca in the Latin epistle he addressed to him,[1] and to this Clement lent a favouring ear, fixing the Jubilee for every fifty years; he also held out vague hopes of re-visiting Rome, and, for the political situation, he showed interest and sympathy, without committing himself to any definite line of action. Rienzi, remaining at Avignon, speedily formed a friendship with Petrarca. There was something of similarity between the two men. Their passion for antiquity was the same, and indeed Cola is said to have been the more accurate and learned antiquarian of the two.[2] Each was well read in the poets and in history; the writings of Livy, Cicero, Seneca, Cæsar, and Valerius Maximus were equally familiar to both; their political ideals coincided, or it may be that Francesco grafted some sort of policy on to the cruder notions of Rienzi, which had not reached much beyond a bitter animosity against the ruling classes. And one failing they undoubtedly had in common—an overwhelming vanity, which, dwarfed and checked in Petrarca by education, experience, by really great qualities, and by that mental humility which is rarely wanting to good scholarship, was fostered and augmented in Rienzi by the marvellous position to which he mounted and which caused his final ruin. The better features of his wonderful career we may fairly attribute to the influence

[1] *Epist. metr.* lib. ii. ep. 6.
[2] Cf. R. Lanciani, *Ancient Rome*, pp. 5-7.

of Petrarca. Rienzi was for some time well received at the papal court, but his strictures on the great Roman houses so offended Cardinal Colonna that he persuaded Clement to withdraw his countenance from the plebeian ambassador, and for some time Cola remained in the city living in the greatest poverty. Petrarca's influence with the Cardinal at length availed to reinstate Rienzi in the Pope's favour, and he was finally awarded the post of notary in the civic Camera, with a salary of five gold florins a month, after which he returned to Rome. The earliest letter we have of Petrarca's to Rienzi obviously relates to this time, and was probably written soon after Cola left Avignon.

" When I recall to my mind the most holy and weighty discourse, which you held with me three days ago before the portals of that ancient and religious temple, I become all enkindled, and am as though I deemed an oracle had issued from the divine sanctuary, and seem to myself to have listened to a god rather than a man. So prophetically did you seem to deplore the present state, nay, rather, the downfall and ruin of the republic, so penetratingly to put the fingers of your eloquence upon our wounds, that, as often as the sound of your words returns to my ears in memory, tears rise to my eyes and grief comes back into my soul. . . . And, if often before, far more often since that day, am I near you; often despair comes upon me, often hope, but often, with my mind wavering between one emotion and the other, I say to myself: Oh, if ever! Oh, if it might happen in my days! Oh, if I might be a partaker in such a splendid work and in so much glory." [1]

In the autumn of this year, 1343, Petrarca was sent on an embassy to Naples, where the government was now in the hands of a council appointed by the late king, Robert, to act as regents until Giovanna should have reached the age of twenty-five. The Pope maintained that this office belonged to him during the queen's minority and was

[1] *De Reb. Fam.* (ed. Fracassetti), *Appendix Litterarum*, ep. 2.

## THE WORLD OF POLITICS

desirous of sending some one acquainted with the place, and likely to be well received at the court, to vindicate the papal rights. It was doubtless Cardinal Colonna who pointed out the poet as a suitable ambassador, and, at the same time, he entrusted him with a private mission—to obtain the release of some political prisoners in whom he was interested. It was a melancholy experience for Francesco to return to Naples under such altered circumstances; three letters to the Cardinal give us some account of his journey and his occupations. He stayed four days in Rome *en route*, and writes:—

"I arrived there on October 4, when it was nearly night . . . and, before taking any rest, I wished to pay a visit to your excellent father. Good God! what virile majesty, what voice, what brow, what countenance, what bearing, what strength of mind, what vigour of body at that age. I seemed to be in the presence of Julius Cæsar or of Scipio Africanus, except that he is far older than either of them, yet to look at him he is just the same as when I left him seven years ago in Rome, or even as when I saw him first in Avignon more than twelve years ago." Then going on to speak of Naples: "Here is no piety, no truth, no faith whatever. . . . In fine, I beg that you will tell the Roman pontiff, in my name, that his words would certainly have been listened to with more veneration at Susa or Damascus, strongholds of the Saracens, than here in Christian Naples."[1]

The difficulties and disappointments that Petrarca met with during his mission were mitigated by intercourse with his old friends, Giovanni Barrili, who had been deputed to accompany him to Rome on the occasion of his coronation, and Marco Barbato di Solmona, the late king's chancellor. So, in his second letter, he says: "I have seen Baiæ with . . . Giovanni Barrili and my Barbato. I never passed a happier day, owing to the company of such friends and to the

[1] *De Reb. Fam.* v. 3.

variety of beautiful things that I have seen." [1] The third letter gives an account of a terrible storm which swept over Naples, and which is noticed by all contemporary historians as one of unprecedented fury. Petrarca writes that never did he see anything so dreadful or so violent. Hardly had he gone to sleep than he was awakened by a sudden terrifying crash; not only the windows, but the walls and the roof, though built of solid stone, being violently shaken to their foundations. When the friars, in whose house he was,[2] rose at midnight, according to their custom, to say the Office, terrified by the sudden disaster, carrying lighted torches in front of them, bearing crosses and relics of the saints, and loudly invoking the Divine mercy, they all crowded into his room, and he, taking courage, went with them into the church, where in tears and prayers they passed the night, thinking from one moment to another that they should all be dead, and everything around them a heap of ruins. It would be impossible to paint, he says, the horrors of that infernal night; rain and wind, and thunder crashing in the sky; tumult on land, and above all the roaring of the sea. Towards the dawn, though it was still little less dark than night, they ventured down to the port, and witnessed the lamentable spectacle of a wreck almost within touch of land. The oldest sailors said that it was an unprecedented sight. Right in the middle of the harbour lay the dreadful wreck; the miserable people in the water, quite close to land, in wild confusion stretched out their arms to grasp it, but were dashed against the rocks by the rushing waves and were broken in pieces like eggshells, and the shore was covered with their mutilated corpses. The cries of men and the wailing of women outdid the noise of the storm and of the sea. It needed courage even to look round, so appalling was the sight of the sky

[1] *De Reb. Fam.* v. 4.
[2] Petrarca was staying in the Convent of San Lorenzo belonging to the Friars Minor.

and of the angry, raging ocean. Great mountains of surge rushed between Naples and Capri, neither blue nor black as it usually is in great tempests, but quite white, and the whole sea seemed to be covered with fierce white foam. There was not a ship that could weather such a tempest, not even in the harbour. Petrarca, who had an unconquerable horror of the sea, and who had been expressly charged by the Cardinal to go by sea to Naples to save time (an injunction which he had not fully carried out), here takes the opportunity of stating that never, to please any one, not the Pope, not his own father if he were still alive, will he make another sea voyage, and concludes: "Birds go through the air and fishes through the sea; I am a land-animal, and, so long as my legs will carry me, I will go by land."[1]

He left Naples at the end of December, having been successful in the business entrusted to him by Cardinal Colonna, but his papal mission was wholly without results. He then returned to Parma, which he found in a much less happy condition than that in which he had left it. The rule of Azzo and his brothers had not been continued with that fatherly care and justice for which its beginning had been conspicuous. One of the brothers had died, and Azzo, quarrelling with the other two, subsequently sold the town to Obizzo d'Este for 60,000 florins, thereby breaking faith with Luchino Visconti, lord of Milan, to whom he had promised to deliver it up after four years; Visconti, however, captured the town from Obizzo. Meanwhile Azzo had made his peace with the Scaligers, who named him governor of Verona. While he was occupying this post, the bastard brother of Can Grande made himself master of the city, and Azzo, who was generally thought to be implicated in the plot, was forced to fly, leaving his wife and children prisoners. He wandered about the north of Italy for some time, until Petrarca, who never lost his friendship for him,

[1] *De Reb. Fam.* v. 5.

was the means of reconciling him with the Visconti, and the fallen tyrant ended his days in peace and comfort in Milan. Francesco dedicated to him his treatise *De Remediis Fortunæ*, with a very interesting prefatory letter which, while showing the poet's estimate of Azzo's character, throws some light on his attitude towards the tyrants in general.

" Having seen you bear yourself well in the one condition and the other . . . you appear to me worthy of this gift. . . . Hardly, to my knowledge, could our age produce a man whom destiny has led and guided through such changes, and by such different ways. . . . As for me, by reason of your courage, not only do you get from me a new and greater love added to the ancient love I gave you . . . but I give you also my pen. He who gives what he has to a friend in necessity, however small it may be, has perfectly fulfilled the duty of friendship; because friendship looks to the mind of him who gives, in the thing given, which, although it be little, may be the token of a great love." [1]

But in 1343, the date of Petrarca's return to Parma, none of these changes of fortune had taken place, only the city was in a state of unrest and discontent. It is generally thought that the winter of 1344-1345 was the occasion of the poet's writing his canzone, *Italia mia*. His high hopes for Parma have been disappointed; there is yet another wound in the body of his beloved Italy, and with all her children he will make lament over it.[2]

[1] Preface to *De Remediis Utriusque Fortunæ*.

[2] The older critics were unanimous in assuming that this canzone was written in 1328, on the occasion of the descent of Lodovico, the Bavarian, on Italy; but, following in the steps of de Sade, it is now generally agreed that its most probable date is 1344-1345, when Parma was besieged by Obizzo, Marchese d'Este, and his allies, supported by an army of German mercenaries, who were popularly called *Bavaresi*. In the absence of complete certainty, other critics have suggested that it was written in 1354, when the war between Genoa and Venice was in progress; while Prof. d'Ancona suggests the date 1370, when Petrarca was ill in Ferrara, as illustrating the line—

" E 'l Po dove doglioso e grave or seggio."

# THE WORLD OF POLITICS

My Italy, though vain is any speech
   The mortal wounds to heal
   Which cover all thy body beautiful,
I would at least that sighs of mine should steal
   To Tiber, and should reach
   Arno and Po where I dwell sorrowful.
O Lord of supreme rule,
I pray the pity, that once brought to earth,
May turn Thee yet to Thy beloved land.
See, Lord, on every hand
What little cause to cruel strife gives birth.

Then, addressing the warring princes, he says:—

You, to whom Fate has put in hand the rein
   Of these fair lands and broad,
   For which it seems no pity stirs your heart,
What makes this throng that wears an alien sword?

   .     .     .     .

   It is your wills at strife
   That spoil the fairest portion of the world.

And he continues with infinite pathos:—

For is not this the land that first I knew?
   And is not this my nest
   Where I was nurtured in such gentle wise;
The country that I trust, within whose breast,
   Mother benign and true,
   The dust of both my parents covered lies?
God grant, as thoughts arise
Like these, your heart may melt, and you may gaze
With pity on the people dolorous

---

For the earliest date assigned—1328—it may well be objected that the finish and perfection of this canzone hardly allow us to think it a very early production; also Petrarca was certainly living in Avignon then, and not in Italy. While against the later dates it must be urged that the poem has always been included in the first part of the *Rime*, which contains nothing later than 1348.

Who only seek repose,
Next after God, from you; and, so your ways
Give any sign of grace,
Virtue 'gainst rage shall start
To arms, and soon the combat shall be sped;
For in the Italian heart
The might of ancient days is not yet dead.[1]

. . . . .

Song, I admonish thee,
Since among haughty people thou must go,
Unfold thine argument right courteously.

. . . .

Thy fortune must be tried
Mid those few noble hearts whom good can please:
Say: Who is on my side?
The while I go forth crying: Peace, Peace, Peace.[2]

---

[1] These are the concluding words of Machiavelli's *Principe*.

[2] " Italia mia; ben che 'l parlar sia indarno,
A le piaghe mortali
Che nel bel corpo tuo sì spesse veggio;
Piacemi al men ch' e' miei sospir sian quali
Spera 'l Tevero e l'Arno
E 'l Po dove doglioso e grave or seggio.
Rettor del ciel, io cheggio
Che la pietà che ti condusse in terra
Ti volga al tuo diletto almo paese.
Vedi, signor cortese,
Di che lievi cagion che crudel guerra:

. . . .

Voi, cui fortuna ha posto in mano il freno
De le belle contrade,
Di che nulla pietà par che vi stringa:
Che fan qui tante pellegrine spade?

. . . .

Vostre voglie divise
Guastan del mondo la piú bella parte.

. . . .

Non è questo il terren ch' i' toccai pria?
Non è questo il mio nido,
Ove nudrito fui si dolcemente?
Non è questa la patria in ch' io mi fido,
Madre benigna e pia,

In spite of very unsettled conditions, which he of all men was least able to bear, Petrarca seems to have remained in Parma until February, 1345, by which time the town was surrounded by hostile forces, and he, with several others, had great difficulty in effecting an escape. They were attacked by robbers near Reggio, but fled under cover of the darkness; the poet, however, had a fall from his horse and bruised his arm badly. After a terrible night, they managed to reach Scandiano, where they found friends, and proceeded to Bologna. It is evident from a letter written thence to Barbato di Solmona that Petrarca was weary of living in a state of siege, and longed to find himself again at large. War and disturbances had made his Italian Helicon (so he puts it) quite distasteful to him, and for some time he had felt allured by the idea of returning to his Transalpine Helicon: so that hatred and longing alike urged him to depart.[1] Leaving Bologna, he went to Verona, where, as we have seen, he had the happiness of finding the

> Che copre l' un e l' altro mio parente?
> Per Dio, questo la mente
> Talor vi mova; e con pietà guardate
> Le lagrime del popol doloroso,
> Che sol da voi riposo
> Dopo Dio spera: e, pur che voi mostriate
> Segno alcun di pietate,
> Vertú contra furore
> Prenderà l'arme; e fia 'l combatter corto:
> Ché l' antiquo valore
> Ne l' italici cor non è ancor morto.
> . . . . .
> Canzone; io t' ammonisco
> Che tua ragion cortesemente dica,
> Perché fra gente altera ir ti convene;
> . . . . .
> Proverai tua ventura
> Fra magnanimi pochi a chi 'l ben piace:
> Di' lor: Chi m'assecura?
> I' vo gridando: Pace, pace, pace."
>
> *Rime*, cxxviii.

[1] *De Reb. Fam.* v. 10.

letters of Cicero, and then returned to Vaucluse. In 1346 Petrarca was offered the post of papal secretary, this being the first of five similar offers that were made to him, but he steadily refused them all, with the idea that such a position would interfere with his personal liberty.

It was the year 1347 that witnessed Rienzi's comet-like course across the horizon of Rome. The episode need only detain us here in so far as it bore the impress of Petrarca's genius; its best aspect was probably inspired by, and certainly identical with, his fondest aspirations; he gave to the unstable ruler his fiery enthusiasm and the support of his eloquence, and, characteristically, did not desert him in his fall. Only three years elapsed between Rienzi's successful mission to Avignon and his popular acclamation on the Capitol as ruler of the people. He had used these three years, on the one hand, in fostering the universal discontent with the oppression of the nobles, the miscarriage of justice, and the violence and robbery, to which all were subjected; and, on the other, by means of popular allegorical representations and by eloquent speeches, he had revived in men's minds the remembrance of former glory, of what Rome had been and might yet be again. And in all this we can discern nothing but true greatness, noble sorrow, and noble scorn. So, too, on that wonderful twentieth day of May, when, after having heard the Mass of the Holy Ghost, accompanied by the Pope's vicar, the Bishop of Orvieto, and thus placing the movement under the protection of the Church, Rienzi ascended the steps of the Capitol, and was hailed by the people as their ruler and deliverer, it was an entirely noble appeal that he made to them. He declared himself ready to die for the Pope and the people, and appealed to the highest that was in them, imploring them to be reconciled with each other for the love of Christ. Very wise were his first laws: he ordained that all murderers were to be punished with death; that no lawsuit was to be protracted beyond fifteen days; that the nobles were to be obliged to preserve the safety of the roads, to refuse shelter to all bandits, and to supply corn to the city; and that all fortresses, bridges, and gates were to be in the hands of guards chosen by the people. Admirable, too, was his treatment of the nobles; they were first summoned to do homage on the Capitol (a summons they obeyed trembling), and then sternly commanded to retire to their estates. Truly, this might be called a great Christian revolution; no drop of blood was shed; peace, not war, was its motive power, and its lasting glory was the mutual reconciliation of hundreds of Roman citizens. And, in the mind of its author, a new creation had taken form—united Italy. To Rienzi, Rome, purified of evil and renewed in strength, was the mother and mistress of nations, and to her he summoned all the surrounding rulers, as being one brotherhood, to take part in a national parliament. If only the man had been equal to his conceptions, the existing history of Italy would have been anticipated by centuries.

From the day when the news of the revolution reached Avignon, Petrarca threw himself heart and soul into the cause, aiding Rienzi with letters and suggestions, and giving him an entire sympathy; and he addressed the following letter to Cola di Rienzo and the people of Rome some time in the June of 1347:—

"I am uncertain, magnanimous man, whether first to congratulate you on the glory of so great an achievement, or the citizens of our delivered native-land on your services and the most blessed acquisition of liberty. I congratulate both equally, and address both at the same time. . . . Liberty is in the midst of you, whose surpassing sweetness and desirableness is never more clearly recognised than by her loss. This great good, known to you by so many years' loss, enjoy now, gladly, soberly, modestly, and peacefully, giving thanks to God the bestower of such gifts, who has not yet forgotten His sacrosanct City, nor endured to behold her any longer a slave, with whom He had set the empire of all the world. Therefore, brave men and successors of brave men, if a sane mind returns with liberty, let each one determine for himself to desert life itself rather than her without whom life is a mockery. Look round with vigilant minds, and take heed that whatever you think, whatever you do, shall savour of liberty. To this alone let your care, your watchfulness, to this alone let every action of every man tend; reckon whatever is done apart from this as either irreparable waste of time, or treachery. Let the undeserved love which by long use you have perchance conceived towards your tyrants, and all memory of unworthy affection, fall from your breasts . . . you were slaves, most illustrious citizens, you whom all nations had been wont to serve; and you, under whose feet kings had been, lay under the tyranny of a few men; and, to add to your grief and augment the shame, you had interlopers and foreigners for your masters. . . . I fear much because I love much, and, for the same reason, I dare much. . . . But you, most valiant man, who have sustained the whole mass of the falling republic upon your pious shoulders, watch in arms against unworthy citizens as against most cruel foes. Younger Brutus, keep ever the image of the elder before your eyes. . . . If you reject not my faithful counsel, you will yield nothing to kindred or private affection. Be assured that he, whom you have perceived to be a foe to liberty, cannot be a friend to you, any more than to himself, while he is striving to take from each his most precious possession. . . . Great and to be feared is the name of the Roman people, howsoever cast down. . . . You, indeed, excellent man, have opened for yourself the way to immortalise your name. You must persevere if you desire to reach the goal; otherwise be assured that, the more splendid the beginning, the darker will the end be. If you must needs fall and sacrifice your life to your country . . . you will mount to heaven, whither virtue and love of your people have prepared the way for you, leaving behind you here the memory of an immortal fame. . . . But do you, who now for the first time are truly citizens, believe that this man is sent to you from heaven; reverence him as a precious gift from God, and expose your lives for his safety. . . . For your children, for your wives, for the grey hairs of your parents, for the tombs of your forefathers, you ought to dare something, and for the good of the republic there is nothing that should not be dared." [1]

Rienzi, in replying to this, said how greatly he desired his friend's company, for, even as a precious jewel enhances the value of a gold ring, so would Rome be adorned and decorated by his presence.[2] In other letters Petrarca tells him how he thinks of him day and night, and shall continue to write to him every day without expecting any answer; he also informs him how eagerly all his communications are looked for; that they are read throughout the papal court and passed from hand to hand, and that many copies are taken; and the poet compliments him on the dignity and eloquence of his style. The canzone, *Spirto gentil*, is considered by many critics to have been addressed to Rienzi. The question is not an easy one to decide. Carducci, while quoting a long list of authors who maintain this opinion, says that it is not an ancient belief, having been first brought forward by Vellutello in 1525. It is a point which will probably never be satisfactorily settled, but, as the canzone certainly seems curiously adapted to the state of things when Rienzi was in power, we will consider it here.[3]

---

[1] *Var.* xlviii.  [2] *Epistolario di Cola di Rienzo*, ep. xv.
[3] There are no less than five competitors for the honour of having inspired this magnificent poem, and each one has found eloquent supporters. Needless to say, all the biographers of Rienzi have appropriated it to him, as also Fracassetti and d'Ancona. Some reasons have been found for imagining the elder Stefano Colonna to be meant. With more likelihood, the younger Stefano Colonna has been suggested, and the claims of the latter are supported by de Sade and Carducci among others, but it is difficult to see any real fitness in either. Two other claimants

Meditating as usual on the past glory of Rome and on her present distress, the poet writes:—

> I, who bewail her wrongs by night and day,
> Have fixed on thee my larger store of hope.
>
> . . . . .
>
> The ancient walls which still inspire the world
> To tremble, love, and fear, when memory
> With backward glance bids her review the past;
> And all the tombs wherein their members lie
> Whose fame until the universe is hurled
> To dissolution, shall for ever last;
> And all that in one ruin now is cast,
> Through thee has hope its every wound to heal.

---

are Paolo Annibaldi and Bosone Raffaelli da Gubbio: the first has little in his favour except the date of his election to office—1335—which corresponds well with the probable date of the poem as argued from its place in the *Canzoniere*. The second is far more plausible. A friend of Dante, a poet and a scholar, a man who had taken no insignificant part in local politics before his election as senator of Rome in 1337, he would certainly have been known to Petrarca by reputation, though, as certainly, he was personally unknown to him, a fact which enables us to get over the stumbling-block of the line—

" Un che non ti vide ancor da presso,"

which it is almost impossible to attach to Rienzi or to either Colonna. Further, the Riccardian MS. 1100, which dates from the earliest years of the fifteenth century, is inscribed: " canzone di messer Franciesco Petracchi a messer Busone." On the other hand, Bosone's great age (for he was nearly eighty), and the facts that he had a colleague, and was only elected for one year, rather militate against his being the subject of such vast hopes. It is certainly tempting to forge another link in the chain that joins Dante and Petrarca, to hand on the poetical tradition, as it were, in a direct succession. But probably the most likely solution, though a disappointing one, is that the canzone, to whomsoever originally addressed, has been so much altered that the personality has been eliminated from it, so that it remains rather the embodiment of an ideal and an aspiration than a direct address to any one. Viewed in this light, it would be useless to try to reconcile discrepancies, for indeed they may be intentional. The canzone probably represents the recurring hopes of various epochs, and is a monument of the poet's undying faith in the greatness of Rome.

## THE WORLD OF POLITICS

> Great Scipios, faithful Brutus, if as yet
> News of that well-filled office penetrate
> Yonder, what great rejoicing will you feel!
> Fabricius (think it well)
> At hearing of the tidings will be fain,
> And say: My Rome shall yet be fair again.[1]

Then follows a moving account of the discord and misery that now rule, and the poet ends with an exhortation to his song to carry his message to the " knight whom all Italy honours " and to tell him:—

> that Rome alway,
> With tender, tearful eyes which sorrow fills,
> Cries for thine aid from all her seven hills.[2]

All through the summer Petrarca had listened with feverish anxiety and interest to every particle of Roman news, admiring the Tribune's justice and sincerity, and entering into all his dangers and difficulties; his heart, indeed, was in Rome, and towards the end of November we

---

[1] " I', che dì e notte del suo strazio piango,
   Di mia speranza ho in te la maggior parte:
   . . . . .
L'antiche mura, ch' ancor teme et ama
E trema 'l mondo, quando si rimembra
Del tempo andato e 'n dietro si rivolve;
E i sassi dove fûr chiuse le membra
Di tai che non saranno senza fama
Se l' universo pria non si dissolve;
E tutto quel ch'una ruina involve,
Per te spera saldar ogni suo vizio.
O grandi Scipïoni, o fedel Bruto,
Quanto v' aggrada, s' egli è ancor venuto
Romor là giú del ben locato offizio!
Come cre' che Fabrizio
Si faccia lieto udendo la novella!
E dice: Roma mia sarà ancor bella."

[2] " Dice che Roma ogni ora
Con gli occhi di dolor bagnati e molli
Ti chier mercé da tutti sette i colli."

*Rime*, liii.

find him setting out for Italy. He was evidently not without apprehension for the future, and perhaps felt that his presence might be the means of averting possible calamities. But, when he had gone no further than Genoa, tidings of Rienzi's extravagant excesses were brought to him, and, writing him a sorrowful letter of remonstrance ("Beware, I implore you, of staining your most splendid fame "[1]), he abandoned his purpose and went instead to Parma, where the Pope had conferred a prebend upon him in the preceding year.

It was too true: Rienzi was hurrying to his fall. His brief reign of seven months came to an end on December 15, 1347; his bright sun of justice set in weakness, cruelty, and extravagance, and his later acts show unmistakable signs of an unhinged mind. While admiring Petrarca as the champion of a movement as full of danger as of glory, one stain yet attaches to him in his treatment of the Colonna family. But, even here, he has not met with entire justice, for many of his biographers seem to consider that, as he was bound to the Colonna by personal friendship and benefits received, he had no right to any political views by which they must suffer. That Petrarca was no politician, that he had not even any standard of political morality, is amply borne out by the record of his changes of residence, hard to understand and, in some cases, harder to justify. But, in so far as he ever attained to a clear understanding of how good government should be brought about, and what were the hindering causes, he seems to have grasped these facts touching Rome, the city dearer to his heart than any other spot on earth. To him, as to Dante, all beauty, all worthiness, was centred in Rome; to make her fair and glorious seemed to him the most noble and most blessed work that man could do; and he appears to have regarded the situation with great discernment and insight. That the people of Rome were to be her salvation, that the

[1] *De Reb. Fam.* vii. 7.

nobles had ever been her bane, he saw clearly, and he saw true. We may fairly believe that he would have poured out his heart-blood for Rome, and he would not spare the blood of others. Writing afterwards of these events, he says that, as regards those two families which were the root of so much evil, towards the one he bore no hatred whatever, while to the other, as every one knows, he was bound, not only by friendship, but by the most intimate familiarity, and no princely house in the world was more dear to him. "But," he concludes, "dearer to me is the public good, dearer is Rome, dearer Italy."[1]

We have no reason to think that Petrarca approved of Rienzi's dealings with the Colonna, which were characterised by cowardice, treachery, and cruelty; but he saw in the great houses the enemies of Rome, and, as such, they had to fall. This is exemplified in his fifth Eclogue, in which the House of Colonna (Martius) and that of Orsini (Apitius) dispute for the lordship of Rome. While they are contending, a messenger arrives in haste to announce that Rienzi is now lord and all look to him. The end of the poem is fine, and in treatment bears a slight resemblance to the canzone *Spirto gentil*, thereby affording a slender proof that that much-disputed poem was addressed to the Tribune.[2] Cola was probably the cause of Francesco's taking the final step and leaving the Cardinal's roof for ever in the autumn of 1347. The parting, to judge from the poet's farewell Eclogue,[3] was cold, almost unkind: perhaps it could hardly be otherwise; and the letter Petrarca wrote to him on the slaughter of so many of his family in their desperate attempt to enter Rome is purely conventional and without feeling.[4] But, with the political struggle, all enmity ceased. It is to the lasting honour of Stefano Colonna, the head of

---

[1] *De Reb. Fam.* xi. 16.

[2] The same may be said of much of the language used by Petrarca in his famous appeal to the people of Rome. Cf. *supra*, p. 87.

[3] *Ecloga*, viii.   [4] *De Reb. Fam.* vii. 13.

the House, and the father of Petrarca's two benefactors, that he never resented the poet's political attitude, disassociating it entirely from private friendship, while in the latter's voluminous correspondence there is abundant evidence that the Colonna family were always first in his affections.

But these momentous choices, political or religious, occur now and then in the lives of men and women, and they leave behind them a scar that can never be effaced; for, however the choice is made, there is always some one to say that it was base, and ungenerous, and unloving; and, however the deed is done, there is nearly always the certainty that it might have been done more wisely and more gently; and, in any event, it is the beginning of one of those divided ways which are the darkest part of life's dark places.

The next few years were truly *Wanderjahre* for the poet; he never remained long in one place. From Parma he proceeded to Verona, where he was when the terrible earthquake occurred in January, 1348.[1] He seems to have spent the greater part of this year in journeying between Parma and Verona, of which the probable cause was that he had placed his son, Giovanni, whose legitimation he had procured in the preceding year, at Verona with Rinaldo da Villafranca. The boy had been there since 1345, and at the end of this year his father brought him to a school at Parma, from which, however, he soon removed him, making him the companion of his many journeys. The death of Laura marks the April of 1348 with a black stone, and, in June, Cardinal Colonna died also.[2] The government of Parma was now in the hands of Luchino Visconti, a ruler of great capacity and of much taste for literature, who eagerly welcomed Petrarca, notwithstanding that the latter had in no wise abandoned his friendship for the late lord, Azzo. It is the honourable part of Francesco's relations with the despots that he never made concessions; on the

[1] *Rer. Sen.* x. 2. [2] *Rime*, cclxix.

contrary, as he says in his Letter to Posterity, he seems rather to be patron than patronised. It has been said that the only way in which a man can accept a favour without degrading himself is by taking it as a right, and this attitude was essentially Petrarca's and constitutes a certain, though not an adequate, justification for his line of action. In the autumn the poet went to Ferrara, Carpi, and then to Padua, at the earnest request of Giacomo da Carrara, of whom he thus writes:—

"My fame procured me the goodwill of a man of such rare excellence that assuredly none of the rulers of his time in Italy could be compared with him. This was Giacomo the younger of Carrara, who, both by messengers and letters sent to me in various parts of Italy, or beyond the Alps, where I was living then, never wearied year after year of begging me to go and make friends with him. . . . So at last I set out and came to Parma, where I was received by this great man, not after the fashion of men, but as I think the blessed do in heaven—with so much delight, so much affection and tenderness, that, as I cannot express it in words, I deem it best to be silent. Among many other things I will relate this, that, knowing I had adopted the ecclesiastical life from my boyhood, in order to bind me more closely not only to himself but to the city, he had a canonry at Padua conferred upon me. And certainly, if his life had lasted longer, my constant journeyings and changes of residence would have come to an end. . . . But two years had scarcely passed when God, who had given him, took him from me, from his country, and from the world." [1]

Giacomo, like so many rulers of his age, had gained his power by violence and lost it in the same manner, being murdered by his nephew in December, 1350. With that astonishing contradiction which makes this period the most bewildering in all history, his reign was marked by justice, moderation, and wisdom; he was a great patron of letters,

[1] *Epist. ad Post.*

and under him Padua enjoyed much prosperity. His son and successor, Francesco, always remained a firm friend of the poet.

It was from Padua, in February, 1350, that Petrarca began that long series of appeals which he poured forth on Charles IV. From the time of Rienzi's first defection, he seems to have conceived no other hope for the restoration of Rome than in turning, like Dante, to the Emperor. To the mediæval mind that world-empire was an alluring idea. It would have been an impossibility, but men had not recognised this: it was still an end to be worked for, an ideal that might be realised. Petrarca had made one step forward in inspiring and upholding Rienzi's enterprise, but, when that failed, he could only fall back on an older tradition; hence his letters to the Emperor. "How is it," he writes, "that you let the time go by in uncertainties and consultations, as though you were master of the future? . . . Among all the sacred and noble duties which press upon you, surely none is more grave and more important than to restore peace to Italy."[1] We thus see the poet in advance of his age in his conception of liberty and popular government, and then, as it were, retrograding; and all the while, if we look at his actions, we find the most curious inconsistency.

In fact, the state of Italy was one huge contradiction. The feudal system, which had never really taken root in the country, was well-nigh dead; politics, as we understand them, were unborn. Italy was a seething mass of individuality, of those most interesting of all things—ideas. In the history of the despots it would be very difficult to apportion to them their share of praise and blame, but their inherent strength and originality is written on what they brought into being. Italy was to develop on intellectual lines: it was but in the realisation of this that any man had a future before him. The despots were the men of the

[1] *De Reb. Fam.* x. 1.

opportunity, those who saw and foresaw; it is only in granting to Petrarca the full appreciation of this truth that we can in any way understand the course of life that he chose out for himself. Meanwhile we see him imbued with the old Dantesque idea of Pope and Emperor. He had never ceased to urge on each successive Pope the duty of returning to Rome, the widowed city who was mourning the loss of her lord. On the accession of Benedict XII., in 1334, the poet addressed two metrical epistles to him; in the first, he implores his return to Rome, whose present desolate state he eloquently contrasts with her former glory; in the second, finding that the Pope is taking no steps to fulfil the promise he had given of return, the poet urges it on him with still greater force, saying:—

> Meanwhile in murmur sad the words rang forth:
> *Rome was.*
>
> . . . . .
>
> And now with eager hope Rome once again
> Invites thee as her spouse, all Italy
> Awaits thee as a father; succour those
> Who thus entreat thee of thine own accord.
> So shalt thou see Christ worshipped through the world,
> While thou dost feed His flock.[1]

With the accession of Clement, in 1342, Petrarca's hopes again rose, and again he addresses the Pope in the name of Rome, who, while she bewails her failure to procure the return of his predecessors, who did but delude her with vain promises, yet, still undaunted, expects to conduct him to the vacant seat of St. Peter.

> Me to thyself and peace to me restore,
> Glory to Italy and all the world,
> And make an end of evils.[2]

If Francesco had really cherished any idea that the new

[1] *Epist. metr.* lib. i. ep. 5.   [2] *Ibid.* lib. ii. ep. 5.

pontiff would forego the luxury of Avignon, and face the dangers and hardships of a return to Rome, he was doomed to disappointment. Clement, of all the Popes of the Captivity, was probably the one who had least intention of putting an end to it. Under him every scandal reached its climax, and the poet poured out his abhorrence of the vices and abuses of the papal court in two of his Eclogues, in one of which Pamphilus (St. Peter) reproves Mitio (Clement) for the bad government of the flock, and in the other, under feigned names, all the Cardinals are passed in review and their characters dissected.[1] Many also of the *Epistolæ sine titulo*, which are all undated, must belong to this time. These letters were the outpouring of the righteous indignation of a Catholic, a patriot, and a poet, against spiritual wickedness in high places. Avignon he calls " the Babylon of the West," " a sink of all crimes and all infamy," " a living hell." It is a place, he says, " where dwells neither piety, nor charity, nor good faith; where pride, envy, luxury, and avarice, with all their frauds, reign . . . where God is despised, money is adored, and the laws are trampled underfoot." And in another place, in almost the same words, he writes:—

" I know by experience that there is no piety, no charity, no faith, no respect, no fear of God; nothing holy, nothing just, nothing honest, nothing sacred, in a word, nothing human. Friendship, modesty, decency, candour, are all banished. . . . Everything is full of lies." [2]

And the same fierce accusations are to be found in four of the sonnets where he inveighs against " impious Babylon," and calls her:—

> A nest of treachery wherein is hatched
> Whatever evil haunts the world to-day.[3]

Unfortunately there is a vindictive tone; the patriotism is marred by jealousy and almost seems to have a note

[1] *Ecloga*, vi. vii.  [2] *Ep. sine Tit.* v. xi. xiv.  [3] *Rime*, cxxxvi.

of mean triumph. Yet is it evident that the burning anger is the effect of faith, not the shipwreck of it: it is an outburst of passionate loyalty both to Church and country. It does not even seem anywhere as if his faith were tried by such an appalling state of affairs, and here we get a point of similarity between Petrarca and his far greater contemporary, St. Catherine of Siena. Her writings—monuments of literary excellence as well as of spiritual wisdom —are as outspoken as his; they are as full of indignation, though in her case tempered with love, in his kindled by scorn; but there is, in each writer, a twin-spirit of untroubled faith and unflinching loyalty: the latter we can find again and again in the subsequent history of the Church, but the former would appear to be the rarer and more transcendent gift. It was this faith which brought Petrarca to Rome in the " much-desired year " of the Jubilee.

Leaving Padua in March, he accompanied the Cardinal-legate to Garda; then passing through Mantua he went to Parma, where he was made archdeacon, and from thence, in the autumn, he set out on his pilgrimage to Rome. On his way, he stopped in Florence, and this was the first time that he found himself within the walls of his own city. Here undoubtedly he saw Boccaccio: the only uncertainty is whether or not this was their first meeting. Rossetti surmises that Boccaccio, who had been living in Naples, was present at King Robert's famous three days' examination;[1] while de Sade inclines to think that they had known each other in Paris as far back as 1333.[2] But Petrarca's own letter really seems to establish the fact that this was the first time they had met face to face, though their names must, of course, have been familiar to each other, and they may even have corresponded. Writing to Boccaccio some years later, Francesco says: " This one thing I shall never be able to forget, that when I was hastily journeying

[1] D. Rossetti, *Petrarca, Celso e Boccaccio*, Parte Terza, N. 11.
[2] De Sade, *Mémoires*, tom. iii. p. 796, note.

through the midst of Italy, although it was already deep winter, you, swift not only in sympathy, which is as it were the movement of the mind, but also in bodily motion, came to meet me, drawn by a wonderful attraction to *a man not yet seen.*"[1] From this period, at any rate, dates their friendship. Petrarca stayed only a few days in Florence, and proceeding on his way, he met with a bad accident near Bolsena, falling from his horse and injuring himself so seriously that he was laid up in Rome for a fortnight. From his sick-bed and " in the deep silence of the night," he wrote an account of his misadventure to his newly-made friend:—

" As you know, having taken leave of you, I went to Rome, where in this year, which we sinners had so longed for, Christians from all parts were assembled. . . . I went thither with a firm intention of putting an end to my sins. . . . It is fourteen years since I first went to Rome from a desire to see its wonders. After a few years' interval, I was drawn thither for the second time by the sweet but perhaps immature desire for the laurel. My third and fourth journeys were occasioned by compassion for my illustrious friends. . . . This my fifth, and it may be my last, Roman pilgrimage is so much happier than the others as the care of the soul is more excellent than that of the body, and eternal salvation more to be desired than earthly glory."

Then, referring to his accident, he says that he consoles himself therefor, thinking it to be the just judgment of God that one who had so long been crippled in soul should now be crippled in body.[2]

Writing later to another friend, Barbato di Solmona, who bewailed the fact that they had not been together in Rome for the Jubilee, Petrarca says that he looks upon that as a special dispensation of Providence, as they would have gone about sight-seeing instead of frequenting the churches

[1] *De Reb. Fam.* xxi. 15.     [2] *Ibid.* xi. 1.

in a spirit of piety and Catholic devotion, and would have been thinking far more of literary than of spiritual things, and one does not arrive thus at one's true end.[1] Wending his way back to Padua, the poet passed through his native Arezzo, where he was received " like a king,"[2] and where certain noble citizens, coming out to accompany him beyond the walls, pointed out to him the house in which he had been born (neither great nor rich, says Francesco, but such as befitted the condition of an exile), telling him that the magistrates had forbidden that any alteration should be made in it. On which Petrarca makes the comment that a stranger is treated far more generously in Arezzo than a citizen in Florence.[3]

Florence, however, was soon to show that she was not unmindful of him. He made another short stay there on his way to Padua, possibly as the guest of Boccaccio, who in the April of 1351 was despatched by the Florentines with honourable letters to him, recalling him from exile, restoring his father's confiscated possessions, and inviting him to fill a post in their newly-founded university. Petrarca's reply contained the following sentence:—

"Truly, most illustrious citizens, this your kindness, as it is to your eternal honour, so it is to my no small consolation, since it restores me to the sweet land of my predilection, in which my father, my grandfather, and my ancestors . . . passed their lives in long succession."[4]

The rest of the letter is distinguished by its vagueness; the poet does not commit himself to any definite date for his return, nor to the occupation of any academical position, and it is most likely that he never contemplated the latter; while the Florentines clearly showed the selfishness of their motives when, failing to attract their great citizen as a lecturer or rhetorician to adorn their university, they cancelled their decree and confiscated his property afresh, on

[1] *De Reb. Fam.* xii. 7.   [2] Lionardo Bruni, *op. cit.*
[3] *Rer. Sen.* xiii. 3.   [4] *De Reb. Fam.* xi. 8.

which account Petrarca would never again set foot within the walls of Florence.

The murder of Giacomo II., lord of Padua, had taken place just at the time of the poet's return thither, in December, 1350. His son and successor, Francesco, was equally friendly, and desirous that his court should be graced by the presence of such an illustrious guest, but Petrarca could not settle down under such altered conditions. In this spring, he made another venture into politics in addressing a letter to his friend, Andrea Dandolo, Doge of Venice, with a view to establishing peace between Venice and Genoa, those sister maritime republics whom jealousy was inciting to war on each other, a sight which the poet-patriot could ill bear. " Italian as I am," he writes, " suffer me to speak of the woes of Italy. Behold! two most powerful people are rushing to arms, two flourishing cities, in a word, two lights of Italy."[1] But in spite of his eloquence, both now and, in the following year, when he appealed to Genoa, the war went on for four years. As a politician, Petrarca was never taken seriously. At Padua he was begged to write the epitaph of the late lord, but it was only on the day fixed for his departure that, going alone to the Augustinian Church where Giacomo was buried, inspiration came to him, and he improvised some dozen lines for the occasion.[2] He then rode to Vicenza, not intending to make any stay there, but found there many people of importance who insisted on detaining him, and with whom he passed the evening. The interest of this lies in the history Petrarca himself has written of it, for it seems that the whole company became involved in a discussion on Cicero, his character and his writings. They all praise him, the poet most of all, but, having extolled his genius and his eloquence, he goes on to say something of his inconstancy and lack of firmness, and when his hearers demur,

---

[1] *De Reb. Fam.* xi. 5.
[2] Epigraphe v. *Poemata minora*, vol. iii. Appendice i.

having with him his own imaginary letters to Cicero,[1] he reads them aloud and converts his audience, with the exception of one veteran who cannot contain his surprise and anguish at hearing a word spoken against his idol, whom he characterises as a god—the god of eloquence. Petrarca, describing the incident, says he is rejoiced to have found some one who loves Cicero even more than he does.[2]

Proceeding to Verona, where he only meant to stay a few days, Francesco is detained there by Azzo and his many friends till the end of May, and, stopping at Mantua and Parma, reaches Avignon late in June.

Thither came Rienzi in the following year, sent by the Emperor; for he had been a prisoner in the hands of Charles IV., to whom he had gone of his own accord for the purpose of inviting him to Rome, and promising him a great future as a reformer of Church and Empire. Since the Tribune's fall, no government had lasted in Rome for any length of time, neither could any one settle the dissensions of the unfortunate city, and, in 1351, Clement VI. appointed four Cardinals to deliberate on the subject and suggest a remedy. In their perplexity they bethought themselves of consulting Petrarca, who answered them in two letters, of which the tenor is that the Roman Senate should be composed solely of Roman citizens; he does not wish that they should share this power with others, but that they should separate themselves completely from the nobles who have insolently deprived them of their rights.[3] It is the pre-eminence of the sovereign people of Rome for which he is never tired of contending, and, when Rienzi was brought a prisoner to Avignon in 1352, it is to the people of Rome that the poet appeals for his relief.

"Invincible people to whom I belong, conquerors of the nations, I have to treat with you privately of a great question in a few words. . . . Your former Tribune, now a

[1] *De Reb. Fam.* xxiv. 3, 4.  [2] *Ibid.* xxiv. 2.
[3] *Ibid.* xi. 16, 17.

captive among strangers, O sad spectacle, like a nocturnal thief or a traitor to his country, pleads his cause in chains, and the means of lawful defence, which have never been refused even to the sacrilegious, are denied to him before those that are judges of the world and the masters of justice. . . . It is laid to his charge as a supreme crime, and one to be expiated on the scaffold, that he dared to affirm that the Roman Empire is still at Rome and belongs to the Roman people. . . . This your admirable citizen does not deny that he affirmed and still affirms it, and this is the grave crime on account of which he is brought in hazard of his life. . . . For your own glory, then, I beseech and exhort you not to abandon your fellow-citizen in this extremity, but show that he is yours by demanding him back by a formal embassy, for, though they strive to snatch from you the title of empire, they have nevertheless not yet arrived at such a pitch of insanity as to dare to deny your jurisdiction over your own citizens. Assuredly, if this man committed an offence, it is at Rome that he committed it; and it cannot be doubted that, touching offences committed at Rome, it is yours to judge, unless the rights of common law are to be taken from you—you the founders and promoters of the laws, who have given to the nations their legal system. . . . Do all that you can and ought to do for your Tribune, or, if that name has disappeared, for your citizen, who has deserved right well of the republic. . . . Succour this man: do not neglect the safety of him who, for your safety, exposed himself to a thousand perils and to eternal hatred. Think on his design and his courage, and remember in what a state your affairs were, and how suddenly, by the counsel and work of one man, not only Rome but all Italy was uplifted in such great hope. How suddenly the name of Italy and the glory of Rome was renewed and purified, how great was the fear and grief of your foes, how great the joy of your friends, how great the expectation of the peoples, how the whole tenor of things was altered, how the face of the world was changed, how the disposition of minds was transformed, how nothing was like itself of all those things which are under Heaven: so wondrous and so sudden was the revolution. For the space of seven months and no more he held the republic by the bridle, so that I deem that hardly since the beginning of the world was anything greater attempted, and, if it had gone on as it had begun, it would have been a divine rather than a human work. . . . It can hardly be doubted that your protection is due to him who has exerted himself so much for your glory and not for his own ambition. . . . Dare something if you would be something; there is nothing less Roman than fear."[1]

In a long and interesting letter to his friend, Nelli, Petrarca enters in detail into his personal feelings about Rienzi, saying how Cola has just arrived as a captive in Avignon, and perhaps hardly deserves pity, seeing that he might have died gloriously on the Capitol, but instead has submitted to be in turn the prisoner of a Bohemian and a Limousin. He then refers to the active correspondence between himself and Cola, and to the eulogies he had showered upon him, but says that he does not regret them, because that which the Tribune designed to do was worthy of the admiration of the whole human race, and the ignominy of the end could not obscure the magnificence of the beginning. Petrarca tells his friend, not without amusement, that Rienzi owes his escape to a rumour that has been circulated to the effect that he is a poet, as to which Francesco states for his own part that, while rejoicing in Cola's liberation and in the esteem in which the Muses are held, he cannot possibly invest the Tribune with the title. He is eloquent and has great powers of persuasion, and is a charming and elegant writer; he is also wonderfully well read in the poets, but a man cannot on this account be called a poet any more than a man can be said to be a weaver who wears garments that another has woven.[2]

[1] *Ep. sine Tit.* iv.  [2] *De Reb. Fam.* xiii. 6.

It is curious that Petrarca never touches on Rienzi's brief return to power and miserable end, but his hopes were now concentrated on the Emperor, and the last time he mentions the hapless Cola is, incidentally, in one of his appeals to Charles: "A very little time ago a humble plebeian, not King of Rome, not Consul, not a patrician, but merely an obscure Roman citizen . . . arose and proclaimed himself liberator of Rome. . . . He chose for himself the title of Tribune, the humblest name among Roman dignities. Now, if there were so much power in the name of Tribune, what should not that of Cæsar be able to do?"[1]

It is clear that, in spite of his writings, Petrarca had not fallen out of favour with Clement VI., since he obtained from him in this year, 1352, a canonry for his son in Verona, and Giovanni was accordingly sent thither, being specially recommended to his former master, Rinaldo di Villafranca, and to Guglielmo di Pastrengo.[2] The Pope also again offered the poet a papal secretaryship, which was again refused,[3] and a similar offer was made to him several years later by Innocent VI., which is interesting as indicating the change which took place in that pontiff's estimate of him. For, before his pontificate, Innocent, being then Cardinal Etienne d'Albret, instructed by a learned Cardinal whose name has not come down to us, believed that Petrarca was a magician.[4] At that time the poet could afford to laugh about it, but after Innocent's accession the affair assumed a different aspect, and he, therefore, resolved to leave Avignon, not wishing to offend the Pope by his sorcery, nor to be offended by his credulity.[5] That the accusation rankled, we see clearly from one of his letters, in which he says that by many he is considered nothing less than a

[1] *De Reb: Fam.* xviii. 1.   [2] Cf. *Ibid.* vii. 17 and xiii. 3.
[3] *Ibid.* xiii. 5. Cf. Fracassetti's note.
[4] *Rer. Sen.* i. 4. Also cf. *De Reb. Fam.* ix. 5, Fracassetti's note.
[5] *Ibid.* i. 4.

sorcerer and a magician, because, forsooth, he is too fond of solitude, and takes immense pleasure in the study of Virgil! While saying that he laughs with rage at these statements, he also confesses that it is a matter of no small moment to him to see the fragile bark of his fame adventuring itself among the rocks of such ignorance. He complains bitterly that such is the way of things: you weary your mind, you sit up whole nights, you write, and, if your writings fall into the hands of such critics as do not understand one word because they are incapable of understanding anything, it will be said that you are a magician.[1] Petrarca's indignation at this ignorance and superstition was probably the main reason of his determination to quit Vaucluse for good. He set off first in the November of 1352, going to Cavaillon to say good-bye to his friend, the Bishop, whom he found very ill. This circumstance, together with the inclemency of the weather, and rumours that the neighbouring country was beset with brigands, so worked on Francesco's habitual irresolution that he determined to return to Vaucluse, at any rate for the present, taking the greater part of his precious books and manuscripts back with him. He never really settled there again, but perhaps the finishing touch was given to his intention of departing by the sudden death of his faithful old servant, Raimond Monet, of which the master has left a touching account.

"The day before yesterday, I left this man—the guardian and custodian of my dearest possessions, who has shared my domestic cares for fifteen years—in his house . . . as I thought slightly indisposed, and yesterday evening . . . he passed from this life to the service of the Master who is in Heaven, who, after so many fatigues in the body, will at length give him rest for his soul. One only thing he had desired and this one grant to him, O Lord Christ, that he, being now a happy dweller in Thy temple after his weary

[1] *De Reb. Fam.* ix. 5

sojourn in heat and cold upon my farm, may be no longer dependent on my will but on Thine, and in Thy house, not in mine, may have his eternal abode." [1]

It was in May, 1353, that Petrarca's long residence at Vaucluse really came to an end; this would seem, therefore, a suitable place to sum up the account of what he owed to Provence, and to see how he acquitted himself of the debt.

[1] *De Reb. Fam.* xvi. 1.

## CHAPTER V

### LA JOYA DE LA VIOLETA

" Brow-bound once with violets like a bride."
                                        A. C. SWINBURNE.

IT would be of great interest if we could know with any certainty how Petrarca regarded his Italian poems at this epoch. It is almost a truism that authors rarely recognise their own best work, and though there is no doubt that his estimate of the *Rime* or *Canzoniere*[1] took a different tone as time went on, we should be inclined to think that, for many years, he looked upon it as by far the least valuable part of his contribution to the world of literature. The fact that he revised, corrected, and almost re-wrote it in his old age, shows clearly that he had then begun to appraise it at its true value, for which we may perhaps find two reasons: first, that, as time removed him further from the restlessness and torment in which all his early Italian poems were produced, he was able to judge of them more calmly and effectually; secondly, that the change wrought by his conversion was marked so broadly on his later work that he could not deem it wholly unworthy.

An exile from the land of his birth and his devotion, we must next consider what Petrarca owed to the country of his adoption, and it is, of course, a significant fact that Provence was the home of poetry. There are few studies more fascinating than the history of the Troubadours and the form of their musical language, which so charmed the ear

---

[1] These two titles are used indiscriminately as the Italian equivalent of Petrarca's own title, *Rerum vulgarium fragmenta* (cf. *rime sparse* in the opening sonnet); the *Canzoniere* as more particularly designating the lyrical poems apart from the *Trionfi* (*Triumphi*).

of Dante that he honoured it with a place in the *Divina Commedia*.[1] The *lengua romana*, with its endless rhyming possibilities, produced at first facile versifiers; then these gave place to the most finished artificers, "smiths of language" (to use Dante's phraseology), who invented the most complicated rhymes and metres. To Arnaut Daniel, in particular, we owe the sestina, the most highly artificial of structures, employed both by Dante and Petrarca, and in our own time with consummate success by Mr. Swinburne, though the rhyme is a later French addition.

The reign of the Troubadours lasted about two hundred years, and nearly coincides with the eleventh and twelfth centuries. At a time when a national spirit was wholly wanting, these wandering poets represent to us the shifting life of courts and camps, the emotions of provincial politics, the jealousies of rival houses, the manners and judgments of the time, and, above all, their own characters. They are normally on the side of right and justice, as all great art always has been; they are full of a fine enthusiasm for great men and noble enterprises, and no less full of a fine scorn for littleness of all kinds. They loom large in the history of the crusades, borrowing from them the consecration of religion, and lending them the lustre of poetry. They were the vital part of the age of chivalry, and in some sort its founders; and though we find few women-singers among their numbers, there is no phase of life upon which women have manifestly left more impress. The Troubadour tradition was one of gentleness; it was his *metier* to idealise and worship, but it was the work of those whose praise he sought to soften and subdue, to give laws and judgments, to set up a standard and an ideal, so that in a rude age there grew up, in an incredibly short time and in a very perfect degree, an obligation to courtesy and gentle manners. Woman, who could not create the art, at any rate created the artist. Of course there is the reverse of the medal, for

[1] *Purgatorio*, xxvi. 140.

the annals of the Troubadours are pre-eminently the annals of lovers—faithful and faithless—but, glancing over the whole period of their existence, the record of these two hundred years is no ignoble one.

There was a natural geographical connection between southern France and northern Italy, and, in the eleventh and twelfth centuries, the relations were drawn closer by the welcome offered by the Marquises of Montferrat and Este and the Counts of San Bonifacio and Savoy to all Provençal singers.[1] Of the long line of great names Arnaut Daniel,[2] Peire d'Alvernhe,[3] Giraut de Borniel,[4] Aimeric de Belenoi,[5] Aimeric de Pegulhan,[6] Folquet,[7] and Sordello[8] are mentioned by Dante, and a far greater number by Petrarca:—

> First among all was Arnaut Daniel,
> Great master he of love, who honours still
> His land with beautiful and polished speech.
>
> Then came those twain, whom love so quickly seized,
> The one and other Peire; the less-famed Arnaut,
> And those whom fiercer warfare did subdue;
>
> I speak of the one Rambaud, and the other
> Who sang of Beatrice in Monferrato;
> And Giraut, and the aged Peire d'Alvernhe.
>
> Folquet, who gave his name unto Marseilles,
> Depriving Genoa; and in the end
> Changed state and habit for a better country.
>
> And Jaufré Rudel, who used sail and oar
> To seek his death; and Guillem who by song
> Brought low his days in flower of his age.

---

[1] Cf. H. J. Chaytor, *The Troubadours of Dante*, pp. xxiv. xxv.
[2] *Purg.* xxvi. 142; *De Vulg. Eloq.* ii. 2, 6, 10, 13.
[3] *De Vulg. Eloq.* i. 10.
[4] *Purg.* xxvi. 120; *De Vulg. Eloq.* i. 9; ii. 2, 5, 6.
[5] *De Vulg. Eloq.* ii. 6, 12.   [6] *Ibid.* ii. 6.
[7] *Par.* ix. 37, 67-108.
[8] *Purg.* vi. 61-79; vii. viii. ix. 58; *De Vulg. Eloq.* i. 15.

And Aimeric and Bernard, Hugues and Ancelme,
And thousand others saw I, to whom speech
Was ever lance and spear, and shield and helmet.[1]

The first of these, Arnaut Daniel, introduced by Dante into the *Purgatorio*, is referred to several times in the *De Vulgari Eloquio*. By his contemporaries he does not seem to have been considered "*fra tutti il primo*," but was rather spoken of for his harsh and unusual rhymes, his strained metaphors, and his *tours de force*. He had received an excellent education, and wrote well in Latin as well as in Provençal, and there are allusions in his poems which show that he was not unacquainted with the great classical masterpieces, which is a rare thing among Troubadours, and is an element in his originality. Arnaut has left more trace on Petrarca than any other Provençal singer.[2] His less famous namesake is Arnaut de Marueil, who is said to have possessed the triple gifts of reading, singing, and poetry. The one and the other Peire are respectively Peire Vidal, a magnetic personality made up equally of wit and folly, the hero of

---

[1] " Fra tutti il primo Arnaldo Daniello,
　　Gran maestro d' amor, ch' a la sua terra
　　Anco fa honor col suo dir novo e bello.
　Eranvi quei ch' Amor sì leve afferra:
　　L' un Piero e l' altro, e 'l men famoso Arnaldo
　　E quei che fur conquisi con più guerra:
　I' dico l' uno, e l' altro Räymbaldo
　　Che cantò pur Beatrice e Monferrato,
　　E 'l vecchio Pier d'Alvernia, con Giraldo,
　Folco, que' ch' a Marsilia il nome à dato
　　Ed a Genova tolto, ed a l' extremo
　　Cangiò per miglior patria habito e stato;
　Giaufrè Rudel, ch' usò la vela e 'l remo
　　A cercar la sua morte, e quel Guillielmo
　　Che per cantar à 'l fior de' suoi dì scemo;
　Amerigo, Bernardo, Ugo e Gauselmo
　　E mille altri ne vidi, a cui la lingua
　　Lancia e spada fu sempre, e targia ed elmo."
　　　　　　　　　*Triumphus Cupidinis*, iii. 40-57.

[2] *Rime*, xxxix. lxx.

many extravagant stories, but of such fame as a Troubadour that when, owing to his wild exploits, the question was debated whether he was a wise man or a maniac, the answer was: " No one without wisdom could have produced such poems "; and Peire Rogier, one of the many singers favoured by Ermengarde, Countess of Narbonne, a famous patroness of poets. His love-songs are addressed to her, and his passion for her obliged him to leave her court: like so many of the Troubadours, he ended his days in a monastery. Rambaut de Vaquairas, who loved Beatrice, the beautiful sister of Bonifacio, Count of Montferrat, was a Crusader, and won fame against the Saracens, taking Salonica from them. Peire d'Alvernhe was one of the very early poets, and called himself the " Master of the Troubadours." He was renowned alike for his character and for his talents, and all women coveted the honour of his praise. His poetry lacks sentiment, but is distinguished for form and seriousness. His hymn to the Blessed Virgin—

> Donna des Angels regina
> Esperanza dels crezens,[1]

is thought to have inspired Petrarca's canzone. Giraut de Borneil was certainly one of the most famous of the Provençals; he was called " the Master "—not by himself, but by the judgment of his contemporaries. Dante names him as the singer of righteousness,[2] but will not allow that in poetry he surpasses Arnaut Daniel.[3] Folquet, a noted Troubadour of the end of the twelfth century, had a memorable and varied career. The son of a Genoese merchant who had settled at Marseilles, the beauty of his person and manners fitted him to be the ornament of courts, and he was patronised by Richard Cœur de Lion, King Alfonso of Castile, Raimon V., Count of Toulouse, and by Sire Barral,

[1] Jehan de Nostredame, *Les vies des plus célèbres et anciens Poètes Provensaux*, p. 163.
[2] *De Vulg. Eloq.* ii. 2.      [3] *Purg.* xxvi. 120.

Viscount of Marseilles, whose wife Alazais he loved passionately and celebrated in noble songs. She did not return his love, but nevertheless grew jealous and expelled him from her court, though he was subsequently recalled. Then, as the story pathetically relates: "It came to pass that the Lady Alazais died, and Barral, her lord and husband, died; and died the good King Richard, and died the good Count Raimon of Toulouse, and King Alfonso of Aragon: and then, because of his grief for his lady, and these princes who were dead, he abandoned the world and entered the Cistercian order."[1] In course of time Folquet became Abbot of Torondet, and subsequently Bishop of Toulouse, and took a prominent part in the war against the Albigenses. As a poet he ranks as one of the great Troubadours.

The next name that meets us is that of Jaufré Rudel, Crusader and lover, the very flower of romance, whose story has drawn poems from the lips of singers of all nations, whose spell is so powerful that it has charmed Browning into music and Mr. Swinburne into piety. Rudel took the cross in 1147, went to the Holy Land, and returned in safety. It was some years later that, enamoured of the fame of Mélisende, the lady of Tripoli, praised alike for her beauty, her courtesy, and her sweet charity, he took sail and oar again, and found death—and life; but, if the story be unknown to any one, he should learn it from none but a poet.

> There lived a singer in France of old
>   By the tideless dolorous midland sea.
> In a land of sand and ruin and gold
>   There shone one woman, and none but she.
> And finding life for her love's sake fail,
> Being fain to see her, he bade set sail,
> Touched land, and saw her as life grew cold,
>   And praised God seeing; and so died he.

---

[1] M. Raynouald, *Choix des Poésies originales des Troubadours*, vol. v. p. 152.

Died, praising God for His gift and grace:
  For she bowed down to him weeping, and said
" Live "; and her tears were shed on his face
  Or ever the life in his face was shed.
The sharp tears fell through her hair, and stung
Once, and her close lips touched him and clung
Once, and grew one with his lips for a space;
  And so drew back, and the man was dead.[1]

Guglielmo is probably to be identified with Guillem de Cabestaing, whose tragic story has been told at great length by all the chroniclers. He was the lover of Marguerite, the beautiful wife of Raimon of Roussillon, and in turn beloved by her. The jealous husband, meeting him in a lonely place, killed him, tore the heart out of his body, and ordered it to be served up to the lady at dinner. After she had eaten, he produced the bleeding head of the Troubadour, and told her of what she had partaken. When the unhappy Marguerite exclaimed that no other food should ever pass her lips to take away the sweetness that the heart of Guillem had left there, her husband rushed upon her with his sword, and she, flinging herself from the balcony, was killed on the spot. Upon this all the knights of the surrounding country, headed by King Alfonso of Aragon, made war upon Raimon, and the king made him prisoner, and kept him in custody all his life. The two lovers were buried in one tomb, and for a long time the day of their death was observed every year, and all true lovers came to pray for their souls.

Of the remaining four Troubadours it may suffice to say that Hugues de St. Cyr was one of the learned men of his age, and that the other three enjoyed at one time or another the favour of Richard Cœur de Lion, Ancelme composing a fine funeral ode in his honour, while Bernard de Ventadour,

[1] A. C. Swinburne, *The Triumph of Time.* Cf. Rostand's romantic play *La Princesse Lointaine.*

a poet of singular tenderness and delicacy, sang the praises of Eleanor of Poitiers, who became Richard's wife.[1]

The great Troubadours had long passed away or ever Petrarca set foot in their country, but lesser poets were abundant (though it is to be noted that neither Dante nor Petrarca makes any mention of them), and in Toulouse, in particular, we come across a most interesting survival. This was *La sobregaya Companhia dels set Trobadors de Tolosa*, subsequently known as the *Académie des Jeux Floraux*, and it is delightful to think that this is still in existence. Monsieur de Ponsan, in his fascinating *Histoire de l'Académie des Jeux Floraux*, has collected all the particulars of the earlier Society. They are gathered from two registers written in Provençal, which consist of treatises on rhetoric and poetry, to which is prefixed an historical note by Molinier, the Chancellor of the Company, setting forth all that took place therein from 1323 to 1356. It is to these registers that we are indebted for our knowledge of the constitution of this, the earliest literary academy, though we are still in doubt as to the date of its foundation, for the proceedings here related would seem to emanate from a society in good working order. It is stated that, in the year 1323, seven wise and good Seigneurs of Toulouse (or Poets—the name seems to have been identical), who desired to help the advancement of poetry, which they called the *gai saber*, issued a letter " written from the Faubourg des Augustins, in the Orchard of the said place, at the foot of a laurel, the Tuesday after All Saints Day, 1323." There is also mention of a palace belonging to them, and of the large hall which it contained. These details, as we have said, point to an existing Society, and not to one that was just being formed.

Molinier takes pains to explain the point of view of the

---

[1] Cf. M. Raynouald, *op. cit.*; F. Diez, *Die Poesie der Troubadours*; M. Fauriel, *Histoire de la Poésie Provençale*; Jehan de Nostredame, *op. cit.*; H. J. Chaytor, *op. cit.*

noble Seven. Gaiety was their characteristic; they wished to enliven learning, and believed that the *gai saber* was good for health of body and peace of mind, and that it led men to virtue. The cultivation of Poetry seemed to them necessary for the spending of innocent and happy days. They wished to be known as the *Gaya Companhia,* and they called the laws of Poetry (*Luys d'Amors—Amors* with an *s* being synonymous with Poetry), *Flora de gai saber.* The letter written by them was sent to all the principal towns of Languedoc, to invite poets to come on a day fixed to Toulouse, that men might make good poems, and compose hymns in honour of God and His glorious Mother, that the art of Poetry might be perfected by discussion, and that they might contribute together to its progress. They further promised to present a golden violet to him who should have made the best poem, and the prize was to be called *La Joya de la Violeta.*

This summons did not fail to meet with a response. A great number of poets came to Toulouse, and the narrative states that on May 1 the seven Seigneurs received all the works, and that on the following day, after having heard Mass, they assembled in their hall of meeting in order to examine and choose out the best. On May 3, the Feast of the Holy Cross, they gave judgment in public, and awarded the Violet to Maître Arnaud Vidal, for a poem he had made on the Blessed Virgin. We are also told that the fête took place in the aforementioned orchard, and that the prize was awarded in the hall of the palace; that the festival was attended by people of all ranks and by many of great importance, among whom were six principal magistrates of the town, who announced that henceforth the *Joya de la Violeta* would be provided out of the revenues of the city. Later, other prizes were added—the brier-rose and the marigold, the Violet always being the prize of honour; and small silver flowers were given at lesser festivals held at other times of the year.

It is sad to have to relate that, owing to wars and disturbances, the orchard of the Gaya Companhia was cut down, and their palace destroyed, about 1356, after which the May festivals seem to have been held in the Hôtel de Ville. It is this circumstance which eventually brings Clémence Isaure to our notice, and the story is so picturesque that it seems impossible to omit it, although it belongs to a much later period.

This lady is one of those phantom figures, such as appear now and again in history, whose personality is so attractive, and at the same time so elusive, that the very fact of existence has been denied them. That she was of illustrious birth and endowed with great beauty and wealth, that she loved literature and flowers, that she flourished in the latter half of the fifteenth century, and died unmarried at the age of fifty—these are the only facts that can be guaranteed about her. She evinced her interest in literature by building a Maison de Ville at her own expense, which she bequeathed, with considerable revenues, to the town of Toulouse, ordering that the "*Jeux Floraux*" should be celebrated there every year, and that at the same time roses should be scattered on her tomb. It is from this date that the former Company took the name of the *Académie des Jeux Floraux,* and to this day they hold their meetings and distribute their prizes every May. To the violet, the brier-rose, and the marigold have now been added the amaranth and the primrose, while the statue of the gracious founder who so loved flowers is crowned annually with roses. Among the poets whom this Academy has honoured have been Ronsard and Baif.[1]

We have wandered far from the age of the greater and lesser Troubadours, and, retracing our steps, there is one phase of court life which we cannot neglect. This was the institution known as the Courts of Love, which probably

---

[1] Cf. G. de Catel, *Mémoires de l'Histoire de Languedoc* ; M. de Ponsan, *Histoire de l'Académie des Jeux Floraux.*

arose out of the favourite Troubadour pastime, the *tenson* or dispute, a form of poetry in which questions—chiefly of gallantry—were debated between two singers. It is manifest that to give purpose to this kind of pastime some tribunal was necessary, and so grew up the Courts of Love held by noble ladies. That of Ermengarde of Narbonne was one of the most famous, but there were many others, those of the ladies of Gascony, of Flanders, of Champagne, and, fraught with interest for us, that of the ladies of Romanin.

Of the Troubadour Bertran d'Allamanon, Jehan de Nostredame relates that: "Il fut amoureux de Phanette ou Estephanette de Romanin, dame dudict lieu, de la mayson du Gantelmes, qui tenoit de son temps cours d'amour ouverte et planière en son chasteau de Romanin près la ville de Sainct Remy en Provence, tante de Laurette d'Avignon de la mayson de Sado tant célébrée par le poète Pétrarque."

And again: "Laurette, yssue de l'illustre famille de Sade, gentil-femme d'Avignon, tant célébrée par François Pétrarque, poète Tuscan, et par aucunys poètes Provencaux, fleurissait en Avignon environ l'an 1341; elle fut aprinse aux bonnes lettres par la curiosité et industrie de Phanette des Gantelmes, sa tante, dame de Romanin, qu'estoit aussi une noble et notable dame. Ces deux dames estoient humbles en leur parler, sages en leurs œuvres, honnestes en leur conversation, fleurissantes et accomplies en toutes vertues, admirables en bonnes moeurs et forme ellégante, et tant bien nourries que chacung estoit convoyteux de leur amour. Toutes deux romansoyent promptement en toute sorte rithme provensalle, suivant ce qu'on a écrit le Monge des Isles d'Or, les œuvres desquelles rendent ample témoignage de leur doctrine. Et tout ainsi que par le passé Estephenette, Comtesse de Provence, Adalazie, Vicomtesse d'Avignon, et autres dames illustres de Provence estimées en savoir, ainsi estoient ces deux dames en Provence, la renommée desquelles avoit emply tout le pays tellement qu'on ne parloit que de leur savoir. Est vrai (dict le Monge) que Phanette comme très excellente en la poésie avoit un fureur et inspiration divine laquelle fureur estoit estimée un vrai don de Dieu. Elles estoient accompagnées de . . . plusieurs autres dames illustres et généreuses de Provence qui fleurissoient de ce temps en Avignon . . . qui s'adonnoient a l'étude des lettres, tenans cours d'amour ouverte et y definissoient les questions d'amour qui y estoient proposées . . . et de leurs belles et glorieuses œuvres leur renommée s'espondit partout jusques en France, en Italie, et Espagne." [1]

We see Laura, then, as the embodiment of Provençal art and manners; a poet, it would seem, or at any rate versed in poetry; learned, gentle, and gracious, the finished product of her time and land: she is, too, the Lady of the Violets. One wonders whether Petrarca was ever attracted by the Joya de la Violeta; we know he passed through Toulouse in the summer of 1330 on his way to Lombez; [2] he may have been there during the May festival; but, certainly, what strikes us most is the little that he has in common with the Troubadours. The chief point of contact is the desire to wed poetry and music. A Troubadour was essentially a singer; his poems demanded a voice and an instrument, and, if he had no facility himself, he was invariably accompanied by a jongleur who supplied the music. Many of these became Troubadours, acquiring the art from their masters; in any event, song could not be divorced from music, and Petrarca, a born musician, would not recite his poems except to the accompaniment of his lute, deeming that indispensable for the right understanding of them.

It is at first sight puzzling that such a literature as that

---

[1] Jehan de Nostredame, *op. cit.* pp. 168, 216-218. It is needless to point out that this is not serious history.
[2] Cf. P. de Nolhac, *op. cit.* i. p. 269 (addenda).

to which Provence gave birth should not have been far more influential than it was; but it perished through its inherent defects. It was nourished on love of glory and love of woman; Chivalry gave it a heart, and the Crusading spirit a soul, but, in the long run, it was fed mainly on court intrigues, on petty wars, on small local jealousies. It had no nation, no foundation of tradition, it had had no past, and scarcely looked to a future; it was only personal and individual, and had the charm and the insidious strength of individuality. When we turn to trace the growth of early Italian poetry, we are in another world: here was a people with an inheritance; from the outset, we get an impression of something calmer and stabler. And Petrarca is the lineal descendant of the early Italians, of Guinicelli and of Cino; he is like them in method, he has their seriousness and their large outlook. The work of the Troubadour was a narrowing one; he sought to extol one woman to the exclusion of every other. But the function of great Art has ever been to open wider the gates of life, so that the lips that are tuned to praise perfectly, exalt not one woman, but all Womanhood; not the loveliness of one, but ideal Beauty; above all, not one petal or leaflet of love, but the perfect rounded Rose: since Art must mean a revelation and not a barren presentment.

It may well be that the existence of that large body of romantic poetry, in which woman played a part so seemingly important and yet so really unimpressive, induced Petrarca to place his Italian poems on a lower level than he would otherwise have done, and that this was a point of view from which he took years to free himself. He was born, as we have noted, as regards Provençal literature in a decadent hour; the poet had become a paid rhymer and the jongleur a mountebank, and, though there lingers a charm round the Gaya Companhia of Toulouse, we can hardly help being conscious that, in their light-heartedness, they were seeing but one side of the shield. Yet, merely externally, it would be impossible to deny that the Provençals had exercised a considerable influence over Petrarca. Apart from the metres for which he was indebted to them, the intricate arrangement of rhymes, in which he sometimes attempted to imitate them (as in lxx. and cxxxv.; and particularly in xxix. and ccvi., where the same rhyme sounds are repeated in each stanza throughout the canzone —a very favourite device of the Troubadours, and one to which their language was specially adapted), there are echoes of no less than fourteen different Provençal poets in the *Canzoniere*, while Bernard de Ventadour and Arnaut Daniel are laid under contribution many times.

In considering the *Canzoniere* we have to bear in mind that probably few of the poems are presented to us, either in order, or in diction, as they were first written. Nearly every one has been submitted to " the long result of years," and only flowers again as the maturer mind of the poet saw fit to allow. Imagination and memory have been at work, and also the will to evoke or to efface, and, for the general effect, this must mean both loss and gain. The crispness, the spontaneity, is in many places gone, and we have an undue impression of arrangement. Something of the same objection has been made to Tennyson's noble elegy, which, begun within a few weeks of Arthur Hallam's death, was continued at intervals until its publication seventeen years later, so that in some parts the sharpness of outline is lost, and the poet almost produces the effect of a man who is experiencing a sort of pleasing pain in thus taking out and examining his emotions: the intensity of feeling is relaxed, though the mine of thought is more fully worked. And in the *Canzoniere* we have a still more direct impression of dalliance, of one who is weaving a garland of fancies, elaborating joys and sorrows, and stringing them together at will; all the music of the verse, all the art of the workmanship, sometimes fail to compensate for this loss of reality.

Poetry, which Wordsworth so magnificently defined as

"the breath and finer spirit of all knowledge . . . the impassioned expression which is in the countenance of all Science,"[1] seems to have worn a somewhat different aspect for Petrarca, who will not dissociate it from rhetoric. He will study ancient forms and reproduce classical imagery and epithets, and the aim that he sets before him is to convince by the vigour and appropriateness of his thought;[2] so he seems to grudge the name of poetry to the pure expression of the imagination, forgetting sometimes that, without this, poetry cannot be said to exist. Both to Dante and to Petrarca the form was of paramount importance; the former devotes a large part of the *De Vulgari Eloquentia* to proving that the canzone is the most noble of all measures, and to laying down rules that shall ensure obtaining the utmost stateliness.[3] The canzone was Provençal in origin, Marcabron and Bernard de Ventadour were the oldest writers of it, and, the language being so rich in rhymes, it was customary to keep those used in the first stanza through all the ensuing ones; there are examples of this method in Dante and Petrarca, but it was never a rule in Italian canzoni. The sestina, as we have seen, was the invention of Arnaud Daniel, and Dante and Petrarca each borrowed it direct from him. The ballata, or dancing song, was of Italian growth; it appeared first in Central Italy about the middle of the thirteenth century, being particularly popular in Florence and Bologna. As we might expect, it is not in this form that Petrarca achieved his greatest successes; it demanded qualities in which he was deficient. The madrigal (more properly *mandriale*, from shepherd or herdsman) was a rustic, pastoral song, and, when adopted by poets in the early part of the fourteenth century, it was always used for celebrating country scenes and sports; it is, in fact, a miniature idyll. Petrarca employed it seldom, but very successfully. The origin of the

[1] Wordsworth, *Preface to Lyrical Ballads.*
[2] Cf. G. Voigt, *Wiederbelebung*, i. pp. 28, 29.   [3] *De Vulg. Eloq.* ii. 3-14.

sonnet has been much disputed, but the best critics now seem to agree that it was indigenous to Italy, as it is to be found in Tuscany in the middle of the thirteenth century, while there is no trace of it in Provence before the end. Dante da Maiano certainly wrote two sonnets in Provençal, but he was a Tuscan himself, and the few Provençals who wrote sonnets wrote them in Italian. The word "sonnet" also is purely Italian; there is nothing to match it in Provençal, where *sonet* merely indicates a lyric, and was applied indiscriminately to all poems that were to be set to music. At any rate, the sonnet acquired no importance until the poets of Central Italy brought it to perfection. It is this perfection which has given the *Canzoniere* its abiding place in literature.

Writing to Pandolfo Malatesta, lord of Rimini, in January, 1373, Petrarca says: "By the hand of this messenger you will receive my wretched little vernacular writings, and I wish I could esteem them as worthy of your perusal and your judgment, as I am certain that you will receive them gladly and eagerly, and give them a corner, however obscure, of your library." And in another letter: "I still have several other vernacular poems, on stray sheets so tattered and worn out that one can hardly read them, and if, from time to time, I have a few days of leisure, I am going to amuse myself by putting them together. But it is only rarely that I can do so, and, for this reason, I have arranged to leave some blank pages at the end of both volumes, and so, if I happened to put together anything else, I would send it on separate sheets to my most sweet and magnificent Signor Pandolfo de' Malatesta." [1]

This places us in secure possession of the fact that the poet went on transcribing and correcting his Italian poems to the day of his death. The complete original collection is the manuscript 3195 of the Vatican Library. It is entitled *Rerum vulgarium fragmenta*, and is in two hand-

[1] *Rer. Sen.* xiii. 10; *Var.* ix.

writings, one being that of Petrarca, and was begun in the poet's house in Milan in 1358; the order and emendations represent his latest intentions, for he was working on them to the end of his life. The Vatican Library also contains another manuscript, 3196, which appears likely to be the remainder of a very rough sketch from which the complete work was elaborated. It is interesting to know that both these were once in the possession of the supreme judge and critic of his time, Pietro Bembo, and, no doubt, the high value that he set on Petrarca's poems, making them the subject both of writings and lectures, had much to do with their measureless popularity. He spoke of the poet as one in whom all the graces of vernacular poetry were collected, and said that "among all well-said things, if there were some minute word that might be put better, Petrarca would change and re-change it till it would be impossible to improve it in any way whatever."[1]

The subsequent history of these precious manuscripts is quite clear; they were left by Bembo to his son, and sold by him to Fulvio Orsini, who presented them to the Vatican Library in 1600; but how Bembo first acquired them is a more difficult question. The most likely supposition seems to be that they had remained in the hands of Lombardo da Serico, a citizen of Padua, Petrarca's very dear friend and secretary, to whom he left the *Africa* and all his Latin books; that the complete manuscript was carefully handed down, its existence and whereabouts being always known, and that in 1544 it was in the possession of a Paduan, Messer Daniello da Santa Sofia, from whom the Cardinal acquired it, and wrote about it to his friend, Girolamo Quirino: " I could not tell you how much I prize it. . . . It is in the author's own hand without doubt."[2]

It is thought that the smaller manuscript disappeared at

[1] *Della Volgar Lingua*, lib. ii. p. 286.
[2] P. Bembo, *Lettere*, vol. iii. lib. ii. p. 43 *v*. (It is not *all* in the author's own hand, however.)

the time of the sack of Padua in 1509, and that much of it was then lost, the remaining leaves having been found in a butcher's shop. Besides these, Beccadelli, when travelling through France, managed to acquire a few sheets containing autograph poems of Petrarca, and thought he could put them to no better use than to make of them a present to Bembo, " who showed the greatest desire to have them,"[1] as the Bishop writes to Carlo Gualterazzi, himself a student of the poet. It is from the Vatican Manuscript 3195 that the final critical editions of Petrarca's works have been compiled—that by G. Mestica in 1896, by Carducci and Ferrari in 1899, and by Salvo-Cozzo in 1904, the text in each case being the same, the only difference consisting in the mode of division. For whereas the other two editors begin the second part of the *Canzoniere* with the canzone *I' vo pensando*, which would seem to have been the poet's own intention, Carducci and Ferrari adhere to the ordinary, time-honoured fashion of naming the two parts, respectively, *In vita di Madonna Laura* and *In morte di Madonna Laura*, and begin the second part with the sonnet *Oimè il bel viso*. The first arrangement would coincide with Petrarca's conversion—a much more real dividing line in the character of his life and work, and is obviously the one intended by himself, the " blank pages," of which he writes to Malatesta, being left between the sonnet *Arbor vittorioso* and the canzone *I' vo pensando*. Following then this division, we have to consider the two hundred and sixty-three pieces which make up the first part of the *Canzoniere*, and, eliminating the political canzoni, and about thirty sonnets which are addressed to friends, or written for special occasions, the problems remain whether all the other pieces were inspired by one woman, and in what sequence they were produced. Signor Cesareo has discussed these questions at great length,[2] and seems to have convinced himself that a

[1] L. Beccadalli, *Monumenti di varia Letteratura*, tom. i. pp. 2, 235, note 38.
[2] G. A. Cesareo, *Su le " Poesie Volgari " del Petrarca.*

considerable part of them celebrates other loves, and that chronology is everywhere to seek; but M. Cochin, with, as we think, more poetical insight, is not prepared to adopt either of these conclusions entirely.[1]

Agreeing with him for the most part, though differing from him somewhat as to time and sequence, the point to be accentuated in this body of verses seems to be its essential unity of purpose. This would not be interfered with, even could it be conclusively proved that certain of these poems celebrated other ladies, just as Petrarca's lifelong worship of Laura does not in any wise cease to be a fact because he was not free from other passions. That any one but the author could establish a real sequence throughout such a mass of imaginative work is not to be thought, nor, perhaps, would it be always possible to him. For, in the region of the imagination, it is not found, as in life, that one thing leads on to another, more or less logically, though often unexpectedly. In reviewing periods of time with their varied events, we can generally see cause and effect, and how one thing was the outcome of another, but, when we have to do with the mind and the fancy, everything becomes more subtle and elusive, and the most unlikely consequences ensue. Thus it would be by no means true to say that the saddest moments produced the saddest songs; on the contrary, grief often gives a revelation, either in memory or in expectation, of the most poignant happiness, while it is rather in joy that our worst apprehensions visit us. A poem is far more often evoked by a suggestion than by an event; the sunshine slanting on a particular angle of the wall, a shadow falling on green grass, a breath of scent or flower, a gesture of some quite indifferent person—any one of these may form the nucleus of the most finished and definite narrative. And as it is a matter of common experience that the things to which we have given an objective form often really come to pass, either because their extreme probability caused

[1] H. Cochin, *La Chronologie du Canzoniere de Pétrarque.*

them to project themselves forward in our imagination, or because our longing is sufficient to create the necessary situation, so these events acquire a dual existence; they live in the shadow-world where we formulated them, and in the real world where they took shape themselves: but the shadow is the more actual of the two. Thus does the work of fancy defy classification, even by the brain from which it emanated; there is too much truth, not too little: it is not that reality is wanting, but that it is multiform. It is enough to feel that, whenever and wherever written, these poems were the outcome of emotions which cannot be catalogued, and we do the author an injustice in supposing that he set himself to relate a concerted story, and forged, in his old age, the links that were wanting. This has been specially urged in the case of the sonnets of presentiment of Laura's death. As, from Petrarca's letters, we know exactly how the news reached him, and how it shocked and surprised him, it has been concluded that these sonnets were written afterwards, for effect, to lead up to the event. But it is, surely, more likely that they were the work of various times, the outcome of the desolation of many partings, either actual or anticipated; or of that inexplicable, unreasoning fear, which has seized on the heart of every lover at some time or other, and which Wordsworth has expressed with such trenchant simplicity:—

"O mercy!" to myself I cried,
"If Lucy should be dead!"

That the pieces were written at long intervals, that they have received numberless alterations, corrections, and new settings (for example, the canzone *Nel dolce tempo* has various notes: *post multos annos*, 1350; *explicit sed nondum correcta et est de primis inventionibus nostris, scriptum hoc* 1351; and *transcripsi in ordine post multos et multos annos, quibusdam mutatis* 1356), and that they are not all presented in order of time, is indisputable; but it is no less sure that the author emended and arranged the series to tell the main story of his life, and to be the apotheosis of her who was his goddess.

It is clear that the opening sonnet, *Voi ch' ascoltate*, was written in the poet's old age, as a preface; it introduces and explains the rest of the work, and shows the conclusions at which he had arrived:—

> Of my wild thoughts repentance is the fruit,
>   And shame, and the most clear intelligence
>   That all that charms the world is a brief dream.[1]

The third sonnet describes the day on which he first saw his Lady, which was Good Friday, 1327, and from thence, all through the long sequence, we are carried through the same recurring emotions. The best landmarks throughout are the anniversary-poems. These were a great fashion among the Provençals; the spring, or Maytime, was their season of inspiration, and they were in the habit of celebrating its return by songs of welcome called *Raverdies*. These are some of the most charming and convincing of all Petrarca's poems; there are about thirty of them, two being often written for the same occasion, and from a large number of them the date may be gathered. The following sestina is a good example:—

> A youthful lady under a green laurel
> I saw, more white and cold than is the snow
> Unmelted by the sun for years and years;
> And her fair face so pleased me, and her tresses,
> And speech, that these remain before my eyes,
> And shall, where'er I go, in every place.
>
> Then shall my thoughts have reached a peaceful place,
> When no green leaf is found upon a laurel;

---

[1] " E del mio vaneggiar vergogna è 'l frutto,
    E 'l pentersi, e 'l conoscer chiaramente
    Che quanto piace al mondo è breve sogno."
                                            *Rime*, i.

When quiet is my heart, and dry my eyes,
We shall get frost from fire and heat from snow.
So many hairs I count not in my tresses
As for that day I fain would wait out years.

But, since time flies and swiftly flee the years
So that one reaches death's appointed place
Or with the brown or with the hoary tresses,
I will pursue the shade of that sweet laurel
Beneath the burning sun or through the snow,
Until the latest day shall close my eyes.

Never before were seen such lovely eyes
Or in our time or in the ancient years,
Which melt me as the sun doth melt the snow:
From whence a rivulet of tears finds place,
Which Love leads to the foot of that hard laurel,
Whose boughs are adamant and gold her tresses.

I fear that change will fall on face and tresses,
Ere with true pity she shall turn her eyes
On me; my idol carved in living laurel.
Since, if I err not, 'tis to-day seven years
That, sighing, I have roamed from place to place,
Both night and day, through summer and through snow.

Having within pure fire, without pure snow,
Alone with these same thoughts, with altered tresses,
I shall go weeping ever in each place,
Haply to kindle pity in the eyes
Of one born after me a thousand years;
If so long life await so praised a laurel.

The gold and jewels sparkling on the snow
Are vanquished by the tresses and the eyes
That speed my years to their last resting-place.[1]

---

[1] " Giovene donna sotto un verde lauro
    Vidi, piú bianca e piú fredda che neve
    Non percossa dal sol molti e molt' anni;
    E 'l suo parlare e 'l bel viso e le chiome

The following sonnet is also obviously an anniversary-poem, but gives no indication of the date:—

> I ever loved and still love ardently,
> And am from day to day to love more fain
> The gentle spot where weeping I complain,

> Mi piacquen sí, ch' i' l' ho dinanzi a gli occhi
> Ed avrò sempre, ov' io sia, in poggio o 'n riva.
>
> Allor saranno i miei pensieri a riva,
> Che foglia verde non si trovi in lauro:
> Quand' avrò queto il cor, asciutti gli occhi,
> Vedrem ghiacciare il foco, arder la neve.
> Non ho tanti capelli in queste chiome
> Quanti vorrei quel giorno attendere anni.
>
> Ma, perché vola il tempo e fuggon gli anni
> Sí ch' a la morte in un punto s' arriva
> O con le brune o colle bianche chiome,
> Seguirò l'ombra di quel dolce lauro
> Per lo piú ardente sole e per la neve,
> Fin che l'ultimo dí chiuda quest' occhi.
>
> Non fur già mai veduti sí begli occhi
> O ne la nostra etade o ne' prim' anni,
> Che mi struggon cosí come 'l sol neve:
> Onde procede lagrimosa riva,
> Ch'Amor conduce a piè del duro lauro
> C' ha i rami di diamante e d' òr le chiome.
>
> I' temo di cangiar pria volto e chiome,
> Che con vera pietà mi mostri gli occhi
> L'idolo mio scolpito in vivo lauro:
> Che, s' al contar non erro, oggi ha sett' anni
> Che sospirando vo di riva in riva
> La notte e 'l giorno, al caldo ed a la neve.
>
> Dentro pur foco e for candida neve,
> Sol con questi pensier, con altre chiome,
> Sempre piangendo andrò per ogni riva,
> Per far forse pietà venir ne gli occhi
> Di tal che nascerà dopo mill' anni;
> Se tanto viver po ben cólto lauro.
>
> L'auro e i topaci al sol sopra la neve
> Vincon le bionde chiome presso a gli occhi
> Che menan gli anni miei sí tosto a riva."
>
> *Rime*, xxx.

Returning where I proved Love's tyranny.
The hour and season love I steadfastly
  Which all mean cares did in my mind displace,
  And most of all her beautiful, bright face,
Through whose example right enamours me.

But who would ever think that all of these
  Should on my heart united onslaught give,
  These that I loved so well, sweet enemies?
Love, with what force to-day thou conquerest!
  Were not the hope by the desire exprest,
  I should fall dead where most I long to live.[1]

As regards Signor Cesareo's contention that many of these pieces are addressed to other ladies, some of those which he selects are so impersonal that it would be difficult to argue anything from them; such are liv., lxxxiii., and lxxxix., and, in the event of these having been inspired by another object, there is no cause for surprise that the poet should have included them here. But, for the most part, the poems are hall-marked as belonging to Laura, either by the constant play on her name, the minute description, we might almost say catalogue, of her beauty and her attributes (the colour of her eyes, however, be it noted, is never mentioned), and the note that is rarely wanting in

[1] " Io amai sempre et amo forte ancora
    E son per amar piú di giorno in giorno
    Quel dolce loco ove piangendo torno
    Spesse fïate quando Amor m' accora;
  E son fermo d'amare il tempo e l'ora
    Ch' ogni vil cura mi levâr d'intorno,
    E piú colei lo cui bel viso adorno
    Di ben far co' suoi essempli m'innamora.
  Ma chi pensò veder mai tutti inseme,
    Per assalirmi il cor or quindi or quinci,
    Questi dolci nemici ch' i' tant' amo?
  Amor, con quanto sforzo oggi mi vinci!
    E, se non ch' al desio cresce la speme,
    I' cadrei morto, ove piú viver bramo."
              *Rime*, lxxxv.

any piece, and is the key-note of most of them—the coldness and cruelty with which the lover is met, causing him the pain of despair.

> If the sharp torture of such agonies
>   Can be resisted, Lady, till I say
>   That I behold, through the years' long array,
> The light grow dim within your lovely eyes,
> And the gold hair take on a silver guise,
>   While garlands and green robes are laid away,
>   And the face pales that made me fear alway
> To make lament for all my injuries.
>
> Then shall Love give me thus much confidence
>   That all my tale of torment shall be told,
>   Counting you up the years, the hours, and days:
> And, if my ardent longings time gainsays,
>   At least my grief shall win some recompense
>   From sighs you cannot any more withhold.[1]

And again:—

> I walk alone through most deserted ways,
>   And, lost in thought, with measured steps and slow,
>   My eyes keep jealous guard lest I should go
> Where print of human foot has left a trace.

---

[1] " Se la mia vita da l'aspro tormento
  Si può tanto schermire e da gli affanni,
  Ch' i' veggia per vertú de gli ultimi anni,
Donna, de' be' vostri occhi, il lume spento;
E i cape' d'oro fin farsi d'argento,
  E lassar le ghirlande e i verdi panni,
  E 'l viso scolorir, che ne' miei danni
Al lamentar mi fa pauroso e lento;

Pur mi darà tanta baldanza Amore,
  Ch' i' vi discovrirò de' mei martíri
  Qua' sono stati gli anni e i giorni e l'ore:
E, se 'l tempo è contrario a i be' desiri,
  Non fia ch' almen non giunga al mio dolore
  Alcun soccorso di tardi sospiri."
                              *Rime*, xii.

To hide me from the people's curious gaze
   I find no other weapon of defence,
   For all my joyless acts give evidence,
Showing without the flames that inly blaze.

So that I now believe both hill and plain
   Of that which tempers all my life are ware;
   So woods and rivers, though 'tis hid from men.
But never can I ways so wild and grim
   Seek out, but what Love always meets me there,
   Holding discourse with me and I with him.[1]

The relations which her poet establishes between his lady and all natural beauty have been already noted. He tells us that the first time he saw her she was dressed in green, and was wearing violets, and the fact has been preserved in two canzoni:—

   Out of the silence comes a gracious sound,
      Wise words which take all other care from me,
      .   .   .   .   .

   On the hillside dark violets are found,
      .   .   .   .   .

---

[1] " Solo e pensoso i piú deserti campi
   Vo mesurando a passi tardi e lenti;
   E gli occhi porto, per fuggire, intenti,
   Ove vestigio uman l'arena stampi.
Altro schermo non trovo che mi scampi
   Dal manifesto accorger de le genti;
   Perché ne gli atti d'allegrezza spenti
   Di fuor si legge com'io dentro avampi:

Sí ch'io mi credo omai che monti e piagge
   E fiumi e selve sappian di che tempre
   Sia la mia vita, ch' è celata altrui.
Ma pur sí aspre vie né sí selvagge
   Cercar non so, ch'Amor non venga sempre
   Ragionando con meco, et io con lui."
                           *Rime*, xxxv.

## LA JOYA DE LA VIOLETA

    And stars of that fair face
    Which lead me by a far serener way
    And all my griefs allay.[1]

Seeing that my inexorable fate
    Far from my greatest good would have me be
    (Wearisome fate, with proud remorseless mien),
    Love only on remembrance feedeth me.
    Wherefore when I behold in child's estate
    The world begin to clothe herself in green,
    Meseems that at that tender age is seen
    The lovely maid who is a woman now.
    Thus when the sun mounts, giving greater heat,
    To Love I liken it,
    Whose fire as lord of noble hearts doth glow.
    But, when the light is low,
    And the day mourns for his departing rays,
    I see that she has reached her perfect days.

Beholding then what time it doth befall
    That cold grows less and better stars gain power,
    Leaf on the bough and springing violet,
    Ever I see the green robe and the flower
    Of violets, that Love was armed withal
    When first he conquered me, and conquers yet.
    The mortal veil so soft and delicate
    That her young, tender limbs were covered by;
    Within which dwells the gentle soul of her;
    Whence all joys else appear
    Vile; for her aspect of humility

---

[1] " In silenzio parole accorte e sagge,
    E 'l suon che mi sottragge ogni altra cura.
    . . . . .
    Le notturne viole per le piagge,
    . . . . .
    E i segni del bel volto
    Che mi conducon per piú piana via
    A la speranza mia, al fin de gli affanni."
                                   *Rime*, cv. l. 61-72.

Remembrance holds so clear;
Which, flowering then, did with the years increase,
Sole cause of my afflictions and my peace.[1]

She is always brought into connection with flowers:—

What gladness in the springtime of the year
To see her walking with her thoughts alone,
Weaving a wreath for her bright curling hair.[2]

---

[1] " Poi che la dispietata mia ventura
　　M'ha dilungato dal maggior mio bene,
　　Noiosa, inesorabile e superba,
　　Amor co 'l rimembrar sol mi mantene.
　　Onde, s'io veggio in giovenil figura
　　Incominciarsi il mondo a vestir d' erba,
　　Parmi vedere in quella etate acerba
　　La bella giovenetta ch' ora è donna:
　　Poi che sormonta, riscaldando, il sole,
　　Parmi qual esser sòle
　　Fiamma d'Amor che 'n cor alto s' endonna:
　　Ma, quando il dí si dole
　　Di lui che passo passo a dietro torni,
　　Veggio lei giunta a' suoi perfetti giorni.

　In ramo fronde o ver vïole in terra
　　Mirando a la stagion che 'l freddo perde
　　E le stelle migliori acquistan forza,
　　Ne gli occhi ho pur le vïolette e 'l verde
　　Di ch' era nel principio di mia guerra
　　Amore armato sí ch' ancor mi sforza,
　　E quella dolce leggiadretta scorza
　　Che ricopria le pargolette membra,
　　Dove oggi alberga l'anima gentile
　　Ch' ogni altro piacer vile
　　Sembrar mi fa; sí forte mi rimembra
　　Del portamento umíle
　　Che allor fioriva e poi crebbe anzi a gli anni,
　　Cagion sola e riposo de' miei affanni."
　　　　　　　　　　　　*Rime*, cxxvii. l. 15-42.

[2] " Qual dolcezza è ne la stagione acerba
　　Vederla ir sola co i pensier suoi 'nseme
　　Tessendo un cerchio a l' oro terso e crespo! "
　　　　　　　　　　　　*Rime*, clx.

## LA JOYA DE LA VIOLETA 137

From many a lovely tree,
  (The memory is sweet)
  Into her lap there fell a rain of flowers;
Mid so much majesty,
  Humbly she took her seat,
  And covered by the amorous bright showers.
Some bloom her robe's hem dowers,
Some fell upon her hair,
  Which seemed that day to hold
  A sheen of pearls and gold;
And some the earth and some the waters bare;
Some on the breeze did move
And circling seemed to say—Here reigneth Love.[1]

Gay happy flowers and grasses born to greet
  My Lady in her meditative walk;
  Meadows that listen to her gentle talk,
Retaining every trace of her fair feet.
Ye trees and budding leaves for springtime meet,
  And darling little violets so pale,
  Ye shady woods, that let the sun prevail,
Made proud and glorious by his light and heat.

O gracious country-side, O river clear
  That bathed her lovely face, her shining eyes,
  And took the radiance of their living light.

---

[1] " Da' be' rami scendea,
    (Dolce ne la memoria)
    Una pioggia di fior sovra 'l suo grembo;
    Et ella si sedea
    Umile in tanta gloria,
    Coverta già de l'amoroso nembo.
    Qual fior cadea su 'l lembo,
    Qual su le treccie bionde,
    Ch' oro forbito e perle
    Eran quel dí a vederle;
    Qual si posava in terra, e qual su l'onde;
    Qual con un vago errore
    Girando parea dir—Qui regna Amore."
                    *Rime*, cxxvi. l. 40-52.

> I envy you those gestures pure and dear!
> Henceforth no stone so hard that in you lies
> But with my fire shall learn to blaze aright.[1]

Two sonnets are inspired by Laura's portrait, which was painted by Simone Martini when he came to Avignon in 1339, at the invitation of Benedict XII. The painter and poet are said to have become great friends, and many authors affirm that Martini executed the frontispiece of Petrarca's famous Virgil, now in the Ambrosian Library at Milan. Francesco further begged of him a miniature portrait of his Lady which he might always carry about with him, and the following sonnet is evidence that the artist acceded to his request:—

> Had Polycletus gazed in rivalry
> With others who were famous in his art,
> Long years, he had not seen the smallest part
> Of that perfection I am conquered by.
> In Paradise was Simon certainly,
> From whence this gentle Lady came, and there
> He saw her, and portrayed her face so fair,
> To give us faith in such divinity.

---

[1] " Lieti fiori e felici e ben nate erbe
    Che Madonna pensando premer sòle;
    Piaggia ch' ascolti sue dolci parole,
    E del bel piede alcun vestigio serbe;
Schietti arboscelli e verdi frondi acerbe;
    Amorosette e pallide vïole;
    Ombrose selve, ove percote il sole
    Che vi fa co' suoi raggi alte e superbe;

O soave contrada, o puro fiume
    Che bagni il suo bel viso e gli occhi chiari
    E prendi qualità dal vivo lume;
Quanto v'invidio gli atti onesti e cari!
    Non fia in voi scoglio omai che per costume
    D'arder co la mia fiamma non impari."
                                *Rime*, clxii.

Truly the work was native unto heaven,
    And there could be conceived, but not with us,
    Where members to the soul for veil are given.
He did a courteous work; nor could have done
    When he had tasted heat and cold, and thus
    To sense of mortal things his eyes were won.[1]

De Sade tells us that in the Maison de Sade at Avignon there is an old portrait which may well be the one painted for Petrarca. Laura is dressed in red (one would rather she had been in green) holding a flower in her hand. There are vague traditions of three portraits of her by Martini's pencil. In the Chapel of St. Jean in the papal palace at Avignon the remains of a fresco show a fragment of a procession, in which three women are walking; one of them is said to be Laura; and there is a tradition that in the Cathedral existed a fresco of St. George, before whom knelt a damsel in green, who was painted from the same lady. Also, among Cardinal Bembo's art treasures, are enumerated portraits of Dante, Petrarca, and Boccaccio; and of Madonna Laura, copied from a fresco of St. Margaret at Avignon which was painted from her.[2]

---

[1] " Per mirar Policleto a prova fiso,
    Con gli altri ch'ebber fama di quell'arte,
    Mill'anni, non vedrian la minor parte
De la beltà che m' have il cor conquiso.
Ma certo il mio Simon fu in paradiso,
    Onde questa gentil donna si parte;
    Ivi la vide, e la ritrasse in carte,
Per far fede qua giù del suo bel viso.

L'opra fu ben di quelle che nel cielo
    Si ponno imaginar, non qui tra noi,
    Ove le membra fanno a l' alma velo.
Cortesia fe'; né la potea far poi
    Che fu disceso a provar caldo e gelo
    E del mortal sentiron gli occhi suoi."
                        *Rime*, lxxvii.

[2] Cf. V. Cian, *Un decennio della vita di Pietro Bembo*, 1521-1531, cap. x. p. 106.

His lady's surpassing beauty is, of course, the theme of innumerable poems:—

> The loveliness divine, incredible,
> Of which I speak.[1]

> The feeble life, which yet remains to me,
> Was the free gift of your so lovely eyes
> And of your voice sweet and angelical.
>    .     .     .     .     .
> For of my heart the one and other key
> Lies, Lady, in your hand.[2]

> The eyes serene beneath the starry brows,
> And lovely mouth angelical, fulfilled
> With roses and with pearls and gracious words.[3]

> For loveliness divine he looks in vain,
> Who never looked upon this lady's eyes,
> How gently she directs her gaze the while.
> Nor knows how one is healed of love and slain,
> Who does not know how sweet are all her sighs,
> And how her speech is sweet, and sweet her smile.[4]

---

[1] " La divina incredibile bellezza
Di ch' io ragiono."
*Rime*, lxxi. l. 63, 64.

[2] " La frale vita, ch' ancor meco alberga,
Fu de' begli occhi vostri aperto dono
E de la voce angelica soave.
  .     .     .     .     .
Del mio cor, donna, l'una e l'altra chiave
Avete in mano."
*Rime*, lxiii.

[3] " Li occhi sereni e le stellanti ciglia,
La bella bocca angelica, di perle
Piena e di rose e di dolci parole."
*Rime*, cc.

[4] " Per divina bellezza indarno mira,
Chi gli occhi di costei già mai non vide,
Come soavemente ella gli gira.

And yet no loss of beauty could alter his love:—

> Her golden hair was lifted by the breeze,
>   And in a thousand gracious knots was twined;
>   The lovely light beyond all measure shined
>   Within her beauteous eyes, where now 'tis less;
> The colour of her face seemed to express,
>   Truly or falsely, pity to my mind;
>   And, since Love's tinder in my breast I find,
>   What wonder if it burned with suddenness?
>
> Her movement was not of a mortal thing,
>   But of an angel; of her words the sound
>   Rang forth as never human voice can ring.
> A living sun, spirit celestial,
>   Was she I looked on, and, though change befall,
>   The loosing of the bow heals not the wound.[1]

He reproaches her incessantly for her coldness, her disdain, and her hard heart which no device of his can soften, and says:—

> Non sa come Amor sana e come ancide,
>   Chi non sa come dolce ella sospira
>   E come dolce parla e dolce ride."
>
> *Rime*, clix.

[1] " Erano i capei d'oro a l'aura sparsi,
  Che 'n mille dolci nodi gli avolgea;
  E 'l vago lume oltra misura ardea
  Di quei begli occhi, ch' or ne son sí scarsi;
E 'l viso di pietosi color farsi,
  Non so se vero o falso, mi parea:
  I' che l'esca amorosa al petto avea,
  Qual meraviglia se di subit' arsi?

Non era l'andar suo cosa mortale,
  Ma d'angelica forma; e le parole
  Sonavan altro che pur voce umana.
Uno spirto celeste, un vivo sole
  Fu quel ch' i' vidi; e se non fosse or tale,
  Piaga per allentar d'arco non sana."

*Rime*, xc.

> I feed on tears, and weeping I rejoice,
> I look on life and death with equal pain.
> To this state, Lady, am I come through you.[1]

And yet his only peace is from her:—

> My life is warfare, full of grief and pain,
> And only thoughts of her bring any peace.[2]

This mood alternates, from the very beginning, with a nobler strain of gratitude for the dignity conferred upon him by the privilege of being his Lady's lover, and a consciousness of the heights to which she would lead him.

> Green robes, or red, or dark, or purple-dyed,
> Did never yet a lady so adorn,
> Nor golden hair in shining braids was twined
> In such fair guise, as this that steals away
> My will, and from the path of liberty
> So draws me, that a yoke less hard to bear
> I could not now endure.
> . . . . .
> Nor for my freedom do I therefore pray,
> Since less direct all other ways do lie
> To heaven's bright realm, nor could one hope to fare
> Thither in bark more sure.[3]

---

[1] " Pascomi di dolor, piangendo rido;
  Egualmente mi spiace morte e vita.
  In questo stato son, donna, per vui."
  *Rime*, cxxxiv.

[2] " Guerra è 'l mio stato, d'ira e di duol piena;
  E sol di lei pensando ho qualche pace."
  *Rime*, clxiv.

[3] " Verdi panni, sanguigni, oscuri o persi,
  Non vestí donna unqu' anco
  Né d'òr capelli in bionda treccia attorse
  Sí bella, come questa che mi spoglia
  D' arbitrio e dal cammin di libertade
  Seco mi tira sí, ch' io non sostegno
  Alcun giogo men grave.
  . . . . .

# LA JOYA DE LA VIOLETA 143

I see a gracious light,
  My gentle Lady, shining in your eyes,
  Which unto me the heavenward path doth show;
And by long habit wise,
Visibly, where alone with Love I sit,
Looking within, I see the heart shine through.
This is the sight which spurs good deeds to do,
And to a glorious end conducteth me;
This from the common herd doth keep me far.
No human words there are
Can tell what feelings the divinity
Of these two lights makes plain,
Both when the winter lets the hoar-frost lie,
And after when the year grows young again
Which was the season of my primal pain.[1]

Whene'er from time to time himself Love shows
  Mid other ladies, shrined in her fair face,
  Seeing how each one lacks her loveliness,
  The longing that inspires me greater grows.

---

    Né quella prego che però mi scioglia:
    Ché men son dritte al ciel tutt'altre strade,
    E non s' aspira al glorïoso regno
    Certo in piú salda nave."
                        *Rime*, xxix.

[1] " Gentil mia donna, i' veggio
    Nel mover de' vostr' occhi un dolce lume,
    Che mi mostra la via ch' al ciel conduce;
    E per lungo costume,
    Dentro là, dove sol con Amor seggio,
    Quasi visibilmente il cor traluce.
    Questa è la vista ch'a ben far m'induce
    E che mi scorge al glorïoso fine;
    Questa sola dal vulgo m'allontana.
    Né già mai lingua umana
    Contar poria quel che le due divine
    Luci sentir mi fanno,
    E quando 'l verno sparge le pruine,
    E quando poi ringiovenisce l'anno,
    Qual era al tempo del mio primo affanno."
                        *Rime*, lxxii.

I bless the time when to such heights arose
   My eyes; the season and the place I bless,
   Saying: O soul, thanksgivings numberless
   One destined to such honour surely owes.

From her thou hast the amorous intent
   Which, while thou followest, to highest good
   Will lead; to what men prize indifferent.
By her the gracious courage too is given
   Which guides thee by a certain path to heaven:
   So walk I proudly with that hope endued.[1]

And the most beautiful of the anniversary sonnets, and the most pathetic of the sestinas, foreshadow the thoughts of the *Secretum*, and are forebodings of the change of life and heart for which we are to look in the second part of the *Canzoniere*.

Father in heaven, after the wasted days,
   After the nights in vainest visions spent
   Of charms found lovely to my detriment
   Through that fierce flame that set my heart ablaze;
Thou, with Thy light, vouchsafe to turn my ways
   To other life and nobler enterprise,
   That, having spread his nets before my eyes
   In vain, my cruel foe may reap disgrace.

---

[1] " Quando fra l'altre donne ad ora ad ora
   Amor vien nel bel viso di costei,
   Quanto ciascuna è men bella di lei,
   Tanto cresce 'l desio che m'innamora.
I' benedico il loco e 'l tempo e l'ora
   Che sì alto miraron gli occhi mei,
   E dico: Anima, assai ringraziar dêi,
   Che fosti a tanto onor degnata allora.

Da lei ti ven l'amoroso pensero
   Che, mentre 'l segui, al sommo ben t'invia,
   Poco prezando quel ch' ogni uom desia:
Da lei vien l'animosa leggiadria
   Ch' al ciel ti scorge per destro sentero;
   Sì ch' i' vo già de la speranza altero."

*Rime*, xiii.

E ra lalor uictoriosa insegna        Non human ueramente, ma diuino
In campo uerde un candido hermellino,   Loro andar era: & lor sancte parole.
Coro fine et topatii al collo tegna.    Beato e ben chi nasce à tal distino.

*Triumphus Pudicitiæ.*
(Fifteenth Century Florentine Engraving.)

See now, O Lord, revolves the eleventh year
  That I have worn the yoke so rigorous,
  Unto the most enslaved most hard to wear.
Have pity on my sorrow and my shame;
  Raise up my wandering thoughts, reminding them
  That Thou to-day wast hanging on the Cross.[1]

So greatly pleased me erst the gentle light,
  That I rejoiced to climb the steepest hills
  That thus I might approach the so-loved branches:
But now the brief life and the place and time,
  Show me another path to turn to heaven,
  And bring forth fruit, rather than flowers and leaves.
Another love and other leaves and light,
  Another climb to heaven by other hills
  I seek (and time it is), and other branches.[2]

---

[1] " Padre del ciel; dopo i perduti giorni,
  Dopo le notti vaneggiando spese
  Con quel fero desio ch' al cor s' accese
  Mirando gli atti per mio mal sí adorni;
Piacciati omai, co 'l tuo lume, ch' io torni
  Ad altra vita et a piú belle imprese;
  Sí ch' avendo le reti indarno tese
  Il mio duro adversario se ne scorni.
Or volge, signor mio, l'undecimo anno
  Ch' i' fui sommesso al dispietato giogo,
  Che sopra i piú soggetti è piú feroce.
Miserere del mio non degno affanno;
  Reduci i pensier vaghi a miglior luogo;
  Ramenta lor com' oggi fosti in croce."
  *Rime*, lxii.

[2] " Tanto mi piacque prima il dolce lume,
  Ch' i' passai con diletto assai gran poggi
  Per poter appressar gli amati rami:
  Ora la vita breve e 'l loco e 'l tempo
  Mostranmi altro sentier di gire al cielo
  E di far frutto non pur fior e frondi.
Altr' amor, altre frondi et altro lume,
  Altro salir al ciel per altri poggi
  Cerco (che n' è ben tempo) et altri rami."
  *Rime*, cxlii.

It is, indeed, a chequered history that we have before us, but it seems that this is what the poet intended; thus these poems are not to be arbitrarily assigned to the lifetime of Laura, but were meant to mirror Petrarca's own life-story. Only with this idea can we understand the introduction of so much extraneous matter, friendships, possible reminiscences of other loves, Rome, Avignon, political odes, religious sonnets—in a word, the man as he was up to the time of his conversion.

It was all this that he brought to his Lady—his art, his genius, his longings, and his love; but weighed down and overshadowed by that haunting restlessness, which was his salient characteristic, which sapped the nobility that was in him, and caused him to be so many times defeated, yet with a will not wholly overcome:—

For Rachel I have served and not for Leah.[1]

---

[1] " Per Rachel ho servito e non per Lia."
*Rime*, ccvi. l. 55.

## CHAPTER VI

### " IN GRACIOUS TWILIGHTS "

" The heart's heart, whose immurèd plot
    Hath keys yourself keep not!
    .   .   .   .   .

Its keys are at the cincture hung of God;
    Its gates are trepidant to His nod;
    By Him its floors are trod."
                          FRANCIS THOMPSON.

THERE is abundant evidence that the year 1342 was a turning-point in Petrarca's life. It was then that he wrote the sonnet *Padre del ciel;* to that year belongs the *Secretum*, and in that year his dearly-loved brother became a Carthusian monk. Gherardo seems to have had this idea in his mind since 1338, when he first visited the monastery of Montrieu, on the occasion of the brothers going together to the grotto of Sainte Baume near which Montrieu is situated. It has been conjectured that this visit took place about a year after the death of his lady, to which event Petrarca's sonnet—

    La bella donna che cotanto amavi [1]

is thought to relate.[2] Gherardo's choice had a great effect on Francesco, who warmly approved and admired it, seeing in his brother the man he had not the means of becoming. " He winged his flight freely," writes Petrarca; " I, without any tie to hamper me, entangled in the snares of bad habits, try in vain to spread my wings. . . . If love do not deceive me, I esteem him the most happy voyager over the

[1] *Rime*, xci.
[2] Cf. G. A. Cesareo, *op. cit.* pp. 70-72; H. Cochin, *op. cit.* pp. 73, 74.

stormy sea of this world, so much cut off from earthly things, and so intent on heavenly, that all his life may be called a song of praise to God. And although I am so different from him, in ways and works, that I ought to blush to find myself so far behind one whom I was born before, yet greater than my shame is my pride and glory to have had the same mother as such a man, and to be closely related to him by the ties of blood."[1] And, writing of him to a friend, he says:—

"Here (at Montrieu) my dearest and only brother lives secluded, in which one can see a proof of what the Psalmist calls *mutatio dexteræ Excelsi*. Since from an idler and libertine, as he was, he has completely changed into a firm and reliable man . . . so that, as he once occasioned me fear and anxiety, he is now the cause of my joy and admiration."[2]

This joy Petrarca must have felt to the full when, some years later, meeting two Carthusian monks in Padua, and being on the point of asking for news of his brother, they related Gherardo's heroic conduct during the plague; for, in spite of the Prior's example and advice, he refused to fly, but remained at his post to minister to his brethren, all of whom died. Gherardo, as though blind to every peril and impervious to all infection, received their last words and embraces, and performed all the last offices for them, digging their graves and carrying them to burial, until he alone of the thirty-four remained alive. Then, with a dog for his sole companion, he watched over the monastery to defend it from the robbers who were harrying all the country round, but, while every other place was attacked, no harm came nigh Montrieu. At the end of their narrative the good monks, observing Petrarca's emotion, and probably noticing some family likeness, exclaimed: "Oh, how happy you are to have such a brother."[3]

To this loved brother Petrarca gave a copy of the book

[1] *De Reb. Fam.* x. 3; xvi. 8.   [2] *Ibid.* xvi. 9.   [3] *Ibid.* xii. 2.

which was before all others his favourite, the *Confessions of St. Augustine*. It was, as we have already seen, his inseparable companion on all his journeys; he had it in such perpetual use that he says it had, so to speak, grown to his hand,[1] and there is a tradition that this was the book he was reading in his study when he died. There seems to have been something peculiarly attractive to him in the character of the great doctor; the genius of their minds was alike; they had the same thirst for knowledge, the same reverence for antiquity; they were haunted by the same restlessness and assailed by the same temptations. In the range of their studies, their appreciation of truth, wherever it was to be found, their longing for an intellectual standpoint which should make life less incomprehensible, their adherence to Christianity as a solution of some of the mysteries of this unintelligible world, we see point after point of resemblance. Among the learned, Augustine seemed to Petrarca the most learned of all,[2] and it was no doubt owing to this intimate attraction that the poet chose him for his censor and judge in those wonderful dialogues which, appearing under various titles—*Dialogi de Contemptu Mundi* and *De Secreto Conflictu Curarum Suarum*—are best known as the *Secretum*, that being the name by which the author elected to call them. "Wherefore you, my little book," he writes in his preface, "stealing away from human society, will rest content with my company only, not forgetful of your proper title, for you are called and you are indeed *my secret,* and in you I shall come to seek for what was spoken of between us."[3] Then he plunges forthwith into the most scathing self-examination that any man ever made. Whether the book was intended for the public we may well doubt, both from the words quoted from the preface, and from the fact that it does not appear to have been published till after the author's death. But however this may be, it remains one of the world's great

[1] *Rer. Sen.* xv. 7.   [2] *Ibid.* viii. 6.   [3] *Secretum, Præfatio.*

monuments of self-revelation, and ranks with the *Confessions of St. Augustine*, on which it was, of course, modelled.

The dialogue-form, when handled with skill, cannot fail to produce an illusion; we cannot easily divest ourselves of the idea that Petrarca is defending himself against another man's accusations, and submitting himself—almost against his own judgment—to the decision of an outside tribunal. But, freeing our mind from this delusion, we have to apprehend that these are the poet's own thoughts, and it is only a transparent honesty of purpose that could have given a man so much insight. It can only be—

Perch' io te sopra te corono e mitrio;[1]

and this conflict of the dual self is of quite peculiar interest.

The *Secretum* is a series of three dialogues which are supposed to take place, on three successive days, between the author and St. Augustine, with Truth for sole arbiter. The first, which is much the shortest, is chiefly occupied in establishing the fact that a man will certainly attain that thing which he ardently desires, and that this ardent desire is entirely different from a mere wish, which may—and probably will—never be fulfilled. The second day's conversation is a more direct attack on Petrarca's faults—his pride of intellect, his sensuality, his satisfaction in his eloquence and beauty, his ambition (and under this head Augustine subtly draws attention to the fact that men renounce many things, not because they despise them, but because they despair of ever obtaining them), and his solicitude about money. In answer to his plea that he only desires " neither to be in want nor to have a superabundance: neither to command nor to serve," Augustine points out that, to achieve this, one must be God rather than man, that neither kings nor the greatest of the earth have attained to this condition, and that he must be content with the common lot of humanity, and cease to dream of the impos-

[1] *Purgatorio*, xxvii. 142.

sible. The last part of the dialogue touches on that form of melancholy to which the poet was peculiarly subject, and to which the name of *accidia* or *ægritudo* is given. This is the sin which Dante punishes in the fifth circle of the *Inferno* :—

>Tristi fummo
>Nell' aer dolce che dal sol s'allegra,
>Portando dentro accidioso fummo:
>Or ci attristiam nella belletta negra;[1]

and of which Chaucer writes in the *Persone's Tale :* "Envye blindeth the herte of a man, and Ire troubleth a man; and Accidie maketh him hevy, thoghtful, and wrawe. Envye and Ire maken bitternesse in herte, which bitternesse is moder of Accidie, and binimeth him the love of alle goodnesse. Thanne is Accidie the anguish of a trouble herte."[2] Augustine again convicts him of ambition, showing that this is the real root of his sadness; he expects too much, while affecting to expect nothing, and does not open his eyes to the fact that he himself is an object of envy to many. He would be independent of fortune, as of riches, but men are born to be members of each other, to live for each other, and true liberty is not to be sought in this arrogant and unattainable independence.

The third dialogue contains the kernel of the matter. "You are bound by two adamantine chains," says Augustine, "Love and Fame." In the first two conversations we feel that the argument is being sustained with a man who lets himself be easily convinced, but now the struggle begins. Here we learn from the poet's own lips the complete story of the part that Laura played in his life. " Her

---

[1] " We sullen were
In the sweet air which by the sun is gladdened,
Bearing within ourselves the sluggish reek;
Now we are sullen in this sable mire."
    LONGFELLOW, *Inferno*, vii. 121-124.

[2] *The Persone's Tale*, Sequitur de Accidia.

soul," he says, "burns with celestial flame, her aspect reveals a divine beauty, she is the model of consummate virtue; there is nothing earthly in her voice, her look, or her bearing. I have loved her body less than her soul; her example has transported me from earth, and made me understand how the citizens of heaven dwell together. If any could behold the image of the love that reigns in me, he would recognise that it is in no way different from that face that I have praised so much, but never yet enough. In my love there has never been anything guilty, except its excess. Endow it with moderation, and nothing more beautiful could be imagined. The little that I am, I owe to her; I should never have attained the small degree of renown that I have acquired if, by her love, she had not made fruitful the feeble seed of virtue that nature had planted in my heart. It is she who has detached my soul from all baseness and forced it to look upwards. The desire of my youth was to please her only, who only had pleased me; and to compass this end, despising the thousand allurements of pleasure, I compelled myself early to undergo countless cares and labours. The love that I have for her has assuredly led me to love God. Though the flower of her beauty has visibly faded, the beauty of her soul has grown with the years, and, as this gave birth to my love, so it gives perseverance to my resolution. My mind is accustomed to admire her, my eyes to contemplate her, and all that is not she seems to me dark and ugly." This is a résumé of one side of Petrarca's statement of his own position, but, forced by his interlocutor, he fills up the picture with darker shades; he acknowledges that from the time when he first saw his Lady his way of life has changed, that his virtues have diminished; that her honourable obduracy has been his safeguard, and not the purity of his own desires; that on her account his days have been passed in torment and his nights in sleeplessness, and that he has been the prey of restless ambition and of incredible vanity.

Here we have again to impress upon our minds that Petrarca is weighing out the measure of the love he had to give, his own cool estimate of its worth and its effects. And this brings us to a new stand-point: this is not what love necessarily is—even in Petrarca's idea—but what he found it, which is a very different thing, and would indeed be a very melancholy thing if we had to think that this was his abiding opinion. But the whole of the second part of the *Canzoniere* and the *Trionfi* unite in contradicting this, and we should therefore regard the *Secretum* as the record of the poet's experiences up to a given time, the humiliating discovery of a strict examination, which so startled and horrified him that he began straightway to reconstruct his life. It is a far greater thing to love well than to be well loved: the nature of a man's love must be commensurate with his character. In Petrarca's love story we do not see a ray of the light that illumines the *Vita Nuova ;* his Lady is in no wise Beatrice, the giver of blessing, but is rather to be identified with Laurea, glory, the insatiable thirst for which was one of the torments of his life. Here, then, is another element of weakness: if his love was wanting in purity, it was no less deficient in passion; it was no consuming, undivided flame that burned within his breast. Rather it flickered this way and that, now fanned by the hope of conferring immortality, and now by the hope of obtaining it; and sometimes chilled, and well-nigh extinguished, by the fear of losing, through it, a fame more to be courted. The classical ideal was already tending to develop an individuality which fell an easy prey to ambition—that quality for which it is most difficult to find a place in the Christian scheme.[1] The latter part of the dialogue is entirely occupied with a dissertation on Fame, in which the emptiness and vanity of it is set forth. But it is plain that the poet is less convinced here than at any other point of contention, and it is certain that " the last infirmity of noble mind " clung to him to the end.

[1] For Dante's treatment of this idea, cf. *Paradiso*, vi. 112-117.

*Secretum enim meum es:* this is the statement of a necessary fact. A man may reveal himself completely, but he cannot give it to others to understand the revelation, nor will all read it alike. In effect, the *Secretum* is as complex as the character of him who wrote it, but, whichever way we regard it, it can hardly appear otherwise than as a conflict between a man's higher and lower self, during the course of which he is, in the main, convinced and converted by his better nature, though he does not wholly surrender on all points, or feel that the end of the struggle has come.

It is from this year, 1342, that Petrarca dates his conversion.[1] Commentators, for the most part, have treated this very lightly and with a certain scepticism, concluding that he remained the same man as before. Yet a careful study of his life and writings seems to establish the fact that he was changed in the only particular in which change avails and has any meaning, that is, in will. For a man's conversion, however sincere, cannot mean a change of temperament; he has to go through life with the same tendencies and the same limitations. Petrarca's conversion was that possible to his character; that of another nature might have been stronger and completer, but Petrarca's was not a strong character; none can be so of which sensuality and vanity are salient points. Dating from this time we may note in him certain radical differences. First, in accordance with the leading of his higher self, he takes refuge for a time in flight—flight from the sight and nearness of the woman he has to learn to love more spiritually, and flight from that other woman whose name has never been known, whose history is hidden, the mother of the son born to him in 1337, and, probably, of the daughter about to be born.[2] Secondly, from this time forth we may date the constant spiritualisation of his poems.

[1] Cf. *Ep. ad Post.*
[2] It is well known that Petrarca had a daughter, and, referring to a passage in the *Secretum*, in which St. Augustine is made to say: *Cadentem*

## "IN GRACIOUS TWILIGHTS"

Closely connected in arrangement, in thought, and feeling with the third dialogue of the *Secretum* is the canzone *I' vo pensando*, chosen by Petrarca to be the opening poem of the second part of the *Canzoniere*, and probably written in the year 1348. Those adamant chains of Love and Fame are again the themes of his reflections, while the sense of his own weakness throws him more and more on the Divine strength. The canzone opens thus:—

> Thoughtful I go, and in my communings
> So strong a pity for myself I see,
> As ofttimes leadeth me
> To other tears than I am wont to shed.
> Since day by day the end nears visibly,
> A thousand times I ask of God those wings
> On which to heavenly things
> The mind can rise that here is prisonèd.[1]

Then three thoughts engage him in turn. The first, speaking from the moral and spiritual stand-point, asks him what are his desires and expectations, and bids him ponder how ignobly time is passing with him, how the world's pleasures will never satisfy him or bring him rest; and then would have him contrast the vain longings and disappointments that his love had brought him with the

---

*et resurgentem vidi, et nunc prostratum misertus, opem ferre disposui*, the date of her birth has been conjectured by de Sade and others as belonging to the year 1343. Cf. de Sade, *Mémoires*, ii. p. 139; also *De Reb. Fam.* vii. 17, Fracassetti's note. (The only possible reference to the mother is in *De Reb. Fam.* ix. 3.)

[1] " I' vo pensando, e nel penser m'assale
    Una pietà sí forte di me stesso,
    Che mi conduce spesso
    Ad altro lagrimar ch' i' non soleva;
    Ché, vedendo ogni giorno il fin piú presso,
    Mille fiate ho chieste a Dio quell' ale
    Co le quai del mortale
    Carcer nostr' intelletto al ciel si leva."
                                        *Rime*, cclxiv.

certain joys attendant on " a more blessed hope." The second thought is both sweet and bitter; it inflames his heart with desire and feeds it on hope. This is the insatiable thirst for fame, from which he cannot free himself, albeit he knows that it is but a vain breath, and, conscious of its unreality, he fears to lose the substance in grasping the shadow. But the third thought, that of Laura, which indeed he does not characterise as a thought, but a will—*quell' altro voler*—is so strong that it overcomes all the rest:

> The light of those fair eyes, that tenderly
> Melts me with heat serene, and doth restrain
> My heart with such a rein
> 'Gainst which nor wit nor force availeth me.[1]

And so he laments that his course is impeded by these two cords of Love and Fame, and, turning to God, he asks why, since He has delivered him from so many other bonds, He does not free him from these. He pleads:—

> I would defend myself but have not arms.[2]

He sees clearly the vanity of his own actions, but cannot decide to do differently:—

> I go reflecting where I turned aside
> From that right path which leads to happy goal.[3]

And so in fear and despondency this noble poem ends, leaving us, however, with the impression that the man who

[1] " E 'l lume de' begli occhi, che mi strugge
Soavemente al suo caldo sereno,
Mi ritien con un freno
Contra cui nullo ingegno o forza valme."
*Rime*, cclxiv.

[2] " E vorrei far difesa e non ho l'arme."
*Ibid.*

[3] " Vo ripensando ov' io lassai 'l viaggio
Da la man destra, ch' a buon porto aggiunge."
*Ibid.*

sees his error so clearly will not fail to be victorious over it.

Another canzone, though probably written towards the close of the poet's life, may fitly be considered here on account of its likeness to the *Secretum*. In that work the conversation was carried on between Petrarca and St. Augustine, with Truth for judge; here we have a colloquy between the poet and Love, and Reason arbitrates. Here Petrarca is the accuser, making use of the same arguments with which Augustine had assailed him on the former occasion. He relates how, in early youth, he had entered into the kingdom of one from whom he had never had aught but anger and disdain:—

> My life is used to so much bitterness
> Through Love's false gentleness,
> Which lured me on among the amorous band.
> I, if I understand
> Aright, was destined high o'er earth to soar:
> He robbed my peace and forced me into war.[1]

He continues with another accusation which the Saint had already pressed upon him:—

> Less than I ought he makes me love my God,
> And careless of myself myself doth make:
> Yea, for one woman's sake
> All thoughts are lost in equal listlessness.
> . . . . .
> Since I was his I know no tranquil hour
> Nor ever hope to know. . . .

---

[1] " In quanto amaro ha la mia vita avezza
   Con sua falsa dolcezza,
   La qual m' atrasse a l'amorosa schiera!
   Che, s' i' non m'inganno, era
   Disposto a sollevarmi alto da terra.
   E' mi tolse di pace, e pose in guerra."
                                    *Rime*, ccclx.

> And hence both many tears and torments be,
> And words and sighs whereby
> Others are haply wearied even as I.
> Be thou the judge who knowest him and me.[1]

After this Love takes up the defence, and tells how only by his means his adversary has risen to such fame as he never could have attained without him:—

> I raised and made him great
> By all the lore I taught him, and by her
> Who in the world stood sole without a peer.
>     .     .     .     .     .
> Also (and this all other gift outweighs)
> To soar above the sky I gave him wings
> By way of mortal things,
> Which, rightly looked on, are the steps to God.[2]

Reason is then appealed to by both to give judgment, but she smiles, and replies that more time is required to decide

---

[1] " Questi m' ha fatto men amare Dio
     Ch' i' non deveva, e men curar me stesso:
     Per una donna ho messo
     Egualmente in non cale ogni pensero.
         .     .     .     .
     Poi che suo fui, non ebbi ora tranquilla,
     Né spero aver. . . .
     Quinci nascon le lagrime e i martíri,
     Le parole e i sospiri,
     Di ch' io mi vo stancando, e forse altrui.
     Giudica tu, che me conosci e lui."
                                          *Rime*, ccclx.

[2] " I' l' esalto e divulgo
     Per quel ch' elli imparò ne la mia scola
     E da colei che fu nel mondo sola.
         .     .     .     .
     Ancor (e questo è quel che tutto avanza)
     Da volar sopra 'l ciel li avea dat' ali
     Per le cose mortali,
     Che son scala al Fattor, chi ben l'estima."
                                          *Ibid.*

*Triumphus Mortis*
(Fifteenth-Century Florentine Engraving)

in such a suit. So we can hardly but conclude that, even in old age, the poet was unable to strike a balance of probabilities in his own mind.

Two other events lead up to the final crisis which terminated Petrarca's sojourn beyond the Alps.

The year 1348 is memorable in the annals of Europe as the year of the great plague, which swept as a scourge over the land, destroying whole populations. Nor was it only destructive of human lives; it uprooted landmarks of tradition and conduct, dislocating society, and altering men's minds and morals. The disease raged in Avignon, where it must be remembered to the credit of Clement VI. that he paid doctors to attend the poor, and did all in his power to lessen the horrors of the situation; but 120,000 people are said to have died in three months. Among these was Madonna Laura, though the cause of her death is not certainly known. On May 19, 1348, when Petrarca was at Parma, he received the news of her death from his friend Socrates; she had died at Avignon on April 6, on the same day, and at the same hour, in which he had first seen her. Whether the sonnets of presentiment (ccxlix.-ccliv.) and the dream of the *Trionfi*[1] have any foundation in fact cannot now be known: as M. Cochin rightly remarks: " Such an exact presentiment is a very rare thing."[2] On the other hand, it is more than likely that some of the poems were really written about this time, for the poet had taken leave of his Lady in the previous November, and, with the pain of parting, his heart may well have been full of foreboding.

> She had put off the charms she used to show,
>   The pearls and garlands and the glad array,
>   And the sweet human speech, and laugh, and song.

---

[1] *La notte che seguì* once reckoned as *Triumphus Mortis*, canto ii., but not now included; see *infra*, chapter x. p. 286.

[2] Cf. H. Cochin, *op. cit.* p. 115.

So all my life to doubt is left a prey;
I am assailed by auguries of wrong,
By dreams and by dark thoughts: God grant they go![1]

Probably the poems were the fruits of many separations, but it is obvious why they have been collected and placed here: they are the fitting introduction to the great sorrow of which Petrarca has left his own most touching record on the fly-leaf of his Virgil—a priceless treasure which is now preserved in the Ambrosian Museum at Milan.

"Laura, illustrious by her own virtues and widely celebrated by my songs, first appeared to my eyes at the beginning of my manhood, in the year 1327, upon the sixth day of April, at the first hour, in the Church of St. Clare at Avignon; and in the same city, on the same sixth day, at the same first hour, but in the year 1348, her light was taken from this light, while I, being by chance at Verona, alas! knew nothing of my fate. The unhappy news, however, reached me at Parma, in a letter from my Ludovico, in the same year on the nineteenth day of May. Her most pure and most beautiful body was laid in the Church of the Friars Minor on the very day of her death at evening. I am persuaded that her soul, as Seneca said of Africanus, returned to heaven from whence it came. I thought fit to write this for a bitter memory of the event, yet with a certain bitter sweetness, especially in this place which often meets my eye, that there should be nothing to please me more in this life, and that I might be warned by the frequent sight of these words and the consideration of the swiftly passing years, that, now that the greater snare is broken. it is time to flee from Babylon, which, by the grace

---

[1] " Deposta avea l'usata leggiadria,
   Le perle e le ghirlande e i panni allegri
   E 'l riso e 'l canto e 'l parlar dolce umano.
Così in dubbio lasciai la vita mia:
   Or tristi auguri e sogni e penser negri,
   Mi danno assalto; e piaccia a Dio che 'n vano."
                                              *Rime*, ccxlix.

of God, will be easy to one who thinks acutely and manfully on the useless cares of former times, their vain hopes, and unexpected end." [1]

This note has been quoted by all biographers since the beginning of the fifteenth century, and, in spite of some modern critics who have tried to maintain that it is a forgery, its authenticity has been confidently asserted by the best authorities, and by it the existence of Laura is proved beyond all doubt.[2] There are certain well-ascertained facts touching the death of Laura de Sade which make it highly probable that she and Petrarca's Laura were one and the same. In the archives of the Sade family it is related how Laura, wife of Hugues de Sade, was taken ill on April 3, that she made her will and received the last sacraments, and died on the morning of April 6, and that the same day at vespers she was taken to the Church of the Friars Minor, and laid in the Chapel of the Cross, which Hugues de Sade had just built for a mortuary chapel for his family. She left nine children, six sons and three daughters.

[1] " Laura propriis virtutibus illustris et meis longum celebrata carminibus, primum oculis meis apparuit sub primum adolescentiæ meæ tempus anno domini 1327 die sexta mensis Aprilis, in Ecclesia Sanctæ Claræ Avenionensis, hora matutina; et in eadem civitate, eodem mense Aprilis, eadem die sexta, eadem hora prima, anno autem 1348 ab hac luce lux illa subtracta est, cum ego forte tunc Veronæ essem heu! fati mei nescius. Rumor autem infelix per litteras Ludovici mei me Parmæ reperit anno eodem, mense maio, die decimanona mane. Corpus illud castissimum atque pulcherrimum in loco fratrum minorum repositum est ipso die mortis ad vesperam. Animam quidem eius, ut de Africano ait Seneca, in cœlum unde erat, rediisse persuadeo mihi. Hoc autem ad acerbam rei memoriam amara quidem dulcedine scribere visum est hoc potissimum loco, qui sæpe sub oculos meos redit, ut scilicet nihil esse deberet quod amplius mihi placeat in hac vita, et effracto maiori laqueo tempus esse de Babylone fugiendi crebra horum inspectione ac fugacissimæ ætatis existimatione commonear, quod prævia Dei gratia, facile erit præteriti temporis curas supervacuas spes inanes et inspectatos exitus acriter ac viriliter cogitanti."—*De Reb. Fam.* vii. 15, Fracassetti's note.

[2] Cf. P. de Nolhac, *op. cit.* i. p. 140.

L

In 1533, Maurice de Sève,[1] poet and antiquary of Lyon, in company with Girolamo Mannelli and M. Bontems, the Vicar of Cardinal de' Medici, Archbishop of Avignon, searching in this Chapel of the Cross, professed to have discovered a leaden casket which contained a medal, on the side of which were these letters, M. L. M. J., and also a sonnet on parchment, stating that this was the grave of Madonna Laura:—

Qui riposan quei caste e felici ossa.

The letters were taken to mean *Madonna Laura Morta Jace*, and for some time the sonnet, though a very indifferent one, was accepted as Petrarca's; but when it was sent to Cardinal Bembo, he entirely refused to believe in its authenticity. Indeed, the whole alleged discovery of the tomb is strongly open to the suspicion of being a falsification.[2]

We have already said that the particulars of Laura's death tend to identify her with Laura de Sade far more than anything that we know of her life. It is, indeed, very immaterial who Petrarca's Lady may have been, but the fact that she was married is fairly well established by this, that Petrarca always calls her *mulier, femina*, in Latin, and *madonna, donna*, in Italian.[3] In any case it is probably true to say that no one has ever formed a clear idea of Laura's appearance or of her personality. She is always beautiful, but even of her beauty we can make no certain picture. In all things she reflects the varying moods of her singer. If we do not find her (as did Christina Rossetti) " scant of

---

[1] Maurice de Sève was born at Lyon in 1510. He was the friend of Clément Marot, and the author of *Délie*, a collection of 449 *dizains* greatly admired by his contemporaries. He was commended by Du Bellay as " a good Petrarchist."

[2] Cf. Letter from Jean de Tournes to Maurice de Sève and the sonnet in de Sade, iii. p. j. 10 and 11; Bartoli, *Storia della Letteratura Italiana*, vii. pp. 198-207.

[3] The argument frequently made use of that he wrote a *Trionfo della Castità* not *Verginità* is no longer available, since we now know that the right title is *Triumphus Pudicitiæ*. See chapter x. p. 273.

attraction," she is at least hard to visualise: at once gentle and haughty, kind and cruel, humble and vain, it is impossible to build up her character. Beatrice, walking in her own intrinsic loveliness, is yet glorified by the dignity and nobility of him who worshipped her; but Laura, in life at least, has to suffer from the restless sensibility of her lover. It would be almost as hard to shed a tear over the *Canzoniere* as to read the *Vita Nuova* with dry eyes. It has been said that " if a man love nobly, he knows love through infinite pity, unspeakable trust, unending sympathy; and if ignobly, through vehement jealousy, sudden hatred, and unappeasable desire";[1] and Petrarca's love varies, inasmuch as it was in his character to partake of all these moods: yet we may mark the persistent preponderance of the higher.

The Jubilee visit to Rome may be looked upon as another step in the poet's conversion, as we see from this passage in a letter to Boccaccio: " Blessed be God, thanks to whom, as said the Apostle, *liberati sumus de corpore mortis hujus*. But as for that which regards this part of human miseries, I hope that the grace of Christ our Lord has entirely delivered me already. Many years since but especially since the Jubilee."[2] His complete change of habits is very fully described in a letter from Avignon in 1351, where he sets forth the difficulty he has in freeing himself from his former companions and way of life; even his tailor and shoemaker will not make for him according to his orders: they promise to alter, but go on just as before. And he deduces from this that there is only one remedy— change of residence—and concludes by saying that he often thinks that old age passes more calmly in a place other than that in which one has spent one's youth.[3]

The sequel to this reflection was the final farewell to Vaucluse, and the following letter, written by the poet to

[1] W. B. Yeats, *The Secret Rose*.     [2] *Rer. Sen.* viii. 1.
[3] *De Reb. Fam.* ix. 3.

his brother a few months before that event, seems to gather up the harvest of the years:—

"Coming at last to speak of myself . . . if I dare not assert that I am already in port, I have done what sailors are wont to do who are overtaken by a tempest on the deep. I have found a refuge from the winds and waves alongside an island, and there, until a safer harbour appear, I lie hid. . . . With the help of Jesus Christ, I have fulfilled the three things that you bade me, and I will endeavour with all my power to carry them out more perfectly every day. I do not say this to boast of myself, for I am still entangled in many miseries; I grieve for the past, I am troubled for the present, and fearful for the future; but I write this for the first fruits of your joy, and that, the better hope you begin to have for me, so much the more fervently may you pray for me. There are these three things in which I have obeyed you. I have faithfully laid bare in salutary confession the hidden stains of my sins which, through fatal negligence and long silence, had become putrified; and I have accustomed myself to do this more often, and thus to show the secret wounds of my soul to the all-powerful physician. Next, I have become so diligent in saying not only daily but nightly lauds to Christ, at His inspiration, that even now that the nights are so short, however tired I may be by the vigil of the evening, the dawn never finds me asleep or silent. That saying of the Psalmist, *Septies in die laudem dixi tibi*, has pleased me so much that, since I have adopted this habit, no occupation of the day has ever once disturbed me from what I have begun. And also that other saying of his: *Media nocte surgebam ad confitendum tibi;* so that daily at that hour I feel, as it were, some one coming to rouse and forbid me to sleep, although weighed down by heavy slumber. Lastly, I now fear more than death itself the society of women, without which I used to think I could not exist, and although I am often assailed by grievous temptations, nevertheless,

## "IN GRACIOUS TWILIGHTS" 165

when I remind myself of what woman is, every temptation straightway vanishes and I return to my liberty and peace. In these things I believe that I have been helped most lovingly by your prayers, and hope still to be helped, and so beseech you by the mercy of Him who deigned to call you back, when wandering in darkness, into His light."[1]

[1] *De Reb. Fam.* x. 5.

# CHAPTER VII

### THE COMPANY OF THE GREAT

" Certain people of importance
(Such he gave his daily dreadful line to)
Entered and would seize, forsooth, the poet."
ROBERT BROWNING.

LEAVING Avignon, as it would seem without any settled plans, Petrarca proceeded to Italy, the land of his predilection, and halted at Milan. Many courses were open to him. He had an ardent desire to settle in Rome, a place for which he had always felt a quite peculiar affection. Writing in later life to Lælius, he relates how, twenty years ago, his sojourn there had delighted him more than anything else, and, if fate would have consented, he should like it to have lasted for ever. He can find no words to convey the reverence which he felt for the glorious fragments and proud remains of the queen of cities — monuments and witnesses of the most splendid virtue; by which are shown to all the ages both the road and the goal of earthly and heavenly glory. Among all the places which he has visited, he says, it is to Rome that love most powerfully impels him; and, having seen it many times as a wandering pilgrim, he would like to become an inhabitant, and find therein that rest that he has so long sighed after. But he appears to have set aside the project as being fraught with too many difficulties. Invitations to Naples from the King of Sicily, and to Paris from the King of France, were also refused by him; and the Gonzaga greatly desired his presence in Mantua, where Virgilian associations somewhat tempted him to go. Florence had shut her gates against him, but he had already established a home in some wise at Parma, and both there, at Pisa, and at Padua, he possessed canonries, and would have been honourably received and welcomed. At any of these places he could have lived his own life undisturbed.

What, then, was Petrarca's motive for deciding to remain in Milan, which of all choices appears the least suited to the genius of his character? Little is open to us in the way of explanation, save his consuming restlessness and love of change, and a certain liking for flattery and the company of the great, which possibly possessed for him this additional charm, that he knew how to accept favours in a different manner and spirit from the usual one. Most men have a conscious pride in the thing that they can do better than others, albeit the thing itself may not be particularly worth doing. Petrarca, while electing, to the scandal of his friends, to live at a corrupt court at the invitation of its rulers, set himself to show to the world the spectacle of a dependent who preserved his liberty, of a courtier who was courted by his hosts—a sight so unusual that we may admire the originality of the man who presented it. Yet while reading his deprecating letters of thin excuse and defence, we cannot but feel that he has taken up life on a lower plane.

The poet's eight years' sojourn in Milan is one of the huge contradictions of his life. That the lover of solitude and tranquillity should have chosen a turbulent city for his home; that he who extolled independence should elect to be a hanger-on of the great; that a man who, in his loyal championship of Rienzi, had identified himself with the cause of freedom should, voluntarily, domesticate himself in the stronghold of the worst tyranny; and that he who had boldly rebuked the corruptions of the papal court should attach himself to rulers whose cruelty and licentiousness knew no bounds—these facts confront us in the guise of riddles to which no satisfactory answer can be found. Nor can we even fall back upon the excuse that the act wore a different complexion to its own age, for there is evidence that to the poet's friends and contemporaries it was as incomprehensible as to ourselves. Letters of expostulation reached him from every side, but of all protests that of Boccaccio was the most vigorous. He says he will begin with the words of another, *loqui prohibeor et tacere non possum*, for, on the one hand, the reverence that he owes to Silvanus [1] bids him keep silence, while, on the other, his indignation at the crime but now committed impels him to speak. He goes on to say that the news was first brought by an old friend, and that he had denied it, saying that it was impossible. " Then a few days afterwards Simonides came by chance to Ravenna, and showed letters written by Silvanus on this matter; and, so made certain, I cried out upon heaven and the crime of Silvanus, and said: If this be so, all things are to be believed. Verily I would rather have deemed that does would subdue tigers, or lambs put wolves to flight, than that Silvanus would act against his own convictions. Who henceforth shall accuse wicked, shameless, lascivious, or avaricious men, after Silvanus has so gone astray? Alas! whither have departed his uprightness, his holiness, his wisdom? He has become the friend of that murderous and inhuman one, whom he was wont to call now Polyphemus, now the Cyclops; and not dragged, not compelled, but of his own free will, he has gone under the yoke of him whose audacity, pride, and tyranny he used indignantly to condemn. . . . Not himself alone hath Silvanus infected by this fall; but you, me, and the rest, who were wont to exalt his life, his character, his songs, and his writing, with all our voices, with all our powers, through all the woods, among all the shepherds—us hath he stained though innocent. . . . And this famous panegyrist and worshipper of solitudes, how will he act surrounded by the multitude? What will he do, who was wont to extol free

[1] This was a favourite name for Petrarca. Cf. *De Reb. Fam.* x. 4.

## THE COMPANY OF THE GREAT 169

life and upright poverty with such sublime praises, when subject to the yoke of another, and adorned with dishonourable wealth? . . . Now, excellent master, since much remains that I could say against him (unless something else is disclosed), what will you say, who have a greater and more eloquent indignation? What will his holy Monicus say?[1] What will his Socrates . . . and many others say, who from afar have watched and wondered at him, and praised him to the skies as a unique example of uprightness among mortals? I think all will condemn him and be tormented with grief. Since, therefore, I am assured that he will believe in you beyond the others, I beseech you to rebuke him, and, by your character, draw him back from so deplorable a crime, and deprive that most cruel man of so splendid an ornament, so sweet a solace, so ripe a counsellor, that you may restore to him his old fame; and to yourself, and to us, and to the woods, our own most pleasant and most beloved friend. Farewell. From Ravenna, July 18, with a fervent and much moved mind.—Your GIOVANNI BOCCACCIO."[2]

Unfortunately the answer to this is not forthcoming, but the arguments contained in it were probably much the same as those that we find in a later letter to Boccaccio (which appears to be a reply to a similar accusation), and in another which may have been addressed either to Boccaccio or to Nelli [3]—the only one of his friends who did not reproach him.[4] The substance of the excuses may be reduced to this. Petrarca says that he perceives that his friends are apprehensive for his liberty, but, for that, they must never fear, for to no man is freedom more essential; a free and quiet life is his first necessity, and to that alone will he sacrifice everything. Therefore, although he may appear to be wearing a heavy yoke, in reality no man is more free than he

---
[1] Petrarca's brother, Gherardo. Cf. *De Reb. Fam.* x. 4.
[2] *Le Lettere di Messer Giovanni Boccaccio*, F. Corazzini, p. 47.
[3] *Rer. Sen.* vi. 2; *Var.* 7. Also *De Reb. Fam.* xvi. 11.
[4] H. Cochin, *Un ami de Pétrarque*, epist. x.

is: free, that is, in soul, for in things of the body a man must perforce be the servant of those who are more powerful than himself. Then, coming to more personal details, he confesses that he had not known how to resist the most gracious requests of this lord (the Archbishop, Giovanni Visconti), the greatest of the Italians, who invited him with such courtesy and honour as he had neither deserved, hoped, nor desired. In vain had he sought to excuse himself on account of his many occupations, and of his aversion to vast assemblages, and, above all, of his ardent desire to live quietly and alone. The Archbishop, as though he foresaw all that would be said, forestalled every difficulty, and promised to furnish the poet with the solitude and repose for which he longed, assuring him that he required no service from him—nothing but his presence, which was sufficient of itself to confer honour on the principality.[1] But, in spite of this, the note of uneasiness is not wanting in Petrarca's letters. That saying of the wisest of the Hebrews, *Cunctæ res difficiles*, he declares, seems to him the truest of all true things. Everything is difficult, but to live wisely is the hardest thing of all, since at every step some obstacle arises.[2] His friends, while apparently profoundly dissatisfied with the course he had adopted, were by no means agreed as to what they would wish him to do. Some would have liked him to go to Padua, some to return to Avignon, others to settle in his own country: each one had something different to suggest.

A house was given him at the extreme west of the town, near the Church of Sant' Ambrogio, which, with its associations with St. Augustine, greatly pleased him. Petrarca stipulated that he was to be the absolute master of his own time, and argues from this that, considering the multifarious occupations of his patron and of himself, the arrangement is not likely to last long. It did last eight years, but with the result that the poet spent large portions of his time in

[1] *De Reb. Fam.* xvi. 12.  [2] *Rer. Sen.* vi. 2.

diplomatic cares.[1] Through it all, he is sensitive to the blame that attaches to him, but says that people will only see what he does and not what he thinks. If he has not done the best thing, he has at any rate done what seemed the least bad; he is yielding to necessity. "So true is it," he writes, "that a man makes no account of himself, but sells his liberty for a vile price.... Do you know what the great apostle Paul said, speaking of himself? *Non enim quod volo bonum, hoc facio; sed quod nolo malum, hoc ago.*"[2]

It is evident that the poet is dazzled by the power and position of the man who flatters him; he shows himself here as one of the many to whom success is a paramount attraction. Perhaps this is a parallel quality with the desire for fame. His is the error of judging by results; it is the wish for something tangible, coupled with the inability to realise that the best things are essentially elusive—out of reach; so that our loftiest aspirations are foredoomed to disappointment, since it is only by foregoing these that we can attain success, which is thus the most complete of failures. It is futile to try and make out for him a better case than he makes out for himself, but, while granting the weakness to which he pleads guilty, we may notice some other determining causes. His nature seems to have had a double need; on the one hand, he craved companionship, on the other, solitude, and the necessity for each was equally imperative. Never was any man less sufficient to himself; the number and variety of his friendships witness to this, and still more the volume of his correspondence. His mind throve and expanded in contact with others; vistas of undiscovered country opened out before him; he obtained brighter lights, wider impressions, from such intercourse and sympathy; but there came also upon him the no less dominating need for retirement and loneliness, to reckon up and utilise his gains. Petrarca's course of life is thus partly the result of obedience to nature, partly the desire to vindi-

[1] *De Reb. Fam.* xvi. 11, 12.   [2] *Ibid.* xvii. 10.

cate his own individuality. For in truth he did what very few could do: he was loaded with favours which he had never courted, he conferred honour rather than received it. This was certainly a new departure in the history of court favourites, but it is one of the redeeming features of the age of the despots. They discerned the signs of the times; understanding that the mind of Italy was awake, they sought out all of intellectual and artistic excellence, both to build up and to adorn the edifice they were raising, and they remained always conscious of their debt: in no age was intellect ever so sovereign.

Thus, with some heart-searchings and misgivings, Petrarca began his eight years' residence in Milan, which, as he seems to have faintly foreboded, was to be at least as full of political as of literary occupations.

"The greatest of the Italians"—this phrase occurs more than once in the poet's letters in reference to Giovanni Visconti, Archbishop and ruler of Milan, and one would like to be able to judge how far the name befits him. The name of Visconti is identified with a career of cruelty and conquest, but, if we consult history, it seems as though Giovanni were blackened by the shadow of his name, for his own character as a ruler will well bear investigation. His powers as a diplomatist were very remarkable; he extended his dominions, but without bloodshed; everywhere his policy was one of conciliation. He recalled his banished nephews, acknowledged them as his heirs, and was above feeling any jealousy of them. His subjects enjoyed the blessings of peace and good government. He only lived for a year and a half after Petrarca's arrival, but, in that short time, he managed to make use of his illustrious guest, and, indeed, his sagacity was never more conspicuously shown than in the manner of his invitation to the champion of Freedom to confer honour on the Milanese court.

In the September of 1353, Cardinal Albornoz, who, with Rienzi in his train, was being sent by Innocent VI. to win

## THE COMPANY OF THE GREAT 173

back the patrimony of the Church, approached Milan. The austere Cardinal and the worldly Archbishop could have had little in common, but Giovanni pursued his usual conciliatory policy and received the Legate with becoming honour, going two miles on the road to meet him, and welcomed him into the city; but he refused him permission to enter Bologna. Petrarca was one of the cortège who went out to receive the Cardinal, and, in the crowd and dust, his horse, getting beyond his management, landed him on the edge of a precipice, and he would, undoubtedly, have been killed but for the courage and presence of mind of Galeazzo Visconti, the Archbishop's nephew. (There are many indications in the course of his history that Francesco was a very indifferent horseman.) Albornoz treated the poet with marked consideration, encouraging him to ask something of consequence for himself; but the latter, with characteristic generosity, contented himself with asking a favour for his friend, Nelli, which he obtained.[1]

It is uncertain whether Petrarca was a member of the Archbishop's Council of State, but he was, at any rate, consulted on all important matters, and, in November, he was sent as ambassador to Venice to negotiate a peace between that republic and Genoa. This was a project the poet had had at heart for a long time. He had already addressed letters to the Doge of each city,[2] and in September had written at length to his friend, Guido Settimo (a Genoese by birth), to condole with him over the defeat his countrymen had just sustained.[3] He tells how, in the first shock of the unexpected news, he had seized his pen, and written to inspire the Genoese with fresh hope and courage from the examples of antiquity; but, before his letter was finished, a report reached him of their proposed submission to Milan. Domiciled as he was with the Visconti, Petrarca must have found himself in a difficult situation: at least, he never despatched his epistle, and, without committing himself to

[1] *Var.* 56.   [2] *De Reb. Fam.* xi. 8; xiv. 5.   [3] *Ibid.* xvii. 3.

either side, he sent Guido a pathetic description of the reception and submission of the Genoese envoys. On this occasion the poet was requested to be the spokesman, but he excused himself, feeling that for such an event the speech would come better from the mouth of the ruler.[1] The Archbishop's next step was to send Petrarca to Venice, which embassy appeared to him a very easy one. Writing to Andrea Dandolo in 1351, he, as an Italian, had deplored that " the two most splendid lights of Italy " should have recourse to arms.[2] It was probably with rhetoric of this kind that he confronted the practical Venetians in his character of ambassador, and produced on them no impression whatever. The patriot-poet was too transcendental in his ideas, which might, indeed, be termed illusions; as a politician, it was impossible to regard him seriously. He could well adorn a court, but was not fitted to build up or to support a kingdom. His eloquence was more useful on such occasions as that of the succession of the three Visconti brothers to their uncle's dominions in 1354, when he harangued the people; or of the baptism of the little son of Bernabò, when he acted as godfather, and presented the baby with a Latin poem [3] and a gold cup.

It was in the October of 1354 that the Archbishop died, and was succeeded by his three nephews, Matteo, Bernabò, and Galeazzo, who divided the dominions between them, holding Milan and Genoa in common: the eldest, however, lived but a short time, and on his death everything was shared between the two remaining brothers. Of these, Bernabò had from his youth a savage and ferocious nature, and as he grew older he became a monster of cruelty and tyranny. Galeazzo was wholly unlike him in character; he was gentle and courteous, loving peace and the society of men of letters. It was he who implored Petrarca to continue to reside in Milan, and he sought his advice on all

---

[1] *De Reb. Fam.* xvii. 4.   [2] *Ibid.* xi. 8. Cf. *supra*, p. 102.
[3] Cf. Corio, *op. cit.* iii. 3.

subjects. The poet had prepared an eloquent speech for the day on which the three Visconti entered on their career as rulers, in which, after bewailing the death of the Archbishop, a loss so great that none could be so dull as not to feel it, he said that, having paid all possible respect to his memory, it was now necessary to consider our new lords and to serve them with the same faithfulness and love as had been given to their predecessor. Here he was inopportunely interrupted by the court astrologer who, announcing that the propitious moment had come for investing the brothers with the insignia of their office, cut short the oration, and then, perhaps taken aback at the obedience of the orator, hesitating and uncertain, invited him to continue his discourse a little longer. Petrarca narrates the incident with some humour and some natural annoyance, arising, no doubt, from his well-known antipathy to astrology; but he seems to have behaved with great good humour and dignity.[1]

Meanwhile, the growing power of the Visconti was the means of bringing about the desire of the poet's heart; Italy in universal disquiet looked towards the Emperor. The Pope hoped that his presence would strengthen the position of Cardinal Albornoz; Florence, who had tried in vain to find other allies, at length turned reluctantly to him; Venice, who had leagued herself with Ferrara, Mantua, and Padua to resist the encroachments of Milan, summoned him; and the Visconti in self-defence offered him the iron crown. Petrarca, since the first fall of Rienzi, had never ceased to appeal to Charles; from Padua, from Avignon, and from Milan his voice had gone forth: " Now to me you are not King of Bohemia, but King of the world, Emperor of Rome, and verily Cæsar."[2] But no such thoughts of world-wide empire dazzled the imagination of the unambitious, scholarly man to whom they were addressed.

[1] *Rer. Sen.* iii. 1. Cf. A. Hortis, *Scritti inediti di Francesco Petrarca,* pp. 137-139, 335-340.
[2] *De Reb. Fam.* xix. 1.

He came to Italy tardily, and probably somewhat against his will, not ill-content, it may be, to acquire the ornaments of the iron and golden crowns, but only with the modest desire of reconciling some factions and remaining at peace with every one. There is something *bourgeois* and cringing in his attitude throughout. Arriving in Mantua, in the depth of an exceptionally severe winter, he sent for Petrarca, who obeyed the summons in the full flush of his enthusiasm.

Of this first interview Francesco wrote a long account to his friend Lælius, whom he subsequently commended to the Emperor. Charles spoke to the great author about his writings, and specially of the *De Viris Illustribus*, asking that it might be dedicated to him, to which Petrarca dauntlessly replied that the Emperor should have it if, by his conduct, he should prove himself worthy of it. Taking this opportunity of presenting him with a collection of coins bearing the effigies of former Cæsars, the poet implored him to emulate their great deeds. Charles, on his side, requested Petrarca to accompany him to Rome, saying that he wished to see the city with the poet's eyes and not only with his own; but Petrarca, though flattered, did not see his way to accepting the invitation.[1] The Emperor passed the winter in Milan, and induced the Visconti to agree to a truce until May, the credit of which arrangement has universally been assigned to Petrarca, though he modestly disclaims it in the above-quoted letter to Lælius. Charles was not anxious to enter Milan, but, on leaving Mantua, was met by Bernabò and Galeazzo with an immense escort, and forcibly brought into the city, where he was crowned with the iron crown in Sant' Ambrogio, and furnished with money for his journey to Rome. There he was duly crowned on Easter Day, but with the humiliating proviso that he was only to enter the city for his coronation and to make no stay in it. If Charles' progress to Rome was like that of a merchant, as says Villani, his return was like that of a fugitive.

[1] *De Reb. Fam.* xix. 3.

Treated everywhere with contempt, he returned to Germany without honour and without credit, the possessor of crowns which symbolised nothing, and taking back, to his shame, a full purse instead of an empty one. Petrarca wrote to him in a strain of bitter disappointment and disillusion,[1] but their intercourse was not destined to end here, for, in the following year, Francesco was sent as ambassador to Prague, rumours having reached Milan that the Emperor was about to form a league with Hungary and Austria against the tyrants of Italy. Petrarca was received with all honour and created Count Palatine,[2] but the expedition was without any political fruit, for Charles would not enter into any negotiations with the Visconti, and, though chiefly occupied with home affairs, continued secretly to favour the league.

Drawn thus into the press and hurry of public events, Petrarca was yet true to the traditions of his character. Even during his first year at Milan we find him retiring to San Colombano, where he delights himself in the wide view, the welcome solitude, and the friendly silence. From there his thoughts travel to Vaucluse, and he writes to Guido Settimo rejoicing to hear that this friend has been spending some days there, using his books and tending his garden, which, he proudly says, has not its equal in the world.[3] Alas! his pleasure in thinking of this favourite retreat was of short duration, for, on the following Christmas Day, it was attacked by thieves, robbed, and burned; only the books were luckily spared and were afterwards sent to their owner in a much injured condition.[4] The repose at San Colombano cannot have been of long duration, but, a few years later, Petrarca procured for himself a country house about three miles out of Milan, and near the Certosa built by Giovanni Visconti. He named his villa Linterno, after that of Scipio Africanus, and, in another letter to Guido

---

[1] *De Reb. Fam.* xix. 12.   [2] *Ibid.* xxi. 2.
[3] *Ibid.* xvii. 5.   [4] *Var.* 25; *Rer. Sen.* ix. 2.

Settimo, has given a full account of his way of life both there and in Milan. He says that day and night he reads and writes alternately, having no other pleasure or diversion, and so the works grow under his hand. He is well suited in his house, which stands at the extreme west of the town, and is too far off to bring him many visitors. He lives the same life that he used to do, and is as sparing of food and sleep. Then, as to his villa, it stands on an elevation, with streams all round. There are orchards and flowers, and all country delights—fishes in the brook, birds, goats, and hares. Close by is the Certosa; he had thought of making this his home, but, as he is obliged to keep servants and horses, he was afraid of inconveniencing the monks, and therefore elected to be their neighbour, rather than their guest: but the church is open to him, and he is free to come and go as he will.[1] One other change he made when, in 1359, he gave up his house near Sant' Ambrogio and went to live in the Convent of San Simpliciano outside the city. " So much," he says, " can love of liberty, of solitude, and of repose effect in me."[2]

What, then, were the works which "grew under his hand"? We may suppose him to have been constantly occupied with his great historical work, *De Viris Illustribus;* in 1357 he began the *Trionfo d'Amore;* in the following year the long philosophical treatise, *De remediis utriusque fortunæ*, written for Azzo da Correggio; while, in 1359, he embarked on the mighty task of selecting and arranging all his Latin letters to his friends, in prose and verse.[3]

Ill-fortune was the constant lot of Azzo, and when, on an accusation of treachery, he was driven out of Verona, Petrarca's son was deprived of his canonry in that city, and it was only restored to him on the very day of his death in 1361.[4] Petrarca's first idea was to keep Giovanni in Milan, and there finish his education, but the boy had no turn for

[1] *De Reb. Fam.* xix. 16.
[2] *Ibid.* xxi. 14.
[3] *Ibid.* xx. 7, Fracassetti's note.
[4] *Var.* 35.

## THE COMPANY OF THE GREAT

study and hated a book as though it were a serpent. His father writes very philosophically that, so long as Giovanni is virtuous, he will be content, for worth without wisdom is better than wisdom without worth.[1] Subsequently he was sent back to Avignon, from whence Simonides wrote to Petrarca imploring him not to be ready to listen to all that was said against the boy, praising his truthfulness and modesty, and showing general approbation of him in the present and hope for the future.[2] When he rejoined his father at Milan troubles began afresh, and he was implicated in the robbing of Petrarca's house at Sant' Ambrogio while the latter was away at Linterno; on which account his father refused to have him any longer to live with him, and wrote two very bitter letters, one to Giovanni himself, and one written about him to Guido Settimo.[3] But there seems some evidence that the boy showed signs of penitence, and was received back into favour. Certainly when he died of the plague, in 1361, his father bitterly lamented him, and wrote of him to Simonides, calling him "my young son whom I seemed to hate when he was alive, and now that he is dead I feel that I love him with my whole heart. . . . Whatever else he was, for you he nourished a warm affection and a deep regard . . . whence I derived one of my most valid arguments for believing that he was improving every day."[4]

Petrarca was happier in his daughter, Francesca. Of her childhood and education we know nothing, but she was married in Milan to Francesco da Brossano, and she and her husband appear to have made their home with Petrarca.

The climate of Milan does not seem to have been very propitious to Petrarca; he suffered every autumn with tertian fever; he also had a long and vexatious illness owing to a neglected wound in his leg, caused by the fall of a heavy manuscript of Cicero's letters. He writes of this

---

[1] *De Reb. Fam.* xix. 17.   [2] H. Cochin, *op. cit.* epist. xviii. xix.
[3] *De Reb. Fam.* xxii. 7; xxiii. 12.   [4] *Rer. Sen.* i. 2.

humorously in two or three places,[1] but the accident was a bad one, and the ill effects lasted more than a year.

An incursion into politics, which he made in 1357, was one of which Petrarca had no cause to be proud, when, at the request of Galeazzo Visconti, he sent a long letter to Fra Giacomo Bussolari exhorting him to resign the lordship of Pavia. The history of the Frate is specially interesting as foreshadowing the career of Savonarola. Villani relates [2] how Bussolari, an Augustinian friar, helped by the Marchese di Monferrato and by a powerful Pavian family, the Beccaria, succeeded in rescuing the city from the clutches of the Visconti; after which, with the countenance of the Marchese, he drove out the Beccaria, who were on the point of becoming lords of the city, and incited the citizens to self-government. The Frate's saintly life and his remarkable powers of oratory gave him a great ascendancy; the people submitted absolutely to him, and, anticipating the great Dominican, he encouraged men and women to strip themselves of their costly garments, to cut off their gold fringes and ornaments, and to lay aside all luxury. Meanwhile, the Beccaria had fled to Milan to demand help from the Visconti, and Galeazzo, not having an army at liberty at the moment, deputed Petrarca to write a letter of remonstrance to Bussolari. The epistle is long and intensely commonplace; it is not without reason and good sense, but, as it is written to order, one cannot say how far the sentiments are genuine; nor can one help feeling that the writer was playing an unworthy part in allowing himself to become the spokesman of the Visconti against local liberties, even if he judged, not unreasonably, that a friar was not a fit person to be despot of a city. ("Turn your eyes upon yourself," he says; "behold your sandals, your girdle, your habit; there is no place for the purple; everything in you announces, not a prince of the world, but a servant of

---

[1] *De Reb. Fam.* xxi. 10; *Var.* 25.
[2] M. Villani, lib. viii. cap. 1-4, 57.

Christ."[1]) The remonstrance was without effect; the Frate continued his despotic government, creating and abolishing offices at will, and obeyed unquestioningly by the people whose idol he was. But, in 1359, Galeazzo was able to send the great general Luchino dal Verme to blockade Pavia, which, threatened with famine, had no choice but to surrender, the Frate setting a seal of nobility to the doubtful wisdom of his political career by making the best terms he could for the city and taking no pains to secure his own safety. He was, of course, made prisoner by the Visconti, and was condemned to perpetual incarceration in a convent of his own order at Vercelli.[2]

In later times Galeazzo, disgusted with his brother's cruelties in Milan, went to reside in Pavia, and there Petrarca spent several summers with him. Galeazzo established a university and induced all the most celebrated professors to come there, and he beautified the city in all ways, building there his immense palace, which was said to be the finest in the world. Petrarca describes it to Boccaccio as standing on the highest point of the city, and built at immense cost by Galeazzo Visconti, " who, excelling many in many things, surpasses all in the magnificence of his buildings." [3]

A more honourable mission fell to Petrarca when, in the next year, he was sent to congratulate King John of France on his release from an English prison—an event to which Galeazzo had contributed by the timely offer of a large sum of money, on condition that the king's daughter, Isabella, should be given in marriage to Visconti's son, Giovan Galeazzo. Francesco was grieved to the heart at beholding the ruinous state of Paris. King John received him with the utmost cordiality and would fain have kept him at his court, but Francesco, though flattered by the wishes of a king who was, he says, " gentle and affable above all monarchs," found it wholly impossible to sever that chain

[1] *De Reb. Fam.* xix. 18. [2] M. Villani, lib. ix. cap. 54.
[3] *Rer. Sen.* v. 1.

which is called the love of country.[1]  Another mark of royal favour was shortly to reach him in the shape of a golden cup sent to him by Charles IV. with an earnest repetition of an invitation already given to settle himself at the imperial court—a request with which the poet only temporises, though, true to his principles, he reminds the Emperor yet again of his destiny in these words: "You call me to Germany and I call you to Italy."[2]

But flatteries were thickly strewn upon Petrarca's path. Long ago Pandolfo Malatesta, having conceived a great admiration for him, had despatched a painter, at great personal expense, to paint the poet's portrait. Pandolfo, coming to Milan, in 1356, as captain of Visconti's cavalry, made it his first care to make the acquaintance of the great man whom he only knew by fame, visiting him numberless times in spite of the multiplicity of his occupations; and, being not wholly satisfied with the former portrait, sent another artist to paint Petrarca unawares among his books, which picture the soldier kept always among his most precious things.[3] Yet another extravagant admirer was Enrico Capra, a Bergamese goldsmith, whose dearest wish was to win the poet's friendship. In every corner of his house he had placed the name, the bust, or the portrait of Petrarca, and he spent large sums in procuring copies of anything and everything that he had written. Finally, he gave up his business and devoted himself entirely to study. The crowning glory of his life was when Petrarca accepted his invitation to pass a night under his roof, when the poet was sumptuously entertained, rather as a king than as a philosopher. His room was adorned with gold and the bed spread with purple, and he was informed that none had slept on it before him, nor should it be ever used by another.[4] One further notice we have of this enthusiast. It seems that he went to Padua to pursue his studies, and Petrarca

---

[1] *De Reb. Fam.* xxiii. 2.  [2] *Ibid.* xxiii. 8.
[3] *Rer. Sen.* i. 6.  [4] *De Reb. Fam.* xxi. 11.

warmly recommended him to his friend, Guglielmo di Pastrengo, telling how the man had given up everything for the sake of learning and prized books above riches and pleasures.[1] This was a characteristic which Francesco well knew how to appreciate.

It was in the spring of 1359 that Boccaccio first visited Petrarca in Milan. Of the pleasure that he derived from this visit the poet writes in two letters to Simonides, telling him first that he has been enjoying the most sweet presence of a mutual friend, and then that he had felt the greatest reluctance to allow such a friend to leave him, and had suffered much anxiety on his account, knowing no peace until he had heard of him as having safely crossed the Po; but, Francesco adds, having crossed the king of rivers he still has to surmount the king of mountains.[2] To which Simonides reassuringly replies that our dear Boccaccio is arrived safe and sound among us.[3]

One subject of conversation during their few days' intercourse we may safely conjecture to have been the writings of the great poet Dante, because, a short time after Boccaccio's return to Florence, he sent Petrarca a complete copy of the *Commedia* written with his own hand, and accompanied by a Latin poem in its praise. This gift is the subject of a very long letter from Francesco to the donor, which throws so much light on his views on language and poetry that it will be considered at length in that connection in a future chapter.[4]

The plague, which visited Milan in 1361, caused Petrarca to depart and establish himself in Padua. During the summer his son died, and also his very dear friend Socrates. It was while he was at Padua that he received, and again refused, an offer of the papal secretaryship from Innocent VI., which, however, gave him great pleasure as contra-

---

[1] *De Reb. Fam.* xxii. 11.   *Ibid.* xx. 6, 7.
[3] H. Cochin, *op. cit.* epist. xxiii.
[4] *De Reb. Fam.* xxi. 15, Fracassetti's note. Cf. *infra*, pp. 227-229.

dicting the opinion the Pope had formerly expressed concerning him. In a letter to Cardinal Talleyrand, Petrarca writes:—

" It cannot be that that man is considered by the Pope a necromancer whom he chooses for his secretary, nor that he supposes him addicted to sorcery whom he esteems worthy to penetrate into the most secret recesses of his mind, and to write in his sacred name. And for such great honour done to me, and for his abandoning his false opinion, I profess myself beyond measure grateful to him." [1]

Not wishing to accept the Pope's offer for himself, Petrarca was very desirous of obtaining it for his friend Simonides, but this plan was frustrated by the death of Innocent in 1362. Urban V., who succeeded him, conferred the post on another Florentine, Francesco Bruni, also a friend of the poet.

In the following summer, Petrarca formed the project of returning to Vaucluse, from which he had been absent ten years; but the unsettled state of the country made such a journey impossible. Doubtful where to go, he then turned towards Germany, from whence he had received so many invitations from the Emperor, which feelings of respect and gratitude prompted him to accept. But thither also war barred the way, and remarking that, to satisfy his duty and the desire of his prince, the will was enough, Petrarca gladly yielded to circumstances, and, the plague having now appeared in Padua, he repaired to Venice.

On the death of Socrates, Francesco had written to Simonides, saying that, being persuaded that his letter-writing could only end with his death, he proposed henceforth to collect all his letters under the title of *Rerum Senilium* and to dedicate them to him.[2] Alas! this friend, too, was taken from him in 1363, together with Lælius and Barbato, and his outlook must, indeed, have been a lonely one. Boccaccio, happily, was to survive him, and, in 1363,

[1] *Rer. Sen.* i. 4.     [2] *Ibid.* i. 2.

# THE COMPANY OF THE GREAT 185

Petrarca had the pleasure of a three months' visit from him in Venice, when he was accompanied by Leontius Pilatus. This man was really a native of Calabria, but liked to pass himself off as a Greek; he seems to have been a half-educated adventurer, of most uncertain temper and character; hideous, unmannerly, and irascible,[1] with nothing to recommend him but his somewhat imperfect knowledge of the Greek language. Boccaccio first met him in 1360, going to Avignon, and persuaded him to go to Florence instead, where, with some difficulty, he induced the professors of the university to receive him and to establish for him the first Greek chair with an adequate stipend, for, though only four or five were found to listen to his lectures, Boccaccio no doubt managed to impress the Florentine magistrates with the idea that commercial and political advantages might accrue to them from the knowledge of Greek. Here for three years Leontius explained the poems of Homer, while Boccaccio took him into his own house and had private lessons from him. But the real work Boccaccio had at heart was that a translation of Homer into Latin should be made. The first difficulty was to procure a copy of the poems, but Petrarca, who was keenly interested in the undertaking, offered his own copy (that one which had been sent him by Niccolò Sigero, which he said was a sealed book to him) and begged that the translation should be made at his expense.[2] Of the nature of the translation we hear in a letter of the poet's to Boccaccio:—

"Well, listen to what Jerome has written on this score in the preface to the book *De Temporibus*, of Eusebius of Cæsarea, which he translated into Latin. . . . *Whoever says* (he writes) *that the graces of the original language are not lost in translation, let him try to translate Homer literally into Latin . . . and he will see that the result will be something*

[1] Cf. Boccaccio, *De Geneal. Deor.* xv. 6.
[2] Cf. *De Reb. Fam.* xviii. 2 and *Rer. Sen.* iii. 6, Fracassetti's notes; *Rer. Sen.* xvi. 1.

*ridiculous, and the most eloquent of poets will speak with a stammering tongue.* I have wanted to say this to you in time that so much labour should not be wasted. For the rest, provided that the thing be done, it will always be most acceptable to me. For such is the hunger that I feel for such noble viands that, like those who are famished, it matters nothing to me in what way the cook prepares them. And, in truth, a small attempt at expressing the first verses of Homer in Latin prose which the same Leontius has done as an experiment, although it demonstrates the truth of Jerome's saying, yet delights notwithstanding, and contains a hidden beauty quite peculiar to itself . . . form is lacking, but savour and odour are not wanting." [1]

Accompanied by Leontius, Boccaccio passed the months of June, July, and August, 1363, with Petrarca in Venice, and, when his affairs obliged him to return to Florence, he wished the teacher to go back with him; but the latter announced his firm intention of setting out for Constantinople. Wilful and obstinate, he would not listen to the requests of either of his patrons, though he remained a short time in Venice, sorely trying Petrarca (who writes to Boccaccio: "This Leontius is certainly a great beast") by his habitual melancholy, and his unmannerly abuse of everything Italian, until the latter gladly suffered him to depart, giving him a copy of Terence for a travelling companion. Subsequently he surprised his host by sending him a letter, "longer and more ragged than his own beard," in which he extolled Italy to the skies and lavished his abuse on Greece and Byzantium.[2] Nearly two years later, Petrarca writes of the tragic death of Leontius, who, having at length decided to come back to Italy, was killed by lightning in a storm on the Adriatic, on his return voyage.[3] His great work—the translation of the *Iliad* and *Odyssey*—does not seem to have come into Petrarca's possession till after this event, and we have the following acknowledgment of it in a letter to

[1] *Var.* 25.  [2] *Rer. Sen.* iii. 6.  [3] *Ibid.* vi. 1.

Boccaccio: "It only remains for me to tell you that your Homer—now turned into Latin—a token of your love and a sorrowful memento of the dreadful death of the translator, has reached me at last, and has filled me with pleasure and satisfaction."[1]

It will be easily understood that a good translation of Homer could hardly be made by a man who, besides having no very profound knowledge of Greek, was destitute alike of poetic feeling and of appreciation of the refinements of language, and whose command of Latin was very limited. Yet the work, such as it was, was a noteworthy possession for the earliest humanists, and it adds a glory to the fame of Petrarca that he was not only the first to desire and to procure such a treasure, but also the first to appraise the worth of Greek literature, and to exalt it to its rightful position. On the other hand, it may be said that Homer, with the poetry left out, tended to strengthen Petrarca in his erroneous contention that the chief beauty of poetry lies in allegory. It was to the allegorical interpretation of the two great poems that he principally confined himself, working out, after the fashion of his age, the different ways by which the hidden meanings could be obtained.[2] He never ceased to comment on and to annotate his Homer, and one tradition maintains that this was the work he was engaged on when the end came.

From Venice is dated the first long letter which Petrarca wrote to Urban V., but, as he still had the return of the papacy as much at heart as ever, it is remarkable that he should have allowed four years to elapse before addressing him. His first letter, written in June, 1366, is so long as to be almost a treatise, and is, as usual, a fervent exhortation to go back to Rome. Recalling how he had written to two former Popes, to the Emperor, and to other kings and princes, he says that his reverence for truth and liberty

[1] *Rev. Sen.* vi. 2.
[2] Cf. P. de Nolhac, *op. cit.* ii. pp. 178, 179; Koerting, *op. cit.* i. p. 474.

imposed this duty on him, for that it was not he that spoke, but his faith, his devotion, his love of the public good. He then goes on to commend all that the Holy Father had done to re-establish order and discipline, attacking the vices of the Curia in the most uncompromising language. But in spite of all that Urban had done, the greatest thing remains undone. He continues thus:—

" Time passes; already the fourth year is flying, and you do nothing; nothing, I say, of that which, being of the utmost importance, you ought to have done first. Our shepherd, I say to myself, and others say it also, our shepherd, though he shows himself in everything a faithful follower of Him who has given him His flock to feed and care for, seems forgetful of one thing only, which is in itself the most serious and the most important: he has no thought of transporting the flock to its proper fold. . . . All goes well in Avignon; everything is done with prudence and sense. I rejoice with you that wherever you are everything succeeds well, so that your presence is a perpetual guarantee of virtuous actions and prosperous events. But tell me, meanwhile, what is your spouse doing? . . . What captain defends her? What counsellors assist her? . . . More than to any other city, you are bound to Rome . . . for she has only you. . . . Of that spouse, then, I ask you: what is she doing? In what condition is she? What are her hopes? And if you are silent, I will answer: Poor, infirm, miserable, abandoned, covered with the garments of widowhood, she weeps day and night, singing sorrowfully with the prophet: *Quomodo sola sedet civitas, plena populo: facta est quasi vidua domina gentium*. . . . She has no rest by reason of your absence; peace is utterly banished from her heart. . . . The queen-city bewails her widowhood, and, what is still more deplorable, she sees that her spouse has fixed his abode in a remote country . . . who might by his return make her at once glorious and happy. . . . Predestined to accomplish this sacred work . . . if you resist the supreme will, think what account you will have to render for such negligence."

Then, in another key, he sets forth the natural beauty of Italy, the easiness of the journey thither, the excellence of the climate, "and all the other things wherein Italy is favoured and happy"; and, returning to his first eloquent strain, he bids him listen to Peter, who says: "I fled from Rome for fear of Nero's cruelty, and the Lord met and reproved me on the way, so that I returned immediately to Rome, where torture and death awaited me. But what Nero or Domitian has forced you to flee?" And finally Petrarca exhorts him to choose whether he will remain in the mire of Avignon, or will not rather come to Rome, which is sanctified by the blood of the martyrs.[1]

How much the Pope was affected by this appeal, fervent, reasoned, and impressive as it undoubtedly was, we can hardly say; but certainly, in less than a year from its reception, Urban bravely set out, in the teeth of the opposition of all the French cardinals, to reinstate the papacy in Rome, and Petrarca sent him a letter of exultant congratulation.[2] After his arrival in Italy, Urban invited the poet more than once to visit him, and, though urging his age and bad health, which were indeed sufficient excuses, Petrarca at length made up his mind to the journey, and started for Rome in April, 1370, but fell dangerously ill at Ferrara, and was unable to proceed.[3] Urban's brief sojourn in Italy, of scarcely more than three years, and his return to Avignon to die, are matters of general history; he has left upon us the impression of a man who had great courage, but not enough—who fell short of the heroic. In his Letter to Posterity, the poet says of him: "Unhappy man! how beautiful it would have been for him to have died before the altar of St. Peter and in his own chair. If his successors had remained there after him, the glory of that happy return would have been all his, but, if they had come away,

[1] *Rer. Sen.* vii. 1.   [2] *Ibid.* ix. 1.   [3] *Ibid.* xi. 16, 17.

so great would have been their fault that his merit would have appeared so much the greater." [1]

One letter more, of noble disappointment and reproach, Petrarca sent to Urban. " Think," he writes, " how Italy turns to you weeping, and says: ' You saw me lacerated by mortal sores, and you hastened compassionately to heal my wounds . . . and began to pour in oil and wine. . . . And behold . . . you leave me and abandon me. . . . Alas! then, stay with me, O Holy Father . . . for, if you are not pleased to give ear to these prayers, you will see Him coming to meet you by whom Peter, also taking flight, was met, and, as by Peter (who asked Him: Lord, whither goest Thou?) so also by you, shall the answer be heard: I go to Rome to be crucified afresh.' " [2]

Of the many appeals that Petrarca addressed to the Holy See this was the last and the most eloquent.

[1] *Ep. ad Post.*
[2] *Var.* 3. The text of this letter was first published by Bandini, *Bibliotheca Leopoldina Laurentiana*, ii. coll. 101-103.

Rhetoric
*Melozzo da Forli.*

## CHAPTER VIII

IN THE FOOTSTEPS OF CICERO

" There is on earth but one Society,
The noble living and the noble dead."
WORDSWORTH, *The Prelude.*

IT is not without a certain pathos that we turn our attention to Petrarca's Latin poems. The world has elected, and perhaps wisely, to know him as the Italian lyrist and the lover of Laura, but not so did he estimate his own claims to immortality. If we can hardly believe him entirely sincere in the little account he professed to make of his vernacular writings, in the light of his careful and perpetual revision and classification of them, there is yet no doubt that for many years, at any rate, his great epic, *Africa*, was his favourite child, while the Eclogues and Epistles came nearer to his definition of poetry than anything to be found in the *Canzoniere*. For, to him, to be a poet meant to be steeped in Latinity, to have appropriated not only the style but the very images of the ancients; to reproduce their line of thought and their manner of speech. And if he was bound by antiquity on the one side, on the other he had not freed himself from a mediæval tradition. To the mind of the Middle Ages, the essence of poetry lay in allegory; every one searched for some hidden signification, and, if there were not one, it was readily invented. The multiplication of interpretations, which seems such a dreary exercise to us, was part of the charm of poetry at that date, and no modern reader ever plunged more heroically into the thickets of Browning, to extract a meaning non-existent in the mind of the poet, than did the intellectualists of that day labour to draw out parables and allegories which the authors had never imagined. Moreover, for Petrarca the end of poetry was morals,[1] and surely, for a poet, it were better that a millstone were hanged about his neck than that he should write under this delusion. As he sharply differentiated between *rime* and poems, and placed no such yoke on the former, the cause of the life that is inherent in them is not far to seek; they were, as all true poetry must be, the spontaneous outcome of the imagination. In his most serious works he could not kill the poet in him, and it may well be questioned whether the *Africa* would have survived if it had not been for these green places where his fancy had full play. The pitiful story of Sophonisba, the detailed description of her charms, for which Laura must have provided the model; the glories of Rome, which lay nearer to Petrarca's heart than aught the world had ever seen; the dying speech of Mago, instinct with modernity—these, and passages like these, have kept the epic alive.

The Latin works bring their author before us in a threefold aspect, as historian, as stylist, and as poet, and in each we owe him recognition and praise. It is, indeed, to his historic sense that the *Africa* is due, born of his devotion to antiquity, to the great men of all kinds and degrees who created " the grandeur that was Rome." The fire of patriotism that was in him lit up the pages of the past; he saw in his compatriots the lineal descendants of Roman greatness, and his aim was so to revivify the past that it must perforce reflect itself in the present. Hence we see his enthusiasm for Rienzi, and find him promising Charles IV. the dedication of his *Lives of Illustrious Men* when the Emperor should have proved himself worthy of it by noble deeds. It is an effort of imagination to think of any one at that time who should have the idea of compiling a history, but Petrarca, with the courage of the scholar, con-

[1] *Rer. Sen.* xii. 2.

ceived the idea of writing a complete history of Rome. Lack of material forced him to abandon the notion, and to content himself with relating the lives of the men who had made history; so we get from him the *De Viris Illustribus*, the *Compendium*, and the *De Rebus Memorandis*, and in this direction, perhaps more than in any other, he is the pioneer of modern authorship.

The *Epitome de Viris Illustribus* began with Romulus and ended with Julius Cæsar. It is Petrarca's longest historical work, and, of the biographies which it contains, that of Julius Cæsar is the fullest and most important, and this has often been separately printed. There is more originality of treatment in this than in any of the other lives. Constant reference is made to the *Commentaries*, and they are always quoted under the name of Julius Celsus, as was the fashion in the Middle Ages,[1] and hence the confusion arose attributing the life to a fabulous author, Giulio Celso.[2] Begun at Vaucluse, the *De Viris* was never finished, but it has a dedicatory letter to Francesco da Carrara, who took a keen interest in the book, and begged the author to make an abridgment of it for him, to illustrate the portraits of great men which were being painted to adorn the principal saloon in the palace at Padua. All the rooms were decorated, some with animals, some with plants, some with historical scenes; but the great hall was given up to portraits of illustrious men, and it is probable that Petrarca suggested the choice of subjects. This hall still stands, and contains the library of the university, but the frescoes with which it is ornamented are all of the sixteenth century; only two panels (repainted) contain full-length portraits of Petrarca and of Lombardo da Serico.[3] This latter, a Paduan, and himself a man of letters, is closely bound up with Petrarca in both these historical works.

---
[1] Cf. P. de Nolhac, *op. cit.* ii. pp. 1–67.
[2] Cf. D. Rossetti, *op. cit.*
[3] Cf. A. Zardo, *Il Petrarca e i Carraresi.*

Turning to the *Secretum*, we find this passage, which seems almost prophetic: " You have undertaken to write a history from King Romulus to the Emperor Titus—an immense work, whether looked at according to the greatness of the undertaking or the amount of time it will require. And without having finished it . . . you have passed on into *Africa*. . . . So in these two things, without mentioning innumerable others, you consume all your time . . . and, haply, death will snatch the weary pen from your hand without allowing you to finish these two works, so that, while greedily pursuing glory by two roads, you may not attain to it either by one or the other."[1] In truth neither of the historical works was ever completed. Of the *Compendium*, Petrarca only wrote fourteen lives, and, for a long time, it was thought that this was all he had achieved of his projected great work; but, early in last century, the researches of Domenico Rossetti, of C. Schwider, and of Professor Gorlitz fully established the fact that Petrarca did compose his history to the number of thirty-one biographies, to which Lombardo added four others; and that this work, though never published, exists in various manuscripts, the most perfect being that preserved in the Vatican. By order of Francesco da Carrara, Lombardo also completed the *Compendium*, adding twenty-one lives and thus bringing up the number to thirty-five, to which he prefixed a dedicatory letter.[2]

In these historical works Petrarca looked to Livy as his first authority: for the idea of the *De Rebus Memorandis*, he seems to have been indebted to Valerius Maximus. This work—also unfinished—is a collection of facts, reflections, characters, and judgments, arranged on a moral basis. It seems to have been intended to illustrate the four cardinal

---

[1] *Secretum*, dial. iii.
[2] For the whole question, cf. D. Rossetti, *op. cit.*, and P. de Nolhac, *Le " De Viris Illustribus " de Pétrarque*. Also *De Reb. Fam.* viii. 8, Fracassetti's note.

virtues, but it breaks off abruptly at the fourth book, while Prudence is still the subject in hand. The work is particularly interesting as setting forth the author's own ideas. The first chapter is called *De Otio*—a favourite subject of his, which recalls two of his other writings; in another chapter, his theory of dreams and portents is explained, and he refers to this in one of his letters.[1] The characters and examples throughout are not drawn only from antiquity; there are anecdotes of Dante and other Italians, and King Robert plays an important part. Such an encyclopædic work must have been most valuable at the time at which it was written, and it is, even more distinctly than the *De Viris*, a forerunner of modern literature.

Ancient history was a religion with Petrarca:[2] he will neither add nor take away. The *Africa* testifies to his close and attentive study of Livy; the subject does not furnish the materials for an epic; it is a mere transcript from history, pages of it being Livy word for word, but it is redeemed by the poet's enthusiasm and gift of vision. Scipio Africanus had always been one of his favourite heroes, and he rightly judged that no more heroic episode could be found than the story of the second Punic war— that struggle for independence when the foreigner was driven out. This expulsion was always dear to Petrarca's heart: the same feeling re-echoes in *Italia mia* :—

   Che fan qui tante pellegrine spade?

But the events of the time do not content him, and by dreams, by narrative, and song, he manages to review the whole history of Roman greatness: it is the apotheosis of the Roman glory that was and is to be.

    Twere easier far to tell
   The number of the stars that deck the night,

---

[1] *De Reb. Fam.* v. 7.    [2] *Ibid.* xxiv. 8.

The ocean-waves, the sands upon the shore,
Than count the names of all those famous men,
Leaders who make the glory of my Rome.[1]

The poem, as we have it, is in nine books, beginning at the time when Scipio resolves to pass over into Africa, and ending with his victorious return; but there is a gap between the fourth and fifth books, which is partly explained by the manner in which we know it to have been composed. Petrarca began it on Holy Saturday, 1339, at Vaucluse, and laboured at it with such diligence as to make himself quite ill, when his friend Philippe de Cabassole, coming to visit him, extorted from him a promise neither to read nor write anything for ten days, and, to ensure fulfilment of the pledge, he locked up the poet's desk and took away the keys. The unfortunate author relates how the first day seemed longer than a year, and how by the third he was in a high fever, so that Cabassole, realising that the remedy was worse than the disease, restored his papers and released him from his promise. The first four books were compiled in hot haste, and then the project was dropped, and it was not until Petrarca found himself at Selvapiana, in 1341, that he resumed the poem. Whether he ever wrote an intermediate part which has been lost, or whether he did not trouble himself to piece events together, we have no means of knowing; but it is certain that the *Africa*, from being his favourite work, fell into disesteem with him, and that in his old age he did not like to have it mentioned, nor would he circulate it among his friends. One cause of this, no doubt, was the annoyance occasioned him by his having given thirty-five lines of the poem to a friend, Barbato di Solmona, who gave the usual futile promise of secrecy, followed by the usual

---

[1] " Stellatæ sidera noctis
Et pelagi fluctus et arenas litoris ante
Enumerem, quam cuncta quibus mea Roma superbit
Nomina clara ducum."
*Africa*, lib. iii.

indiscretion. Barbato seems not only to have shown the passage, but to have had it copied and widely distributed, and one of these copies, reaching Florence, was subjected to much adverse criticism, to all of which Petrarca replies in a long letter to Boccaccio.[1] The lines in question were those on the death of Mago, in the sixth book, and were censured by the Florentines as being eminently unsuitable as the utterance of a dying youth, and especially of a pagan, while the author indignantly vindicates them as being natural to all men everywhere.[2]

> Alas for mighty honour's giddy height,
> Fallacious hopes of men, false flatteries
> That serve to hide a glory that is vain.
> Alas for life uncertain, given up
> To ceaseless labours, and alas for death
> Of whose sure day no man makes sure enough.
> Alas for man, born to an evil fate.
> All animals repose, but restless man,
> Anxious through all his years, is hurrying down
> The road to death. O death, the best of things,
> The errors and the dreams of vanished life
> Thou only dost discover and dispel.[3]

It is indeed universal utterances such as this, and small

---

[1] *Rer. Sen.* ii. 1.

[2] It is curious that, four centuries after the death of Petrarca, he was accused of having borrowed these same lines from Silius Italicus. Cf. *Rer. Sen.* ii. 1, Fracassetti's note.

[3] " Heu tremulum magnorum culmen honorum,
Spesque hominum fallax, et inanis gloria fictis
Illita blanditiis. Heu vita incerta labori
Dedita perpetuo! semperque heu certa, nec unquam
Sat mortis provisa dies. Heu sortis iniquæ
Natus homo in terris! Animalia cuncta quiescunt;
Irrequietus homo perque omnes anxius annos
Ad mortem festinat iter. Mors, optima rerum,
Tu retegis sola errores et somnia vitæ
Discutis exactæ."

*Africa*, lib. vi.

personal touches, which make the *Africa* possible reading. There is a fine passage in the second book which is full of Petrarca's own particular melancholy:—

> Time will go by, this body will decay
> And all its members in the ignoble tomb.
> The tomb will go to ruin, and the name,
> Though cut in marble, perish utterly,
> And thou shalt suffer thus a second death.
> Grafted indeed on works felicitous
> Great fame may know long life, but ne'ertheless
> 'Twill pass into the dark; the coming age
> Will speak thy praises till she heedless grow,
> Or fall to silence wearied out by time,
> And future ages shall but breed for thee
> Forgetful generations.[1]

In this, passages of the *Trionfi* are clearly foreshadowed.

In the sixth book he gives us a detailed description of the coast of Genoa—very rare at that time in the appreciation and observation displayed. The ninth book contains the prophecy of the poet to come, who will sing Scipio's praise and who will be crowned even as Ennius was. The whole poem sets Petrarca before us as a great Roman: therein lies its interest. A great epic poet he was not, nor was the pastoral form much more suited to his genius. He has written twelve Eclogues, and all of them suffer from want of correspondence between the form and the matter. They are over-weighted with allegory, so much so that the poet

---

[1] " Transibunt tempora, corpus
Hoc cadet, et cedent indigno membra sepulcro;
Mox ruet et bustum, titulusque in marmore sectus
Occidet: hinc mortem patieris, nate, secundam.
Clara quidem libris felicibus insita vivet
Fama diu, tamen ipsa suas passura tenebras.
Ipsa tuas laudes ætas ventura loquetur;
Immemor ipsa eadem, seu tempore fessa, tacebit,
Immemoresque dabit post sæcula longa nepotes."
*Africa*, lib. ii.

explains, in a letter, that no one can understand them without being furnished with the key—a ponderous method of entertainment. Two are polemics against the papal court, which we have noticed already; two more are connected with Rienzi, and have been dealt with in their place. The second Eclogue celebrates the death of King Robert. Laura, of course, is alluded to, more than once, in these pastorals. The third, which is one of the best, describes Petrarca's devotion to poetry, and gives an account of his coronation. He speaks to Daphne (Laura) of his love, implores her pity, and vows to dedicate himself to music and song for her sake. In the tenth Eclogue Fame (*Laurea*) and Laura are woven into an inextricable allegory, and the eleventh is a touching lament over his Lady's death, and an asseveration of her two-fold immortality.

In the metrical Epistles, composed between 1333 and 1361, in which critics have considered that Petrarca has given us his finest Latin, we find ourselves, as it were, in another country. Though dealing in many instances with the same themes as the Eclogues, the spirit is wholly different. There is no room here for allegory; all is natural and spontaneous. We have already spoken of the charming letters to Cardinal Colonna, one thanking him for his gift of a dog, the other describing, at great length, the poet who would fain be a gardener entering into an unequal contest with the Naiads of the valley.[1] We get another full description of the coronation, written to the friend who should have borne a part in it, and containing a message to King Robert, to inform him that the *Africa* is growing under the influence of his name.[2] Yet another deals with the plague, and another with poetry; one is a patriotic address to Rome; while the most interesting of all is to the Bishop of Lombez, relating all his sufferings at the hands of love during the last ten years, the journeys he has undertaken in vain, the impossibility of winning freedom.

[1] *Epist. Metr.* lib. iii. 1, 2, 3, 4.   [2] *Ibid.* lib. ii. 1.

Then he describes his retreat to Vaucluse, and ends with a delightful account of his quiet dwelling, his many books, and the peace that is settling down upon his life.[1] It is in such landscape-painting that Petrarca excels; nor is Vaucluse the only picture; Parma and Selvapiana are also commemorated, and a letter to Socrates ends thus:—

> Truly 'twill be more grateful when at last,
> Weary with wandering, this foot shall tread
> Italian soil, and with more joy our stars
> And our clear skies these eyes shall then behold.[2]

There are two of Petrarca's Latin works that may be fitly called companion-pictures; these are the *De Vita Solitaria* and the *De Otio Religiosorum*; the former was begun in 1346 and the latter in 1347, but neither was finished until ten years later, nor was the *De Vita Solitaria* sent to Philippe de Cabassole, to whom it was dedicated, until 1366.[3] This work was the outcome of the author's life at Vaucluse; it is divided into two books; the first praises the solitary life, the second confirms the praises by the examples of great men. The first book is by far the more interesting, though the one-sided comparison of the city-man given up to vices and the recluse to devotion must provoke a retort. All solitaries are not saints, nor are all dwellers in cities reprobates, and the idea seems at length to have dawned upon the writer, for, in and after the eighteenth chapter, he allows that it is a great thing to live in the world for the good of others, and says that he is writing only for himself and will not judge other men, but that, for those who are in love with letters, the solitary life is not only more peaceful, but higher and safer. *Otium*—that liberty and leisure of the mind—is the fountain of letters and of the liberal arts. The second book is compiled after the manner of the *De Rebus Memorandis*, and consists of illustrations in support

---

[1] *Epist. Metr.* lib. i. 7.　　　　[2] *Ibid.* lib. iii. 32.
[3] *Rer. Sen.* vi. 5.

of the argument, drawn from sacred and profane history. One chapter is devoted to St. Mary Magdalen and refers to her grotto at Ste. Baume, on which Petrarca had already composed a poem.[1] Another is concerned with Pope Celestine, who resigned the high dignity of the papacy, and to whom Dante is thought to have referred when he wrote:—

> Vidi e conobbi l'ombra di colui
> Che fece per viltate il gran rifiuto.[2]

Petrarca would seem to have had this in his mind, for he says: Let who will attribute this act to the *vilitas animi* of the solitary and holy father, he, for his part, can award him nothing but admiration for the small store he set by worldly greatness, and for his long love of solitude. Such an act must have proceeded from a soul very perfect and very free, and the choice could not have been made but by a man who esteemed human things at their just value, and who had trodden pride under his feet.[3] Petrarca ends his treatise by saying: "My first idea was to have written a letter and I have written a book"; and he expresses the fear that Cabassole will think that solitude has made him more loquacious than city-life.

That this book was a favourite with his friends, we can see by the many references to it throughout his letters,[4] and, in particular, we get, by means of it, one interesting bit of self-revelation. Writing to Francesco Casini da Siena (one of his many friends in the medical profession of whom he records: "I have known and been most friendly with many doctors who were eloquent, cultured, learned in many

---

[1] *Rer. Sen.* xv. 15; *De Reb. Fam.* iii. 10. Cf. Fracassetti's note.

[2] "I beheld the shade of him
Who made through cowardice the great refusal."
LONGFELLOW, *Inferno*, iii. 59, 60.

[3] *De Vita Solitaria*, lib. ii. tract. iii. cap. 18.
[4] *Var.* 4, 12, 14; *Rer. Sen.* v. 4; vi. 5, 9; x. 1.

sciences, but only of no account as doctors "[1]), Petrarca says:—

"You tell me you were moved to tears while reading that passage in the *Vita Solitaria* in which I award the palm of a triple solitude to that blessed Francis whose name we both bear.[2] But the love of that name, and not any merit in my book, was capable of producing that effect upon you. But, however it may be, I am content. Men are ordinarily bad judges of their own productions, because self-love twists their judgments, and everything that is theirs appears good to them. I am a bad judge of my things, but for the contrary reason: I am never content with what I do, and my desire to do well is so great that I feel I never reach the mark at which I aim. So that, if my work be approved by some man of merit, I begin to make some account of it myself, and to think I see something good in it. . . . It is true that my book of the *Vita Solitaria* received so much praise from that learned man to whom I dedicated it that never did I see the truth of that saying—the judgments of lovers are wholly blind—more clearly manifested. It is enough to tell you that . . . he desired that this book should be read aloud while he was sitting at table with distinguished persons, at which time it is customary only to read the sacred Scriptures. Now, if you can praise it, although it is dedicated to another, I am all the more pleased as there are fewer extrinsic reasons to make it acceptable to you. The opinions of others have great power over the mind of the writer, especially when they are free from every suspicion of adulation or malice."[3] And to another friend he writes:—

"As for my book of the *Vita Solitaria* . . . I have written to tell my priest at Padua to send it to you. I will allow you to read, but not to copy it, because I have not yet put the finishing touches to it. You know my habits; I am

---

[1] *Rer. Sen.* v. 4.    [2] *De Vita Solitaria*, lib. ii. tract. iii. cap. 11.
[3] *Rer. Sen.* xvi. 3.

like Protagoras, who could not keep his brush off the canvas." [1]

The treatise *De Otio Religiosorum* was the immediate result of Petrarca's visit to his brother, Gherardo, in the Carthusian monastery at Montrieu; it was written at the request of the monks and was dedicated to them. It was no doubt also the product of that attraction to the monastic life which he undoubtedly had, for, though there is no evidence that he ever thought of adopting it, there are many indications that he felt he had in some sort missed his chance. The little work is a development of the words in Psalm xliv., *Vacate et videte*, with numberless digressions and illustrations from classical history, from the Fathers, and notably from St. Augustine. Monks, Petrarca says, are the slaves of Christ and herein their liberty consists. Theirs by right is that *otium* which other men can so rarely enjoy: it is their portion, but it has to be won, and he compares it to Rachel, for whom Jacob was to serve seven years—Rachel, of course, being the favourite mediæval type of the contemplative life.[2] The Petrarca of the *Secretum* and of these treatises is one and the same man, but in these last there is an absence of struggle and a more certain hold on peace. By the time they were completed he had served for Rachel more than twice seven years, and we may think that he had won her at last. To the same class of composition belong the *Psalmi Pœnitentiales*—sets of pious ejaculations closely modelled on the Psalms, of which Petrarca has left it on record that he wrote them in a time of great unhappiness and all in one day. Their date is uncertain, but when sending them to Sacramore in 1367 or 1368, the poet says they were written "many years ago."[3] This kind of writing was evidently attractive to him, and in one of his letters to his brother we have this charming sentence: "All theology is a poem with God for its subject."[4]

[1] *Rer. Sen.* v. 4.
[2] Dante, *Inferno*, ii. 102; *Purg.* xxvii. 104-108.
[3] *Rer. Sen.* x. 1.    [4] *De Reb. Fam.* x. 4.

The *De Remediis Fortunæ*, to which reference has already been made, is perhaps the least readable of all the Latin works. Dedicated to Azzo da Correggio, for whom Fortune's wheel had made more revolutions than for most men, it is divided into two books, the first dealing with good and the second with evil Fortune, and written in the dialogue-form, which is always liable to become wearisome. Hope and Joy converse with Reason in the first book, Fear and Pain in the second, and the various goods and ills of life, from the least to the greatest, are discussed. Beauty, Intellect, Liberty, Games, Gardens, Love of Country, Glory, Weakness, Poverty, Loss of Friends, Old Age, and Death are some few of the subjects dealt with, and we might expect to find much of interest in the discussions. But, to say truth, they are always prosy, and a very great deal of chaff must be sifted to obtain a grain or two of wheat. In the chapter on *Intellect*, we get the rather obvious statement: " Nothing is more odious to wisdom than too much subtlety. Often a great intellect has been the source of great evils." On *Liberty* : " He who dies free, not he who is born so, can truly be called free. Fate has much power against him who is born, but can do nothing against him who dies; fate conquers the strongest cities and defeats armed hosts, but the tomb is an impregnable fortress." On *Magnificent Buildings* : " The fine house is an honour to him who made it, not to him who lives in it." On *The Death of a Friend* : " Wise men say that true friendships are immortal, for they cannot in any wise be taken away. Death can take away the body, but not the friend or the friendship; these are of the things which are not subject either to death or to fate, but only to virtue." On *Old Age* : " You have made a difficult and disagreeable journey. It is a wonder if you do not wish to rest, and if you do not joyfully expect your approaching end, which is death. He is a foolish traveller who, being tired with his journey, wants to turn back and make it over again." These are some of the least flat of the platitudes with which Petrarca here provides us. The *De Vera Sapientia* (if it be a genuine work) is also a dialogue, written to maintain that true wisdom consists in the fear of God and the knowledge of self, and that the only wise man is he who knows his own ignorance.

In the *Itinerarium Syriacum*, we have yet another presentment of the poet's many-sided character—his keen interest in nature and art, and his remarkable powers of observation. The date of this charming little guide-book is not known, but it was compiled for Giovanni di Mandello, who had asked Petrarca to accompany him on a pilgrimage to the Holy Land, which the latter's unconquerable horror of the sea made him decline. Fearful, however, lest his friend should miss any of the sights and associations of the journey, he wrote this book for him. Though not free from geographical errors, and wanting in vividness of description in that part of the journey that was unknown to him, it yet puts the author before us as a pioneer in vast fields of beauty and interest little explored or understood in his day. History and geography are made to go hand in hand, the one enriching the other, and, so long as we are on Italian ground, the landscape lies before us. The Riviera is again described and praised with special reference to the laurel that flourishes there, and in Naples the traveller is bidden on no account to neglect to see the pictures in the royal palace, " in which a fellow-citizen of mine, formerly the first painter of our age, has left a great monument of his handiwork and genius." [1]

In the course of so long a life it is hardly to be expected that Petrarca should never have been entangled in dispute or controversy, and accordingly, on three separate occasions, we find him entering the inglorious lists. The event which gave rise to his first controversial work was the grave illness

[1] This chapel was in the Castel Nuovo, which was the royal residence of King Robert, and was situated near the " artificial harbour " which Petrarca mentions. He refers, of course, to Giotto.

of Clement VI., in 1352, when the poet (whose distrust of doctors is abundantly evident throughout his correspondence) wrote to warn him of his peril:—

"I know that your bed is besieged by doctors, and this is the principal cause of my fears . . . for there is no doubt that all doctors, whoever they may be, traffic in our lives, in the hope of becoming famous through making new discoveries. . . . The doctor is the only person who is allowed to kill with impunity." In conclusion, he tells Clement that he ought to guard his life from a doctor as he would from an assassin![1] The Pope having unwisely shown this letter to his physicians, one of them entered into a correspondence with Petrarca, accusing him, among other things, of being a heretic and schismatic.[2] To this accusation Petrarca opposed his four *Invectivæ contra Medicum*, in which abuse, wanting in reason and proportion, is hurled against the medical profession. But, if his invectives are singularly unprofitable, the remarks on doctors and medicine scattered profusely through his letters are very amusing reading. In a letter to Boccaccio he writes:—

"Some time ago, I do not remember when, you wrote me word that you had been very ill and that, by the grace of God and the skill of the doctor, you were well again. And I have not forgotten that I replied that I wondered very much how, with your great intelligence, you could accept such a vulgar error; God and your good conscience had done everything, for the doctor could have done nothing. . . . Now you write to me that, having fallen ill again, you did not call in any doctor, so I do not wonder that you have recovered quickly. There is no shorter road to recovery than to keep the doctor at a distance. . . . Not every one is able to boast of having killed five thousand men, which is the number the Romans exacted before awarding the honour of a triumph. It is enough to-day to have killed a good number, as the quality of the slain

---

[1] *De Reb. Fam.* v. 19.  [2] *Ibid.* xv. 6.

makes up for the quantity; since in the first case enemies were exterminated, but now citizens and friends. . . . ' He has a great practice,' they say, ' he has great experience'; which means: he has contracted the habit of killing with assurance. . . . Many are the doctors whom I have had as friends . . . and I can assure you that they are all learned and courteous men, excellent speakers, clever in argument, skilful in persuading, such men in fact that they kill people most agreeably and naturally, and always know sufficiently how to excuse and defend their action. . . . Now, if I happen to fall ill, I always receive all these in my house as friends, but as doctors never. I always delight in the society of my friends, and I think nothing is more efficacious than their presence and company for maintaining or restoring health. If they prescribe something for me that I like, I do it and am grateful to them; if what they order is not to my mind, I let them talk and go my own way." [1]

Describing his severe illness at Ferrara, Petrarca writes:—

" A crowd of doctors immediately assembled round my bed . . . and after having contradicted each other for some time according to their wont, they pronounced that I should die at midnight. A quarter of the night was already gone, so you see what a little time remained to me to live, if the nonsense of these Hippocrates was to come true. . . . They decided that the only way to prolong my life a little was to bind me with some sort of cord, so as to prevent my sleeping, and in this way they might hope to keep me alive till dawn. What a tedious business for such a poor result! And I believe that depriving me of sleep, in such a condition, would have been equivalent to killing me. But no one there would heed their prescription, because I had already implored my friends, and given strict injunctions to my servants, that nothing that the doctors ordered should ever

[1] *Rer. Sen.* v. 3.

be carried out on me; or, if they wanted to do anything, it must be the contrary to what they had been told by the doctors. So I passed the whole of that night in a most profound sleep.... Certain that I must have breathed my last at midnight, the doctors returned in the morning, possibly with the intention of assisting at my funeral, and found me busy writing. Amazed at the sight, and not knowing what to say, they exclaimed that I must be a marvellous man."[1]

It must not, of course, be forgotten that in Petrarca's time the science of medicine was closely bound up with necromancy and astrology, for which he felt a hatred and contempt far in advance of his age. Renan rightly says that in those days medicine, Arabism, Averroism, astrology, incredulity, were nearly synonymous terms,[2] and this brings us on to Petrarca's second controversy, that with the Averroists. The philosophy of Averroes (Ibn Rushd), who had died at the end of the twelfth century, was then a great power in Western Europe. His commentary on Aristotle had been welcomed by Thomas Aquinas, but his general teaching was rejected as being contrary to Christianity; still his opinions were widely diffused, and in particular he had a great following in Padua and Venice. Petrarca, who had established himself in Venice in 1362, could not fail to be a centre of attraction to the busy and cultivated city. His house was the rendezvous for all, both residents and travellers, who had any claim to distinction, either of talent and wisdom, or merely of birth and position; hence he was often annoyed by uncongenial visitors. So he writes piteously to Boccaccio of " this new school " who have the audacity to despise Cicero and Virgil, and call the style of Livy and Sallust harsh and unpolished. Scarcely less repugnant to him is that " monstrous band " who speak of Ambrose, Augustine, and Jerome as ignorant chatterers. " Of Augustine, they say that he saw much

[1] *Rer. Sen.* xiii. 8.  [2] Renan, *Averroes*, p. 259.

but knew little." One of these men who came to his study, and to whom he quoted some passage of Scripture, had the effrontery to reply: "Keep your miserable Fathers to yourself. . . . Oh, if you would read Averroes, you would see how he surpasses all your babblers "—on which the poet promptly turned him out of the house.[1] It is evident that Francesco's aversion to the Arabian philosophy arose from two causes; the deepest, no doubt, was that it had identified itself with infidelity and materialism; the second, that he could not brook that Arab learning should bear the palm over Greek and Latin.[2] This wounded him in his dearest feelings, for he was never more modern than in his devoted attachment to the ancient world.

Disputes like the one related above must have been tolerably frequent, and we hear in particular of four young men (Leonardo Dandolo, Tommaso Talenti, Zaccaria Contarini, all Venetians, and Guido da Bagnolo of Reggio) who used frequently to visit the poet, sometimes two by two, sometimes altogether, and weary him with their arguments. Now these four finally held a conclave and solemnly decided that Petrarca was a good man but without learning, *sine litteris, virum bonum*.[3] This judgment being duly reported to the subject of it, filled him with indignation. One is surprised that, at his age and with his very great reputation, he could have minded the *ipse dixits* of these young upstarts, but his vanity was wounded, and, as we have other means of knowing, he never could be patient under adverse criticism. Silence would have been his most dignified course, but that was never easy to him, and so, in self-defence, he broke out into the treatise *De sui ipsius et multorum Ignorantia*. It was written at the instance of his friend Donato Appenninigena, and dedicated to him.

Petrarca begins rather pathetically by saying that he is not fighting friends or enemies, but simply envy; that

[1] *Rer. Sen.* v. 3.  [2] *Ibid.* xii. 2.
[3] *De Reb. Fam.* v. 12, Fracassetti's note.

these four men are envious of him, and why? Not of riches, for he has them not; not of friends, for death has robbed him of the greater number; not of strength or beauty, for the years have taken from him whatever he may have had. Why, then, is he the cause of envy? The really interesting point in the treatise is the author's estimate of Aristotle, the special idol of the Averroists. Petrarca had the originality to protest against the worship of the Stagirite, saying that, though he was a great man, he was but a man, and not only did not know everything, but held a good many erroneous opinions; and he proceeds to award the first place to Plato. Aristotle, he says, is admired by the greatest number, but Plato by the greatest minds; Plato rises higher into divine things. So does Petrarca oppose the hard and pedantic tone of Venetian materialism. And his Platonism is the more surprising as we know how little real acquaintance he actually had with him. The Greek edition was an ornament to his library, but he never acquired enough Greek to be able to read it, and knew only the Timæus, quoting Plato for the rest from Cicero and St. Augustine. It was a sort of divine instinct of taste which directed his judgment right, and made him yet again the herald of the coming day:—

> Plato I saw,
> Who of that band pressed closest to the mark
> Which those attain whose gift it is from heaven.[1]

At the very end of his life, probably in 1372,[2] he was again involved in controversy, owing to his correspondence with Urban V. A French Cistercian monk, whose name has not been preserved, resenting the part Petrarca had played in the departure of Urban from Avignon, loaded him and his arguments with contempt, and, in particular, indulged in such abuse of Rome as the poet could not refrain from refuting. His *Apologia contra Gallum* is as bitter

[1] *Triumphus Famæ*, iii. 4-7.   [2] *Var.* 3, Fracassetti's note.

as his other invectives, but has the merit of being patriotic rather than personal. But the crowning glory of Petrarca's contributions to Latin literature is undoubtedly his collection of Letters; for fine passages, for general interest, and for originality they bear the palm. If, as has been objected, his Latin is not so perfect as that of Poliziano or Erasmus, we must give him double honour as a pioneer. He used the language as it had never been used before, for small things as well as great, for the commonplaces of daily life, for simple narrative and description, and he showed himself a master-worker in the adaptation of his instrument. The correspondence is immensely large: we have the *De Rebus Familiaribus* in twenty-four books, the *Rerum Senilium* in seventeen books, the *Epistolæ variæ* in one, and the *Sine Titulo* in one; also the unfinished autobiographical fragment entitled *Epistola ad Posteros*. The value of this vast collection cannot be over-rated; if we had to eliminate from our knowledge of the writer all that we gain from his letters, the very shadow of a man would be all that would remain to us. No one ever lived more in his friends than did Petrarca, and it is in this connection that we shall consider the greater part of the letters in our next chapter: here we will only notice those to dead authors, and the much-quoted *Epistola ad Posteros*.

The writing of imaginary letters or conversations has always been a favourite pastime, but, probably, to few writers were their ghost-correspondents as real as they were to Petrarca. His devotion to Cicero and to Virgil, to Livy and to Seneca, was so much a part of himself, that these friendships were scarcely less real to him than those of ordinary human life. So, in the metrical letter to Virgil, he writes:—

>Of glorious Rome, our common mother, now
>Suffer my silence; let me only tell
>How green is still the laurel on thy brow.[1]

---
[1] *De Reb. Fam.* xxiv. 11.

And, in the long letters to Cicero, the blame so reluctantly meted out, and the praise so lavishly awarded, do not seem to belong to past time, but to the living present. The same is even more true of the letter to Seneca, where it is difficult to think that the reasoned argument, against his remaining at the court of Nero, is formulated concerning an action performed hundreds of years ago. Other letters are to Homer, Quintilian, Horace, and many more, of which perhaps the most interesting is addressed to Livy:—

"O why did not the Fates allow me to live in your times, or you in mine? . . . Now I see you such as your books show you to me; not complete, because the slothfulness of our age does not permit of your being completely known, since of a hundred and forty-two books, that we know you to have written about the affairs of Rome, at the cost of much care and labour, only thirty have been preserved to us. . . . I have said thirty, because every one says it; but really there are only twenty-nine; that is, three decades of the first, the third, and the fourth books, of which latter one is missing. And over these I pore and delight myself when I wish to forget these times and customs, and I feel my heart consumed with anger against the men of to-day, who prize nothing except gold and silver, and the gratification of vile pleasures. . . . Rather would I now render you eternal thanks for many things, but especially that, owing to you, I have often become oblivious of present evils; while reading you, I think I see Cornelius, Scipio Africanus, Camillus, beside me, and so, by a pleasing illusion, I fancy I am living in the midst of these great ones, and not among the knaves who really surround me. And O! if I had been able to find you complete, how many other names would have brought gladness into my life, helping me to forget the present age. . . . Farewell for ever, supreme preserver of the memories of the past.

"From the world of the living, in Italy, and in that city which gave you a cradle and a grave, and which is my present abode; in the hall of St. Justina and in sight of your tombstone, February 22, of the year 1350, of the birth of Him whom you might perhaps have seen, or of whose birth you might have heard, if your life had lasted a little longer." [1]

The Letter to Posterity is an interesting bit of autobiography, but unfortunately it breaks off short, and does not extend beyond the poet's forty-seventh year. As mention is made in it of the death of Urban V., which took place in December, 1370, the letter must have been written in the last years of Petrarca's life. We have already drawn on it for various pieces of information, and will only now quote the writer's estimate of himself from an intellectual point of view:—

" My intellect was rather just and well-balanced than keen, inclined to all good scholarship, but specially attracted to moral philosophy and to the art of poetry. This, however, in the course of years I laid aside, delighting myself in sacred literature, finding a hidden sweetness in what I had hitherto despised, so that I no longer occupied myself with poetical studies, except by way of recreation. The study of antiquity pleased me above every other, for I have always so loathed the present age that, if it had not been for the love of those dear to me, I would rather have been born in any other time than this; wherefore I strive to make myself forgetful of every one, and I live in spirit among the ancients. And so I have taken the greatest delight in history. . . . My style has been praised as being clear and pointed; to me it has always seemed weak and obscure. In familiar intercourse with my friends I never set myself to appear eloquent . . . but, when the place, the subject, or the audience seemed deserving of it, I did everything in my power to succeed in that particular; whether I did so I do not know; it is for those who heard me to judge. . . . My mind, like my body, was rather alert than strong, and

[1] *De Reb. Fam.* xxiv. 8. Cf. Fracassetti's note.

hence it has happened that I have undertaken many things with alacrity, and then abandoned them through fatigue."[1]

If Petrarca accomplished less than he desired and projected, all his struggles with copyists must not be overlooked. First, he suffered from the difficulty of procuring them; secondly, from the inefficient manner in which they worked. Writing from Arquà, in 1372, he says that he usually employs five or six copyists, and, though he has but three at that time, this is on account of the extreme difficulty of finding good ones.[2] He speaks more than once of the great scarcity of men capable of doing the work, so that a book written in a few months cannot be copied in the same number of years; and he further remarks on the incompetence of those men who, instead of copying what is given to them, set down something quite different; and he complains that they always deceive and take advantage of him, and that he is distracted from important studies by their carelessness and want of consideration.[3]

One copyist indeed he had, dear to him as a son, who has acquired additional interest because he has been thought by some to be identical with Giovanni da Ravenna (sometimes called de' Malpaghini or di Convertino), of whom Coluccio Salutati wrote to Carlo Malatesta that he had been a friend and disciple of Petrarca, and had lived with him for fifteen years.[4] On close investigation this theory does not seem tenable, though it is certainly strange that Petrarca should have had an accomplished scholar and Latinist with him for so long a time without ever mentioning him in any of his letters: but this is not the first problem of the kind with which we have been confronted.[5]

[1] *Epist. ad Post.*  [2] *Var.* 15.
[3] *De Reb. Fam.* xviii. 12; *Rer. Sen.* v. 1; *Var.* 22.
[4] " Hic autem fuit quondam familiaris atque discipulus celebris memorie Francisci Petrarce, apud quem cum ferme trilustri tempore manserit."—*Epistolario di Coluccio Salutati*, lib. xii. 18.
[5] For this much discussed question, cf. G. Voigt, *op. cit.* i. pp. 210-217, and P. de Nolhac, *op. cit.* i. pp. 74, 75.

In any case, the minute account of the copyist of Ravenna, whose name is never told, given at great length in a letter to Boccaccio, and the details of his career that we are able to pick out from subsequent letters, do not in any wise tally with the *trilustrum* spoken of by Salutati. Petrarca's letter to Boccaccio (which bears internal evidence of having been written in 1365) states that the copyist had arrived the year after Boccaccio's departure. Now the date of Boccaccio's visit to Venice was 1363, so, even if the youth had remained until his master's death, we should only have a period of eleven years; but we know, on Petrarca's own authority, that after the date of this letter he was with him little more than a year.[1] His story, however, is somewhat dramatic. He was a native of Ravenna and of humble birth and fortune, but of great intellectual powers and possessed of a wonderful memory, of which he gave evidence by learning Petrarca's twelve eclogues by heart in eleven days. He was also something of a poet himself, and had an overwhelming admiration for Virgil. He made himself specially useful to his master in copying and collating all the prose epistles, which had become so numerous, and were in such confusion, that the writer was almost in despair of ever completing the collection. It is evident that the young man was extraordinarily congenial, as well as useful, to the poet, and so we can well understand the keen disappointment occasioned by his conduct, described in two letters to Donato Appenninigena.[2] For it appears that this boy, whom Petrarca calls his "beloved friend" and "adopted son," and who seems to have been even dearer to him as a potential scholar and poet than as a secretary, seized with a sudden restlessness and desire for change, suddenly announced to his master that he must leave him immediately—that he could not stay with him any longer. Petrarca was ready to make any concession,

---

[1] *De Reb. Fam.* xxiii. 19. Cf. Fracassetti's note.
[2] *Rer. Sen.* v. 5, 6.

and implored him to remain, not as a scribe but as a son;
but it is manifest that the boy was thoroughly unsettled
and bent on seeing the world. No feelings of gratitude or
affection could restrain him. The poet had no choice but
to let him go, and makes every excuse for his youth and
inexperience, while lamenting his unsteadiness and fickleness of purpose, for he had neither aim nor object in his
wanderings. Within a year he returned, sick and penniless,
to his benefactor, who had nothing but kindness for him,
though he confesses that he could not welcome him with all
his former love. Nor even after this experience was the
boy willing to settle down, and, while deploring his restlessness, Petrarca cannot withhold his sympathy from one
whose most earnest desires were to see Rome and to learn
Greek. A year's delay was all he could obtain when every
argument was exhausted, and at the end of that time the
youth again set out on his travels, Petrarca writing on his
behalf to Ugo da San Severino and to Francesco Bruni,[1]
secretary to Pope Urban V., and it seems likely that, after
many vicissitudes, the wanderer settled down in the employment of the latter as secretary. It may fairly be conjectured that the letter entitled *Vago cuidam*[2] was addressed
to him, and in it Petrarca rejoices characteristically with his
vagabond secretary that he has, at any rate, *seen Rome.*

[1] *Rer. Sen.* xi. 8, 9.      [2] *Ibid.* xv. 12.

## CHAPTER IX

### THE EUGANEAN HILLS

" They went then till they came to the Delectable Mountains. . . . Now there were on the tops of these mountains shepherds feeding their flocks . . . the Pilgrims therefore went to them and . . . asked, *Whose Delectable Mountains are these?*

*Shepherd.* These mountains are *Immanuel's Land,* and they are within sight of His City."

BUNYAN, *The Pilgrim's Progress.*

IF it be true to say of Petrarca that he lived in his friends, it is truer still to say of many of them that they live by him. Popes, cardinals, and bishops, ruling princes, the great House of Colonna—these all have their assured place in history and gain only an additional interest in being remembered as friends of the poet; but what would history know of Lodovico di Campinia, and Lello Stefani, and Francesco Nelli, if the names of *Socrates, Lælius,* and *Simonides* had not become synonyms for friendship by means of Petrarca's letters? Looking through these precious volumes, we gain an insight into the tastes and characters of these men and of many others, and, naturally, in a greater degree, the writer manifests himself. The essentials of Friendship are sympathy and similarity of aims; the essentials of friendships are, besides these, adaptability and many-sidedness. The man of many friends is necessarily a different being from the man of few: he has wider sympathies and quicker feelings, and, above all, more need for response. He is like a musical instrument which cannot reveal its own excellence, but whose latent harmonies must be called out by another. There is something tenderly human in this kind of character, and it is all the more attractive when we find it in a man of very remarkable intellectual powers. For he is, so to speak, at the world's mercy; he is dependent on what the world will give him, and of such a one it may be said that whoever has loved him worthily, and corresponded generously to his affection, becomes an effective part of the genius that is evoked.

All through Petrarca's life the sense of obligation to his friends was upon him. It is, indeed, to his love of Socrates that the preservation of his letters is due. In the prefatory letter to the *Epistolæ de Rebus Familiaribus*, dedicating them to this first and earliest friend, the writer tells us how he was, though reluctantly, on the point of destroying them all, when he fell to considering them with regard to his friends, and, remembering their wishes, he decided to make two collections, giving the prose to Socrates and the verse to Barbato, for he seemed to see these two standing beside him and imploring him not to disregard his promises and their hopes. And this was the sole cause of their preservation, " for, without this, believe me, they would have been burned with the rest."[1] Well for us that this did not happen! Of all the friendships, perhaps, that with Socrates is the most charming. There is something very naïve in Francesco's repeated wonder that a " barbarian " should be so delightful, and he asserts that, though born out of Italy, there is no man more Italian in heart and mind, and reckons among his many excellences that " his great love for me had made him almost an Italian." Their common passion for music must have been another bond, and, on this account, Petrarca says he deserved to be called Aristocles, but, by common consent, his other qualities earned him the name of Socrates.[2] This is further enlarged upon in the *De Vita Solitaria*, where it is said of him: "While the others were our companions, this one was a part of ourselves. He was dear to us by the faith of a firm and stable friendship, and noble on account of his great familiarity

---

[1] *In Epist. Rer. Fam. Præfatio.*   [2] *De Reb. Fam.* xx. 13; ix. 2.

with the sacred Muses. The strength of his imagination and the vigour of his mind were such that no cloud of melancholy ever obscured them; his brow was always smooth, and in him was to be seen and loved that uniformity and constancy which, with the greatest admiration, we are accustomed to praise in the ancient Socrates."[1]

Lælius, a friend of the same date, was scarcely less dear, and, when these two quarrelled, Petrarca knew no rest until he had effected a reconciliation, and the letters which concern this, touching a subject which he had so much at heart, show the naturalness of his style better than any others. It would seem that some unknown person had told Lælius that Socrates had spoken ill of him in a letter to Petrarca, and the latter, writing to Lælius, says:—

"Believe—and you already believe it, I trust—that Socrates would not write harm of anybody; and if he would of any, yet never of you; and if he could of you, he might write it to others, but never to me. You ask the reason? He knows well that I should not believe it, and that I should be indignant with him rather than with you. Truly I may say that you are two whom I should believe in everything save in this one thing alone, that is, if either should accuse the other, and especially of an offence committed against me, or my reputation, or my state. . . . All things can be said, but not all should be believed. . . . Men that are friends, among whom the name of Lælius was always most famous and supreme, have their ears deaf to informers, and reject all things which are adverse to true friendship. . . . After you have once decided upon a friend, there must be no doubt concerning the friendship. . . . There must be now no mistrust, no fear. For when minds are united by the bonds of friendship, and two (as it is said) become one, it is meet that each should cherish the same hopes for his friend as for himself. . . . For your sake, for mine, I pray you take from me as soon as possible

[1] *De Vita Solitaria*, lib. ii. tract. x. cap. 1.

this anxiety which is pressing, burning, and tormenting me; and if you love me, or have ever loved me, straightway, before these letters have left your hands, either go or send to Socrates. This I beg of you, this is an easy thing. . . . Now I shall see if you really love me."[1]

After the reconciliation had taken place, Petrarca wrote to Lælius, assuring him that never, in the whole course of his life, had he given him so much pleasure; and to Socrates he wrote: "Our one theme to-day is the friendship which has been restored between you and Lælius at my exhortation; I am rejoicing to hear of it from your letter, from his, and from those of many others, and I am more delighted at this reconciliation than at any other thing in the world."[2]

This pair of friends receives honourable mention in the *Triumphus Cupidinis* :—

> Scarce had I issued from the common way,
> When Socrates and Lælius first I saw.
> With them I must a longer journey go.
>
> O what a pair of friends! whom neither rhyme,
> Nor prose, nor verse can ever praise enough,
> If, as is due, bare virtue is esteemed.
>
> In company with these I sought the heights,
> Walking together 'neath the self-same yoke;
> To these my wounds were openly displayed.
>
> From them (as is my hope and my desire)
> Nor time nor place can ever me divide
> Until the ashes of the funeral pyre.
>
> With them I gathered haply ere the time
> That glorious branch with which I crowned my brows
> In memory of her I love so well.[3]

---

[1] *De Reb. Fam.* xx. 13.  [2] *Ibid.* xx. 15.

[3] " Poco era fuor de la comune strada,
   Quando Socrate e Lelio vidi in prima.
   Con lor più lunga via conven ch' io vada.

Socrates is also the subject of one of the pathetic entries on the fly-leaf of the Virgil. Petrarca chronicles the news of " the death of Socrates, my friend, companion, and best of brothers, who is said to have died at Babylon or Avignon last May. I have lost the comrade and the solace of my life. Receive, Christ Jesus, these two [his son, Giovanni, and Socrates] . . . into Thy eternal tabernacles, that these who can no longer be with me, by a most blessed exchange, may be with Thee."[1]

Petrarca's earliest friend, in order of time, was Guido Settimo, of whose boyhood and early studies with Francesco we have already written, and who became Archdeacon of Genoa and, subsequently, Archbishop. But he passed nearly all his life in Avignon, and once Petrarca lived with him, on and off, for about a couple of years, probably from 1351 to 1353, during the poet's last sojourn in France. We plainly infer from one letter of Petrarca that Guido had begged to be mentioned in his letters, of which request the poet says that it is a proof, not of his intellect, but of the friendship of Guido, who wishes thus to find a place in his memory, and, careless of the hospice, is thinking wholly of the host. Francesco modestly continues that he must receive his

> " O qual coppia d'amici! che nè 'n rima
>     Poria, nè 'n prosa ornar assai, nè 'n versi,
>     Se, come dee, vertù nuda se stima.
>
> " Con questi duo cercai monti diversi,
>     Andando tutti tre sempre ad un giogo;
>     A questi le mie piaghe tutte apersi.
>
> " Da costor non mi pò tempo nè luogo
>     Divider mai (sì come io spero e bramo)
>     Infino al cener del funereo rogo.
>
> " Con costor colsi 'l glorioso ramo
>     Onde forse ançi tempo ornai le tempie
>     In memoria di quella ch' io tanto amo."
>                        *Triumphus Cupidinis*, iii. 67-81.

[1] *De Reb. Fam.* vii. 15, Fracassetti's note.

friend according to his own ability and not according to the honour due to him; the house is narrow, but the love is very great. Finally, since the nobleness of the company may compensate for the obscurity of the inn, he is to consider that rulers, monarchs, emperors, and pontiffs have shared the same place, and, what is more, philosophers and poets, and, what is still more again, virtuous men.[1]

Two other very dear friends of early days were Luca Cristiano and Mainardo Accursio (the latter nicknamed Olimpio); it is probable that they all studied law together in Bologna, and afterwards formed part of the household of Cardinal Colonna in Avignon. In later years Petrarca's favourite project was that they and Socrates should come and live in Italy with him, and we have three separate letters urging the plan on each of them in nearly the same words.[2] Why, he asks, should we allow seas, hills, and rivers to divide us? Why should not one house unite those who are united in will? But Socrates, though "almost an Italian," would never consent to live in that country; the other two might have acceded to the request, but while travelling together in 1349, Olimpio was murdered by a band of ruffians near Florence; the agony which this occasioned to Petrarca was increased by the uncertainty which hung, for some time, over the fate of Cristiano. The latter, however, had escaped and returned to Avignon, and to him the poet resigned the canonry of Modena, which had been conferred on himself. Olimpio's death is another of the sad records to be found on the fly-leaf of the Virgil.

To Vaucluse, Francesco owed his friendship with Philippe de Cabassole, who, as Bishop of Cavaillon, was a near neighbour. From this obscure little town, Cabassole was summoned, in 1343, to the court of Naples, and remained there until the death of Giovanna's first husband, Andrea of Hungary. He was twice sent as papal legate to

[1] *De Reb. Fam.* xix. 8.
[2] *Ibid.* viii. 4, 5, Fracassetti's note; *Ibid.* ix. 2.

Germany, but his diplomatic missions were not successful, and Petrarca, writing to congratulate him on his return to his flock at Cavaillon, impresses upon him to refuse to act again in an official capacity, making the state of his health and his age an excuse, and naïvely advises him to make himself a little older than he really is, for that any one adding to his years is sure to be believed.[1]

In 1361, Cabassole was made Patriarch of Jerusalem; Urban V. created him Cardinal, and, in 1369, he became Bishop of Sabina. It was through him that this Pope sent one of his oft-repeated invitations to Petrarca, who, urging his bad health, asseverates that he is cut off from his most ardent desires, that of seeing the Pope—" not on account of the loftiness of his dignity, but for the singular merit of his person "—and of being reunited to his early friend whom he has not seen for an age.[2] Indeed, the two never met after the poet's final farewell to Vaucluse, but, when Cabassole came to Perugia as Cardinal-legate in 1371, Petrarca made a strenuous effort to visit him, but was unable even to mount his horse; and so he writes bitterly that death has taken away nearly all his friends, and that distance robs him of the few that remain.[3] Cabassole died in August, 1372, just two years before Petrarca.

The poet's journey to Naples, in 1341, to interview King Robert was the means of gaining him two lasting friendships, with Giovanni Barrili, who was high in the service and favour of the king, and was deputed to represent him at Petrarca's coronation, and with Barbato di Solmona, the Chancellor, himself a poet. With these two Francesco entered into life-long relations and frequent correspondence. To Barbato, in 1347, he addressed an agitated letter concerning the state of Naples after the murder of Andrea, begging him to make good his escape and come to Parma, for Louis of Hungary, brother of the murdered prince, had invaded the kingdom in order to avenge the crime.

[1] *De Reb. Fam.* xxii. 5.   [2] *Rer. Sen.* xiv. 16.   [3] *Ibid.* xv. 4.

"Among the many cares with which I am beset," writes Petrarca, "not the least is that which keeps me anxious and uneasy on your account. And what could I have more tenderly at heart than that which concerns my Barbato? . . . For behold, what I have always feared is now confirmed: that it was not possible that the horrible misdeed should remain unpunished; and so vengeance does but come more tardily than I had expected. O God! pour out Thine anger upon the author of the crime . . . but have mercy on the faithful and the good, for the miserable people is innocent, and innocent the sacred soil of Italy. . . . Already the report has come that . . . Solmona has fallen into the hands of the enemy. Alas! the generous city which was your birthplace and Ovid's. . . . I greatly fear for you, but I do not see how to give you advice or help of any kind. . . . It is true that I am in the good graces of the Tribune . . . and also that I enjoy the favour of the Roman people . . . if then I can do anything with that Tribune or that people to help you in your present peril, my goodwill and my pen are entirely at your disposal. Besides that, I want to tell you that I possess a house in a corner of Italy, remote and secure from these disturbances. It is small, certainly, but for two who are friends, and have only one soul, no house is ever narrow. Therein are no hurtful riches, no poverty, no cupidity, but a great abundance of books. . . . I have nothing else to offer you. As to the house to which I invite you, you know where it is and how it is situated; in a healthy place where fear cannot come, with a most pleasant aspect, and, above all, well-adapted to study. Whichever course you decide upon, may God make you fortunate and happy, and grant that my fears may prove fallacious. . . . But my mind cannot be at rest until either I see you come, or know by your letters that you are come, safe to shore, out of these tempestuous waters."[1]

[1] *De Reb. Fam.* vii. 1.

But, in spite of the peril of remaining in the besieged city, Barbato did not accept Francesco's invitation, and, though their friendship was of the closest, it seems that they never met again, for Petrarca, writing of his friend's death, says that they had been separated for twenty-two years. As a literary friend, Barbato occupies a specially prominent place; all the metrical Epistles were dedicated to him, and to him alone was confided a portion of the unpublished *Africa*. One of Petrarca's letters to him mentions the ardour and diligence with which he endeavoured to collect all the poet's writings. In this same letter we have one of Petrarca's most illuminated sayings on the power of friendship to annihilate time and space: " It is true that I have you always present, and that, though far off, by force of love I hear you and see you. The Apennines may divide persons, but distance cannot divide souls. Although the Alps, the Caucasus, the mountains of Atlas, and Olympus higher than the clouds, should interpose, and even the immense ocean itself, we should be always side by side. . . . A warm and most powerful affection . . . holds us inseparably joined and close together." [1]

Neither was Petrarca's sojourn in the north barren of friendships, even excluding, as he does himself, those with princes. Sacramore, the Emperor's confidential messenger, became a close friend of the poet, to whom his resolution to enter the Carthusian order was but another bond of union. Padua also furnished a devoted friend and fellow-scholar in the person of Lombardo da Serico, of whom we have already spoken in connection with the completion of the *De Viris Illustribus*. Ungrateful Florence, besides contributing Francesco Bruni, Lapo da Castiglionchio, Zanobi da Strada, and a character scarcely less congenial to Petrarca than Socrates and Lælius—Francesco Nelli (the Simonides to whom the *Rerum Senilium* were dedicated),

[1] *Var.* 22.

was to bestow on her exiled son the most famous and the most interesting of all his friends—Giovanni Boccaccio.

To our ears Dante, Petrarca, and Boccaccio form a natural triumvirate of the ruling names in Italian literature; but it is curious to notice how little consciousness had the third of the place that would be assigned to him, and, on the other hand, how blind was Petrarca to the distance by which he himself was separated from Dante. Devoted to learning and a profound scholar, a born poet inasmuch as a great part of his prose is the purest poetry, there is no trait more charming in the character of Boccaccio than his generous appreciation of others, coupled with a very real humility. There was no room in his mind for jealousy, and the praises he lavished on his great contemporary and his still greater predecessor were in proportion to the warmth and sweetness of his nature. In the *Genealogia Deorum*, we find this passage about Petrarca: " Francesco Petrarca, Florentine, my most honoured teacher, father, and lord . . . of whom I will not say that all the Italians, of whom he is the singular and immortal honour, but that all France, Germany, and England to the remotest corner of the world . . . have recognised him as a unique poet."[1] The beginning of their friendship may be dated with tolerable confidence from 1350, when they met at Florence in the year of the Jubilee.[2] Although it seems likely, from another passage in the *Genealogia Deorum*, that Boccaccio was in Naples during Petrarca's famous examination by King Robert, as he relates that the king had set little store by Virgil until Petrarca had explained it to him—" and I heard him say with my own ears that he had never imagined there was such excellent and sublime meaning in poetry "[3]—yet it may well have been that Boccaccio, being then unknown to fame, had no opportunity of becoming acquainted with the laureate-elect. The sentence in his letter of condolence to

[1] *De Geneal. Deor.* xv. cap. 6.   [2] *Supra*, p. 99.
[3] *De Geneal. Deor.* xiv. cap. 22.

Francesco da Brossano on Petrarca's death, in which he says that he had been devoted to him for forty years, need not imply a personal acquaintance of that length of time, but merely a knowledge and admiration of the poet's works; and, indeed, we know that they exchanged poems shortly before the meeting in Florence,[1] and that, as early as 1347, Boccaccio had transcribed several of Petrarca's Latin poems.[2]

From that time their friendship steadily increased; numbers of letters remain to us in proof of it, and there are many things to show how congenial they were in taste and mind; each gave the other of his best. It is a comfort to know that death, who robbed Francesco of so long a roll of friends, spared this favourite to the end. Boccaccio was eight years younger than Petrarca, but survived him little more than a year. Their Greek studies and the important work of obtaining a translation of Homer are, of course, the subject of much correspondence.[3] Besides this, we find Boccaccio sending his friend several works of Cicero and Varro copied with his own hand,[4] and a magnificent volume containing the works of St. Augustine[5]—a gift singularly acceptable to Francesco. But by far the most interesting present sent was a copy of the *Divina Commedia*, also in Boccaccio's own hand, which was accompanied by a Latin poem in praise of Dante,[6] and, apparently, by a letter in which, while excusing himself for having perhaps lavished too much praise on the author, Boccaccio seems to accuse Francesco of jealousy. The very long reply is important from many points of view. First, it contains a long paragraph bearing directly on Dante, though not mentioning him by name, in which Petrarca states that it must be

---

[1] *Lettere*, p. 471; *De Reb. Fam.* xi. 2, Fracassetti's note.
[2] Cf. H. Hauvette, *Notes sur des manuscrits autographes de Boccace à la Bibliothèque Laurentienne*. Rome, 1894 (Ecole Française: Mélanges, Année 14).
[3] *Var.* 25; *Rer. Sen.* iii. 5; v. 1; vi. 2.
[4] *De Reb. Fam.* xviii. 4.      [5] *Ibid.* xviii. 3.      [6] *Lettere*, p. 53.

noted that he never had any reason to hate a man whom he only saw once, in the days of his childhood. He then draws out a parallel between this man and his own father, who were companions in misfortune, and were alike in their abilities and their studies, though the latter neglected these in exile, being distracted by domestic cares; while the other, on the contrary, tenacious of purpose, and with no other thought but that of making a great name, gave himself up to the pursuit of learning, and is therefore worthy of the praise and admiration of all, because neither the insults of his fellow-citizens, nor exile, nor enmity, nor poverty, nor the love of woman, nor the affection of children, could make him turn aside from the path on which he had set out. " Therefore," he continues, " you will understand that the hatred on my part towards him, which some persons have invented, is both hateful and ridiculous; since, as you see, I have no grounds for hate, but many for love—his country, to wit, and his friendship with my father, and his genius, and his style, excellent in its kind, which, far and wide, preserves him safe from contempt." [1]

Secondly, Petrarca goes on to say that it has been urged against him that, though he was collecting every kind of book from his earliest youth, he has never troubled to procure this man's works, of which he affirms the reason to be this: that as he was then devoting himself to writing in the vernacular, he was afraid that, if he read the compositions of this writer, he might unwittingly imitate them. " Now, however, I care no more for those studies, and since I have turned from them entirely, and the fear is removed by which I was held, I can apply myself with all my mind to all such works, and to his above them all . . . and I judge that I should easily assign the palm of vernacular eloquence to him. They are liars who say that I carp at his renown. . . . For my part, I admire and love him, instead of scorning him. And I may fairly say that, if it had been

[1] *De Reb. Fam.* xxi. 15.

granted to him to reach this age, he would have had few warmer friends than myself, provided that his character delighted me as much as his genius delights. . . . You will believe me when I swear that I am charmed with the genius and the style of this man, and that I never speak of him save with the highest praise." [1]

Petrarca's assertion that he had refrained from reading Dante's vernacular poems has been called in question, and kindred passages from the works of each have been laboriously sought out,[2] but probably there is little foundation for the charge of plagiarism. The habit of thought, the turn of expression, was in the mind of the time; nor would Petrarca have claimed an absolute ignorance of poetry which, as he says in this very letter, was constantly to be heard on the lips of the people. One statement which does not ring quite true is the assertion of the contempt with which he affects to treat his own compositions in the vernacular. For though it is certain that he always regarded Latin as the proper vehicle for literature, yet the care and labour that he bestowed on the *Canzoniere* to the end of his life does not let us believe that he held it in small estimation. Touching the charge of jealousy, Petrarca naïvely inquires why he should be jealous of a writer who ended, so to speak, where he began—who devoted his life to things which were to him a mere pastime; how could there be a suspicion of envy between them? And, indeed, it is probable that Petrarca was really free from envy, because of his narrow unconsciousness that there was anything of which to be envious. He is to be accused of a want of generous appreciation, rather than of jealousy: but generosity is rarely the companion of excessive vanity.

More remarkable even than Petrarca's ignorance of

---

[1] *De Reb. Fam.* xxi. 15.
[2] Cf. G. A. Cesareo, *op. cit.* p. 132. Also Moschetti, *Dell' Ispirazione Dantesca nelle rime di F. Petrarca*, and F. Lo Parco, *Il Petrarca nel Casentino* (Rivista d' Italia, April, 1906, Rome).

Dante appears the fact that he never read the *Decameron* —the work of his most intimate friend—till the very end of his life. This we know from one of his letters written in 1373:—

"The book which, as I believe, you wrote in our mother tongue in your early years, has come into my hands, I know not how nor from whom. I should lie if I said I had read it, for the size of the volume, and the fact that it is written in prose for the people, caused me not to interrupt my more serious studies on its account. . . . I ran through it rapidly. . . . Thus skimming it, your book pleased me immensely; and if sometimes something that was too free and licentious offended me, I reflected that the age at which you wrote it might serve you for an excuse, also the language, the style, the lightness of the subject, and, above all, the kind of reader for which it was destined. . . . Among many light and amusing stories, I came upon some that were grave and edifying; of which, however, I cannot give you an exact opinion since I have not taken them into serious consideration. But, as one generally does when making a hasty examination, I dwelt longer on the beginning and on the end of the book; and I saw there described the horrible plague which, in a new and unexampled manner, filled our century with mourning and miseries; and the ability with which you have painted and deplored that awful disaster to our country seemed to me really unique. Then I read, at the end, the last of your stories, which seemed to me very different from all the others, and it pleased and delighted me so much that . . . I wished to learn it by heart." [1]

This was the story of Griselda which Francesco translated into Latin and transmitted to the author, saying: "I cannot doubt that you will be pleased for me to translate your things, when I certainly should not do it for those of any one else." The poet's enthusiastic admiration for

[1] *Opera Omnia* (1581), tom. i. p. 540.

the history of Griselda possesses an additional interest for English readers, since it was from his version, and possibly from his lips, that Chaucer learned the story which appears among the *Canterbury Tales*, and is there ascribed to Petrarca.

Boccaccio's opinion of his own work we may gather in some sort from Francesco's answer to a letter of his, which told of a message conveyed to him by a Carthusian monk of Siena, Gioacchino Ciani. Shortly before his death, in 1361, Pietro Petroni, then a monk in the Sienese Certosa of Maggiano, had a vision of Christ, in which he was shown the spiritual lives of Hell, Purgatory, and Paradise. In that high vision the secret condition of many living souls was revealed to him, and he believed himself charged with a mission to admonish and convert them. On his death-bed he commanded his disciple, Gioacchino Ciani, to perform this duty for him. Boccaccio was apparently one of those named, and, finding him the nearest at hand (he was then at Certaldo), Gioacchino went to him in the spring of the following year.[1] What were the exact terms of the message we do not gather from the narrative in the life of Petroni; but it is evident that the effect on Boccaccio was very great, and that he conceived himself not only called to repentance and a change of life, but to a renunciation of his books and poetical studies. The latter idea Petrarca combats; with the former he was in entire sympathy. Perhaps the attitude of Boccaccio is the more admirable as being the more generous; at the same time, Francesco's well-balanced comment is full of interest and good sense. After referring to the message and the circumstances of its delivery, he writes:—

"As regards yourself, you reduce everything to two heads: first, that death is already hanging over you and that you have but a few more years to live; secondly, that you ought to renounce the study of poetry. . . . But

[1] Bartholomæus Senensis, *Vita B. Petri Petroni*, iii. 1, 2, 11.

neither the love of virtue nor the thought of approaching death ought to divert us from the study of letters, which, if it is carried on with good intentions, awakes the love of virtue, and diminishes and destroys the fear of death. . . . Because learning is no impediment to him who, with a well-disposed mind, endeavours to acquire it; and letters are not a hindrance in the difficulties of our earthly journey, but a comfort and a help. . . . Many attain to the highest degree of sanctity without learning; but learning never hindered any one from being holy. . . . Now, if I may be allowed to speak my mind freely, I should say that the road which leads to virtue by the way of ignorance may, perhaps, be plain and easy, but conduces to sloth and idleness. The goal of all good men is the same, but many and diverse are the roads which lead to it. One man goes slowly, another proceeds more quickly; these in the light, those in the darkness; one remains lower, another higher. The path of all these is blessed, but that is the more glorious which, with a fuller illumination, mounts higher. . . . Try to quote me the greatest saint you can who was ignorant of letters, and I will undertake to match him with a learned man who shall be still more holy." [1]

The rest of the letter is concerned with the purchase of Boccaccio's books, and contains the first mention of Petrarca's idea of leaving his library to Venice. In 1362, he drew up an address to the Venetian government stating his desire to leave all his books, albeit neither numerous nor valuable, to " that glorious city," in hopes that they might be the nucleus of a famous library. In return, he asks for a small house for himself and the said books. In September 1362, the Grand Council accepted his offer, and awarded him the palace of the Due Torri, situated on the Riva degli Schiavoni, at the corner of the Ponte del Sepolcro. The house, though much altered, is still standing. The affair of the Averroists,[2] however, disgusted Petrarca with Venice as

[1] *Rer. Sen.* i. 4.    [2] Cf. *supra*, pp. 208, 209.

## THE EUGANEAN HILLS

a residence, and he left it in 1367, nor does it seem that his books were ever presented to San Marco, though this has been the subject of many conjectures. Some have thought that, owing to the poet's change of residence, he considered that his legacy had lapsed; others, again, believed that the books were really remitted to Venice and allowed to perish in a damp room. Monsieur de Nolhac denies both these theories, and has better ones to advance. It is noteworthy that when Petrarca made his will, in 1370, before setting out on his abortive journey to Rome, he makes mention of no books whatever, except of a breviary, which is left to Giovanni da Bocheta, priest of the church of Padua.[1] Now, if he had not regarded his library as already disposed of, it is inconceivable that he should not have made it the subject of special bequest. We may then conclude that it remained his intention to benefit San Marco; but, at the time of his death, there was great jealousy between the Carraresi and Venice, and it is likely that Francesco da Carrara took no steps for having the books conveyed thither. They were certainly in Padua in 1379, for we find Coluccio Salutati corresponding about them with Brossano and Lombardo da Serico.[2] After that date they would seem to have been dispersed, for they were found scattered in all parts—Rome, Mantua, Verona. It is certain that Francesco kept a large number for himself, for when, in 1388, Padua fell a prey to the united forces of Venice and the Visconti, the palace being despoiled, a large quantity of Petrarca's books were found and taken to Pavia.[3]

[1] Cf. P. de Nolhac, *op. cit.* vol. i. pp. 62, 63. It was once in the possession of the Borghese family, from whom it has passed into the Vatican Library. That this breviary was large and inconvenient we gather from a letter of Nelli's (H. Cochin, *Un Ami de Pétrarque*, Lettero xii.), who had evidently wished to give Petrarca a more portable one, and, when the latter demurred at taking such a valuable gift, told him that he must not always confer favours, but must also know how to accept them.

[2] *Epistolario di Coluccio Salutati*, lib. iii. 25; lib. iv. 1, 2, 5, 18. Cf. also lib. iii. 18, 23.

[3] P. de Nolhac, *op. cit.* vol. i. pp. 93-98.

Although Boccaccio never acceded to his friend's often-expressed wish that he would go to live with him, we have already seen that he passed three months with him in Venice in 1363. Another time he went there and had the misfortune to find Petrarca absent, but to this circumstance we owe a most charming letter, throwing much light on the poet's home and surroundings. His daughter and son-in-law were then living with him, and one little grand-daughter, Eletta. Boccaccio relates how, hearing on the way that Petrarca had gone to Pavia, he was inclined to turn back, but the fear of disappointing his friends, and the great desire he had to see " Tullia " (as he and her father seem to have called Francesca, after the daughter of Cicero) and her husband, whom he had never seen yet, induced him to continue his journey. On the way he met Petrarca's son-in-law, and says how charmed he was with his appearance and manners. " At the first glance I judged how highly praiseworthy had been your choice. But could there be anything done by you which I should not find most worthy of praise? . . . When I had rested a little, I went to Tullia's house to greet her, and hardly had she heard of my arrival than she at once ran out to meet me, as gladly as though you yourself were returning, and as soon as she was beside me, blushing a little and casting her eyes to the ground, with modest and filial affection she embraced me and received me with open arms. O good God! I immediately perceived that she was fulfilling your orders, and I knew the confidence you placed in me, and congratulated myself that I am so much yours. When we had talked a little of some few things and of the latest news, we went down into your orchard and sat there with a few friends. Then with matronly gravity, and in the most frank and gentle words, she offered me the house, the books, and everything that was yours, and everything that was hers. And, in the middle of these offers, with a more sedate step perhaps than became her age, your delight, your Eletta, came up to us, and, before she knew who I was, she looked at me laughing, and I threw my arms round her, not merely gladly but eagerly. At the first glance I seemed to see my own baby again.[1] Your Eletta's face is just like that of my little girl; the smile is the same, the vivacity of the eyes, her gesture, her walk . . . only my child was rather bigger and a little older, for she was just five and a half when I saw her for the last time."[2]

Besides this girl, a son, Francesco, was born later, who was the special joy of his grandfather; but he only lived two years. Petrarca wrote most pathetically of his death to his friend Donato Appenninigena, who had been the child's godfather:—

"Named after me and after both his parents, he was the fourth Francis of my house, the delight of us all, and the hope and treasure of the family. And, so that the grief of his loss might be all the more cruel, nature had endowed him with beauty and with extraordinary intelligence." He was wonderfully like his grandfather. "This every one said; and I remember that you yourself once wrote to me that in him, a baby of hardly a year old, you seemed to see my perfect portrait. . . . As for me, although I know, and it is never out of my mind, that he has gained eternal happiness without labour, and that, in leaving me, he has taken from me an occasion of continual anxiety . . . yet, when I see myself deprived of the sweetness that he brought into my life, I confess that I cannot but be greatly affected by it."[3] The poet erected a monument to the child in the Church of San Zeno at Pavia and composed the epitaph himself.[4]

---

[1] This little daughter (possibly the child of Fiammetta) was called Violante and died in Naples. Her father seems to have called her Olimpia or Celeste and wrote his fourteenth eclogue to deplore her loss. Cf. G. B. Baldelli, *Vita di Giovanni Boccaccio*, p. 193 and note.

[2] *Lettere*, p. 122.   [3] *Rer. Sen.* x. 4.

[4] *Poemata Minora*, vol. iii. Epigraphe iv. and Appendice i. pp. 66-68.

Donato Appenninigena, or Albanzani, to whom reference has already been made as the man to whom Petrarca dedicated his *De sui ipsius et multorum Ignorantia*, would seem to have been a friend of Venetian days. He was a professor of Latin in Venice for many years, and a devoted admirer of the poet, whom he loaded with gifts sorely against his will.[1]

There are two correspondents of Petrarca whose names we cannot willingly omit, because they link him with the greatest personality of his age, one who, conjointly with him, was the most famous letter-writer of the century—St. Catherine of Siena. We have one letter of hers to Francesco Casini, "Medico di Siena di grande fama,"[2] and to him Petrarca addresses two letters, the second of which gives some interesting particulars about the *De Vita Solitaria*, and vindicates his well-known hatred of the medical profession, though allowing that he has more friends in it than in any other. He objects that famous doctors have warned him against fasting, against eating fruit, and drinking water, except what is tepid and has been boiled, and concludes: "I, however, am determined to live as I have lived hitherto, according to the rules laid down by God and indicated by reason, and, when I shall have paid my tribute to nature, I shall begin to think myself sure of perpetual health."[3]

The other link with St. Catherine is Fra Bonaventura Badoara, an Augustinian hermit, of whom Petrarca said that he and his brother were lights of their religion and singular ornaments of the city of Padua.[4] Urban VI. created him Cardinal in 1378.[5] The only letter addressed to him by the poet, that remains to us, is one of condolence

---

[1] *Rer. Sen.* x. 5.; xiv. 9.   [2] *Epist.* 227 (ed. Gigli).
[3] *Rer. Sen.* xv. 2, 3.
[4] St. Catherine's letter (30, ed. Gigli) is addressed to him at Florence after he became a cardinal. Cf. also E. G. Gardner, *Saint Catherine of Siena*, p. 376, note 2.
[5] *Rer. Sen.* viii. 6.

on the death of his brother, Fra Bonsembiante.[1] Another Augustinian friar with whom the poet was on terms of intimacy was Luigi Marsili, whom he first knew as a child in Padua. To him Petrarca gave his cherished copy of St. Augustine's *Confessions*,[2] and also incited him to write against the Averroists. Marsili wrote a commentary on the *Italia mia* and on some of the sonnets: but it was rather his personality than his authorship that impressed his contemporaries; he exercised a great moral influence and had an immense reputation. One of his friends and disciples was Coluccio Salutati — himself a direct product of Petrarchan influence. At one time appointed coadjutor to Francesco Bruni in his work as apostolic secretary, he afterwards became Chancellor to the Republic of Lucca, and, in 1375, was nominated to the same post in Florence. Here he attached himself to Marsili; they were the leading spirits of the brilliant literary circle that met in the gardens of Antonio degli Alberti, but Coluccio surpassed his master in his writings, criticisms, and general erudition. Petrarca praises his style, and tells him that he had long loved him although he had never seen him.[3] It would be impossible even to enumerate the long list of Petrarca's friends and ardent admirers; but Niccolò Acciaiuoli, Grand Seneschal of the kingdom of Naples, deserves mention as being closely connected with the poet during a long period of years, and for being nearly successful in his endeavours to persuade Petrarca to settle in Naples when he finally bid adieu to Avignon.[4] Of his poet-friends, Franceschino degli Albizzi and Sennuccio del Bene, both mentioned in the *Trionfi*,[5] something should be said. The former, who was also a relation, came to Avignon in 1345, on his way to the university at Paris, and formed such a strong friendship with Francesco that, for two years, he could not make up his

[1] *Rer. Sen.* xi. 14.     [2] *Ibid.* xiv. 7.     [3] *Ibid.* xi. 4.
[4] *De Reb. Fam.* xii. 2, Fracassetti's note.
[5] *Triumphus Cupidinis*, iii. 37, 38.

mind to separate from him. After this, he carried out his project of studying in Paris, and then returned to Avignon, where, hearing that Petrarca was in Italy, he set out to join him, but fell ill and died on the way. His ballata, beginning *Per fuggir riprensione*,[1] is of such finished perfection that it would not have disgraced Petrarca himself. This loss of a relative, a friend, and a brother-poet, Francesco bitterly laments in one of his letters.[2] Sennuccio must have been a very intimate friend and confidant of Petrarca, as we see from the only remaining letter to him,[3] and from the two sonnets (cxii., cxiii.) addressed to him. He was so great a poet that one of his canzoni (*Da poi ch' i' ho perduto ogni speranza*[4]) was honoured by being for a long time attributed to Dante.

It is from Francesco's sojourn in Milan that a change in his trend of thought and study can be traced. While there he seems to have added considerably to his theological library: the Scriptures and the Fathers occupy henceforth a more important place.[5]

It was in 1363 that he began the custom of passing some months every year at Pavia, while he was always constant to spending Easter at Padua to fulfil the duties attached to his canonry. And here it might not be amiss to give a list of the benefices enjoyed by Petrarca, as much confusion prevails concerning them. It is certain that he never possessed more than four, and at the end of his life he only retained two. The canonry of Lombez was given him by Benedict XII. in 1335; the priory of S. Niccola di Migliarino in the diocese of Pisa by Clement VI. in 1342; the same pontiff also gave him a prebend in the Church at Parma in 1346, and nominated him Archdeacon in 1350; and,

---

[1] *Rime di M. Cino da Pistoia e d'altri del Secolo XIV.*, ed. G. Carducci, p. 225.
[2] *De Reb. Fam.* xii. 7 and Fracassetti's note.
[3] *Ibid.* iv. 14.   [4] *Rime di M. Cino, etc.* p. 233.
[5] *De Reb. Fam.* xxii. 10. Also cf. Nolhac, *op. cit.* ii. pp. 194-195.

in 1349, Giacomo da Carrara conferred upon him a canonry at Padua. Besides these, in 1352, a canonry at Modena was given him, but he resigned it immediately in favour of his friend Luca Cristiano. Also, in 1365, the Florentines, hoping to entice their illustrious citizen back to them, begged Urban V. to bestow on him a canonry in Florence or in Fiesole; but the Pope, who desired to attract Petrarca to himself, proposed instead to offer him one at Carpentras. This intention was frustrated by the often-repeated report of the poet's death, which caused Urban to bestow not only the canonry of Carpentras on another, but also those benefices which Petrarca already held, though they were subsequently restored to him.[1] It is extraordinary to notice the many occasions on which the news of his death was circulated and believed, so that he says himself that, since 1343, not a single year passed without the report being spread. If he were in Italy, in France they believed him dead; if in France, Italy would lament him; or, in Italy itself, the people in one part would see him alive, and in another they would be about to bury him.[2]

Roughly speaking, the last ten years of his life were spent in Padua; Boccaccio visited him there in 1368.[3] But the life of a town was what could never suffice Petrarca for long, and, in 1365, we find him ill at the neighbouring Bagni d'Abano,[4] and the following year he establishes himself at Arquà, dating his letters *From the Euganean hills.* He seems to have spent his first summer there in the house of the Augustinian friars,[5] and afterwards to have built a house for himself. The residence at Arquà takes us back to the poet's best days at Vaucluse. There is a touch of the same austerity and simplicity; a conscious aloofness from the world, its cares, and its fetters. He writes that he has built himself a modest house among the Euganean hills, where he will pass what little remains to him of life in peace;

---

[1] *De Reb. Fam.* xiv. 4, Fracassetti's note.  [2] *Rer. Sen.* iii. 6.
[3] *Ibid.* x. 4, 5.  [4] *Var.* 18.  [5] *Rer. Sen.* xi. 14.

that he has no anxiety except for those whom he greatly loves, and no desires except for a good death, and that he flies from a multitude of servants as he would from a host of enemies; that, if he could, he would have none, but this is impossible owing to his age and weakness. He says he is still desirous, as of old, for quiet and solitude; he wishes to read, and write, and meditate, being assured that the study of letters is the most noble, as it is the most enduring, of pleasures.[1] And to his brother he writes: " So as not to be too far from my Church, I have built myself a tiny but charming house here among the Euganean hills, not more than ten miles from Padua, with a vine and an olive which produce enough for a small but modest household. And here, although weak in body, I live tranquil-minded, far from tumult, noise, and care: always reading and writing, and giving God thanks and praise, alike for the good and for the evil which he sends me."[2] And again: " I am no longer living either in Venice or in Padua, but in a solitary and delightful retreat in the Euganean hills, in a healthy and delicious situation, where very often the magnificent lord of Padua is pleased to pay me a friendly visit, attracted by the beauty of the place and the love he bears me."[3] To this " magnificent lord " Francesco addressed, at the very end of his life, one of the longest of his letters, which is indeed a treatise on the art of government.[4]

Questions and events of public importance never ceased to interest Petrarca. In 1364, he assisted at the fête held in Venice to celebrate the victory over Crete, which had revolted from the mother-city, but was reduced to submission in three days by an army commanded by the famous Luchino dal Verme. Of this event the poet writes that the august city of Venice exults—she who is in our days the only harbour of liberty, justice, and peace; a city rich in

[1] *Rer Sen.* xiii. 7, 9; xvi. 2.   [2] *Ibid.* xiv. 6.   [3] *Var.* 31.
[4] Cf. Petrarca's letter to him, *De Repub. optime administranda* (*Opera Omnia*, tom. i.), ed. cit. p. 372.

M a per la turba a grandi errori aueza  
Doppo la lunga era sia il nome chiaro  
Che e questo pero che si appreza.

T anto uince & ntoglie il tempo auaro  
Chiamasi fama, & e morir secondo.  
Ne piu che contro al primo e alcun riparo

*Triumphus Famæ*
*(Fifteenth Century Florentine Engraving.)*

gold but richer in renown, powerful in strength but more powerful in virtue, founded upon solid marble, but standing firm and immovable on a still more solid basis of civil concord, and fortified and secured by the prudence and wisdom of her children. He goes on to say that, when tidings of the victory arrived, the Doge desired that all the people should render homage of thanks and praise to God; and the most solemn festival that had been held within the memory of man was celebrated, the whole city being magnificently decorated, and especially the Basilica of St. Mark the Evangelist. There was a gorgeous procession all round the Church and the Piazza, in which not only the people and all the clergy took part, but also foreign prelates. And when these religious demonstrations were over, the whole population gave themselves up to games and pageants. Petrarca witnessed these sights from a place of honour, sitting at the Doge's right hand in his marble loggia, which was richly decorated for the occasion.[1]

In 1368, at the request of Galeazzo Visconti, he went to Pavia to conclude a treaty with Cardinal Anglico, and then proceeded to Milan to assist at the marriage of Galeazzo's daughter, Violante, with Lionel, Duke of Clarence, when he was treated as a highly honoured guest. In 1371, in spite of very failing health, he accompanied Francesco da Carrara to the solemn requiem for Pope Urban V. at Bologna, and in the following year, when war broke out with Venice, local disturbances obliged him to leave his retreat at Arquà and to move into Padua. The struggle was a disastrous one for the Carraresi, who were forced to sue for peace and accept any terms that Venice would grant them. One of the articles of the treaty was that Francesco, or his sons, should appear in person at Venice to ask pardon and swear fidelity. Francesco sent his son on this humiliating mission, and Petrarca accompanied him, and both wrote and delivered the set speech for the occasion.[2]

[1] *Rer. Sen.* iv. 2.   [2] A. Zardo, *op. cit.* pp. 165-170.

This was the poet's last journey. He retired to Arquà to " pursue the silent tenor " of his doom, resuming his habits of continuous study, and writing to Boccaccio that he was immovable in his purpose of working and learning to the end, and that he should wish death to find him " either reading or writing, or, better still, if God will, praying and weeping." [1] And even thus it came to pass. On July 18, 1374, the scholar passed away among his books. One tradition tells that he was engaged in annotating his Homer, another that he was correcting his life of Cæsar,[2] a third that he was poring over his beloved St. Augustine; while yet another asserts that he died in the arms of his friend and secretary, Lombardo da Serico. But the most commonly accepted account is that he died in his library during the night of the 18th, and was found dead by his servants early the next morning, his head bowed upon the book that he had been reading. He was buried with great pomp in Arquà, on July 24, by order of Francesco da Carrara; an immense concourse of people attended the ceremony and the funeral oration was pronounced by Fra Bonaventura Badoara. The Bishops of Padua, Verona, Vicenza, and Treviso assisted at the funeral, and the coffin, covered with a pall of gold tissue, was borne by sixteen doctors of the law. Whether the dead poet was robed in the state garment that King Robert had presented to him for his coronation, or in the red soutane of his canonry, is a disputed point. In any case, the ceremony must have been in complete contradiction to the wish so clearly expressed in his will: " This frail and mortal body, the heavy burden of noble minds, I would have restored to the earth from whence it sprang; and this without any pomp, but with the utmost humility and lowliness possible. I pray, I beseech, I supplicate, I conjure my heir and all my friends, by the tender mercy of our God, and by the love they have borne me, not to neglect this because of any false hope of honour-

[1] *Rer. Sen.* xvi. 2.     [2] Cf. P. de Nolhac, *op. cit.* i. p. 88, note 2.

ing me. Should they, perchance, violate this, may they be held answerable to God and to me at the day of judgment." From the same document we learn his intention of erecting a little chapel at Arquà in honour of the Blessed Virgin, where he desires to be buried; but he never carried out this plan. His body, therefore, was laid in the parish church, but was removed six years later to a marble sarcophagus that Francesco da Brossano erected to his memory at a short distance from the church.[1]

Petrarca's daughter and son-in-law were his sole heirs, but many small legacies were left. His servants were duly remembered; to Francesco da Carrara he left his picture of the Madonna, " the work of that supreme painter Giotto ";[2] to Tommaso Bambagia[3] the best of his lutes, " that he may play upon it, not for the vanity of the fleeting world, but to the praise of eternal God "; to Lombardo da Serico his golden cup (the Emperor's gift), " which he can use for water which he drinks gladly, much more gladly than wine." " To Messer Giovanni da Certaldo or Boccaccio I leave (and I am ashamed to leave such a little thing to such a great man) fifty gold florins of Florence, to buy a winter gown for his studies and nocturnal meditations."

Boccaccio's letter to Brossano on the death of his master and friend is full of noble sorrow:—

" I received your sad letter, most beloved brother, and, not knowing the writing, I broke the seal, looked hurriedly for the name of the sender, and, as soon as I read yours, I

---

[1] *Exemplum testamenti a Francisco Petrarcha conditi. Opera Omnia,* ed. cit. iii. p. 116.

[2] " Prædicto magnifico Domino meo Paduano, quia ipse per Dei gratiam non eget, et ego nihil habeo, dignum se, dimitto tabulam meam sive iconam Beatæ Virginis Mariæ, operis Joctii pictoris egregii, quae mihi ab amico meo Michaele Navis de Florentia missa est, cuius pulchritudinem ignorantes non intelligunt, magistri autem artis stupent: hanc iconam ipsi magnifico Domino lego, ut ipsa Virgo benedicta sit sibi propitia ad filium suum, Jesum Christum."—*Ibid.* p. 117.

[3] *Rer. Sen.* iv. 2.

understood what I should find therein, namely, the happy passing away of our illustrious father and master, Francesco Petrarca, from this earthly Babylon to the heavenly Jerusalem, of which ... I had already heard to my utmost sorrow, and had wept several days unceasingly, not for his flight, but at finding myself miserable and forsaken. It is no wonder: for none on earth was more bound to him than I. And to hide nothing from you, I had it in my mind to come to you, in order to pay my debt of tears to your grief and mine, and to pour forth with you my lamentations to Heaven, and haply to say my last farewell at the tomb of such a father. ... Since I have received and read your letter, my sorrow is renewed; I have again wept the whole night, not compassionating, I confess, this most excellent man (because remembering his goodness, his way of life, his fasts, vigils, and prayers, and his innate piety, his love of God and his neighbour, I am certain that, having laid down the tribulations of the wretched world, he has soared into the presence of the eternal Father, and there possesses his God and eternal glory), but bewailing myself and his friends, deserted in this tempestuous land. ... And while I think on the agitations of my own breast, I can easily understand the state of your mind and of Tullia's (your wife and my beloved sister, whom I have always held in honour), pierced, as I doubt not, by a far bitterer affliction. ... Our Silvanus has done that which we must do in a short time: he has died full of years; wherefore he has not died, but has preceded us, going forth to the seats of the blessed, that he might pity our miseries, praying the merciful Father to give to us pilgrims strength against our vices, and, when the end comes, to grant us a peaceful and happy release. ... Which things, to make no further digression, if you will consider, the lovers of this so glorious man ought not only to cease from weeping, but to feel joy and hope of future salvation; which consolation I pray you to impress upon Tullia by your devotion and our friendship. ...

You add that he ended his days near the village of Arquà, in the district of Padua, and that he enjoined that in the same place his ashes should be transferred to their last rest, and that you yourself are going to raise a beautiful and magnificent tomb for his everlasting remembrance. Alas! I confess my crime, if crime it be, to say that I, a Florentine, am envious, seeing that, by reason of another's humility rather than for any merit of her own, such great felicity should be reserved to Arquà, as that to her should be committed the body of him whose illustrious mind was the most acceptable home of the Muses and of all Helicon. . . . On which account Arquà, though ignored by the Paduans themselves, shall be known henceforth to strangers and to nations afar off, and her name shall be had in honour by all the world, no otherwise than by us are the hills of Posilipo . . . because at the foot of them are laid the bones of Virgil. . . . And I doubt not that the mariner returning laden with riches from the extreme bounds of the ocean, ploughing the Adriatic Sea, when he catches sight of the high peaks of the Euganean hills, will not fail to venerate them, saying within himself or to his friends: Behold the hills which enclose within them the ornament of the world, he who was once the temple of all truth, Petrarca, the sweetest poet, once crowned by the Senate in the Eternal City with the triumphal laurel; of whom remain so many excellent books, and such a music of noble and sacred fame.[1] . . . O unhappy country! to whom it was not given to preserve the ashes of so illustrious a son, to whom such a wonderful glory was denied. In truth thou art unworthy of so much splendour, thou who didst omit, while he

---

[1] " As the love from Petrarch's urn,
Yet amid yon hills doth burn,
A quenchless lamp by which the heart
Sees things unearthly."
SHELLEY, *Lines written among the Euganean Hills.*
Cf. also Samuel Rogers, *Italy: Arquà;* Byron, *Childe Harold's Pilgrimage,* canto iv. 30, 31, 32.

lived, to draw and fold him to thy bosom as he deserved. . . . Nevertheless, I could have wished, whatever thou art, that to thee, rather than to Arquà, this honour might have fallen. . . .

"That which concerns his munificence to his friends I cannot describe in a few words. . . . If, after that departure to a better life, which we call death, people love their friends, I believe that he loves me and will love me, not, certainly, because I deserve it, but because it was his habit carefully to keep whomsoever he had once taken for his own, and for forty years and more I was his. . . . I should much like to have heard how the valuable library of this illustrious man has been disposed of. But what most especially torments me is that a part of the books composed by him should be destroyed, and especially of that *Africa*, which I consider a celestial work; whether it still exists and is to remain lastingly, or has been delivered to the fire, with which, as you know, he threatened it while he lived—very often too severe a judge of his own things. I hear that the examination of this, as of the other books, has been committed to certain persons, I know not by whom, and that those which they declare worthy are to remain. I marvel at the ignorance of whoso gave this charge, but much more at the temerity and baseness of those who received it. May God, I pray, look down and protect the poems and other inventions of our master." [1]

To Boccaccio we are also indebted for the following sonnet on Petrarca's death:—

> Thou art ascended now to that abode,
>   Dear master mine, where every soul expecteth
>   Her sure ascent whom God thereto electeth,
>   The journey ended o'er life's evil road.
> Now thou art where thou oftentimes hast trod
>   Urged by desire to look upon Lauretta;

---

[1] *Lettere*, p. 383.

Now thou art where my beauteous Fiammetta
With her is seated in the sight of God.

With Dante, Cino, and Sennuccio now
  Thou dwellest sure of everlasting rest,
  Beholding things we cannot yet appraise.
Ah! if thou lov'dst me wandering below,
  Now draw me after thee, with joy to gaze
  On her who first lit love within my breast.[1]

The poet passed away in the summer of 1374: the following winter, it is said, all the laurels in Italy died.

[1] " Or sei salito, caro signor mio,
  Nel regno al qual salire ancora aspetta
  Ogn' anima da Dio a quello eletta
  Nel suo partir di questo mondo rio:
Or se' colà dove spesso il desio
  Ti tirò già per veder Lauretta;
  Or sei dove la mia bella Fiammetta
  Siede con lei nel cospetto di Dio:

Or con Sennuccio e con Cino e con Dante
  Vivi sicuro d'eterno riposo,
  Mirando cose da noi non intese.
Deh! se a grado ti fui nel mondo errante,
  Tirami drieto a te, dove gioioso
  Veggia colei che pria d'amor mi accese."
*Rime di M. Cino da Pistoia e d' altri del Secolo XIV.*, ed. cit., p. 385.

# CHAPTER X

## THE CROWN OF VIOLETS

" With the flower of song held heavenward for the violet of her crown."
A. C. SWINBURNE, *Athens*.

IT has already been noticed that the second part of the *Canzoniere* should begin with the canzone, *I' vo pensando*, thus marking the division between the two parts, not by an arbitrary event such as the death of Laura, but by the most intimate fact in the poet's own life—his moral conversion which left ineradicable traces on his mind and work.[1] In this collection we have before us a body of poetry which forms a far more connected whole than did the first part. With scarcely an exception, one purpose seems to run through it: it is to be the apotheosis of Laura, the record of her two victories, the eternal life that she has won for herself and that that she will obtain for her lover. Unlike the preceding poems, which were a record of conflicting emotions and desires, of a vacillating will, and an uncertain mind, the present work is a perpetual progress, and there can be no doubt that this was the author's definite intention. It is tolerably certain that *I' vo pensando* was written in 1348; of the remaining poems, the notes in the Vatican MS. 3196 furnish us with dates for some half dozen pieces, and these are nowhere inserted chronologically. Further, Mestica was the first to point out that the last thirty-one pieces have been renumbered on the margin of the MS.,[2] and the order there given makes the last sonnet but one (which, however, M. Cochin connects with the one following as being but two parts of the same prayer [3]) an

---
[1] Cf. Mestica, *Le Rime di F. Petrarca*, p. vii.   [2] *Ibid.* pp. vii. viii.
[3] H. Cochin, *La Chronologie*, p. 146.

anniversary-poem which bears its own date, for it states that Petrarca had loved and hoped for his lady for twenty years and had wept her for ten; it must, therefore, belong to the year 1358, and is certainly not the latest written.

Having thus established the fact that chronological sequence was no part of the poet's design, it is not difficult to follow his line of thought. He is like a man engaged in mortal combat who, pressed by foes on all sides so that he despairs of overcoming them, suddenly finds that he has but one enemy left to deal with: the relief is so great as to be almost equivalent to conquest. So with Petrarca; he has been torn in two with conflicting desires; now they are merged in one; the goal is the same and the way thither. His is not a mind ever to free itself from doubt and torment; something will always grieve, always torture him, but he is to be led henceforth along a simpler path. He has always been a prey to emotion rather than to passion, and his deep vein of sentiment is specially adapted to the illusive presence of his Lady, which he is now to celebrate. Here he shows himself as much painter as poet. He will move in a kingdom of shadow, but he will inform it with sufficient substance for us to grasp it. His touch is so delicate that he almost evolves the soul; his symbolism is so real that we forget the symbol. Hitherto Laura has been the creature of Petrarca's dreams, feignings, inventions; Bartoli says of her: " Such a woman has not a story of her own." Compare her with Beatrice: each lives for us solely in her poet's representation; no single fact of the life of either would have existed for us otherwise, and yet the one stands out clear-cut, definite, the most actual of all the women who have ever walked this earth; while the other is intangible. She is a tissue of contradictions, a mass of incompatible qualities and defects, so that the one conviction that remains with us is that, whatever Laura was, she was not the creature of Petrarca's imagination, for such a being would be a sheer impossibility. And it is this fact that accounts for the weariness bred of the first part of the *Canzoniere;* it is in the second part that Laura really begins to be; we can apprehend her in heaven far better than on earth, for it is only when she has become pure spirit that she is verily human. Although she is in heaven, she shines more brightly than ever upon his heart [1]:—

> The breath that was my life from me is gone,
> That spirit fair and pure heaven's height has won
> And thence reigns over me and gives me strength.[2]

But though earth is deprived of her presence he seems to see and hear her, and she answers his sighs and tenderly bids him not to weep for her to whom death has given everlasting life.[3] She tells him that formerly she was only cruel for their mutual good,[4] and he recognises that her conduct was the root of his salvation,[5] that so he might have " brief war and eternal peace."[6] Very often she returns to visit him, drying his tears and bidding him grieve no more, for he ought to live since she is not dead [7]:—

> My lady comes to comfort so much grief,
> For her compassion leads her back to earth.[8]

The contents, then, of the second part of the *Canzoniere* may be stated to be, with scarcely an exception, the narration of Petrarca's desolation without his Lady, a desolation haunting him night and day, but gradually lightened by

---

[1] *Rime*, cclxxvii.

[2] " È l'aura mia vital da me partita
E viva e bella e nuda al ciel salita:
Indi mi signoreggia, indi mi sforza."
*Rime*, cclxxviii.

[3] *Rime*, cclxxix.   [4] *Rime*, cclxxxix.   [5] *Rime*, cccxli., cccli.
[6] *Rime*, ccxc.   [7] *Rime*, cccxlii., cccxliii.

[8] " Ben torna a consolar tanto dolore
Madonna, ove pietà la riconduce."
*Rime*, cclxxxiii.

the consolation she comes to bring him, infusing into him the courage to follow her, and renewing and strengthening the love of God in his heart. This courage and love visibly increase all through the long series of poems, until the cries of penitence and humiliation culminate in the glorious prayer to Our Lady; of which contrition and hope are the key-notes.

At the outset, he asks of Love what he should do since his Lady is dead and has taken his heart with her; he despairs of ever seeing her again, and all sweetness has vanished from his life.[1] Now that she has gone from him he is left desolate:—

> Thy weapons were the eyes which erst let fly
>   Arrows whence issued fire invisible,
>   Fearless of reason, well
> Knowing that human arms 'gainst heaven are naught.
> The thought and silence, the sweet words that fell,
>   The modest air, the laugh and gaiety,
>   And speech of courtesy,
> Of a base soul a gentle would have wrought.
>     .    .    .    .
>   These could thy conquest of hard hearts ensure:
>   And now thou art disarmed and I secure.
>     .    .    .    .
>   In truth no fears arise,
>   Love, lest thou wound me with thy hand again.
>   Vain is the bow, the arrow flies in vain;
>   Its force was spent when closed those lovely eyes.
> Death has released me, Love, from all thy laws:
>   She who was once my lady dwells on high
>   Leaving my life free and in misery.[2]

---

[1] *Rime*, cclxviii.

[2] " L'arme tue furon gli occhi onde l'accese
    Saette uscivan d'invisibil foco
    E ragion temean poco,
    Ché 'n contra 'l ciel non val difesa umana;

Perhaps the saddest of all his complaints is in the double sestina, which is a wonderful *tour de force*, but flags both in thought and expression in the second part, of which only a few stanzas are given here:—

> My so fair fortune and my life so glad,
>   The beautiful bright days and tranquil nights,
>   The sighs so gently-breathed, and the sweet style,
>   That used to ring in verses and in song,
>   Suddenly changing into grief and tears,
>   Now make me loathe my life and long for death.
>
> Inexorable, bitter, cruel Death
>   Doth give me cause to be no longer glad,
>   But rather all my life to spend in tears,
>   The days be dark and sorrowful the nights.
>   My heavy sighs are now attuned to song,
>   And my fierce anguish mastereth my style.
>
> Now to what use is put my amorous style?
>   To speak of wrath, to hold discourse of death.
>   Where now are gone the verses and the song
>   Whereby the gentle heart was once made glad
>   And thoughtful?  Where the dreams of love at nights?
>   I neither think nor speak of aught but tears.

> Il pensar e 'l tacer, il riso e 'l gioco,
>   L'abito onesto e 'l ragionar cortese,
>   Le parole che 'ntese
>   Avrian fatto gentil d'alma villana.
>
> .   .   .   .   .
>
> Con quest' armi vincevi ogni cor duro:
>   Or se' tu disarmato, i' son securo.
>
> .   .   .   .   .
>
> Certo omai non tem'io,
>   Amor, de la tua man nove ferute:
>   Indarno tendi l' arco, a vòto scocchi;
>   Sua virtú cadde al chiuder de' begli occhi.
> Morte m'ha sciolto, Amor, d' ogni tua legge:
>   Quella che fu mia donna, al cielo è gita,
>   Lasciando trista e libera mia vita."
>
> *Rime*, cclxx.

## THE CROWN OF VIOLETS

For me erewhile desire made sweet my tears,
   Thus tempering with sweetness my harsh style,
   And making me keep vigil all the nights;
But now my tears are bitterer than death,
Hopeless to meet the gaze so pure and glad,
The lofty subject of my lowly song.

Love set a manifest signal for my song
   In those fair eyes: he sets it now in tears,
   Remembering in grief the time so glad;
Wherefore with heavy thoughts that change my style
I wander forth entreating thee, pale Death,
That thou wouldst take me from such painful nights.

Sleep is a fugitive from my sad nights,
   And wonted melody from my harsh song,
   Which cannot treat of anything but death;
And thus my singing all is turned to tears.
Love's kingdom has not such a varied style,
As mournful now as ever it was glad.

None ever lived till now than I more glad:
   None lives more sorrowful through days and nights:
   Redoubled grief redoubles thus my style,[1]
Which from the heart draws forth such plaintive songs.
I lived on hope but now I live on tears,
Nor against Death have any hope but death.

      .    .    .    .    .

Love, I have passed so long a time in tears,
   Weeping my heavy loss in dolorous style,
   Nor do I hope from thee less cruel nights;
And therefore am I moved to ask of Death
That he would take me hence and make me glad
There where she dwells for whom I weep in song.

      .    .    .    .    .

---

[1] The idea of the double sestina being that the thought is too great to be expressed in the one scheme of rhymes, but requires that they should be doubled.

Make me then glad ere passed are many nights;
And in harsh style and in my mournful song
I pray my tears may find an end in Death.[1]

---

[1] " Mia benigna fortuna e 'l viver lieto,
    I chiari giorni e le tranquille notti,
    E i soavi sospiri e 'l dolce stile
    Che solea resonare in versi e 'n rime,
    Vòlti subitamente in doglia e 'n pianto
    Odiar vita mi fanno e bramar morte.

Crudele, acerba, inessorabil Morte,
    Cagion mi dài di mai non esser lieto,
    Ma di menar tutta mia vita in pianto
    E i giorni oscuri e le dogliose notti.
    I miei gravi sospir non vanno in rime,
    E 'l mio duro martír vince ogni stile.

Ove è condutto il mio amoroso stile?
    A parlar d'ira, a ragionar di morte.
    U' sono i versi, u' son giunte le rime
    Che gentil cor udia pensoso e lieto?
    Ov'è 'l favoleggiar d'amor le notti?
    Or non parl' io né penso altro che pianto.

Già mi fu co 'l desir sí dolce il pianto,
    Che condia di dolcezza ogni agro stile
    E vegghiar mi facea tutte le notti;
    Or m'è 'l pianger amaro piú che morte,
    Non sperando mai 'l guardo onesto e lieto,
    Alto soggetto a le mie basse rime.

Chiaro segno Amor pose a le mie rime
    Dentro a' belli occhi; et or l' ha posto in pianto
    Con dolor rimembrando il tempo lieto:
    Ond' io vo co 'l penser cangiando stile,
    E ripregando te, pallida Morte,
    Che mi sottragghi a sí penose notti.

Fuggito è 'l sonno a le mie crude notti,
    E 'l sòno usato a le mie roche rime,
    Che non sanno trattar altro che morte;
    Cosí è 'l mio cantar converso in pianto.
    Non ha 'l regno d' Amor sí vario stile;
    Ch'è tanto or tristo, quanto mai fu lieto

Nesun visse già mai piú di me lieto,
    Nesun vive piú tristo e giorni e notti:
    E doppiando 'l dolor, doppia lo stile,

# THE CROWN OF VIOLETS

And the whole country-side is aware of his anguish:—

> There is nor shoot nor stone upon these hills,
>   Nor on the slopes a single branch or leaf,
>   Nor hath the valley blade of grass or flower;
> No drop of water from the stream distils,
>   Nor any beasts so wild the forests scour,
>   But each one knows how bitter is my grief.[1]

Again he sees Laura walking among the violets;[2] he appeals to the valleys and the streams, the hills and the paths, where Love used to lead him, to see how he is made a hostel of infinite grief.[3] He is like a wild beast wandering about a world which has become to him a desert.[4] Erewhile it had been far otherwise, for—

> What time in this low world of ours she stayed
>   Which, truly, for her dwelling was not meet,
>     .   .   .   .   .

---

>     Che trae del cor sí lacrimose rime.
>     Vissi di speme; or vivo pur di pianto,
>     Né contra Morte spero altro che morte.
>         .   .   .   .   .
>   Amor, i' ho molti e molt' anni pianto
>     Mio grave danno in doloroso stile;
>     Nè da te spero mai men fere notti;
>     E però mi son mosso a pregar Morte
>     Che mi tolla di qui, per farme lieto
>     Ove è colei ch' i' canto e piango in rime.
>         .   .   .   .   .
>   Far mi po lieto in una o 'n poche notti:
>     E 'n aspro stile e 'n angosciose rime
>     Prego che 'l pianto mio finisca Morte."
>                                    *Rime*, cccxxxii.

[1] " Non è sterpo né sasso in questi monti,
  Non ramo o fronda verde in queste piagge,
  Non fiore in queste valli o foglia d' erba,
  Stilla d'acqua non vèn di queste fonti
  Né fiere han questi boschi sí selvagge,
  Che non sappian quanto è mia pena acerba."
                                    *Rime*, cclxxxviii.

[2] *Rime*, ccclii.   [3] *Rime*, ccci.   [4] *Rime*, cccvi.

The wood and water, earth and rocks she made
Green, clear, and soft; and where her foot did pass
And her hands press, so proudly grew the grass,
And her fair eyes set all the fields in flower,

. . . . .

And clearly showed the world so deaf and blind
How much the light of heaven within her shined.[1]

In one of his most charming sonnets he condoles with the bird that has lost its mate:—

Fair bird that goest singing on thy way,
　Or maybe weeping for the time gone by,
　Seeing that night and winter are come nigh,
　And day behind thee lies and springtime gay.
If, as thou canst thine own affliction weigh,
　Thou couldst discern how similar my state,
　Thou'dst nestle in my breast disconsolate
　To share with me the darkness of thy day.

I know not if our portion equal be;
　The friend thou mournest haply liveth yet,
　While death and heaven of mine were covetous.
But hour and season less felicitous,
　And memory of bitter years and sweet,
　Urge me, compassionate, to speak with thee.[2]

---

[1] " Com' ella venne in questo viver basso,
　　Ch', a dir il ver, non fu degno d' averla,

. . . . .

　Legno, acqua, terra o sasso
　Verde facea, chiara, soave, e l' erba
　Con le palme o co i piè fresca e superba,
　E fiorir co i belli occhi le campagne,

. . . . .

　Chiaro mostrando al mondo sordo e cieco
　Quanto lume del ciel fusse già seco."

*Rime*, cccxxv.

[2] " Vago augelletto che cantando vai,
　O ver piangendo il tuo tempo passato,
　Vedendoti la notte e 'l verno a lato
　E 'l dí dopo le spalle e i mesi gai;

# THE CROWN OF VIOLETS

The laurel, too, preserves its old significance, as we see from the following simile:—

> Within a grove the sacred branches spread
>  Of a young laurel grown so straight and tall,
>  It seemed to be a tree of Paradise;
> And from its shade such sweet songs issuèd
>  Of various birds and such delights withal,
>  As rapt the world completely from my eyes.
> Watching it in fixed wise,
> The heavens were changed, the skies grew dark amain,
> The lightning fell, uprooting suddenly
>  That erst so happy tree:
> And since that time my life is full of pain
> For such sweet shade may ne'er be found again.[1]

He speaks of—

---

> Se, come i tuoi gravosi affanni sai,
>  Così sapessi il mio simile stato,
>  Verresti in grembo a questo sconsolato
> A partir seco i dolorosi guai.
>
> I' non so se le parti sarian pari;
>  Ché quella cui tu piangi è forse in vita,
>  Di ch' a me Morte e 'l ciel son tanto avari:
> Ma la stagione e l' ora men gradita,
>  Co 'l membrar de' dolci anni e de li amari,
>  A parlar teco con pietà m'invita."
>
> *Rime*, cccliii.

[1] " In un boschetto novo i rami santi
 Fiorian d'un lauro giovenetto e schietto,
 Ch'un de li arbor parea di paradiso;
 E di sua ombra uscian sì dolci canti
 Di vari augelli e tant' altro diletto,
 Che dal mondo m' avean tutto diviso:
 E mirando 'l io fiso
 Cangiossi 'l cielo in torno, e tinto in vista
 Folgorando 'l percosse, e da radice
 Quella pianta felice
 Subito svelse: onde mia vita è trista,
 Ché simile ombra mai non si racquista."
  *Rime*, cccxxiii.

> My sweet laurel where was wont to dwell
> All ardent virtue and all loveliness.[1]

And again:—

> The breath and scent, the shelter and the shade
> Of the sweet laurel and her flowering face,
> Of my tired life the light and resting-place,
> Are his who desolate the world has made.[2]

But, all the time, he is receiving comfort from his lady's presence, and thus addresses her:—

> Blest soul that oftentimes returnest here
> To bring some solace to my weary night,
> With eyes where death has nowise quenched the light
> But made them above measure lovelier.
> How I rejoice thou shouldst consent to cheer
> My days, that are so mournful, with thy sight;
> Thus I begin to find thy presence bright
> In places where thy wonted dwellings were.
>
> Where I went singing thee so many years,
> Weeping thee now, as thou mayst see, I go;
> Ah! no, not thee; but only that in tears
> I find repose in so much wretchedness.
> When thou return'st I see thee and I know
> By footstep and by voice, by face and dress.[3]

---

[1] " Dolce mio lauro, ove abitar solea
   Ogni bellezza, ogni vertute ardente."
                                   *Rime*, cccxxxvii.

[2] " L' aura e l' odore e 'l refrigerio e l' ombra
   Del dolce lauro e sua vista fiorita,
   Lume e riposo di mia stanca vita,
   Tolto ha colei che tutto 'l mondo sgombra."
                                   *Rime*, cccxxvii.

[3] " Alma felice che sovente torni
   A consolar le mie notti dolenti
   Con gli occhi tuoi, che morte non ha spenti
   Ma sovra 'l mortal modo fatti adorni;

Another time he has an ecstatic vision of her:—

> I raised myself in thought to mansions where
>   Is she I seek on earth and no more find;
>   Mid those whom the third circle's limits bind,
>   I saw her stand, less proud and far more fair.
> She took my hand and said: Within this sphere,
>   Unless desire deceive, thou'lt share my life;
>   For I am she who caused thee so much strife,
>   And closed my day before the night drew near.[1]

But the thought of her beauty would be too overpowering, if he did not believe that she would obtain for him the grace to be with her where she is:—

> From the most lovely face, the brightest eyes
>   That ever shone, and from the loveliest hair
>   That made both gold and sunlight seem less fair,
>   From sweetest speech and smile sweet in likewise,
> From hand and arm that had won victories
>   And made Love's most rebellious foes retreat

---

> Quanto gradisco ch' e miei tristi giorni
>   A rallegrar di tua vista consenti!
>   Così comincio a ritrovar presenti
>   Le tue bellezze a' suoi usati soggiorni.
> Là 've cantando andai di te molt' anni,
>   Or, come vedi, vo di te piangendo;
>   Di te piangendo no, ma de' miei danni.
> Sol un riposo trovo in molti affanni;
>   Che, quando torni, ti conosco e 'ntendo
>   A l' andar, a la voce, al volto, a' panni."
>          *Rime*, cclxxxii.

[1] " Levommi il mio penser in parte ov' era
>   Quella ch'io cerco e non ritrovo in terra:
>   Ivi, fra lor che 'l terzo cerchio serra,
>   La rividi più bella e meno altera.
> Per man mi prese e disse—In questa spera
>   Sarai ancor meco, se 'l desir non erra:
>   I' son colei che ti die' tanta guerra,
>   E compiei mia giornata inanzi sera."
>          *Rime*, cccii.

Without a blow; from beautiful swift feet,
  And from the form fashioned in Paradise,
My spirit drew its life: these now delight
  The heavenly King and each winged messenger,
  And I am left below forlorn and blind.
One only comfort in my grief I find,
  That she who sees my every thought aright,
  May win me grace that I may be with her.[1]

And she visits him to assure him of this:—

What time my gentle, faithful comforter
  To give repose unto my weary days,
  With wonted words of wisdom and of grace,
  Doth on the left hand of my bed appear.
Quite pale with passion of pity and of fear:
Whence comest thou, O blessed soul? I say.
And then she draws a spray
Of laurel from her breast and one of palm.
The empyrean calm
And holy place of heaven I left, saith she,
And only am come down to comfort thee.

I thank her then in gesture and in speech
  Right humbly, while I ask: How canst thou know

---

[1] " Da' piú belli occhi e dal piú chiaro viso
  Che mai splendesse, e da' piú bei capelli
  Che facean l'oro e 'l sol parer men belli,
  Dal piú dolce parlare e dolce riso,
Da le man, da le braccia che conquiso
  Senza moversi avrian quai piú rebelli
  Fûr d' Amor mai, da' piú bei piedi snelli,
  Da la persona fatta in paradiso,
Prendean vita i miei spirti: or n'ha diletto
  Il re celeste, i suo' alati corrieri;
  Et io son qui rimaso ignudo e cieco.
Sol un conforto a le mie pene aspetto;
  Ch' ella, che vede tutt' i miei penseri,
  M'impetre grazia ch' i' possa esser seco."
                                    *Rime*, cccxlviii.

## THE CROWN OF VIOLETS

My state? And she replies: The mournful flow
Of tears insatiate, and the breath of each
Long sigh thou heavest, through all space can reach,
And pass to heaven, and do disturb my peace.
Doth it so much displease
That I have gone from trouble and from strife
Unto a better life?
Which thing should please thee, if thou lov'd'st me well
As all thy looks and words would seem to tell.

I answer her: It only is for me
I weep, left here in darkness and in woe,
Always most sure that thou to heaven didst go,
As sure as of such things that men can see.
For how could God and nature cause to be
In thy young heart so many virtues rife,
If everlasting life
Were not the prize of thy good actions here?
Soul, of rare souls the peer!
Who while with us didst live so loftily
And suddenly hast winged thy flight on high.

But I, what should I do but weep alway,
Alone and sad who without thee am naught?
Would I had died an infant, nor been brought
To know the heat of love's tempestuous day.
And she: Why dost thou weep and faint away?
Better it were from earth to raise thy wings;
And all brief, mortal things,
And all thine idle fancies, vain and sweet,
In a just balance mete,
And follow me, if love be still so strong,
Plucking these boughs as thou dost pass along.

I answer her: To ask thee I am fain
Of these two leaves what may the meaning be?
And she: Thy very self doth answer thee
Who one hast greatly honoured with thy pen.
The palm is victory; and youthful then

The world and self I conquered: laurel is
For triumph, and of this
Worthy am I, through Him who made me strong.
Thou, if assailed by wrong,
Turn thee to Him and ask Him for His grace,
That we may be with Him when ends thy race.

Is this the golden knot, this the bright hair,
I said, which binds me still, the lovely eyes
That were my sun? Err not with fools, she cries,
Nor in their speech and faith have any share.
I am pure spirit, glad in heavenly air;
That which thou seek'st is dust these many years;
Only to stay thy tears
'Tis given me to look thus. I yet shall be,
Both far more dear to thee,
And far more fair, the same who, cold and pure,
My own and thy salvation did secure.

I weep; and with her hands
She dries my face, and sighing tenderly
She then rebuketh me
With words that had been fit to break a stone:
And, after that, she and the dream were gone.[1]

---

[1] " Quando il soave mio fido conforto,
  Per dar riposo a la mia vita stanca,
  Ponsi del letto in su la sponda manca
  Con quel suo dolce ragionare accorto;
  Tutto di pièta e di paura smorto
  Dico—Onde vien' tu ora, o felice alma?—
  Un ramoscel di palma
  Et un di lauro trae del suo bel seno,
  E dice—Dal sereno
  Ciel empireo e di quelle sante parti
  Mi mossi, e vengo sol per consolarti.—

  In atto et in parole la ringrazio
   Umilemente, e poi demando—Or donde
   Sai tu il mio stato?—Et ella—Le triste onde
   Del pianto, di che mai tu non se' sazio,
   Co l'aura de' sospir, per tanto spazio

## THE CROWN OF VIOLETS

A careful study of the last thirty-one pieces will further accentuate Petrarca's idea of progression; step by step we are led through growing hope, and thankfulness, and faith, to the final notes of penitence which usher in Petrarca's

    Passano al cielo e turban la mia pace.
    Sì forte ti dispiace
    Che di questa miseria sia partita
    E giunta a miglior vita?
    Che piacer ti devria, se tu m'amasti
    Quanto in sembianti e ne' tuoi dir mostrasti.—
Rispondo—Io non piango altro che me stesso,
    Che son rimaso in tenebre e 'n martire,
    Certo sempre del tuo al ciel salire
    Come di cosa ch' uom vede da presso.
    Come Dio e natura avrebben messo
    In un cor giovenil tanta vertute,
    Se l'eterna salute
    Non fusse destinata al tuo ben fare?
    Oh de l'anime rare
    Ch' altamente vivesti qui fra noi
    E che súbito al ciel volasti poi!
Ma io che debbo altro che pianger sempre,
    Misero e sol, che senza te son nulla?
    Ch' or fuss 'io spento al latte et a la culla,
    Per non provar de l'amorose tempre!—
    Et ella—A che pur piangi e ti distempre?
    Quanto era meglio alzar da terra l'ali,
    E le cose mortali
    E queste dolci tue fallaci ciance
    Librar con giusta lance,
    E seguir me, s'è ver che tanto m'ami,
    Cogliendo omai qualcun di questi rami!—
—I' volea demandar—rispond'io allora—
    Che voglion importar quelle due frondi.—
    Et ella—Tu medesmo ti rispondi,
    Tu la cui penna tanto l'una onora.
    Palma è vittoria; et io, giovene ancora,
    Vinsi il mondo e me stessa: il lauro segna
    Triunfo, ond'io son degna,
    Mercé di quel Signor che mi diè forza.
    Or tu, s'altri ti sforza,
    A lui ti volgi, a lui chiedi soccorso;
    Sì che siam seco al fine del tuo corso.—

*Ave*—one of the devotional treasures of literature, and breathing such a personal and intimate piety that, as has been said, to read it is almost like overhearing some one's confession:—

> Beautiful Virgin, clothèd with the sun,
>   And crowned with stars, and to the Sun supreme
>   So pleasing that He hid His light in thee;
>   Love urges me to choose thee for my theme,
>   But naught without thine aid can be begun
>   And His who dwelt in thee by love's decree.
> Her I invoke who answers certainly
> To every cry of faith.
> Virgin, if mercy hath
> Ere moved thee for the utmost misery
> Of human things, to my petition lean:
> Win for my struggle worth,
> Though I am earth and thou of heaven the queen.
>
> Wise Virgin, one of that fair company,
>   And first of those, the prudent virgins blest,
>   Thou art the one whose lamp gives clearest light.
>   O sure, protecting shield of folk distrest

---

> —Son questi i capei biondi e l'aureo nodo—
> Dich'io—ch'ancor mi stringe e quei belli occhi
> Che fûr mio sol?—Non errar con li sciocchi,
> Né parlar—dice—o creder a lor modo.
> Spirito ignudo sono, e' n ciel mi godo:
> Quel che tu cerchi, è terra già molt' anni:
> Ma per trarti d'affanni
> M'è dato a parer tale. Et ancor quella
> Sarò, piú che mai bella,
> A te piú cara, sí selvaggia e pia,
> Salvando inseme tua salute e mia.—
>
> I' piango; et ella il volto
> Co le sue man m'asciuga; e poi sospira
> Dolcemente, e s' adira
> Con parole che i sassi romper pònno:
> E, dopo questo, si parte ella e 'l sonno.
>
> *Rime* ccclix.

## THE CROWN OF VIOLETS

Against the darts that Death and Fate let fly,
'Neath which secure we triumph in the fight!
Subduer of that ardour lacking sight
That heats a world unwise;
Virgin, those beauteous eyes,
That sorrowing saw the marks of cruel spite
Upon the members fair of thy dear Son,
Turn now upon my doubt
For I without advice to thine would run.

Virgin most pure and wholly undefiled,
  Daughter and mother of thy noble Son;
  Light of this life, splendour the next displays.
  Window of heaven, O high and shining one,
  Through thee the supreme Father's and thy child
  Came down to save us in these latter days;
  And of all dwellings found in mortal ways,
  He chose from all the rest
  Thee only, Virgin blest,
  To turn the plaint of Eve to happy praise.
  Make, as thou canst, me worthy of His grace,
  Thou blest without all bound,
  Already crowned in the supernal place.

O holy Virgin, every grace is thine,
  Who by a true and lofty humbleness
  Didst soar to heaven, whence now thou hearest me.
  Thou didst bring forth the Fount that flows to bless,
  The sun of justice who arose to shine
  Upon a world of dense obscurity.
  Three sweet and precious names unite in thee,
  Of Mother, Daughter, Spouse;
  O Virgin glorious,
  Lady of Him who us from bonds set free,
  And made a world of liberty and rest:
  In His sweet wounds, I pray
  That thou alway wilt ease my heart, Most Blest.

Sole Virgin in the world without a peer;
  Heaven was enamoured of thy loveliness,

Nor first nor second like thee was there found.
Within thy fruitful Virginhood by grace
Of holy thoughts and deeds was fashioned there
A living temple wherein God was throned.
Through thee my life with gladness may be crowned,
If, Mary, at thy prayer,
Virgin most sweet and dear,
Where sin abounded grace may more abound.
In mind before thee I am fain to bend,
Be thou my guide, I pray,
My crookèd way   lead to a blessed end.

   Bright Virgin, stably fixed eternally,
     And of this sea tempestuous the star,
     Of every trustful pilot trusted guide.
     Think what dread storms assail me near and far,
     As lone and rudderless my course I ply,
     And the last agony will soon betide.
   But always shall my soul in thee confide.
   Sinner, I can but say,
   Virgin, but thee I pray
   That never may thy foe mine ill deride.
   Remember, it for sin of ours befell
   That God for our escape
   Took human shape   within thy virgin-cell.

   Virgin, how many tears have I let fall,
     What arts and what vain prayers I now deplore
     Made but for grievous hurt and punishment!
     Since first I saw the light by Arno's shore,
     Seeking now here, now otherwhere, in all
     I found but weariness where'er I went.
   Gesture and speech and human beauty blent,
   These all have filled my mind.
   Virgin most pure and kind,
   Delay not for my years are well-nigh spent;
   My days run on swifter than arrow's flight,
   Through misery and sin
   Their course they win   with only Death in sight.

# THE CROWN OF VIOLETS

Virgin, lo! she is dead and grieves my heart,
  Who living ever made my tears to flow;
  Of all my thousand woes not one she knew,
  And, had she known, these things had still been so,
  Since from aught other wish upon her part
  Must death to me and shame to her accrue.
  But thou, Lady of Heaven, our goddess too
  (If I speak fittingly),
  Virgin, of wisdom high,
  Thou seest all, and nothing can subdue
  Thy mighty power, albeit hers could naught;
  End thou my grief, and be
  Honoured by me    in my salvation wrought.

Virgin, on whom my every hope is set,
  Who canst and wilt my utter need supply,
  Do not at my last end abandon me.
  Weigh not my worth, but mark the image high
  Of Him who deigned to fashion me, that it
  Move thee to care for one so vile to see.
  Medusa and my sin have made me be
  Stone whence vain drops distil:
  Virgin, do thou fulfil
  With holy tears my heart that cries to thee,
  That so at least my last lament may rise
  Earth's stain without
  And all-devout    unlike my former cries.

Virgin, pride's foe, and human like to us,
  Let our same origin induce thy love;
  Pity a heart that humbly mourns its wrong.
  If me a little mortal dust could move
  To love even with a faith miraculous,
  What must to thy pure gentleness belong?
  If but thy hands to raise me up are strong
  From my so piteous state,
  Virgin, I dedicate
  My sighs and tears, and purge my heart and tongue,
  My mind and pen, even as thy name inspires.

Guide me a better way,
And let me pay  to thee my changed desires.

The day draws on, nor long it tarrieth,
　So swiftly pass the years;
　Virgin without compeers,
　Now conscience pricks my soul, now haply death.
　Commend me, Lady, to thy Son's dear grace,
　True God and man, that He
　May welcome me  at my last breath in peace.[1]

---

[1] " Vergine bella, che di sol vestita,
　　Coronata di stelle, al sommo Sole
　　Piacesti sí che 'n te sua luce ascose;
　　Amor mi spinge a dir di te parole,
　　Ma non so 'ncominciar senza tu' aita
　　E di colui ch' amando in te si pose.
　　Invoco lei che ben sempre rispose
　　Chi la chiamò con fede.
　　Vergine, s' a mercede
　　Miseria estrema de l'umane cose
　　Già mai ti volse, al mio prego t'inchina;
　　Soccorri a la mia guerra,
　　Bench' i' sia terra,  e tu del ciel regina.

　Vergine saggia, e del bel numero una
　　De le beate vergini prudenti,
　　Anzi la prima e con piú chiara lampa;
　　O saldo scudo de l'afflitte genti
　　Contr' a' colpi di Morte e di Fortuna,
　　Sotto 'l qual si trïunfa, non pur scampa;
　　O refrigerio al cieco ardor ch'avampa
　　Qui fra i mortali sciocchi;
　　Vergine, que' belli occhi,
　　Che vider tristi la spietata stampa
　　Ne' dolci membri del tuo caro figlio,
　　Volgi al mio dubio stato,
　　Che sconsigliato  a te vèn per consiglio.

　Vergine pura, d'ogni parte intera,
　　Del tuo parto gentil figliuola e madre,
　　Ch' allumi questa vita e l'altra adorni;
　　Per te il tuo figlio e quel del sommo Padre,
　　O fenestra del ciel lucente, altera,
　　Venne a salvarne in su li estremi giorni;

# THE CROWN OF VIOLETS

To pass from the study of the second part of the *Canzoniere* to that of the *Trionfi* is in some measure a descent, if not in purpose, at any rate as regards poetry; it is prob-

>     E fra tutt' i terreni altri soggiorni
>   Sola tu fosti eletta,
>   Vergine benedetta,
>   Che 'l pianto d' Eva in allegrezza torni.
>   Fammi, ché puoi, de la sua grazia degno,
>   Senza fine o beata,
>   Già coronata   nel superno regno.
>
> Vergine santa, d' ogni grazia piena,
>   Che per vera et altissima umiltate
>   Salisti al ciel, onde miei preghi ascolti;
>   Tu partoristi il fonte di pietate,
>   E di giustizia il sol, che rasserena
>   Il secol pien d'errori oscuri e folti:
>   Tre dolci e cari nomi ha' in te raccolti,
>   Madre, figliuola e sposa;
>   Vergine glorïosa,
>   Donna del Re che nostri lacci ha sciolti
>   E fatto 'l mondo libero e felice:
>   Ne le cui sante piaghe
>   Prego ch'appaghe   il cor, vera beatrice.
>
> Vergine sola al mondo, senza essempio,
>   Che 'l ciel di tue bellezze innamorasti,
>   Cui né prima fu, simil, né seconda;
>   Santi penseri, atti pietosi e casti
>   Al vero Dio sacrato e vivo tempio
>   Fecero in tua verginità feconda.
>   Per te po la mia vita esser joconda,
>   S' a' tuoi preghi, o Maria,
>   Vergine dolce e pia,
>   Ove 'l fallo abondò la grazia abonda.
>   Con le ginocchia de la mente inchine
>   Prego che sia mia scorta,
>   E la mia torta   via drizzi a buon fine.
>
> Vergine chiara e stabile in eterno,
>   Di questo tempestoso mare stella,
>   D' ogni fedel nocchier fidata guida;
>   Pon' mente in che terribile procella
>   I' mi ritrovo, sol, senza governo,
>   Et ho già da vicin l' ultime strida.

able, however, that Petrarca considered these as his most
serious work in the vernacular, and it seems likely that the
growing fame of Dante incited him to the composition of an

> Ma pur in te l' anima mia si fida;
> Peccatrice, i' no 'l nego,
> Vergine; ma ti prego
> Che 'l tuo nemico del mio mal non rida.
> Ricorditi che fece il peccar nostro
> Prender Dio, per scamparne,
> Umana carne   al tuo virginal chiostro.
>
> Vergine, quante lagrime ho già sparte,
>   Quante lusinghe e quanti preghi indarno,
>   Pur per mia pena e per mio grave danno!
>   Da poi ch' i' nacqui in su la riva d'Arno,
>   Cercando or questa et or quell'altra parte,
>   Non è stata mia vita altro ch' affanno.
>   Mortal bellezza, atti e parole m' hanno
>   Tutta ingombrata l'alma.
>   Vergine sacra et alma,
>   Non tardar, ch' i' son forse a l'ultimo anno.
>   I dí miei, piú correnti che saetta,
>   Fra miserie e peccati
>   Sonsen andati,   e sol Morte n' aspetta.
>
> Vergine, tale è terra e posto ha in doglia
>   Lo mio cor, che vivendo in pianto il tenne,
>   E di mille miei mali un non sapea;
>   E, per saperlo, pur quel che n'avenne
>   Fôra avvenuto; ch' ogni altra sua voglia
>   Era a me morte et a lei fama rea.
>   Or tu, donna del ciel, tu nostra dea
>   (Se dir lice e convènsi),
>   Vergine d' alti sensi,
>   Tu vedi il tutto; e quel che non potea
>   Far altri è nulla a la tua gran vertute,
>   Por fine al mio dolore;
>   Che a te onore   et a me fia salute.
>
> Vergine, in cui ho tutta mia speranza
>   Che possi e vogli al gran bisogno aitarme,
>   Non mi lasciare in su l'estremo passo:
>   Non guardar me, ma chi degnò crearme;
>   No 'l mio valor, ma l' alta sua sembianza
>   Ch' è in me ti mova a curar d' uom sí basso.

important poem in *terzà rima*.[1] Certainly the most interesting feature of the *Trionfi* is that they exhibit the author in his two-fold capacity of poet and humanist. They are steeped in classicism; they show his vivid appreciation of classical learning, and his wonderful knowledge of ancient history. The long list of classical names (over three hundred are mentioned), however commonplace it

> Medusa e l' error mio m'han fatto un sasso
> D' umor vano stillante:
> Vergine, tu di sante
> Lagrime e pie adempi '1 mio cor lasso;
> Ch'almen l' ultimo pianto sia devoto,
> Senza terrestre limo,
> Come fu '1 primo   non d' insania vòto.
>
> Vergine umana e nemica d' orgoglio,
>   Del comune principio amor t'induca;
>   Miserere d' un cor contrito, umíle:
>   Ché se poca mortal terra caduca
>   Amar con sí mirabil fede soglio,
>   Che devrò far di te, cosa gentile?
>   Se dal mio stato assai misero e vile
>   Per le tue man resurgo,
>   Vergine, i' sacro e purgo
>   Al tuo nome e penseri e 'ngegno e stile,
>   La lingua e '1 cor, le lagrime e i sospiri.
>   Scorgimi al miglior guado,
>   E prendi in grado   i cangiati desiri.
>
> Il dí s' appressa, e non pòte esser lunge,
>   Sí corre il tempo e vola,
>   Vergine unica e sola;
>   E '1 cor or consc͏ïenzia or morte punge
>   Raccomandami al tuo Figliuol, verace
>   Omo e verace Dio,
>   Ch' accolga '1 mïo   spirto ultimo in pace.

[1] For much of the information contained in this and the succeeding chapter, I am indebted to the kindness of Mr. Edmund Gardner, who allowed me to consult two of his unpublished articles. To one of these I owe the whole conception of the purport of the *Trionfi*, the idea of the general and particular allegory contained in them, and the minute details in which they emphasise not only events, but also tendencies and predilections in the poet's life.

may seem to us, meant to the author the research and the patient study of years; it meant also the intelligent interest that he had awakened and the taste that he had created. It is much to furnish men with ideas, and no one is required to furnish the brains to comprehend them, but Petrarca did both these things. Nor does the singer of Laura fail her in his latest work. Though he never rises to the highest level of the *Canzoniere*, he never, in the passages that concern Laura, departs from the region of great poetry. And yet another side of his character is brought into prominence —his sense of Friendship and the high value that he sets upon it. Socrates and Lælius are here, and Cardinal Colonna and King Robert, and Sennuccio and Franceschino *che fûr sì humani*. Laura herself is surrounded by a band of friends whose lamentation over her death is one of the most beautiful parts of the whole.

Begun in the spring of 1352 or 1353, during his last residence at Vaucluse, we know that Petrarca was working on the *Trionfi* to the end of his life, and that they had not received his ultimate corrections and amendments. There is, therefore, no authoritative text for them as for the *Canzoniere*, although there were some autograph manuscripts containing copious notes and corrections in the poet's own hand, which were preserved up to the beginning of the sixteenth century, and seem to have been dispersed after the sack of Padua in 1509. Two cantos in this form, from the Vatican manuscript 3196, were published by Ubaldini in 1642. Both Ludovico Beccadelli and Bernardino Daniello have left us particulars of various copies which are not to be found; but in 1897 Flaminio Pellegrini discovered a valuable manuscript at Parma, the work of a sixteenth-century transcriber who collated his text with two autograph manuscripts of Petrarca. Herr Carl Appel, the author of the latest critical edition, brought out in 1901, tells us that he has consulted two hundred and fifty codices of the *Trionfi*, and in his exhaustive and learned work all that can be known of the chronology and sequence of the cantos, and of their definitive number and text, is to be found.¹ The *Trionfi*, six in number, were finally composed of only ten cantos, making two groups of five, which balance each other thus: on the one hand, the *Triumphus Cupidinis* has three cantos, the *Triumphus Pudicitiæ* one, and the *Triumphus Mortis* one; on the other hand, the *Triumphus Famæ* has three, the *Triumphus Temporis* one, and the *Triumphus Æternitatis* one. It was, perhaps, this idea of proportion which prompted Petrarca to discard three other cantos; it is not easy otherwise to account for their suppression, except in the case of the second canto of the *Triumphus Mortis*, which, while reminding us of the canzone *Quando il soave mio fido conforto*,² seems to breathe a different atmosphere from the other *Trionfi* and to introduce quite another point of view; he may well have felt that this did not harmonise with the rest.³ Seven *terzine*, which introduced the *Triumphus Mortis*, were ultimately rejected as interfering with the balance of the whole.

The following is the manner in which they are now presented to us:—

I. *Triumphus Cupidinis.*
   1. Al tempo.
   2. Era sí pieno.
   3. Poscia che mia.

II. *Triumphus Pudicitiæ.*
   Quando vidi.

III. *Triumphus Mortis.*
   Quella leggiadra.

IV. *Triumphus Famæ.*
   1. Da poi che Morte
   2. Pien d'infinita.
   3. Io non sapea.

V. *Triumphus Temporis.*
   Del aureo.

VI. *Triumphus Æternitatis.*
   Da poi che sotto.⁴

---

[1] Cf. Carl Appel, *Die Triumphe*, pp. 2-9, 98-105, 121-147.
[2] *Rime*, ccclix.
[3] Herr Appel seems to have convinced himself (on rather slight grounds) that this was written long after Laura's death. Mestica (p. xvii), on the other hand, regards it as one of the earliest, as it stood first in the original collection of the *Trionfi*. It seems, rather, to bear internal evidence of having been an independent composition. [4] Carl Appel, *op. cit.*

The order given thus by Herr Appel would seem to be that intended by Petrarca at the time of his death, though it is, of course, possible that, had he lived, he would have made further alterations. The very varied order in which the cantos have been found is accounted for in two ways. In the first place, there is no doubt that they were not written in sequence, and, as each individual canto was finished, the poet, *more suo*, circulated it among his friends. When these fugitive pieces came to be collected, it was manifest that a different arrangement was required, and this may have been planned both by Petrarca and by the numerous friends to whom he had submitted his work, which would explain the great variety in the distribution. The titles of the *Trionfi* have also been matters of dispute, but Mestica (pp. xiii., xiv.) considers it probable that Petrarca gave them their Latin names. These do not appear in all the MSS.; sometimes they are only numbered, and sometimes the titles are given in Italian, when a certain diversity arises, *Triumphus Cupidinis* being rendered *Trionfo d'Amore*, and *Triumphus Pudicitiæ, Trionfo della Castità;* while the *Triumphus Æternitatis* appears sometimes as *Trionfo della Divinità* or *della Trinità*, thereby losing its signification as the pendant and contrast to the *Triumphus Temporis*.

Petrarca's six Triumphs of Love, Purity, Death, Fame, Time, and Eternity must be regarded as a single poem, for they are governed by one intention. Following in the footsteps of Dante, the idea in Petrarca's mind would seem to be to present, like him, in epic form a double allegory, capable both of a general and personal application. As Dante, while describing his own life and spiritual experiences, also stands forth as the symbol of mankind in general, set free from misery and led into blessedness, so Petrarca, in giving an idealised picture of his own history—his early studies, his passion for Laura, his struggles and wanderings, the effect of his Lady's example and the desolation caused by her death, his longings for fame and disillusionment concerning it, and his final conversion to God—wishes at the same time to present man in general, enslaved by passions in youth, liberated by grace, overtaken by death, living yet awhile in Fame which Time conquers, and finding his only rest in Eternity. But while Beatrice becomes Divine Philosophy, Laura is always the type of ideal Womanhood. Petrarca's poem, in spite of its universal applicability, remains absolutely subjective. The purpose of each Triumph is to relate the impression produced upon the poet's heart and mind, and the references to personal experience are minute and subtle. It is this which lends the chief interest to this sequence of events, set forth, as it is, in lines of very unequal merit, and certainly lacking the spontaneous sweetness of the *Canzoniere*. But though the descriptions are often laboured and lengthy, they in no wise produce the impression that the poet is writing for effect: on the contrary, we get a poignant impression of reality, such as we hardly find in the earlier work, and from time to time the real man reveals himself more vividly than he has ever done elsewhere.

The very name and conception of a Triumph would have had a singular attraction for a mind imbued with classical and historical associations; but the idea in poetry was no new thing. Already Jacopo (or possibly Piero) di Dante had written the *Trionfo della Morte*, and Boccaccio in his *Amorosa Visione* had introduced five Triumphs of Wisdom, Glory, Riches, Love, and Fortune. It is possible that Petrarca borrowed something from this work, which is earlier in date than the *Trionfi*, as there is a marked resemblance between the two; yet, as he had never read the *Decameron* till the year before his death, he may have been equally ignorant of the *Visione*. A more probable source of inspiration lies in the *Divinæ Institutiones* of Lactantius, where the following passage occurs:—

"It was not without humour that a certain poet wrote of the triumph of Cupid: in which book he not only represented Cupid as the most powerful of the gods, but also as their conqueror. For having enumerated the loves of each, by which they had come into the power and dominion of Cupid, he sets in array a procession, in which Jupiter, with the other gods, is led in chains before the chariot of him, celebrating a triumph. This is elegantly pictured by the poet, but is not far removed from the truth. For he who is without virtue, who is overpowered by desire and wicked lusts, is not (as the poet feigned) in subjection to Cupid, but to everlasting death." [1]

In the springtime, and on the memorable April 6, the anniversary of the day when his Lady was first shown to him, and when, too, death deprived him of her, Love leads the poet back to Vaucluse, *al chiuso loco*, and, overcome by sleep, a vision is vouchsafed to him. He sees passing before him a Triumph such as was bestowed upon a Roman conqueror. The victor, Cupid, is armed only with bow and arrows, and has on his shoulders vast myriad-coloured wings; he is seated upon a flaming chariot drawn by purple-winged steeds, far more white than snow, and around the car is an innumerable multitude of victims, some slain, some wounded, some captive. Now the poet looks round him to see if there is any one known to him, and one comes towards him saying: *This is the reward of love.* There have been many conjectures as to the personality of this figure; he is never named, but he declares himself to be a Tuscan and a friend of Petrarca's. Among the many names which have been suggested are those of Dante, Cino, Sennuccio, and Franceschino. It would be particularly interesting to think that Dante was intended, but there does not seem sufficient reason for this idea, as the speaker certainly implies some intimate knowledge of the poet in early youth. Also, the fact that Petrarca sees all these, a little later in the vision, walking in a green meadow, seems out of harmony with the notion that he had already been

[1] *Divin. Instit.* i. 26, Dr. Fletcher's translation.

addressed and guided by one of them. Another suggestion has been that his brother, Gherardo, was intended, but Gherardo's being the younger is a great difficulty, nor is it very likely that Petrarca would have placed the Carthusian among the band of Love's captives. Francesco Nelli is another candidate, but, as his friendship with the poet only dates from 1350, this idea cannot seriously be entertained, and the same objection would, in some measure, apply to Boccaccio, whose personal acquaintance with Petrarca dates also from that year; but he had long known and admired his work, and may even have seen him at Naples as far back as 1341. Still, difficulties remain in their respective ages and mode of address: *figliuolo* and *padre* would have to be reversed.

Indeed, this matter of the date furnishes the only explanation of the strange fact that Boccaccio receives no mention in the *Trionfi*. That the poem was begun during Petrarca's last residence at Vaucluse (1351-1353), and was continually worked on until his death, are incontrovertible facts, but it is no less true that it was conceived as a vision culminating in the year of Laura's death. That the poet wished to preserve the unity of time is certain from his constant rearrangement of the separate cantos, and his discarding those portions which seemed to interfere with such a plan. Boccaccio's friendship was no part of the history of that time, and hence it is likely that Petrarca would not give him a place in it. Two other names deserve some consideration. Guido Settimo, the friend of earliest times, sharer of school-days and holidays and of the student-life at Montpellier and Bologna, was a constant companion and correspondent; and that he is the person meant gains some colour from the fact that Petrarca was probably staying with him at the time when he began the *Trionfi*. Guido was not a Tuscan by birth, but Petrarca sometimes uses this epithet loosely for Italian. But the most likely solution, on the whole, seems to be that Convenevole was intended. He was the poet's earliest master, and loved him above all his other pupils; he must have known his character and capabilities, and no doubt formed high expectations of him, and though in no sense an heroic figure, yet, as scholar and poet, Petrarca must have owed much to him, and it would not be unlikely that he should choose this manner of acknowledging his debt.[1]

The figure, whoever he may be, fulfils the office of a guide and an interpreter, and exclaiming: "Oh, what a flame is lit for thee, my son!" continues:—

> Lo! this is he whom the world calleth Love,
> A bitter lord as thou shalt clearly see,
> When he shall rule o'er thee as now o'er us.
> . . . . .
> Some doth he slay, some, neath more grievous laws,
> Untimely lead a life of bitter days
> Under a thousand chains and thousand keys.[2]

Then the procession of prisoners passes; first come the Roman emperors, then the Greek heroes, and the pagan gods and goddesses—

> And laden with innumerable chains
> Great Jove himself is harnessed to the car.[3]

---

[1] Cf. In *Rassegna Bibliografica della Letteratura Italiana*, Pisa, 1905, vol. xiii.; Francesco Lo Parco, *L'Amico duce del Petrarca nel Trionfo d'Amore*. Also Carl Appel, *Zur Entwickelung Italienische Dichtungen Petrarcas*.

[2] " O figliuol mio, qual per te fiamma è accesa!
. . . . .
Questi è colui che 'l mondo chiama Amore:
Amaro, come vedi, e vedrai meglio
Quando fia tuo, com' è nostro signore.
. . . . .
Qual è morto da lui, qual con più gravi
Leggi mena sua vita aspra ed acerba
Sotto mille catene e mille chiavi."
*Triumphus Cupidinis*, i. 76-78, 85-87.

[3] " E di lacciuoli innumerabil' carco
Ven catenato Giove innançi al carro."
*Ibid.* 159, 160.

More heroes and heroines pass along, and Jacob, and David, and others mentioned in the Scriptures; then come the knights and ladies of the Arthurian legends, Lancelot and Tristram, Guinevere and Iseult, and following them Francesca and her lover. This part of the pageant would seem to represent Petrarca's early studies and reading before Laura had dawned upon his life. Now she appears:—

> Purer by far than is a snow-white dove.
> She took me captive; I, who would have sworn
>   To guard myself against a man full-armed,
>   By words and gestures now was straitly bound.
>
>         .   .   .   .   .
>
> And blind and deaf to every other joy,
>   Along such perilous paths I followed her
>   That still I tremble when I think thereon.
> Since then with tearful eyes that seek the ground
>   And thoughtful heart, I use to dwell alone,
>   Mid streams and fountains, rocks, and woods, and hills.
>
>         .   .   .   .   .
>
> From then till now I know what things are done
>   Within Love's cell, and how one hopes and fears;
>   Can any read, 'tis writ upon my brow.[1]

---

[1] "Pura assai più che candida colomba.
Ella mi prese; ed io ch' avrei giurato
  Difendermi d'un uom coverto d'arme,
  Con parole e con cenni fui legato.

         .   .   .   .   .

Ad ogni altro piacer cieco era e sordo,
  Seguendo lei per sì dubbiosi passi
  Ch' i' tremo ancor, qualor me ne ricordo.
Da quel tempo ebbi gli occhi humidi, e bassi,
  E 'l cor pensoso, e solitario albergo
  Fonti, fiumi, montagne, boschi e sassi.

         .   .   .   .   .

Da indi in qua so chi si fa nel chiostro
  D'Amore, e che si teme, e che si spera,
  E, chi sa legger, ne la fronte il mostro."
        *Triumphus Cupidinis*, ii. 90-93, 109-120.

He complains that he is bound, while his lady is free, and then consoles himself with the thought that this is the universal law of Love, and is as old as the world. He reckons up all the knowledge that he has gained from Love; he knows now how the heart can make peace and war, and hide her own wounds; he has learnt that the snake is hidden among the flowers; he lives upon long sighs and brief laughter, and can deceive himself a thousand times a day. He knows how Love strikes and flies away, and how empty are his promises. This is the most complete description of the lover of the first part of the *Canzoniere;* almost every line might be illustrated by a sonnet; nowhere are the torments and passions of Love set forth with more fidelity.

From henceforth, then, he is deprived of liberty; he, too, must be led as a captive in the van of Love's triumphal car. But before the nerves of liberty are cut, he looks round him once again to see if he can recognise any of the famous ones of ancient or modern times, and beholds a group of great lovers and poets. Here are Orpheus and Anacreon, Virgil, Catullus, Sappho, and many others. Gazing still more intently, he sees a band of people wandering in a green meadow, talking of Love. Here is Dante with Beatrice, Cino with Selvaggia; here are the first Bolognese singers and their Sicilian predecessors, together with the earliest singers of the *dolce stil nuovo*. With them is a long line of Troubadours, headed by Arnaut Daniel, " the great master of love," and here Francesco immortalises his own chosen friends.[1] All these, it would seem, are Love's votaries, and not his slaves, and Petrarca's place is not with these. His destiny it is to follow the sound of the purple pinions, and to be dragged in chains across forests and mountains, over a thousand obstacles till the home of Venus is reached, the island of Cyprus. It is a very lotus-land to which he has come, and, in the picture that he draws of its seductions and their effects, we cannot but recognise the snares that en-

[1] *Triumphus Cupidinis*, iii. 29-81.

# THE CROWN OF VIOLETS

trapped him, the dangers to which he fell a victim, the wanderings and confusions, which, on his own confession, made up his life until his fortieth year:—

> I saw unto what servitude, what death,
> What torture goes the man whom love ensnares.
>  .      .      .      .      .
> In such a dark and narrow prison cell
> Was I enclosed . . .
> But all the while, dreaming of liberty,
> My soul, made light and quick by great desire,
> I comforted by looking on past things.[1]

This may be taken as an indication of the part Petrarca's classical studies played in his life-history. The *Africa* had no slight influence on his career; it always claimed a large part of his time and devotion. There was another canto of this Triumph, sometimes placed second, and sometimes third, but now omitted in accordance with Petrarca's own final desire. In it the poet speaks with Masinissa and Sophonisba, and by some this has been considered one of the finest passages; it is, at any rate, interesting as linking Petrarca's love of ancient history and of his own special hero, Scipio, with the years he spent in Love's prison, and it makes the introduction of Scipio in the second Triumph a little less irrelevant and surprising.

The Triumph of Purity, besides its obvious meaning that grace and virtue deliver man from the slavery of his passions, and besides showing forth that Laura, by her purity and goodness, triumphed over the unworthy side of her

[1] " E vidi a qual servaggio, ed a qual morte,
A quale stratio va chi s'innamora.
   .      .      .      .      .
In così tenebrosa e stretta gabbia
Rinchiusi fumo . . .
E'ntanto, pur sognando libertate,
L'alma, chel gran disio fea pronta e leve,
Consolai col veder le cose andate."
*Ibid.* 137, 138, 156-163.

lover's devotion (as is amply borne out by passages in the *Secretum* and by many parts of the *Canzoniere*), seems to be thickly sown with allegorical reminiscences personal to the poet. In construction it may owe something to Giotto's fresco of Chastity, painted in one of the divisions of the vaulted roof over the high altar in the lower Church of Assisi; Cleanness of Heart and Fortitude are there shown presenting a neophyte with lance and shield, while Chastity, above in a tower, is praying, and two angels offer her a book and a palm. In the poem, Laura, in the strength of her transcendent purity and surrounded by a band of armed Virtues, conquers Love, and, aided by a troop of ladies, despoils him and plucks out his feathers. Lucretia stands on Laura's right hand, Penelope on the left; Virginia is there, and Judith, and many other valiant women. Among them, strangely enough, the poet has placed Piccarda, she who took the veil and whose fair purpose was frustrated by the violence of others. The loveliest figure in almost the loveliest canto of Dante's *Paradiso*, uttering words of the deepest significance, which have become part of the religious inheritance of the ages, we feel it a sacrilege for Petrarca to have brought her here; he should have left her in the lowest sphere, giving eternal testimony that " everywhere in heaven is Paradise." [1]

The Triumph now proceeds to Baiæ, passes by Cumæ, the ancient abode of the Sibyl, and by Linterno, famous as the retreat of Scipio. At this spot they meet the hero himself, and he accompaniès them to Rome, where the spoils are hung up in the temple of Pudicitia:—

> Here were displayed to view the glorious spoils
> By the fair conqueror: and here she laid
> Her sacred and victorious laurel-crown.[2]

---

[1] *Paradiso*, iii. 88, 89.
[2] " Ivi spiegò le gloriose spoglie
La bella vincitrice; ivi depose
Le sue victoriose e sacre foglie."
*Triumphus Pudicitiæ*, 184-186.

It cannot but be thought that, in this triumphal progress from Naples to Rome, the poet had some thought of his own coronation; in the preceding Triumph he had already mentioned—

> the glorious branch
> With which, too soon perhaps, I crowned my brows
> In memory of her I loved so well,[1]

and, if this were in his mind, it would be fitting that his great hero should head the company. But it is likely that more than one journey is here intended. It seems to be the normal experience of every one that whatever has very greatly appealed to him becomes a part of himself, and will inevitably be reproduced in speech or writing, in conduct or character. There are emotions and impressions from which we cannot free ourselves; they have cut into us and are bound to reappear some time or other. Now all Petrarca's journeys to Rome were in some sort pilgrimages; they had for him a moral significance, and Rome herself was a multiform allegory. He never approached her in other than a religious spirit. He worshipped her ancient greatness and those who had created it; the laurel that he coveted would have been bereft of half its significance if it had been bestowed upon him anywhere else. It is in Rome that he records a special struggle between religion and love:—

> The sacred aspect of your land hath riven
>     My heart for all the ill-spent past with woe,
>     Crying: Arise, poor wretch, what dost thou do?
>     And showing me the way to mount to heaven.
> But with this thought another one hath striven,

---

[1] " il glorioso ramo
Onde forse ançi tempo ornai le tempie
In memoria di quella ch' io tanto amo."
*Triumphus Cupidinis*, iii. 79-81.

> That says to me: Why wilt thou haste to go
> Since 'tis the time, as memory will show,
> When to behold our lady it is given.
>
> I, giving heed unto his argument,
> Am turned to ice within, as he might be
> To whom some sudden evil news is sent.
> Then doth the first displace the second thought.
> I know not which shall have the victory,
> But ofttimes to this hour the twain have fought.[1]

The identical journey of this Triumph is one that he made in all its details (only in the inverse order) in 1343, and of which he wrote a minute account to Cardinal Colonna;[2] he was then approaching his fortieth year, which we know was a turning-point with him, and it is not without importance that his visit to Rome during the Jubilee would seem to mark the final triumph of Purity in the poet's own life.[3]

The Triumph of Death contained at one time two cantos; the first only is now admitted, and there can be no doubt that the poem gains in dignity and unity by the omission of the second. Laura, surrounded by that chosen company

---

[1] " L'aspetto sacro de la terra vostra
   Mi fa del mal passato tragger guai
   Gridando:—Sta' su, misero: che fai?—
   E la via di salir al ciel mi mostra.
Ma con questo pensier un altro giostra,
   E dice a me—Perché fuggendo vai?
   Se ti rimembra, il tempo passa omai
   Di tornar a veder la donna nostra.—

I', che 'l suo ragionar intendo, allora
   M'agghiaccio dentro in guisa d'uom ch' ascolta
   Novella che di súbito l'accora.
Poi torna il primo, e questo dà la volta.
   Qual vincerà, non so; ma in fino ad ora
   Combattut' hanno, e non pur una volta."
                                   *Rime*, lxviii.

[2] *De Reb. Fam.* v. 4.    [3] *Rer. Sen.* viii. 1.

who had assisted at her triumph, crowned with roses and violets, returns on her victorious way and is confronted by a giantess robed in black, who accosts her with threatening words. So does Petrarca visualise the awful figure of the Black Death which was sweeping over the lands and claiming victims on every side.[1] He sees the whole country full of the dead:—

> Here too were those once reckoned fortunate,
>   Rulers were here, and popes, and emperors;
>   Now they are naked, destitute, and poor.
> Where are their riches now, their honours where?
>   Their jewels and their sceptres and their crowns?
>   Where are their mitres and their purple pomp?[2]

The poet moralises thus over the vanity of possession where all things must return to the ancient mother, and men's names shall hardly be had in remembrance; and then he turns from this thought to chronicle how, on the fatal sixth day of April, the last hour had come of " that brief, glorious life." Laura dies, surrounded and lamented by her friends, and, amid so much sighing and weeping, she alone is silent and glad:—

> She was not pale, but whiter than the snow
>   That falls untouched by wind upon the hill;

---

[1] It seems likely that Petrarca drew some inspiration for this description from the famous fresco of the Triumph of Death in the Campo Santo at Pisa, painted early in the fourteenth century by the brothers Lorenzetti. Death is there represented as a woman with wild streaming hair, and the mighty of the earth—kings, bishops, warriors—lie dead beneath her feet.

[2] " Ivi eran quei che fur detti felici:
   Pontefici, regnanti, imperadori;
   Or sono ignudi, miseri e mendici.
     U' sono or le richeçce?   U' son gli honori?
     E le gemme, e gli sceptri e le corone,
     E le mitre e li purpurei colori? "

*Triumphus Mortis*, 80-85.

So did she lie as though for weariness.
And when the spirit was from her gone forth
Then that which fools call death appeared to be
Like a sweet slumber on her beauteous eyes,
And death looked lovely in her lovely face.[1]

The rejected canto, *La notte che seguì*, is in no sense a Triumph, nor is it in harmony either with the foregoing canto or with the poem as a whole. It is quite manifestly of another phase of feeling, and was almost certainly a separate composition, written at a time when he could treat his grief in a plaintive, meditative manner, elaborating it and giving his fancy full play. Charming as a piece of writing, it was doubtless greatly admired by all to whom it was submitted; and for this reason was interpolated into the *Trionfi*, where it is wholly out of place and strikes a false note, which must have jarred on the poet and led him to exclude it. But, read as a poem apart, it has much grace, and throws light on Laura's relations with Petrarca, or, at any rate, on the manner in which he came to regard them.

The Triumph of Fame specially recalls the *Secretum* in reminding us of the two chains with which St. Augustine accused Petrarca of being bound.[2] This Triumph, divided into three cantos, seems to be the least inspired in the whole poem. Death, "pale, proud, and horrible," departs and gives place to her "who draws men from their graves and keeps them alive." This is Fame, who comes like the morning star, followed by a long procession of honourable

[1] " Pallida nò, ma più che neve bianca,
   Che sença venti in un bel colle fiocchi,
   Parea posar come persona stanca.
   Quasi un dolce dormir ne' suo' belli occhi,
   Sendo lo spirto già da lei diviso,
   Era quel che morir chiaman li sciocchi.
   Morte bella parea nel suo bel viso."
                                    *Triumphus Mortis*, 164-172.

[2] *Secretum*, iii.

## THE CROWN OF VIOLETS

people, among whom the poet recognises many of those who had been Love's captives. On her right hand are all those who had been great rulers and had won fame in battle; first come all the Roman heroes, headed by Julius Cæsar and Scipio, down to Romulus and the early kings of Rome; then the great warriors of other nations; after them, in a place apart, some of the Old Testament heroes, followed by the Amazons and other warlike women. After many kings and conquerors, Godfrey de Bouillon comes alone, giving Petrarca occasion for one of his passionate outbursts against the present generation of miserable Christians, who are content to leave the sepulchre of Christ in the hands of the infidel. Petrarca's enthusiasm for a Crusade is the point at which he most nearly touches St. Catherine of Siena.[1] Then two friends and patrons are commemorated:—

> And two I saw who went but yesternight
>    From this our state and out of this our land;
>    Who closed the number of this honoured throng:
> The good Sicilian king who fixed his aim
>    On lofty things and looked with Argus-eyes;
>    And on the other side my great Colonna,
> Gentle, high-souled, and firm, and liberal.[2]

The poet then hears a voice bidding him look on the left hand, since fame is not only acquired by force of arms.

---

[1] Cf. *Rime*, xxvii. and xxviii. with St. Catherine, *Epist.* 311, 312, 313, 314 (ed. Gigli), and E. G. Gardner, *St. Catherine of Siena*, pp. 138, 139, Appendix, letter i.

[2] " E vidi duo che si partir iersera
   Di questa nostra etate e del paese;
   Costor chiudean quella honorata schiera:
Il buon re cicilian che 'n alto intese
   E lunge vide e fu veramente Argo;
   Dall' altra parte il mio gran Colonnese,
Magnanimo, gentil, constante e largo."
                        *Triumphus Famæ*, ii. 157-163.

There, occupying the first place, he sees Plato, and after him comes Aristotle: this is an interesting example of Petrarca's own judgment, which led him to differ from Dante in assigning the precedence to Plato. Philosophers, poets, historians, follow in quick succession; none of them is minutely described or elaborated, and the list ends abruptly with the Stoics. The whole procession is depicted in such a spiritless manner that we can only feel that the chain of which Augustine spoke has been loosened, and that Petrarca is no longer fettered by it in any dangerous degree.

In the Triumph of Time there is far more actuality than in the preceding Triumph; the poet seems to be setting down, somewhat bitterly and reluctantly, the conclusions to which life has brought him. Dante deals with the same subject in the eleventh canto of the *Purgatorio* with fuller intelligence and without bitterness. Petrarca sees victorious Time fly onward leaving all behind him:—

> I saw the ice and close to it the rose.

> What is our mortal life more than a day?
>   Cloudy, and brief, and cold, and full of woe,
>   And nothing worth, though fair it may appear.

Those, too, who were famous in themselves, or whose writings had conferred fame on others, may not be spared by envious Time; their name too shall vanish:—

> A doubtful winter, an inconstant sky,
>   Such is your fame which a light mist obscures,
>   Great Time of great names is the great destroyer.
> Your triumphs and your glories fade away
>   And kingdoms also pass and sovereignty;
>   For Time doth shatter every mortal thing.

> On flying feet he whirls the earth with him,
>   Nor ever rests nor stays nor turns aside
>   Till he returns you to a little dust.

he più dun giorno e lauita mortale	Cosi fuggendo ilmondo seco uolue:
Nubile: breue: fredda: & pien dinoia:	Ne mai sipofa ne sarefta o torna
Che può bella parer: ma nulla uale.	In fin che ua condotti in poca peluc

*Triumphus Temporis*
*(Fifteenth Century Florentine Engraving.)*

Covetous Time wins and recaptures all;
   What men call Fame is but a second death,
   And, like the first, it knows no remedy.
Thus triumphs Time o'er names and o'er the world.[1]

Thus Love (or rather *Cupiditas,* Desire) conquers the world, Purity conquers Desire, Death conquers Purity, Fame triumphs over Death, and Time over Fame; the world with its joys, its treasures, and its wisdom has come to naught; the last and final Triumph must be the Triumph of Eternity.  This is how an English poet saw it:—

I saw Eternity the other night,
Like a great *Ring* of pure and endless light,
   All calm as it was bright;
And round beneath it, Time, in hours, days, years,
   Driv'n by the spheres,
Like a vast shadow mov'd, in which the world
   And all her train were hurl'd.[2]

---

[1] " I' vidi il ghiaccio, e lì stesso la rosa.

Che più d'un giorno è la vita mortale?
   Nubil' e brev' e freddo e pien di noia,
   Che pò bella parer, ma nulla vale.

Un dubbio hiberno, instabile sereno
   È vostra fama, e poca nebbia il rompe,
   E 'l gran tempo a' gran nomi è gran veneno.
Passan vostri triumphi e vostre pompe,
   Passan le signorie, passano i regni;
   Ogni cosa mortal Tempo interrompe.

Così, fuggendo, il monde seco volve,
   Nè mai si posa, nè s'arresta o torna,
   Fin che v' à ricondotti in poca polve.

Tutto vince e ritoglie il Tempo avaro;
   Chiamasi Fama, ed è morir secondo,
   Nè più che contra 'l primo è alcun riparo.
Così il Tempo triumpha i nomi e 'l mondo."
      *Triumphus Temporis,* 49, 61-63, 109-120, 142-145.
[2] Henry Vaughan, *The World.*

T

Not quite with Vaughan's simplicity and directness, Petrarca writes:—

> I seemed to see a world
> New, and eternal, and immovable;
> The sun and all the heaven with all its stars,
> The earth, too, and the sea were brought to naught,
> And were remade more joyful and more fair.
>     .     .     .     .     .     .
> To-morrow, yesterday, evening, and morn,
> And then and now, like shades shall pass away.
> No place be found for past or future things,
> Only the present is, to-day, and now,
> And all included in Eternity.[1]

It is characteristic of Petrarca to dwell on the dissolution of past and future into one perfect present. All through his life he has been at the mercy of shifting hopes and fears; remorse has shed darkness over the past, and haunting longings have embittered the future; restlessness has been the torment of his life: now the long struggle is over, and the victory is with God. All the jarring chords are resolved, and among the blessed ones he sees how Laura is the most blessed, among all the fair ones the fairest. For, to the end, Petrarca is only an earthly lover. Probably it is only a few, and they great saints, who reach the Divine immediately; most men have need of many stepping-

---

[1] " Veder mi parve un mondo
Novo, in etate immobile ed eterna,
E 'l sole e tutto 'l ciel disfar a tondo
Con le sue stelle, anchor la terra e 'l mare,
E rifarne un più bello e più giocondo.
    .     .     .     .     .     .
Diançi, adesso, ier, deman, matino e sera,
Tutti in un punto passeran com' ombra.
Non avrà loco fu, sarà ned era,
Ma è solo, in presente, ed ora, ed oggi,
E sola eternità raccolta e'ntera."
*Triumphus Æternitatis*, 20-24, 65-69.

stones, and to the larger number human love is the angel that prepares the way for Divine love. Human love spiritualised, as St. Catherine has told us in her *Dialogo*,[1] is at once a test and a witness, and, having received that testimony and applied that test, souls are empowered to mount higher: the beauty of the Divine shines forth so immanently that the human chains fall off. So it was with Dante when Beatrice had led him into Paradise. But no such unfettered heart was ever Petrarca's; his heaven is, as it ever was, in his lady's eyes. So even the Triumph of Eternity only ends with Laura, with a touching relation of his long fidelity and its certain reward:—

> Love for her sake in so long war engaged me
> That still my heart preserves the memory.
> O happy stone that hides her lovely face!
> And when she hath resumed her beauteous veil,
> If he were blest who saw her upon earth,
> What will it be in heaven again to see her.[2]

And this conclusion is rendered even more pathetic by what we know of its final revision. These last lines were written, as we learn from the poet's own marginal notes, at the very end of his life, in the February of 1374: *Explicit Dominica carnis privij* 12 *Febr.* 1374 *post cenam;* the last line standing:—

> Che porà essere a vederla in cielo?

---

[1] *Dialogo,* cap. cxliv.

[2] " Amor mi diè per lei sì lunga guerra
  Che la memoria anchora il cor accenna.
 Felice sasso che 'l bel viso serra!
  Che, poi che avrà ripreso il suo bel velo,
  Se fu beato chi la vide in terra,
 Or che fia dunque a rivederla in cielo! "
  *Triumphus Æternitatis,* 140-145.

Then, some time between that date and his death in the July of the same year, he substituted for this a more emphatic and triumphant conclusion:—

> Or che fia dunque a rivederla in cielo!

And, writing below this *Hoc placet*, he thus set the seal to his life's work.

## CHAPTER XI

### IN PETRARCA'S SCHOOL

" Hark yet again, like flute-notes mingling rare,
   Comes the keen sweetness of Petrarca's moan."
A. H. Hallam.

It is a happy thing that Italy cast her spell over the father of our poetry: from that moment a different genius presided over the evolution of English song. There is, indeed, good reason for believing that Chaucer and Petrarca had personal knowledge of each other, though it cannot be ascertained with certainty. Chaucer's own words:—

> I wol yow telle a tale which that I
> Lerned at Padowe of a worthy clerk,
> As preved by his wordes and his werk.
> He is now deed and nayled in his cheste,
> I prey to God so yeve his soule reste!
> Frannceys Petrark, the laureat poete,
> Highte this clerk, whos rethoryke sweete
> Enlumined al Itaille of poetrye,[1]

being put into the mouth of the Clerk cannot be regarded as strictly autobiographical, but the circumstances of the poet's life give ground for supposing that they were so. It is matter of history that he was sent to Italy by the king in the December of 1372, returning to London in the November of the following year, and that he visited Genoa, Pisa, and Florence. Of other travels there is no record, but, at a time when the whole country was ringing with the fame of Petrarca, we cannot suppose that his name was unknown to

---
[1] The Canterbury Tales, *The Clerk's Prologue.*

a brother-poet. That Chaucer should have left Italy without visiting her laureate would be almost incredible, but there is a further reason for believing that the interview really took place. The Clerk asserts of his tale that he learned it at Padowe: now Arquà had been Petrarca's place of residence since 1370, but in the year 1373, owing to the unsettled state of the country, he had moved into Padua, and his residence there synchronises with Chaucer's sojourn in Italy.

To establish the material intercourse, so to speak, between these great men is not without interest, but the study of Chaucer's works supplies an incontestable proof of the " meeting of true minds," which is far more essential. Indeed, Chaucer's debt to the great Tuscans—Dante, Petrarca, and Boccaccio—is incalculable. To his unending praise be it spoken, it was Dante who had the greatest influence over him, who extorted his fullest admiration, waked the clearest echoes in his heart, and left the profoundest traces on his work. But, born story-teller as he was, probably the genius of Boccaccio was nearest akin to his. And here we come to another puzzling feature in the life and writings of Chaucer, that he nowhere makes mention of the author of the *Decameron* from whom he borrowed so largely, unless his personality is hidden, as is generally supposed, under the name of Lollius, twice referred to by Chaucer, in his *Troilus and Criseyde*,[1] as the orginal author of the story which is founded on Boccaccio's *Filostrato*. The first reference, however, is to a sonnet of Petrarca's, *S'amor non è, che dunque è quel ch' io sento*.[2] On this Professor Lounsbury[3] has based a curious theory, that Chaucer, though familiar with many of Boccaccio's writings, believed them to be Petrarca's. This view he points out would eliminate certain difficulties, namely, the total omission of

[1] *Troilus and Criseyde*, book i. line 394; book ii. lines 14-20.
[2] *Rime*, cxxxii.
[3] J. R. Lounsbury, *Studies in Chaucer*, vol. ii. pp. 224 ff.

Boccaccio's name, the "Lollius" in *Troilus and Criseyde*, the reference to Petrarca as the author of Cenobia in the *Monke's Tale*, which is really taken from Boccaccio's *De Claris Mulieribus*, and the epithet "maister"[1] in the same poem, since Boccaccio was far more truly his master than Petrarca. Yet it would not account for Lollius, or explain the strange fact that Chaucer should not have heard of Boccaccio, when, at the very time of the English poet's sojourn in Florence, the chair of Dante had just been established at the university, and Boccaccio, who was then living at Certaldo, had been chosen to fill it.

As the first lecture was delivered on October 23, 1373, Chaucer could hardly have been present, for he was back in England on November 22, but he could scarcely have failed to hear of the chair and the lecturer. Furthermore, this theory would surely deprive us of the right to believe that Chaucer and Petrarca met, and that the former heard the story of Griselda from the laureate's lips, for Petrarca must have told that Boccaccio was the author and himself only the translator. Rather than part with this pious belief, we would sooner suffer all the riddles to be left unread, and let Lollius remain what Professor Lounsbury calls him—"the Junius of English poetry."[2]

Chaucer's debt to Boccaccio is chiefly to his Italian poetry and his Latin works; it is even possible that he was not acquainted with the *Decameron*, as the subject-matter of many of the stories was common property, and he may have derived them from various sources. Even Petrarca, as we have seen, had never read the volume until the June

---

[1] *The Monke's Tale*, 3515, 3516.

[2] *Op. cit.* p. 41. Dr. R. G. Latham, in a letter in the *Athenæum*, October 3, 1868, says that it is his opinion that "in the beginning of the Second Epistle of the First Book of Horace we find the germ of the subsequent confusion. Horace is writing to his friend *Lollius about the writer of the Trojan War*, meaning *Homer*. . . . I submit that by the time of Chaucer the name of the person thus addressed had become attached to the person written about."

of 1373,[1] when, attracted by the story of the patient Griselda, he made a free Latin translation of it, to which we are indebted for Chaucer's version. It is in the story told by the Clerk in *The Canterbury Tales*, and in the song of Troilus:—

> If no love is, O God, what fele I so [2]

(three stanzas which are a translation and amplification of *Rime* cxxxii.), that the direct influence of Petrarca is chiefly to be detected. Widely different in character and in their outlook on life, we should look in vain for any marked analogy in the writings of the two poets. The Englishman is more robust, more natural, more joyous; he has not the Italian's deep vein of sentiment, nor his inherent gracefulness: Chaucer has a grace of his own, but it is of quite a different order from Petrarca's. But the debt of English poetry to Italy was of no narrow and individual kind; it was a spiritual endowment of greater insight and greater breadth of view, and an emancipation from an insufficient vocabulary and an exhausted line of thought; it was the appreciation of form, the sense of taste, and the birth of the critical faculty.

Chaucer never attempted a sonnet, nor did he ever write a true canzone, but his hymn to the Blessed Virgin, called *An A. B. C*, and mainly a free translation from Guillaume de Deguileville's *Pèlerinage de la Vie*, approaches nearer to a canzone than anything that had yet been found in English poetry, or was to be found again for a century and a half. Nobler and more devotional than the French original, it reminds us more than once of Petrarca's invocation—

> Vergine bella che di sol vestita,[3]

though, as the date of Chaucer's poem is uncertain, and

[1] *Rer. Sen.* xvii. 3.  [2] Book i. line 400.  [3] *Rime*, ccclxvi.

Petrarca's is known to be one of his latest works, it cannot be decided whether the resemblances are real or accidental. Of another poem, the *Compleint to his Lady*, the opening stanzas recall Petrarca's sestina—

A qualunque animale alberga in terra,[1]

which was to be produced later in sonnet form by Wyatt and Surrey. Professor Skeat rightly calls the *Compleint* a succession of metrical experiments. The first two stanzas correspond to those of the sestina, and then follow two fragments in *terza rima*, unique in English literature until the sixteenth century. But while the genius of Chaucer assimilated the idea of the values of music and metre, it is to be noted that his immediate successors fell further and further behind their master, becoming ever more rough, more careless, and less musical. The Petrarchan tradition, in so far as it was a poetical one, seemed to be lost; to Skelton and the rest he was a " famous clerk "[2] and naught else.

Turning to the history of poetry in Italy, we see that for a time Petrarca won his fame as he would have desired to do. He was the pioneer of classicism, reviving the classical taste, and leading men back to the well-springs of great literature. He inaugurated that severely classical movement which was faithfully carried on by his immediate disciples and successors, Coluccio Salutati and Luigi Marsili, and further developed by Niccolò Niccoli, Lionardo Bruni, Carlo Marsuppini, Poggio Bracciolini, and Palla Strozzi, preserving an unbroken tradition down to the time of Ficino and the neo-Platonist school; and, meanwhile, as an original poet he was comparatively little regarded. But he who had heralded the dawn of the early Renaissance had his resurrection in the Renaissance proper, when men, turning their attention to the Italian tongue and resolving to use it

[1] *Rime*, xxii.   [2] Skelton, *Garlande of Laurell*.

in its very purest form, reverted, with a common instinct, to Petrarca, hailing him as their guide and model, even to the extent of refusing to make use of any word that could not be found in his writings. In this way did Petrarca the poet gradually supersede Petrarca the humanist, and it should be our object to do him justice in both capacities and to award him a double crown.

The sixteenth century in Italy, in France, and in England is marked by the great Petrarchan revival. In the former country, guided by Bembo, an immense group of Petrarchists arose, of whom Jacopo Sannazaro, Luigi Alamanni, Annibale Caro, Francesco Molza, Giovanni della Casa, and Gaspara Stampa were among the most important. The French school we shall have occasion to notice later. In our own land, although it might seem that the torch lighted by Chaucer had well-nigh flickered out, yet, indeed, Italian influence had never decayed. A constant stream of English scholars were always travelling to Italy; many were so attracted by what they found that they made their home there, while others returned to enrich England, and notably Oxford, with the fruits of their knowledge. Humphrey, Duke of Gloucester, deserves honourable mention for having fostered learning, and for having welcomed Italian scholars who came to England in search of manuscripts: he also formed a library, which he presented to Balliol College, and Petrarca's works are to be found among the volumes. There was also a copy of them in the library at Peterhouse in 1426. The fifteenth century may thus be regarded as the seed time that was to bring forth the abundant harvest of the succeeding age. For, in the sixteenth century, the love of all things Italian became a veritable passion: Italian art, music, manners, language, and finally letters, became the first necessities of gentle life, and poetry awaked from her long sleep to breathe forth Italian melody through the lips of Wyatt and Surrey.

The Petrarchan influence is nowhere more visible than in

these two poets. Puttenham, in his *Arte of English Poesie*, says: " In the latter end of the same king's raigne (Henry VIII.) sprong up a new company of courtly makers, of whom Sir Thomas Wyat, the elder, and Henry Earle of Surrey were the chieftaines, who having travailed into Italie and there tasted the sweete and stately measures of the Italian Poesie as novices newly crept out of the schooles of Dante, Arioste, and Petrarch, they greatly pollished our rude and homely manner of vulgar Poesie, from that it had bene before, and for that cause may justly be sayd the first reformers of our English meetre and stile." And again: " Henry Earle of Surrey and Sir Thomas Wyat, betweene whom I finde very little difference, I repute them (as before) for the two chief lanternes of light to all others that have since employed their pennes upon English Poesie; their conceits were lofty, their stiles stately, their meetre sweete and well proportioned, in all imitating very naturally and studiously their Maister Francis Petrarcha."[1]

Friends and companions, Wyatt and Surrey are always spoken of together, and it is difficult to dissociate their work, though, indeed, it has marked differences. Surrey is the smoother and the more successful poet, but to the older man belongs the glory of the pioneer; also Wyatt was the more original thinker, and yet, hampered and often defeated by difficulties of form and expression, he was the more servile imitator of the two. The greater number of his thirty-eight sonnets are either direct translations from Petrarca, or else very obvious imitations, while one sonnet—

My hart I gave thee, not to do it pain,[2]

is made up of two strambotti of Serafino dell' Aquila,[3] on whom many of the shorter pieces are modelled; and one satire in *terza rima* is a free translation from Luigi Alamanni.

[1] Puttenham, *Arte of English Poesie*, lib. i. cap. 31.
[2] Cf. Tottel's *Miscellany*, p. 71.
[3] *El cor ti diedi* and *La donna di natura*. Opere. Strambotti.

Born in 1503, Sir Thomas Wyatt was educated at Cambridge, where he no doubt began his Italian studies, and subsequently perfected them by travelling in Italy when the rage for Petrarchism was at its height. Every one used to carry about a pocket edition of the *Canzoniere*, and a hundred and seventy-seven editions of Petrarca's poems are said to have been published in the sixteenth century.[1] No one of his contemporaries or successors owes more to the Italians; none is so steeped in Petrarca, none borrows more from him so directly, or imitates him so continuously. There he had a hard task to perform. The English tongue was still singularly rough and undeveloped, without any settled rhythmical system, and full of Gallicisms which it was the poet's aim to root out. Following the Petrarchan tradition, Wyatt adopted a definite metrical structure, but, plunging boldly into sonnet-writing, the rudeness of the language was often too much for him, and the result is that the roughness of his metre often obscures the beauty of the thought, while it also happens that the exigencies of rhyme sometimes hamper the thought's expression. That he had a wonderfully musical ear many of his poems attest, and notably his most pathetic invocation to his lute:—

> My lute awake, performe the last;[2]

but as a translator he specially commands our admiration; he is undertaking to transfer the expression and idiom of a singularly rich language into one which was as yet rough-hewn, while, at the same time, his own thought is too vigorous to be a mere tool. For instance, in—

> My galley charged with forgetfulnesse,[3]

which is a very literal translation of Petrarca's clxxxix., in one line he has bettered the original:—

> The starres be hidde that leade me to this payne;

---

[1] Cf. C. Segré, *Studi Petrarcheschi*, pp. 297-299.
[2] Cf. Tottel's *Miscellany*, p. 64.  [3] *Ibid.* p. 39.

while—
> The piller perisht is whereto I lent [1]

follows Petrarca's cclxix. closely until the last three lines, which are replaced by a sharp cry of self-reproach, supposed to have reference to the death of Cromwell, for whose fall Wyatt felt himself in some sort to blame. Perhaps the most literal, and one of the most effective, translations is of Petrarca's ccxxiv., which will also serve as a good example of Wyatt's style:—

> If amourous fayth, or if an hart unfained
> A swete languor, a great lovely desire:
> If honest will, kindled in gentle fire:
> If long errour in a blinde mase chained,
> If in my visage ech thought distayned,
> Or if my sparkelyng voyce, lower, or hier,
> Which fear and shame so wofully doth tyre:
> If pale colour, which love alas hath stayned:
> If to have another then my self more dere,
> If wailyng or sighyng continually,
> With sorowful anger fedyng busily,
> If burnyng a farre of and fresyng nere,
> Are cause that I by love my selfe destroy:
> Yours is the fault, and mine the great annoy; [2]

and the first sestina (xxii.) is rather charmingly echoed in—

> Some fowles there be that have so perfit sight. [3]

As regards the sonnet form, it must be noted that Wyatt rarely attains the metrical arrangement, and still less frequently grasps the idea, of the Petrarchan sonnet. The structure of the Italian model is simple. The sonnet must consist of fourteen decasyllabic lines, divided into an octave and a sestet. The octave consists of two quatrains which follow a prescribed rhymical arrangement:—

A–B–B–A–A–B–B–A.

---

[1] Cf. Tottel's *Miscellany*, p. 72.   [2] *Ibid.* p. 70.   [3] *Ibid.* p. 38.

The sestet consists of two tercets, in which there can be either three rhymes or two, and there is endless variety in the arrangement of them, but the use of a rhymed couplet at the close of the sonnet is comparatively rare in Italian literature. Petrarca's favourite disposition of the sestet is—

or—
C-D-E-C-D-E

C-D-C-D-C-D.

Only four of his sonnets end in a rhyming couplet.

But the idea of the sonnet is a far more difficult thing to grasp, and has constantly eluded our best writers. The narrow limits of the sonnet are fitted to contain one thought. In the octave this thought has to be presented, developed, elaborated; in the sestet it has to be summed up and concluded: but in the true Italian spirit it is not to come to a crisis, to be wound up to an abrupt finish, as in the rhyming couplet; it is rather to be resolved into a clear and harmonious conclusion. This definiteness of idea we may look for in vain in the work of Wyatt, and it is less to be wondered at, inasmuch as, in his struggle to use an unfamiliar instrument, he would not do anything to increase the difficulty. His use of the rhyming couplet is more surprising, but it may be accounted for by his familiarity with the work of Serafino dell' Aquila, whose strambotti always end thus; and also by the inherent lack of sensitiveness in the English ear.

But it was not only sonnets for which our poet was indebted to Petrarca; three of the canzoni are also reproduced. The most literal of the three is the " Complaint upon Love to Reason, with Love's answer." [1] It is written in Chaucer's " rithme royall," and it is a fairly accurate translation of Petrarca's ccclx., though missing much of the grace of the original, especially in the second part, where Love's beautiful answer—

---
[1] Cf. Tottel's *Miscellany*, p. 46.

> Io no, ma' chi per sé la volse,

is inexplicably given—

> Not I, but price: more worth than thou (quod he),

a rendering so far from the text as to suggest that the translator had not understood it.

> Perdy I sayd it not[1]

is an extremely skilful paraphrase of Petrarca's ccvi., not keeping very close to the model except in the conclusion:—

> For Rachel have I served,
> For Lea cared I never:
> And her I have reserved
> Within my hart for ever.

Petrarca's early canzone (xxxvii.)—

> Sí è debile il filo a cui s'attene,

is very loosely translated in a measure of Wyatt's own invention, which consists of a series of rhyming couplets, the first an Alexandrine, and the second a longer line of fourteen syllables and seven accents, to which Gascoigne gave the name of Poulter's measure.[2] Some of this translation is very graceful:—

> The life so short, so fraile, that mortall men live here:
> So great a weight, so heavy charge the bodies that we bere:
> That, when I think upon the distaunce and the space,
> That doth so farre devide me from my dere desired face,
> I know not, how tattain the winges, that I require,
> To lift me up, that I might flie, to folow my desyre.

---
[1] Cf. Tottel's *Miscellany*, p. 66.
[2] *Certayne Notes of Instruction concerning the making of Verse or Ryme in English.*

> Thus of that hope that doth my life somethyng sustayne,
> Alas! I feare, and partly fele: full litle doth remain.
> Eche place doth bring me griefe: where I do not behold
> Those lively eyes: which of my thoughts were wont ye keys to hold.

This is sufficiently Petrarchan, but the concluding lines furnish another instance of the fact that English thought had not yet grown her wings. Petrarca wrote:—

> Canzon, s' al dolce loco
>   La donna nostra vedi,
>   Credo ben che tu credi
>   Ch' ella ti porgerà la bella mano
>   Ond' io son sì lontano:
>   Non la toccar; ma reverente ai piedi
>   Le di' ch' io sarò là tosto ch' io possa,
>   O spirto ignudo od uom di carne e d'ossa;

which with Wyatt becomes:—

My song: thou shalt attain to finde that pleasant place:
Where she doth live, by whom I live: may chance to have this grace
When she hath red and sene the grief, wherein I serve:
Betwene her brestes she shall thee put: there shall she thee reserve:
Then tell her that I cumme: she shall me shortly see:
And if for waighte the body fayle, the soule shall to her flee.[1]

Wyatt, as we have said, was a pioneer, and such men may fairly be described as those who have the courage to make mistakes. Thought and intelligence were never wanting to him, but, in his struggle after a form and diction which were almost beyond his strength, we feel that his sense suffers, as does all poetry where the power of thought is greater than the power of expression. Browning wilfully courted this failure, and is already paying the penalty; but Wyatt's was one of those noble failures which proclaim

[1] Cf. Tottel's *Miscellany*, p. 73.

the hero. With painful labours he prepared the way for our great procession of poets, and, following close on his footsteps, Surrey was the first to reap an inherited glory. With less force and originality, it is difficult to think to what he would have attained without his forerunner, but, with the path in some sort made straight for him, he has given us very perfect work. He is a far less direct imitator of Petrarca than Wyatt, which is perhaps accounted for by the fact that he had never travelled in Italy, but no one in England, at that date, could escape Italian influence. Yet there is something in his genius which seems to be of native growth—an inherent love of nature, a breath of the spirit of Chaucer—which, amid all his Petrarchisms, makes him a distinctly national poet. He is pre-eminent for style; with more sweetness and facility than Wyatt, he would not allow himself any word but the right one, any term of expression that was harsh, or wanting in grace. To compass this end, he devised a new form of sonnet, arranging the fourteen lines in three quatraines, followed by a rhymed couplet, thus:—

A–B–A–B–C–D–C–D–E–F–E–F–G–G;

a form which remained popular for a long time, and was, of course, used by Shakespeare.

Surrey is rarely a direct translator: he imitates Petrarca, but more often he echoes him. He must have had a most intimate acquaintance with the *Canzoniere*, of which the images and way of thought are reproduced again and again. Surrey's Laura was the fair Geraldine, really Lady Elizabeth Fitzgerald, whose family was said to have been a branch of the Florentine Geraldi:—

> From Tuskane came my Ladies worthy race:
> Faire Florence was sometyme her auncient seate;[1]

---

[1] Cf. Tottel's *Miscellany*, p. 9.

and her lover celebrates her, bewails her, and complains, in the true Petrarchan fashion.

> Set me wheras the sunne doth parche the grene [1]

is a tolerably close translation of Petrarca's cxlv., and—

> I never sawe my Ladye laye apart [2]

of his canzone—

> Lassare il velo o per sole o per ombra.[3]

Again—

> Alas, so all thinges nowe doe holde their peace,[4]

with the fine line—

> Calme is the Sea, the waves worke lesse and lesse;

and—

> The soote season, that bud and blome furth bringes [5]

(the most Chaucerian of Surrey's sonnets), are a kind of paraphrase of Petrarca's clxiv. and cccx. There is one sonnet, Petrarca's cxl., which Wyatt and Surrey both attempted, and it is interesting to place these renderings side by side:—

| WYATT | SURREY |
|---|---|
| The longe love, that in my thought I harber, | Love that liveth, and reigneth in my thought, |
| And in my hart doth kepe his residence, | That built his seat within my captive brest, |
| Into my face preaseth with bold pretence, | Clad in the arms wherin with me he fought, |
| And there campeth, displaying his banner. | Oft in my face he doth his banner rest. |

---

[1] Cf. Tottel's *Miscellany*, p. 11.  [2] *Ibid.* p. 12.  [3] *Rime*, xi.
[4] Cf. Tottel's *Miscellany*, p. 10.  [5] *Ibid.* p. 4.

| WYATT | SURREY |
|---|---|
| She that me learns to love and to suffer, | She, that me taught to love, and suffer payne, |
| And willes that my trust, and lustes negligence | My doutfull hope and eke my hote desyre, |
| Be reined by reason, shame, and reverence, | With shamefast cloke to shadowe and refraine, |
| With his hardinesse takes displeasure. | Her smilyng grace converteth straight to yre. |
| Wherwith love to the hartes forest he fleeth, | And cowarde Love then to the hart apace |
| Leavyng his enterprise with paine and crye, | Taketh his flight, whereas he lurkes and plaines |
| And there him hideth and not appeareth. | His purpose lost, and dare not shewe his face. |
| What may I do? when my maister feareth, | For my lordes gilt thus faultlesse byde I paynes. |
| But in the field with him to live and dye, | Yet from my lorde shall not my foote remove, |
| For good is the life, endyng faithfully.[1] | Swete is his death that takes his end by love.[2] |

But these Petrarchan echoes are even more insistent in Surrey's canzoni, of which there are several; none of them is a translation or a paraphrase, but nearly all of them contain passages collected now from one poem, now from another. In the long piece in *terza rima*, beginning—

The sonne hath twise brought furth his tender grene,[3]

the first three stanzas of the sestina, *A qualunque animale*,[4] are substantially reproduced, and also several lines from the sonnet—

Solo e pensoso i più deserti campi ;[5]

while the influence of the canzone, *Di pensier in pensier*,[6] is

[1] Cf. Tottel's *Miscellany*, p. 33.   [2] *Ibid.* p. 8.   [3] *Ibid.* p. 3.
[4] *Rime*, xxii.   [5] *Rime*, xxxv.   [6] *Rime*, cxxix.

clearly to be felt. *A qualunque animale* is again recalled in Surrey's masterpiece written in Poulter's measure: "If care do cause men cry, why do not I complaine?"[1] which is also full of Petrarchan similes. Palgrave has said of this poem that it is "perhaps the most delicate song Surrey has left us of youthful melancholy, of high-bred reverie, almost persuading me that the passion was truly felt as well as truly painted."[2] Finally—

Suche waiward waies hath love, that most part in discord,[3]

draws largely on Petrarca's *Triumphus Cupidinis*, ii., from which whole lines are borrowed.[4]

In this connection it is interesting to note that Lord Berners, who is said to have made the earliest translations of Petrarca's sonnets, and Henry Parker, Baron Morley, who translated the *Trionfi* in 1554, were both connections of the House of Howard. The poems of Wyatt and Surrey were first published in Tottel's *Miscellany* in June 1557, when Wyatt had been dead fourteen and Surrey two years. The rest of the collection consists of poems by Nicholas Grimald, and over one hundred pieces of uncertain authors, of whom some are known to have been Lord Vaux, Edward Somerset, and John Heywood. Nearly all show traces of Petrarca's influence, and there are two direct tributes to him in sonnets, one of which begins:—

With Petrarke to compare there may no wight,
Nor yet attain unto so high a stile;

and the other runs thus:—

O Petrarke, hed and prince of Poets all,
Whose lively gift of flowyng eloquence,

---

[1] Cf. Tottel's *Miscellany*, p. 220.
[2] F. T. Palgrave, *Essay on the Minor Poems of Spenser*, Grosart's edition, vol. iv.
[3] Tottel's *Miscellany*, p. 6.   [4] *Triumphus Cupidinis*, ii. 1150 to end.

> Well may we seke, but finde not how or whence
> So rare a gift with thee did rise and fall,
> Peace to thy bones, and glory immortall
> Be to thy name and to her excellence,
> Whose beauty lighted in thy time and sence
> So to be set forth as none other shall.
> Why hath not our pens rimes so perfit wrought,
> Ne why our time forth bringeth beauty such
> To trye our wittes as golde is by the touche,
> If to the stile the matter aided ought?
> But ther was never Laura more then one,
> And her had Petrarke for his paragone.[1]

Although—

> Sweete Surrey suckt Parnassus springs
> And Wiat wrote of wondrous things,

there was to be an arid season: nearly a quarter of a century was to pass before the full flood of Petrarchan influence was to be felt, and then, strangely enough, it was from France that the fresh wave of song visited our shores. Under Charles VIII., Louis XII., and Francis I., the French had traversed Italy from end to end, and, with their quick intuition and gift of discernment, they began to assimilate something of the culture around them. French monarchs coveted the artistic and intellectual wealth of Italy, decoying painters and architects to France, and offering a welcome to Italian courtiers and *literati*, and a shelter to all who needed it. The constant intercourse which was necessitated by diplomatic relations, and the residence of such men as Luigi Alamanni at the French court owing to political troubles at home, must have been no small factor in the spread of Italian influences. Melin de Saint-Gelais (1487-1558), who had studied law for several years at Bologna and Padua, was saturated with the Petrarchan spirit. It has been

[1] Cf. Tottel's *Miscellany*, p. 178.

disputed whether he or Clément Marot (1497-1544) first introduced the sonnet into France, though it is now generally agreed that the honour belongs to Marot, who also translated six sonnets and one canzone from Petrarca.[1] But it was that brilliant constellation the Pléiade, that, by raising a standard of taste and defining the laws of composition, brought into being a noted school of poetry. Ronsard (1524-1585), the favourite poet of Mary Queen of Scots, may be called the head of the school; Du Bellay, by his manifesto, *Défence et illustration de la langue française*, was its voice. To Pontus de Thyard is due the first French sestina. These men and their companions had all travelled in Italy, they knew Petrarca by heart, and they had no ambition but to reproduce his spirit and his art, inspired by a heart-whole devotion. Of him Du Bellay said, praising his grace and sincerity: " Pour le sonnet donc tu as Petrarque . . . sonne moy ces beaux sonnets, non moins docte que plaisante invention italienne."[2] Such an outpouring of literature could not but have a far-reaching effect, and indeed the second revival of Italian poetry in England was inaugurated by the study and translation of the French Petrarchists. The one poetic link between Wyatt and Surrey and the Elizabethans is the figure of George Gascoigne. Not a great poet, he was yet an interesting writer. He called himself—

Chaucer's boye, and Petrark's jorneyman,[3]

and in his Posies, published in 1575, of which the title is: *A hundred sundry Flowers bound up in one small Posy, gathered partly by translation in the fine Outlandish Gardens of Euripides, Ovid, Petrarch, Ariosto, and others*, he says:—

---

[1] Clément Marot, *Œuvres Complétes*, tome iii. pp. 146, 148.
[2] Du Bellay, *Défence et illustration de la langue française*, iime. partie, chapitre iv.
[3] *The Griefe of Joye*, a poem modelled, as Gascoigne tells us in the preface, on Petrarca's *De Remediis*.

If any verse doe passe on plesant feet
The praise thereof redownd to Petrark's lore.[1]

He also recalls his master in his poem *The Arraignment of a Lover*, in which, however, not Beauty but Reason is the judge.[2]

To Gascoigne we are also indebted for *Certayne Notes of Instruction concerning the making of Verse or Ryme in English*, which contains the excellent advice: " Do rather searche the bottome of your braynes for apte wordes, than chaunge good reason for rumbling rime "; and also gives the definition of a sonnet—not unneeded in an age when the word was to be so much abused. " Then have you sonets," he writes; " some are apte to thinke that all poemes being short may be called sonets . . . but yet I can beste allowe to call those sonets whiche are of fourteen lines, every line conteyning tenne syllables." A little later it had become so usual to call any kind of song a sonnet, that the cumbersome word *quatorzain* came into fashion.

The Elizabethan age was pre-eminently the age of the sonnet; it has been estimated that between the years 1591 and 1597 over two thousand sonnets appeared;[3] among the long list of authors the names of Sidney, Spenser, and Watson stand supreme. In order of time Watson's poems appeared first. His earliest published work (1582) was entitled the Ἑκατομπαθια or *Passionate Centurie of Love*, each poem being called a passion; for the most part the pieces are not sonnets, having eighteen lines each. Watson was a very honest plagiarist, for each line is prefaced by an explanation and an acknowledgment of the source from which it is taken or imitated. He is known to have travelled in France when young, and, from his elaborate confessions, we can see that he was very greatly indebted to the French school, and particularly to Ronsard; but though he did not

[1] *The Griefe of Joye.*
[2] George Gascoigne, *The Complete Poems*, 2 vols. 1869, vol. i. p. 36.
[3] Cf. Sidney Lee, Introduction to *Elizabethan Sonnets*.

go into Italy, he was well acquainted with the Italian language and the poets, old and new. He is said to have translated all Petrarca's sonnets into Latin, but of this great undertaking only a few specimens have been preserved, and we have them as Latin Passions in the 'Εκατομπαθια. The sonnet which is prefixed to the collection, and which is written by a friend and panegyrist of the author, says:—

> The starr's which did at Petrarch's byrthday raigne
> Were fixt againe at thy nativity,
> Destening thee the Thuscan's poesie,
> Who skald the skies in lofty quatorzain.

The preface to Passion v. says: " All this Passion (two verses only excepted) is wholly translated out of Petrarch, where he writeth *S'amor non è* "[1]*;* and that to vi.: " This Passion is a translation into Latine of the selfe same sonnet of Petrarch which you red lastly alleaged, and commeth somwhat nerer unto the Italian phrase then the English doth." Passion lxvi., he tells us, is borrowed from Petrarch's *Hor che 'l ciel,*[2] and xc. paraphrased from *Tennemi amor,*[3] while the last sonnet is an epilogue to the whole work: " and more like a praier than a Passion: and is faithfully translated out of Petrarch, where he beginneth: *I' vo piangendo i miei passati tempi,*[4] etc." [5]

Watson's next publication was *Italian Madrigals Englished* (1590), in which he translated Italian words which had been set to music. One of these madrigals is the octave of Petrarca's sonnet *Zefiro torna.*[6] This work is interesting as showing how the increasing taste for music tended still further to popularise Italian song. In a little work on music published in 1597, the author defines a madrigal as " a kind of musike made upon songs and sonnets such as Petrarke and menie Poets of our time have excelled

---
[1] *Rime,* cxxxii.  [2] *Rime,* clxiv.  [3] *Rime,* ccclxiv.
[4] *Rime,* ccclxv.  [5] Thomas Watson's *Poems,* Arber's Reprint.
[6] *Rime,* cccx.

in," and further says that " our countrymen will highly esteem whatsoever cometh from beyond the seas, and specially from Italy."[1] Watson's last work, *The Tears of Fancie*, was published the year after his death in 1593, and is a collection of genuine sonnets, in which Petrarca's influence is everywhere to be found: the spring-time sonnets specially recall him, and the sestina *A qualunque animale*, which seems to have attracted every English Petrarchist, was no less irresistible to him, and is reproduced in sonnet lii.:—

    Each creature ioyes Apollos happie light.

It is to be noted that nearly all Watson's sonnets follow Surrey's model.

Sir Philip Sidney's sonnets were not printed until 1591, four years after his death, but they had been already circulated among his friends. The very embodiment of Castiglione's *Cortegiano*, whatever was noble or beautiful of all lands had contributed to the fashioning of Sidney's mind and manners. Travelling through France to Italy, he had stayed some time in Venice, where he made the acquaintance of Tintoretto and Paolo Veronese, and had his portrait painted by the latter. He resided some time at Padua, where he studied philosophy and music, and then proceeded to Genoa, but was dissuaded from visiting Rome. Though Ronsard is obviously one of his masters, and the *Arcadia* was suggested by Sannazaro's work of the same name, and though he made no direct translations from Petrarca, Philip Sidney is more thoroughly Petrarchan than any other Elizabethan. His Stella is another Laura, the relations between the lovers are the same, and the whole scheme matches with the earlier portion of the *Canzoniere*, so that the author of *Astrophel and Stella* came to be spoken of as the " Petrarch of our time." But though

[1] Thomas Morley, *A Plain and Easy Introduction to Practical Music*, 1597.

in this sonnet-sequence he is a very Petrarchist, lacking originality, and most often recalling the Italian poet's host of imitators in their most fantastic moods, now and again he seems to get back to nature, and to remind us of Petrarca at his strongest and simplest. In one respect, Sidney follows him more faithfully than any other sonneteer of the time: he recurs to the Italian metrical arrangement, writing in very many instances—

A–B–B–A–A–B–B–A,

and, at any rate, rarely allowing himself more than two rhymes in the octave, while in the tercets he avoids the rhyming couplet in twenty-one sonnets.

Sidney's last sonnet is, beyond doubt, his most impressive one, in matter though not in metre:—

> **Leave me, O love, which reachest but to dust!**
>   And thou, my mind, aspire to higher things!
>   Grow rich in that which never taketh rust;
>   Whatever fades, but fading pleasure brings.
> Draw in thy beames, and humble all thy might
>   To that sweet yoke where lasting freedomes be;
>   Which breakes the clowdes, and opens forth the light
>   That doth both shine, and give us sight to see.
> O take fast hold! Let that light be thy guide
>   In this small course which birth drawes out to death:
>   And think how evill becommeth him to slide,
>   Who seeketh heav'n, and comes of heav'nly breath.
>     Then farewell, world! Thy uttermost I see!
>     Eternall Love, maintaine Thy life in me!

This is the appropriation of Petrarca's ultimate conclusions, but it is not, like the greater part of the *Astrophel* sonnets, an imitation which has filtered through hundreds of minds and been tortured into innumerable shapes, so that the thought has become emasculated before it ever reaches us.

It is, on the contrary, clear and resonant; like a strong reflection and not a far-off whispered echo. This keen breath of nature and reality is everywhere to seek in the mass of Elizabethan sonnets. It is hardly necessary here to dwell on the voluminous work of Daniel, Constable, Drayton, Barnes, and a host of others, since it is known that they drew their knowledge of Petrarca mainly from French sources. The production of a sonnet-sequence seemed to be required of every would-be poet, but there was little original about them — not even their ladies' names, which were persistently borrowed from French authors: thus Daniel's Delia had a prototype in the *Délie* of Maurice de Sève, and Drayton's Idea was borrowed from *L'Idée* of Claude de Pontoux.[1]

Passing then to Spenser, we find that it is in him that the Petrarchan influence is seen at its widest and fullest; though in his case, also, it is probable that France led the way to Italy, for the earliest poetical compositions of his that we know of were entitled *The Visions of Bellay* and *The Visions of Petrarch*, and appeared in 1569, in a miscellany called a *Theatre for Worldlings*, compiled by a refugee Flemish physician, one John van der Noodt. The fact that these were reproduced with slight alterations in 1591, in a volume of Spenser's poems published with his consent, establishes the certainty of their authorship. Now the collection of sonnets called the *Visions of Petrarch* is really a translation of the canzone—

Standomi un giorno solo a la fenestra,[2]

which Clément Marot had already translated in the same form, giving it the title of *Visions :* it is, therefore, reasonable to suppose that Marot, and not Petrarca, was the source of Spenser's inspiration. Nor was this his only debt to the forerunner of the Pléiade. Marot had also written

[1] Cf. Sidney Lee, *op. cit.* pp. xlix.-lxxxv.   [2] *Rime*, cccxxiii.

eclogues, and it is evident that the study of these prompted the writing of the *Shepherd's Calendar*, since the eleventh and twelfth eclogues are largely imitated from two of Marot's.[1] But there are also reminiscences of one of Petrarca's eclogues,[2] and the Italian influence dates from the time Spenser went to Cambridge, as we see from the letters exchanged between him and Gabriel Harvey. "What newes al this while at Cambridge?" writes the latter; "Petrarch, Boccaccio in every man's mouth." And again: "I dare saye you wyll holde your selfe reasonably wel satisfied if your Dreams be but as well esteemed of in Englande as Petrarche's Visions be in Italy";[3] while E.K.'s prefatory letter to the *Shepherd's Calendar*, written to Harvey, says that the author has been moved "rather in Æglogues than otherwise to write . . . following the example of the best and most aunacient Poetes which devised this kind of writing . . . at the first to trye their habilities. . . . So flewe Theocritus . . . so flewe Virgile, as not yet well feeling his winges. . . . So Petrarque. So Boccace. So Marot, Sanazarus, and also divers other excellent both Italian and French Poetes, whose foting this Author everywhere followeth."

In his *Pierces Supererogation* Gabriel Harvey has a fine panegyric of Petrarca: "Petrarke's Invention," he says, "is pure love it selfe. . . . All the noblest Italian, French, and Spanish poets have in their severall veines Petrarchised . . . and it is no dishonour for the daintiest or divinest Muse to be his schollar, whom the amiablest Invention and beautifullest Elocution acknowledge their master. All posterity honour Petrarke that was the harmony of heaven; the lyfe of Poetry; the grace of Arte; a curious frame of exquisite workmanship; nothing but neate Wit, and refined Eloquence."[4] Spenser's Muse was

[1] Clément Marot, *De Madame Loyse de Savoie, Mère du Roy, en forme d'églogue, Au Roy soubs nom de Pan et Robin*.
[2] *Ecloga*, x.   [3] Grosart's *Spenser*, vol. i. p. 69.
[4] *Pierces Supererogation*, ed. Grosart, pp. 92-94.

in a very complete sense Petrarca's "schollar"; we can trace the master's influence from the very beginning; in imagery, in cadence, in line of thought, it is constantly brought to our mind. In the *Visions*, the *Eclogues*, the *Fowre Hymnes;* in the *Faerie Queene*—Raleigh's exaggerated compliment to which does but accentuate the presence therein of "the soul of Petrarch"[1]—in the *Amoretti* and the Marriage Odes, the work of Spenser is one long tribute to Petrarca. But the debt is a wholly different thing from that of the vast tribe of Elizabethan sonneteers; they, for the most part, are mere copyists, and most often they are copying imitations. Spenser, on the other hand, assimilates; his own genius is in no wise limited or crushed out, but is simply inspired and directed. More than the *Astrophel and Stella*, the *Amoretti* recall Petrarca, but it is in the manner more than in the matter; for, though in very many sonnets (xv., xxx., lxxxi., for examples) we have exact Petrarchan images, we find in the treatment more force and individuality than we have met with heretofore in this class of English poetry. It may well be that there was more reality, for these are really love-sonnets written for that Elizabeth—

> My love, my life's last ornament,
> By whom my spirit out of dust was raysed,[2]

who became the poet's wife, and for whom was written that most perfect Wedding Song which caused Aubrey de Vere to call her "the best sung of women except Beatrice."[3]

---

[1] "Me thought I saw the grave where Laura lay,
  Within that Temple where the vestall flame
  Was wont to burne; and passing by that way
  To see that buried dust of living fame,
  Whose tumbe faire Love and fairer Vertue kept,
  All suddeinly I saw the Fairy Queene;
  At whose approch the soule of Petrarke wept."

[2] *Amoretti*, lxxiv.

[3] Aubrey de Vere, *Characteristics of Spenser's Poetry*, Grosart's *Spenser*, vol. i.

The extraordinarily beautiful stanza used by Spenser in his *Epithalamion* and *Prothalamion* is probably fashioned to some extent upon that of Petrarca's canzoni, *Nel dolce tempo* and *I' vo pensando*,[1] and is one of his great legacies to English metre.

Meanwhile, as regards form, English sonnets were getting further and further away from the Petrarchan model. Spenser, indeed, restricted himself in rhyme, for, though he used three quatrains and a concluding couplet, he made the first line of the second quatrain rhyme with the last line of his first, and the first line of his third quatrain rhyme with the last of his second, thus having only five rhymes in the sonnet. Shakespeare reverted to the four quatrains rhyming alternately, and the concluding couplet; but even his magnificent cycle of sonnets need not detain us now, for though they are full of Petrarchan expressions (notably Sonnets xxiii., xxiv., xcvii., xcix., cxv., cxlvii.), such had become so familiar to all English writers of the time that very little direct foreign influence need be conjectured. For the rest, like all Shakespeare's borrowings, they were so permeated with his own personality that we cease to regard them as other than his own. It is strange, however, that, steeped as he was in Italian influences—names, places, music, allusions of all kinds—there is only one direct mention of Petrarca in all his plays, and that is in *Romeo and Juliet*, when Mercutio, mocking Romeo, says: " Now is he for the numbers that Petrarch flowed in: Laura to his lady was but a kitchen-wench—marry, she had a better love to be-rhyme her."[2] The sonneteering mania is scornfully alluded to in several plays; in *Much Ado about Nothing*, when Benedick deplores his inability to rhyme, and where finally the lovers are each comforted with their own " halting sonnets " ;[3] in *Henry V.*, where the Dauphin says of his charger: " I once wrote a sonnet in his

---

[1] *Rime*, xxiii., cclxiv.  [2] *Romeo and Juliet*, ii. 4.
[3] *Much Ado about Nothing*, v. 2, 4.

praise and it began thus: *Wonder of Nature,"* and the Duke of Orleans replies: " I have heard a sonnet begin so to one's mistress."[1] In *Love's Labour's Lost,* two extravagant sonnets are circulated, which draw forth from Biron the remark: "Tush, none but minstrels like of sonneting";[2] and, in the *Two Gentlemen of Verona,* Proteus advises Thurio to write—

> Wailful sonnets, whose composed rhymes
> Should be full fraught with serviceable vows.[3]

After Shakespeare, there is no remarkable addition to English sonnet-literature, until the work of William Drummond of Hawthornden. It may well be that what we know of the man's life and character has invested his poetry with an additional interest, but certainly his writing has a very special charm. For any one who has spent a sunny day wandering in Hawthornden, the poet can never henceforth be dissociated from the place which in itself might have been sufficient for his inspiration. But solitude and natural beauty were not Drummond's only masters; Love—" a more ideal artist he than all "—was his chief teacher, and the pathetic story of his love and sorrow are enshrined in his best work. He was engaged to a beautiful girl, Mary Cunningham, who died on the eve of their wedding, and the *Poems,* divided into two parts, of which Part I. deals with the perfections of his lady while she lived, and Part II. with his grief and desolation after her death, bear the impress of Petrarca's influence.[4] The author is known to have been a very proficient Italian scholar, and many Italian poets are borrowed from and imitated. But, besides direct translations from Petrarca, of which there are a considerable number, we are constantly reminded of the *Canzoniere.* The sonnets are interspersed with songs and

---
[1] *Henry V.,* iii. 7.  [2] *Love's Labour's Lost,* iv. 3.
[3] *Two Gentlemen of Verona,* iii. 2.
[4] Cf. *The Poems of William Drummond of Hawthornden.*

madrigals, and there are two sestinas. The long philosophic poem—

> It autumn was, and on our hemisphere,[1]

reminds us forcibly of Petrarca's canzone—

> Quando il soave mio fido conforto,[2]

though the whole argument is different; but it is the atmosphere that is thoroughly Petrarchan.

Drummond, recounting one of his conversations with Ben Jonson, says that the latter " cursed Petrarch for redacting verses into sonnets, which he said were like that tyrant's bed where some who were too short were racked, and others who were too long cut short "; to which Drummond affixed a note: " All this was to no purpose, for he neither doth understand French nor Italian."[3] For himself he says: " The best and most exquisite Poet of the subject (Love), by consent of the whole Senate of Poets, is Petrarch. . . . The French have also set him before them as a paragon. . . . Among our English Poets Petrarch is imitated, nay surpast in some things, in Matter and Manner. In Matter none approach him to *Sidney*, who hath songs and sonnets in Matter intermingled. In Manner the nearest I find to him is *W. Alexander*, who, insisting in these same steps, hath Sextains, Madrigals, and Songs, Echoes and Equivoques, which he hath not. . . . After which two next (methinks) followeth *Daniel* for sweetness in rhyming second to none. *Drayton* seemeth rather to have loved his Muse than his Mistress; by I know not what artificial similes this showeth well his Mind, but not the Passion."[4] In the latter judgment Drummond would seem to have forgotten that masterpiece of Drayton's—

> Since there's no help, come let us kiss and part,

---

[1] *The Poems of William Hathornden*, vol. i. p. 124.   [2] *Rime*, ccclix.
[3] *Conversations of Ben Jonson with William Drummond*, p. 14.
[4] *Work of W. Drummond*, p. 226. Edinburgh, 1711.

of which it is so hard to conceive of any one but Shakespeare as the author.

It is to be noted that all Drummond's sonnets follow the Shakespearean and not the Petrarchan model, but a master was to arrive who should, at any rate, restore the Italian metrical tradition. Milton, who owed so much to the language and literature of Italy, and was a most finished Italian scholar, shows everywhere traces of Tuscan models, especially in *Lycidas* and in his Sonnets. But he does not seem to have been directly influenced by Petrarca, though certainly he writes of his sonnet *On his being arrived at the age of twenty-three* as " a Petrarchan stanza ": but this was probably only because it was a sonnet. Yet, in one important particular, he reverted to the true Petrarchan type, and rhymed his octaves—

<blockquote>A–B–B–A–A–B–B–A,</blockquote>

permitting himself much variety in his tercets, but only once adopting the rhyming couplet at the end. He also grasped the necessity of the sonnet expressing one single independent emotion; his sensitive ear and classical taste led him surely to these conclusions. The break between the octave and the sestet, the *volta*, that pause for the resolution or the return—the sonnet obeying, as Mr. Watts-Dunton has taught us, the same laws as the ebb and flow of a wave [1]—does not seem to have struck his imagination in the same degree, and thus, according to Mark Pattison's criticism, " he has missed the very end and aim of the Petrarchan scheme." [2] Even the idea of embodying a single emotion sometimes deserts him, and, though he never falls into the error of conceiving of the sonnet as a mere rhyming meditation or description, he has yet admitted an anti-climax in the sonnet to Cromwell, and is often guilty of obscuring his meaning in a tangle of conflicting thoughts.

---

[1] Encyclopædia Britannica, *The Sonnet*.
[2] Milton's Sonnets, ed. Mark Pattison, *Introduction*.

Yet, even so, he attains nearer to the Italian model than any English poet had done before him, and he also increases our obligation to him in that he redeemed the sonnet from being the mere expression of conventional love, and set it free to inshrine great principles and lofty ideas: so, in many ways, he " gave the notes to glory."[1]

From Milton's time to that of Wordsworth the sonnet seems to have dropped out of favour. With Wordsworth it revived, and with it, unfortunately, that notion, which seems to have been fastened on the English mind, that to poetise, or moralise, or even to prose, in fourteen lines is to compose a sonnet; to which is due such a series as that to the river Duddon. But Wordsworth has given us many noble sonnets, of which, perhaps, the one *Composed upon Westminster Bridge* is the most perfect.

It remained for two poets of the latter half of the nineteenth century, Dante Gabriel and Christina Rossetti, to bring into being the true Petrarchan sonnet. It has been objected that their work was English in form and Italian in thought: truly the contrary might be urged with more justice. The thought is entirely English, in some of Christina's poems it might be called aggressively so, while the pure passion of the *House of Life* is of all things least Italian. The structure, rhythm, and form are directly and, for the first time, completely transplanted from the Italian. These poets were both discoverers and creators; they found in the English tongue a subtlety and pliability of which it had been thought incapable, and they created such liquid lines, such strains of pure music, as no other singers have given to us. In them the Petrarchan sonnet has found its true expression; cultivated, imitated, sought after, from the days when Wyatt first essayed it; transposed, altered, diverted, passing from hand to hand, sustaining both gain and loss, it has come now to its full perfection and has put on immortality.

[1] W. S. Landor.

Beati spiriti: che nel sommo choro
Si troueranno, & truouano in tal grado
Che sia memoria eterna il nome loro.

O felice colui che truoua el guado
Di questo aspetro & rapido torrente
Cha nome uita : & a molti e si a grado.

*Triumphus Æternitatis.*
(Fifteenth Century Florentine Engraving.)

One other splendid trace of Petrarca's influence remains to us in the *Triumph of Life* of Shelley, which is one of the few sustained pieces in *terza rima* that our language possesses. It has all the pathos of an unfinished poem, with the added interest that, as the best critics have judged, if it had been completed, it would have given us the author's mature views on Life and Death. It is, like the *Trionfi*, an epic of human life, and it is a very tragedy of existence, for it is the downfall of the idealist and the reign of disillusion; and the poet, with hope destroyed and at the mercy of blind destiny, ends with the bewildered question: " Then what is life? " Had Shelley lived to think this out with his maturing powers, we might, perhaps, have found in his answer the same advance on the crudity of his early philosophy that the craftmanship shows when compared with his earlier work in the same metre, *Prince Athanase*. Shelley was no pessimist, and, if the ideal of the human was shattered, we cannot but think that the light of the Divine would have broken upon him, and that he, like Petrarca, might have come to look for a fulfilment of the Triumph of Life in Eternity.

## CHAPTER XII

### THE TWOFOLD CORONAL

" My heart is at your festival,
My head hath its coronal."
WORDSWORTH.

To Petrarca belongs the honourable, but in some measure thankless, part of the pioneer. Living as he did before the shining of the earliest ray of the Renaissance, to him may be applied the Eastern epithet, *Subh-i-Kazib*, the dawn before the dawn—that first faint light which is obliterated and forgotten as soon as the daylight has visited us. Yet the *Subh-i-Kazib* truly heralds the dawn, and the dawn is not without it.

Petrarca had something new to say to his own age, and the eternal truth of his message is attested by the fact that it is no less important to ours. Like every pioneer, he made mistakes—even fatal ones—but he hewed out the road along which future generations have marched in triumph. From that time to this, great acquisitions in knowledge have been made, there has been much progress, much achievement, but the literary standard unfolded by Petrarca remains with us. Turning to the classics as the source from which all inspiration is to be drawn, he was saturated with the idea that it is a folly to stop short of perfection: he engaged men to the worship and the pursuit of what was highest in art and purest in taste, and hence it is that his ideal abides with us, and that our generation, no less than his own, has to acknowledge itself intellectually his debtor.

Petrarca has been called " the first modern man," and, indeed, there is about him a sense of freedom and emancipation; he gives the impression of one who is peculiarly conscious of his own individuality and who has conquered a world for himself. His many-sidedness, too, is intensely modern; poet, scholar, musician, letter-writer, collector, copyist, traveller, botanist, politician, solitary and man of society, nature-worshipper and art-lover. Apart from his genius, one hardly knows which to admire most, his versatile interest or his enormous industry; the mind whose first need was solitude, or the heart that could not live without friendship. This very complexity of character should make him a study particularly sympathetic to our time, when all literature demonstrates that, like Browning, we feel that little else but the development of a soul is worth studying.

In the character of Petrarca there is a total lack of the obvious and the consistent, and this it is, perhaps, which makes him so perennially interesting. There is nothing flatter in life than the people who are so like themselves, of whom we can predicate what they will say and do on all occasions, and the line of conduct they are sure to pursue. Francesco must have been as constant a surprise to his friends as he is to posterity. Neither a great nor a profound thinker, he is yet both original and individual, a fact to which his tastes, his choices, and his judgments bear perpetual witness. He broke away from traditions of education and scholarship; he cut himself free from surroundings which might have fettered many a stronger man. He not only looked around him with a breadth of vision very uncommon at his time, but he opened out new horizons for those about him: he had the power of imposing his own point of view and of communicating his enthusiasm. Never was there in any one so much of the unexpected and the incompatible. If we study him as the scholar and the recluse, we do, indeed, find in him every valuable quality of the man of letters, and the untiring, patient devotion of the student: but with these we have to take into consideration his diversity of tastes, his astonishing agility of mind, his ardent friendships, and his need for reciprocity. If we look at him as poet and lover, we come to understand, indeed, that he was the victim rather of emotions than of passions, the singer of sentiments rather than of ideas; that he had in a rare degree the art of seizing the moment, of moulding a fugitive fancy and a passing impression into an immortal poem (and it is this which makes him the supreme master of the art of sonnet-writing); but, on the other hand, not Schopenhauer himself was more imbued with the sense of the nothingness of life, or realised more completely the futility of mortal things. It is not his woes as a lover, but it is the sorrow beyond and outside, the sorrow of humanity at large, and of all unattainable ideals, that has made Petrarca the voice of his own and succeeding generations.

With the inherited taste of ages, it is difficult to go back in imagination to the days when such a standard had been well-nigh lost, and the work of the man who set it up again can be called nothing less than genius. The literary progress made between the birth and death of the poet is a wonderful monument to his greatness. He was, in the highest sense of the word, an educator, for he not only taught but evoked a desire for learning, and there grew up a band of men whose aim was to discover and to disseminate knowledge. Petrarca would never specialise; he extended the range of study; in all fields of research he restored lost or forgotten ideals, and looked for a high level of general culture. Steeped in the classics, he had thoroughly assimilated their ideas and entered into their spirit, and he extended the domain of study by bringing in new aims and a desire for perfection. It was not so much the quality of his knowledge as the manner of it that ushered in the new era. As critic he was even more remarkable than as scholar; dowered with a perfect sense of form, a musical ear, and a fine taste, his ambition was to instil these into his followers, to whom he revealed antiquity as the supreme school of art, making them realise that the intellectual future of the race depended on their assimilation of the classics and their conformity to the laws of harmony and beauty. He gave back to mankind the sense of proportion, and, with his passion for perfection, none was ever more fitted to be a guide in the high places of culture.

It is remarkable that it was his philosophy rather than his poetry that most struck Petrarca's contemporaries. The Middle Ages had, to a great extent, lost the perception of beauty of form: it was Dante's task to give it back to them, and Petrarca enriched the gift; albeit in this passion for the musical side of language there lay a snare. A veritable poet-painter, we are conscious sometimes of his idolatry of words: it is only given to the greatest minds perfectly to unite form and thought, and, when the latter is the weaker power of the two, the former will sometimes evaporate into sentimentality. Here, as in other ways, Petrarca has suffered from his imitators; they could not but recognise that he invariably chose the exact, right epithet, and so it became with them a rule to use only such words as the master's hand had consecrated, and thus the false note struck from time to time by Petrarca becomes one long discord in the work of the Petrarchists.

With Petrarca's worship of antiquity, with his abandonment to classical ideas and ardent desire to enter into their spirit, we find a strong strain of individuality—his national feeling, his pride in the land and people of Italy. Doubtless, the glories of the ancient times took on fresh splendour for him when he thought of them as the birthright of Italy. This love of all things Italian is one of his most touching characteristics—the ancient history, because it immortalises and may yet be reproduced in the race—the Latin literature, because it is native to Italy—the ancient monuments, because they testify to the greatness of Rome. It is on this account that Rienzi's enterprise appeals to him. It is that Rome may be restored, made great and fortunate, that he will win back the Popes to the Eternal City and invite the Emperor to the seat of empire. The glory of Rome and the primacy of Italy, these were his central ideas, and from these result a kind of fantastic outlook which has nothing solid about it, and which makes him, as a politician, a contradictory and elusive personality. Every writer in turn has drawn a parallel between his political standpoint and that of Dante. They are, indeed, alike in their faith in the supremacy of the Roman People, which Dante duly sets forth in the second book of the *De Monarchia* and Petrarca in various letters.[1] There is also a superficial resemblance in their attitude towards Pope and Emperor, but Dante's highly speculative and philosophic mind had built up for itself a well-reasoned and sharply-defined system. His political creed may be summed up from a passage in the *De Monarchia*, where he says that Providence has set two ends before man: the blessedness of this life, and the blessedness of eternal life; and that man has need of a twofold directing power according to his twofold end; to wit, the Supreme Pontiff to lead the human race to eternal life, and the Emperor to direct to temporal felicity; which can only come about by the disposition of Him who so pre-ordained it that He in His providence might weave all things together, each in its due order. It is thus clear that the authority of the temporal monarch descends upon him without any mean from the fountain of universal authority, though it is not to be thought that the Roman prince is in nothing subordinate to the Roman pontiff; since mortal felicity is, in a sense, ordained with reference to immortal felicity.[2] This, then, defines Dante's attitude both to the papacy and the empire, and explains his impassioned invocation of Henry VII. as "the minister of God, the son of the Church, and the promoter of Roman glory";[3] and, when his hopes were destroyed by Henry's

---

[1] *De Reb. Fam.* x. 1; xiii. 6; *Var.* 38; *Ep. sine Tit.* iv.
[2] *De Monarchia*, iii. 16.   [3] *Epistola* vii.

death, he still looks for the defender that is to be, since the empire is of divine appointment and the true leader must be to come.[1]

But, though it is probable that Dante's letter to Henry inspired Petrarca's numerous appeals to Charles IV., we look in vain in the latter for a scheme of consistent policy. To the champion of Rienzi the supreme authority of the Emperor had faded into the background; then the Tribune's failure again brings Charles into the political arena, but, even while inciting him to come and take his crown, Petrarca would seem to be half-attracted by the vast schemes of conquest that were taking shape in the minds of the Visconti rulers. Francesco's opinions are always fluid; one outlook disappears as the next comes into view, thus he was ever at the mercy of circumstances. The fundamental difference in the attitude towards the Emperor of the two poets is that Petrarca limited himself to a local and historic standpoint; he wished to revive former greatness and ancient customs, to re-clothe Roman story and literature with their old grandeur and importance: history fills his horizon, it is to him poetry and inspiration. But the greater poet was also the profounder philosopher: his was a universal and not a national ideal; he dreamed of a power and a righteousness that should reform the world.[2]

There is far more resemblance in the point of view from which they regarded the papacy and the popes—the office and the men who filled it. Here we find in both an absolute loyalty to the supreme governing power, which, in each poet, finds its expression in the most fearless denunciation of prevalent abuses and scandals; for, as history witnesses, it was the Reformation which first deprived men of freedom of thought and speech, and Cantù, in writing of Dante's time, says: " In those days men used a frankness in censuring the abuses and the personal faults of men in high places, of which the empty servility of to-day has lost the

[1] *Purg.* xxxiii. 37-44.   [2] Cf. Zumbini, *Studi sul Petrarca*, pp. 241-255.

very idea." [1] Dante's letter to the Italian cardinals,[2] and his denunciations of popes,[3] clergy,[4] and religious orders;[5] Petrarca's Eclogues [6] and *Epistolæ sine Titulo ;* and St. Catherine's *Trattato delle Lagrime* [7] all bear witness to this. But, whenever we compare the writings of Dante and Petrarca, we find a marked difference in character, those of the former being distinguished by a far greater sharpness of outline and objectivity of vision. We have no doubt in our minds as to the prerogatives and the exact position that Dante's pope is to hold. In the third book of the *De Monarchia*, he clearly sets forth that the temporal power is no part of the Church, " for every divine law is contained in the bosom of the two Testaments; in which bosom I cannot find that solicitude or care for temporal things was commended to the priesthood, first or latest. Nay, I find that the priests of the one were expressly removed from it, as is clear through God's precepts to Moses, and the priests of the other, through Christ's injunctions to His disciples. For the form of the Church is none other than the life of Christ, as it is comprehended both in His words and in His deeds. For His life was the idea and exemplar of the Church militant, especially of pastors, and most of all of the supreme pastor, whose it is to feed the lambs and sheep. . . . But Christ in the presence of Pilate renounced any such regimen as that in question: ' My kingdom,' said He, ' is not of this world.' . . . It is therefore of the very nature of the Church to say and to hold the same." [8] But with Petrarca we do not get these clear-cut statements. It is not easy to see the exact position he destined for the

---

[1] C. Cantù, *Il Secolo di Dante*, p. 8.  [2] *Epistola* viii.
[3] *Inf.* xi. 8; xix. 52, 96-105; xxvii. 85; *Purg.* xix. 97; xxxii. 149; xxxiii. 45; *Par.* xxvii. 17.
[4] *Inf.* xxxiii.; *Par.* ix. 52-54; xxi. 130-132; xxix. 103-126.
[5] *Par.* xi. 124; xii. 103-120; xxii. 74-93.
[6] *Eclogæ*, vi. vii.
[7] Cf. E. G. Gardner, *op. cit.* pp. 354 *n.*, 361, 362.
[8] *De Monarchia*, iii. 14, 15.

Pope, when he should be reinstated among the "sovereign Roman people" and confronted with the successor of the Cæsars. It is as before: Petrarca sees no further than the historic and the picturesque. He was no politician and was never seriously considered as such; he carried no weight; on the other hand, his contradictions and his vacillations were leniently regarded, because men felt that he was not a force with which they need reckon. He is concerned with things limited by space and time, while Dante is the herald of the supremacy of the spiritual.

The most salient point of resemblance in these two great poets was undoubtedly the desire for fame which burned in each of them, yet the manner in which this is manifested throws the strongest light on the intrinsic difference of their characters. Dante's estimate of his own greatness is unequivocal; he tells us how the master-poets received him into their company;[1] how his old teacher, Brunetto Latini, prophesies to him:—

>      Se tu segui tua stella,
> Non puoi fallire al glorioso porto;[2]

and, more than once, he promises himself the laurel crown.[3] His sin, if sin it be, is pride—the assurance of his own unequalled merit, and for this he seems to foresee his own punishment.[4] Petrarca, on the other hand, together with a consuming thirst of glory, has, at the same time, a consciousness of its futility, and of the way in which it fights against his highest interests. We have here the difference between a proud man and a vain one. In the first we may find haughtiness and scorn, but the restless torment that

[1] *Inf.* iv. 97-103.
[2] "If thou thy star do follow,
Thou canst not fail thee of a glorious port."
*Inf.* xv. 55, 56.
[3] *Ecloga*, i. 42-44; *Par.* i. 13-27; xxv. 1-9.
[4] *Purg.* xiii. 136-139.

afflicts the other is far from him. It would seem to be rather a question of relative than of abstract right, for a thing not wrong in itself may be wrong to the mind before which it looms as a danger and a degradation, and the mere unquietness which it produced in the soul of Petrarca fought against his peace, and limited and weakened his powers; and yet he is lovable in his very limitations. If the lover of Beatrice walks, as indeed he does, on a higher plane; if he has scaled the furthest heights of mortal love, and looked into the highest and deepest mysteries of the Divine; if he has written of Beatrice " what hath not before been written of any woman," and if he has expressed the loftiest love and worship in his invocation to the Virgin Mother; Petrarca can yet tell us something on the human side. The lover of Laura does not, indeed, waft us to the heights of Paradise. He—much rather than Dante—might be called—

> Plucker of amaranths grown beneath God's eye
> In gracious twilights where his chosen lie;[1]

for, as he leads us through the mazes of the *Canzoniere*, we feel that the whole devious road is a gradual ascent, and that it closes fitly in the prayer to Our Lady, ineffable in its tenderness and its humility.

Of a truth, Dante belongs to the whole world: his genius is a universal thing. Petrarca belongs first to Italy, and then to the new world that was to be; and he both anticipated and accelerated the coming dawn. He anticipated it, perhaps, most strikingly by turning his back on the schoolmen, by ridiculing their subtlety, their pedantry, and their worship of Aristotle. His attitude towards Plato was somewhat in the nature of a divination: he was led to it by no accurate knowledge, but rather, as some men have the instinct for discerning true gems from false, his intuitive sureness of touch guided him to the comprehen-

[1] R. Browning, *Sordello*.

sion of Plato's supremacy. He broke away from scholastic methods because he saw in them the enemies of that general culture, which he was the first to initiate, and for which we are so much more indebted to him than for any specific knowledge. It was his manner of doing things that was so modern—his tastes, his travels, his collections, above all, his letters. Coloured as they are with his own individuality, steeped in introspection, often transparently written for effect, polished and altered for posterity, the writer had yet too much imagination to be a pedant, too much feeling and too much learning to be overshadowed by his harmless vanity. Though Cicero and Virgil were pre-eminently his favourites, as a letter-writer Seneca influenced him most, and, in his reversion to these models, he re-endowed the Latin language with something of its former eloquence, and put an end to the monotonous style of the Middle Ages. For it is with the Latin of his own time that his should be compared, and not with that of Erasmus, who said of him that his Latin diction showed the rudeness of his age; but, as has been justly said: "If Petrarch had never written Latin, it may be questioned if Erasmus would have been so good a judge of Latinity." [1]

Even as in letter-writing he was the first to realise the value and interest of personal details and everyday events, so was he the first in poetry to seize the importance of the moment of emotion, the song inherent in the fugitive joy or sorrow of an hour. It was not so much that he had something new to say, as that his manner of speech was a novelty; the Renaissance in Italy found its first expression in him. The heart of the new world was to beat with a fuller life; poetry, sculpture, painting, architecture, were to bloom forth as never before, springing out of the manifold intelligence and power of a rapidly developing people: but that many-sided vitality had blossomed in the mind of Petrarca, and the vigour of his personality held up a mirror to suc-

[1] Thomas Campbell, *Life of Petrarch*.

ceeding times, and revealed to each man his own independence, his own individuality, and his own loneliness. In this manner Petrarca is so supremely modern; for, while man has become accustomed to his kind, he has never become accustomed to himself; he is to himself a constant surprise, an unknown quantity, an undiscovered country.

Crowned, then, as scholar and humanist, it is yet rather as poet that we should acclaim him; for to the artist above other men, and to the poet above other artists, belong the grace of self-revelation and the gift of prophecy. Essentially a creator, he is no less essentially a seer. In the story of the ages, in scholarship, in science, in politics, one achievement gives place to another, one view vanishes as another comes into the foreground, but in Art it is not so. The ultimate truth, the absolute ideal, have there an assured existence, and within that temple Petrarca has found an immutable resting-place, wearing, like the Lady of his love, both the palm and the laurel.

# BIBLIOGRAPHY

Affò, I.—*Cronichetta Parmigiana.* 1784.
Aleardi, Aleardo.—*Discorso su Francesco Petrarca.* Padua, 1875.
Allodi, G. M.—*Serie cronologica dei Vescovi di Parma.* 1856.
Alscher, R.—*Sir Thomas Wyatt und seine Stellung in der Entwickelungsgeschichte der englischen Literatur und Verkunst.* Vienna, 1886.
Ancona, A. d'—*Il Concetto dell' Unità politica nei poeti italiani.* Pisa, 1876.
Ancona, A. d'—*Studj sulla Letteratura Italiana.* Ancona, 1884.
Ancona, A. d', and Bacci.—*Manuale della Letteratura Italiana* vols. i. and ii. 1904.
Appel, Carl.—*Zur Entwickelung Italienischer Dichtungen Petrarcas.* Halle, 1891.
Appel, Carl.—*See under* Petrarca.
Appel, Carl.—*Provenzalische Chrestomathie.* Leipzig, 1895.
Aquilano, Serafino.—*Opere.* Venice, 1508.
Arullani, V. A.—*Pei Regni dell' Arte e della Critica.* Turin, 1903.
Baldelli, G. B.—*Vita di Giovanni Boccacci.* Florence, 1806.
Baldelli, G. B.—*Del Petrarca e delle sue Opere.* Florence, 1707.
Barbieri, V.—*Dell' Istoria della Volgar Poesia.* Venice, 1730.
Bartoli, A.—*Storia della Letteratura Italiana,* vol. vii. Florence, 1884.
Bartsch, Karl.—*Chrestomathie Provençale.* Marburg, 1904.
Bartsch, Karl.—*See under* Diez.
Beccadelli, L.—*Monumenti di varia Letteratura.* Bologna, 1797.
Beccadelli, L.—*Vita del Petrarca.* Padua, 1722.
Bembo, P.—*Opere,* 12 tom. Milan, 1810.
Bene, Sennuccio del.—*In Il Petrarca con narrazione del suo Coronamento.* London, 1796.

BINDI, E., and FANFANI P.—*Le Rime di Messer Cino da Pistoia.* Pistoia, 1878. (This contains two short articles by Carducci and Carl Witte.)

BISTICCI, V. DA.—*Vite di Uomini illustri del Secolo XV.* Florence, 1859.

BOCCACCIO, G.—*L' Amorosa Visione.* Venice, 1549.

BOCCACCIO, G.—*De Genealogia Deorum.* Venice, 1472.

BOCCACCIO, G.—*Le Lettere edite e inedite di Messer Giovanni Boccaccio.* F. Corazzini. Florence, 1877.

BORGHESI, P.—*Petrarch and his Influence on English Literature.* Bologna, 1906.

BRUNI, L.—*Le Vite di Dante e del Petrarca.* Florence, 1672.

BURY, H. BLAZE DE.—" Laure de Noves " (*Revue des deux Mondes,* 15 juillet, 1874).

BURY, RICHARD DE. — *Philobiblon.* Edited and translated by E. C. Thomas. London, 1888.

BURCKHARDT, J.—*Die Kultur der Renaissance in Italien.* Leipzig, 1908.

CALVI, E.—*Bibliografia analitica Petrarchesca.* Rome, 1904.

CAMPBELL, THOMAS.—*Life of Petrarch,* 2 vols. London, 1841.

CANELLO, U.—*La Vita e le Opere del Trovatore Arnaldo Daniello.* Halle, 1883.

CANTÙ, C.—*Dante e il suo Secolo.* Florence, 1868.

CARDUCCI, G.—*Petrarca e Boccaccio.* Rome, 1884.

CARDUCCI, G.—*Opere,* vols. i. and viii. Bologna, 1889-1898.

CARDUCCI, G.—*Jaufré Rudel.* Bologna, 1888.

CARDUCCI, G.—*Rime di M. Cino da Pistoia, etc.* Florence, 1862.

CARDUCCI, G.—*See under* PETRARCA.

CARLINI, A.—*Il Pensiero filosofico religioso di F. Petrarca.* Jesi, 1904.

CARRARA, ENRICO.—" Il Sesto Centenario Petrarchesco " (*Giornale Storico della Letteratura Italiana,* vol. 47). Turin, 1904.

CASINI, T.—*Manuale di Letteratura Italiana,* 4 parts. Florence, 1886-1892.

CASINI, T.—*Le Forme Metriche Italiane.* Florence, 1900.

CASTELLI, G.—*Cecco d'Ascoli e Dante.* Rome, 1903.

CATEL, G. DE.—*Mémoires de l'Histoire de Languedoc.* Toulouse, 1633.
CESAREO, G. A.—*Su le " Poesie Volgari " del Petrarca, nuove ricerche.* Rocca S. Casciano, 1898.
CHAYTOR, H. J.—*The Troubadours of Dante.* Clarendon Press, 1902.
CHIAPPELLI, L.—*Lo Studio Bolognese.* Pistoia, 1888.
CIAMPI, S.—*Vita e Poesie di Messer Cino da Pistoia.* Pisa, 1813.
CIAN, V.—*Un decennio della vita di M. Pietro Bembo, 1521-1531.* Turin, 1885.
CIPOLLA, A.—*Commemorazione di F. Petrarca.* 1905.
CIPOLLA, C.—*Storia delle Signorie Italiane dal 1313 al 1530,* 2 vols.
CITTADELLA, G.—*Storia della Dominazione Carrarese in Padova.* Padua, 1842.
CITTADELLA, G.—*Petrarca a Padova e ad Arquà.* Padua, 1874.
COCHIN, H.—*Boccace.* Paris, 1879.
COCHIN, H.—*Le Texte des Epistolæ de Rebus Familiaribus de F. Pétrarque.* In *F. Petrarca e la Lombardia.* Milan, 1904.
COCHIN, H.—*La Chronologie du Canzoniere de Pétrarque.* Paris, 1898.
COCHIN, H.—*Le Frère de Pétrarque.* Paris, 1903.
COCHIN, H.—*Un Ami de Pétrarque.* Paris, 1892.
CORAZZINI, F.—*See under* BOCCACCIO.
CORAZZINI, G. O.—*La Madre di Francesco Petrarca.* Florence, 1903.
CORIO, B.—*Storia di Milano,* 3 vols. Milan, 1855.
CORRADINI, F.—*See under* PETRARCA.
COURTHOPE, W. J.—*History of English Poetry.* London, 1895.
CRESCIMBENI, G. M.—*L'Istoria della volgar Poesia.* Rome, 1698.
CRESCINI, V.—*Studi sul Boccaccio.* Turin, 1887.
CROWE and CAVALCASELLE.—*A New History of Painting in Italy,* edited by Edward Hutton, vol. i. London, 1908.
DANTE.—*Tutte le Opere.* Oxford, 1904.
DARU, P.—*Histoire de la République de Venise.* Paris, 1853.
DEGUILEVILLE, G. DE—*Le Pèlerinage de Vie humaine.*
DIEZ, F.—*Die Poesie der Troubadours.* Leipzig, 1826.

Diez, F.—*Leben und Werke der Troubadours.* Zweite vermehrte Auflage von Karl Bartsch. Leipzig, 1884.

Doni, A. F.—*Prose antiche.* Florence, 1547.

Drummond, William.—*Poems,* 2 vols., edited by W. C. Ward. London and New York, 1894. See under Masson.

Du Bellay, J.—*Défense et illustration de la langue française.* Paris, 1549.

Einstein, Lewis.—*The Italian Renaissance in England.* New York, 1902.

Faguet, Emile.—*Histoire de la littérature française.* Paris, 1900.

Farnell, Ida.—See under Mahn.

Fauriel, M.—*Histoire de la Poésie Provençale,* 3 vols. Paris, 1846.

Finzi, G.—*Petrarca.* Florence, 1900.

Fioravanti, A.—*Francesco Petrarca e Roma.* Modena, 1905.

Flamini, F.—*Studi di storia letteraria italiana e straniera.* Livorno, 1895.

Foscolo, Ugo.—*Essays on Petrarch.* London, 1823.

Fracassetti, G.—See under Petrarca.

Fracassetti, G.—*Il Secolo di Dante.* See under Cantù.

Fuzet, A.—*Pétrarque à Vaucluse.* Rouen, 1904.

Galvani, G.—*Osservazioni sulla Poesia dei Trovatori.* Modena, 1829.

Gardner, Edmund G.—*St. Catherine of Siena.* London, 1907.

Gardner, Edmund G.—See under Wicksteed.

Gascoigne, George.—*Certayne notes of instruction concerning the making of verse or ryme in English.* 1575.

Gascoigne, George.—*Complete works,* edited by W. Hazlitt, 2 vols. 1869.

Gaspary, A.—*Storia della Letteratura Italiana,* vol. i., tradotta da N. Zingarelli. Turin, 1887.

Gebhart, E.—*Les Origines de la Renaissance en Italie.* Paris, 1879.

Geiger, L.—*Petrarka.* Leipzig, 1874.

Ginguené, P. L.—*Histoire littéraire d'Italie.* Paris, 1778.

Gosse, E.—"Essay on English Pastoral Poetry." *Complete works of Edmund Spenser,* edited by Rev. A. Grosart, vol. iii. London, 1884.

Graf, A.—*Attraverso il Cinquecento.* Turin, 1888.

# BIBLIOGRAPHY 339

Gramont, C. de.—*Sextines.* Paris, 1872.

Gregorovius, F.—*Geschichte der Stadt Rom im Mittelalter.* Stuttgart, 1867.

Hallam, A. H.—*Remains in Verse and Prose.* London, 1863.

Harvey, Gabriel.—*The Works of Gabriel Harvey,* edited by Rev. A. Grosart, 3 vols. 1884, 1885.

Harvey, Gabriel. Letters from Edmund Spenser to G. Harvey. *See* Grosart's *Spenser,* vol. ix.

Haslewood, J.—*Ancient critical essays on English poets and poesy,* 2 vols. Edited by J. Haslewood. London, 1811-1815.

Hauvette, H.—*Le Professeur de Grec de Pétrarque e Boccace.* Chartres, 1891.

Hauvette, H.—*Notes sur des manuscrits autographes de Boccace à la Bibliothèque Laurentienne.* Rome, 1894.

Hauvette, H.—*Un exilé florentin: Luigi Alamanni.* Paris, 1903.

Hortis, A.—*Scritti inediti di Francesco Petrarca.* Trieste, 1874.

Hueffer, F.—*The Troubadours.* London, 1878.

Jonson, Ben.—*Conversations of Ben Jonson with William Drummond,* edited by P. Sidney. London, 1906.

Kirner, G.—*Sulle opere storiche di F. Petrarca.* Pisa, 1890.

Koerting, G.—*Geschichte der Literatur Italiens im Zeitalter der Renaissance,* 3 bds. Leipzig, 1878-1881.

Lee, Sidney.—*Elizabethan Sonnets,* 2 vols. London, 1904.

Lee, Sidney.—*Life of William Shakespeare.* London, 1905.

Lizio-Bruno, L.—" Il Petrarca e Tommaso da Messina " (*Il Propugnatore,* vol. ix.). Bologna, 1876.

Lo Parco, F.—" Dei Maestri canonisti attribuiti al Petrarca " (*Revue des Bibliothèques*). Paris, 1906.

Lo Parco, F.—" Il Petrarca nel Casentino " (*Rivista d'Italia, Aprile* 1906. Rome).

Lo Parco, F.—" L' Amico duce del Petrarca nel Trionfo d' Amore " (*Rassegna Bibliografica della Letteratura Italiana,* Ann. xiii.). Pisa, 1905.

Lounsbury, J. R.—*Studies in Chaucer,* 3 vols. London, 1892.

Mahn, C. A. F.—*The Lives of the Troubadours,* translated from the Mediæval Provençal by Ida Farnell. London, 1896.

MALMIGNATI, A.—*Petrarca a Padova, a Venezia, e ad Arquà.* Padua, 1874.

MANNI, D. M.—*Istoria del Decamerone di Giovanni Boccaccio.* Florence, 1742.

MAROT, CLÉMENT.—*Œuvres complètes,* 4 vols. Paris, 1875.

MASSÉNA, V., ET MÜNTZ, E.—*Pétrarque, ses études d'art.* Paris, 1902.

MASSON, D.—*Drummond of Hawthornden.* London, 1873.

MAZZONI, G.—" La Lirica del Cinquecento." See *La Vita Italiana nel Cinquecento.* Conferenze tenute a Firenze nel 1893.

MEHUS, L.—*Specimen historiæ litterariæ Florentinæ,* 1747.

MELODIA, G.—*Studio su i Trionfi del Petrarca.* Palermo, 1898.

MÉLY, F. DE.—" Pétrarque et le symbolisme antique." (*Société nationale des Antiquaires de France,* Centenaire, 1804-1904. Recueil de Mémoires. Paris.)

MENEGHELLI, A.—*Saggio sopra Petrarca.* Venice, 1812.

MENEGHELLI, A.—*Del Canonicato di Messer F. Petrarca.* Padua, 1818.

MESTICA, G.—*See under* PETRARCA.

MEZIÈRES, A. J. F.—*Pétrarque.* Paris, 1868.

MILTON, JOHN.—*Epistolarum familiarium liber.* London, 1674.

MILTON, JOHN.—*Sonnets,* edited by Mark Pattison. London, 1883.

MOSCHETTI, A.—*Dell' ispirazione dantesca nelle rime di F. Petrarca.* Urbino, 1894.

MUNARON, G.—*Della casa abitata in Padova dal Petrarca.* Padua, 1904.

MÜNTZ, E.—*See under* MASSENA.

MURATORI, L. A.—*Rerum Italicarum Scriptores,* vol. xix.

NOLHAC, P. DE—*Pétrarque et l'Humanisme,* 2 vols. Paris, 1907.

NOLHAC, P. DE—*Le " De Viris " de Pétrarque.* Paris, 1891.

NOLHAC, P. DE—" Pétrarque à Bologne au temps d'Azzo Visconti." In *F. Petrarca e la Lombardia.* Milan, 1904.

NOSTREDAME, JEHAN DE—*Les Vies des plus célèbres et anciens Poêtes Provensaux.* Lyon, 1575.

# BIBLIOGRAPHY

NOVATI, F.—" Il Petrarca ed i Visconti." In *F. Petrarca e la Lombardia*. Milan, 1904.

PALGRAVE, F. T.—*Landscape in Poetry*. London, 1897.

PALGRAVE, F. T.—" Essay on the Minor Poems of Spenser." See *Complete works in verse and prose of Edmund Spenser*, edited by Rev. A. Grosart, vol. iv. London, 1884.

PAOLETTI, V.—*Cecco d' Ascoli*. Bologna, 1905.

PAPENCORDT, F.—*Cola di Rienzo und seine Zeit*. Hamburg, 1841.

PARIS, GASTON.—*Les origines de la Poésie lyrique en France au moyen âge*. Paris, 1892.

PETRARCA, FRANCESCO.—*Opera Omnia*. Venice, 1501 : Basle, 1581.

PETRARCA, FRANCESCO.—*Epistolæ de Rebus Familiaribus et Variæ*. Giuseppe Fracassetti, 3 vols. Florence, 1859-1863.

PETRARCA, FRANCESCO.—*Lettere di F. Petrarca delle cose familiari libri ventiquattri, lettere varie libro unico*. Giuseppe Fracassetti, 5 vols. Florence, 1892.

PETRARCA, FRANCESCO.—*Lettere senili di F. Petrarca*. Giuseppe Fracassetti, 2 vols. Florence, 1892.

PETRARCA, FRANCESCO.—*Poemata Minora*, edited by D. Rossetti, 3 tom. Milan, 1829-1834.

PETRARCA, FRANCESCO.—*Africa Francisci Petrarcæ nunc primum emendata curante F. Corradini*. Padua, 1874.

PETRARCA, FRANCESCO.—*Sonetti canzoni e triomphi di Messer Francesco Petrarca con la spositione di B. Daniello*. Venice, 1549.

PETRARCA, FRANCESCO.—*Rime di F. Petrarca con l'interpretazione di G. Leopardi*. Milan, 1826.

PETRARCA, FRANCESCO.—*Le Rime di F. Petrarca sopra argomenti storici, morali e diversi*. G. Carducci. Livorno, 1876.

PETRARCA, FRANCESCO.—*Le Rime di F. Petrarca*. Giovanni Mestica. Florence, 1896.

PETRARCA, FRANCESCO.—*Le Rime di F. Petrarca*. Commentate da G. Carducci e S. Ferrari. Florence, 1899.

PETRARCA, FRANCESCO.—*Le Rime di F. Petrarca*. G. Salvo-Cozzo. Florence, 1904.

PETRARCA, FRANCESCO.—*I Trionfi secondo il Codice Parmense* 1636. Fl. Pellegrini. Cremona, 1897.

PETRARCA, FRANCESCO.—*Die Triumphe Francesco Petrarcas.* In kritischem Texte herausgegeben von Carl Appel. Halle, 1901.

PIÉRI, M.—*Le Pétrarquisme au XVI$^{me}$ Siècle.* Marseille, 1896.

PLOETZ, G.—*Etude sur Joachim Du Bellay.* Berlin, 1874.

PONSAN, M. DE—*Histoire de l'Académie des Jeux Floraux.* Toulouse, 1764.

PROTO, E.—*Nuovi abozzi di rime edite ed inedite di Francesco Petrarca.* Naples, 1907.

PUTTENHAM, G.—*The Arte of English Poesie.* London, 1589.

QUINET, E.—*Les révolutions d'Italie.* Paris, 1848.

RAYNOUALD, M.—*Choix des Poésies originales des Troubadours,* 6 vols. Paris, 1817.

RE, ZEFIRINO.—*La vita di Cola di Rienzi scritta da incerto autore nel secolo decimo quarto.* Con note da Z. Re. Forlì, 1828.

REEVE, HENRY.—*Petrarch.* London, 1878.

RENAN, ERNEST.—*Averroes.* Paris, 1866.

RIENZO, COLA DI—*Epistolario di Cola di Rienzo a cura di A. Gabrielli.* Rome, 1887.

ROBINSON, J. H., and ROLFE, H. W.—*Petrarch.* New York, 1898

RODOCANACHI, E.—*Cola di Rienzo.* Paris, 1888.

ROMUSSI, C.—*Petrarca a Milano.* Milan, 1874.

RONSARD, P. DE—*Œuvres.* Paris, 1891.

ROSSETTI, D.—*Petrarca, Celso, e Boccaccio.* Trieste, 1828.

RUDEL, J.—*Der Troubadour Jaufré Rudel, sein Leben und seine Werke.* A. Stimming. Kiel, 1873.

SADE, ABBÉ DE—*Mémoires pour la vie de François Pétrarque,* 3 vols. Amsterdam, 1764.

SAINT GELAIS, MELIN DE—*Œuvres complêtes,* 3 vols. 1873.

SALUTATI, COLUCCIO.—*Epistolario.* A cura di F. Novati. Rome, 1891.

SALVO-COZZO, G.—*See under* PETRARCA.

SANCTIS, F. DE—*Saggio critico sul Petrarca.* Naples, 1869.

SANDYS, J. E.—*History of Classical Scholarship,* vols. i. and ii. Cambridge, 1903 and 1908.

## BIBLIOGRAPHY

SANDYS, J. E.—*Harvard Lectures.* Cambridge, 1905.

SCARONA, N.—*Fonti Provenzali e Italiane della lirica Petrarchesca.* Turin, 1899.

SEGRÈ, C.—*Studi Petrarcheschi.* Florence, 1903.

SIDNEY, Sir PHILIP.—*The Complete Poems of Sir Philip Sidney,* edited by A. B. Grosart, 2 vols. 1873.

SIDNEY, Sir PHILIP.—*An Apologie for Poetrie* (E. Arber, English Reprint. 1868).

SOLERTI, A.—*Le Vite di Dante, Petrarca, e Boccaccio scritte fino al secolo decimosesto.* Milan, 1904.

SPENSER, EDMUND.—*Complete works,* edited by Rev. A. Grosart, 9 vols. London, 1882-1884.

TEN BRINK, B.—*Geschichte der englischer Litteratur.* Strasburg, 1899.

TIRABOSCHI, G.—*Storia della Letteratura Italiana.* Milan, 1824, etc.

TOMLINSON, C.—*The Sonnet.* London, 1874.

TORRACA, F.—*Discussioni e ricerche letterarii.* Livorno, 1888.

TOTTEL, R.—*Miscellany.* Arber's Reprint. 1895.

TOMASINI, G. F.—*Petrarcha Redivivus.* 1650.

TRENTA, G. J.—*Mosaici del Duomo di Pisa.* Florence, 1896.

TUCKER, J. G.—*The Foreign Debt of English Literature.* London, 1907.

VAGANAY, HUGUES.—*Le Sonnet en Italie et en France au XVI$^{me}$. Siècle.* Lyon, 1903.

VATTASSO, M.—*Del Petrarca e di alcuni suoi amici.* Rome, 1905.

VERE, AUBREY DE.—"Characteristics of Spenser's Poetry." *Complete Works of Edmund Spenser,* edited by Rev. A. Grosart, vol. i. London, 1884.

VERRI, P.—*Storia di Milano,* 2 vols. Florence, 1851.

VEYRIÈRES, LOUIS DE.—*Sonnettistes anciens et modernes.* Paris, 1869.

VILLANI, G.—*Historie Fiorentine.* Venice, 1559.

VOIGT, GEORG.—*Die Wiederbelebung des classischen Alterthums,* 2 vols. Berlin, 1893.

WATSON, THOMAS.—*Italian Madrigals Englished.* 1590.

WICKSTEED, P. H., and GARDNER, EDMUND G.—*Dante and Giovanni del Virgilio.* London, 1902.
    WITTE, CARL.—*Cino da Pistoia, Giurista.* See under BINDI.
    WOODWARD, W. H.—*Studies in Education.* Cambridge, 1906.
    WYNDHAM, G.—*Poems of Shakespeare.* London, 1898.
    WYNDHAM, G.—*Ronsard et la Pléiade.* London, 1906.
    ZARDO, M. A.—*Il Petrarca e i Carraresi.* Milan, 1887.
    ZENATTI, O.—*Dante e Firenze.* Florence, 1902.
    ZUMBINI, B.—*Studi sul Petrarca.* Florence, 1895.

# INDEX

## A

ACCIAIUOLI, Niccolò, 237
Accursio, Mainardo, 222
Aimeric de Belenoi, 111
Alamanni, Luigi, 298, 299, 309
Alberti, Antonio degli, 237
Albizzi, Franceschino degli, 237, 272, 276
Albornoz, Cardinal, 172, 173, 175
Alexander, W., 320
Ambrose, St., 208
Ancona, A. d', 7 n.
Andrea, Giovanni d', 12, 13
Andrea of Hungary, 222, 223
Anglico (Cardinal de Grimouard), 241
Anguillara, Orso, Conte dell', 42, 43, 67
Annibaldi, Paolo, 90 n.
Appel, Carl, 272, 273 n., 274
Appenninigena, Donato, 209, 215, 235, 236
Aquila, Serafino dell', 299, 302
Aquinas, St. Thomas, 208
Arnaut de Marneil, 112
Aristotle, 60, 208, 210, 288, 332
Atticus, 58
Augustine, St., 60, 149, 150, 151, 203, 208, 210, 286
Augustine, St., *Confessions*, 31, 34, 40, 41, 149, 227, 237, 242
Averroes, 208, 209

## B

BADOARA, Fra Bonaventura, 236, 242
Badoara, Fra Bonsembiante, 237
Bagnolo, Guido da, 209
Bambagia, Tommaso, 243
Barbato da Solmona, Marco, 79, 85, 100, 184, 196, 197, 218, 223, 225
Bardi, Roberto de', 30, 66
Barlaam, 60, 61, 62
Barrili, Giovanni, 67, 79, 223
Beatrice, 10, 20, 153, 163, 249, 275, 280, 291, 317, 332
Beccadelli, Ludovico, Cardinal, 126, 272
Bembo, Pietro, Cardinal, 125, 139, 162, 298
Bene, Sennuccio del, 68 n., 237, 238, 276

Benedict XI., 5 n.
Benedict XII., 35, 76, 97, 238
Bernard de Ventadour, 122
Bertram d'Allamanon, 119
Boccaccio, Giovanni, 2, 11, 54, 61, 62, 99, 101, 163, 168, 169, 181, 183, 187, 197, 206, 208, 226, 227, 231, 234, 242, 243, 246, 277, 294, 295, 316
Bocheta, Giovanni da, 233
Bontems, 162
Bosone, Raffaelli, 90 n.
Bouillon, Godfrey de, 287
Bracciolini, Poggio, 297
Brossano, Francesco da, 179, 227, 233, 243
Browning, Robert, 15, 114, 191, 304, 325
Bruni, Francesco, 184, 216, 225, 237
Bruni, Lionardo, 2 n., 297
Burckhardt, J., 68 n.
Bury, Richard de, 24
Bussolari, Fra Giacomo, 180

## C

CABASSOLE, Philippe de, 55, 196, 200, 201, 222, 223
Cæsar, Julius, 31, 77, 79, 193, 287
Caloria, Tommaso di, 74
Campinia, Lodovico di (Socrates), 10, 22, 76, 159, 160, 169, 183, 200, 217-222, 225, 272
Canigiani, Eletta, 1, 13 n., 14
Capra, Enrico, 182
Carducci, G., 89 n., 126
Carrara, Francesco da, 96, 102, 193, 194, 241-243
Carrara, Giacomo da, 95, 102, 239
Caro, Annibale, 298
Casa, Giovanni della, 298
Casini, Francesco, 201, 236
Castiglionchio, Lapo da, 225
Catherine of Siena, St., 99, 236, 287, 291
Catullus, 59, 280
Cecco d'Ascoli, 12
Celestine, Pope, 201
Celsus, Julius, 193
Cesareo, G. A., 126, 132
Charles IV., 96, 103, 175, 176, 182, 192, 329
Charles VIII., 309

345

Chaucer, Geoffrey, 151, 231, 293-296, 298, 302, 310
Ciani, Gioacchino, 231
Cicero, 6, 7, 9, 14, 18, 35, 48, 58, 77, 102, 103, 179, 208, 211, 212, 227, 234, 333
Cino, *see* Sinibuldi
Clémence, Queen, 65
Clement VI., 76, 77, 97, 98, 103, 106, 159, 206, 238
Cochin, H., 127, 159, 248
Colonna, Agapito, 23
Colonna, Agnese, 42, 43
Colonna, Giacomo, Bishop of Lombez, 18, 19, 21, 33, 34, 35, 42, 43, 67 *n.*, 74, 199
Colonna, Giovanni, Cardinal, 5, 21, 23, 31, 33, 43, 44, 50 *n.*, 53, 56, 65, 66, 71, 76, 78, 79, 81, 94, 199, 222, 272, 284, 287
Colonna, House of, 19, 23, 34, 92, 93, 217
Colonna, Stefano, 21, 42, 79, 89 *n.*, 93
Colonna, Stefano (the younger), 89 *n.*
Contarini, Zaccaria, 209
Convenevole, 4-7, 65, 277, 278
Convertino, *see* Giovanni da Ravenna
Coreggio, Azzo da, 35, 36, 46, 70-73, 75, 81, 82, 94, 103, 178, 204
Correggio, Guido da, 35
Cristiano, Luca, 222, 239

D

Dandolo, Andrea, 102, 174
Dandolo, Leonardo, 209
Dante, 1, 2, 10, 20, 28, 49, 92, 110-112, 123, 139, 183, 195, 201, 226-229, 247, 270, 274, 276, 280, 282, 291, 294, 327, 328, 330, 331
Dante, Jacopo di, 275
Daniel, Arnaut, 110, 111, 112, 113, 122, 123, 280
Daniello, 315, 320
Daniello, Bernardino, 272
Deguileville, G. de, 296
Dionisio da Borgo San Sepolcro, 31, 36, 62-65, 75
Doni, A. F., 11
Drayton, Michael, 315, 320
Drummond, William, of Hawthornden, 319-321
Du Bellay, J., 162 *n.*, 310

E

Eletta (Petrarca's grand-daughter), 234, 235
Erasmus, 211, 333

Ermengarde, Countess of Narbonne, 113, 119
Este, Obizzo d', 81

F

Fiammetta, 235 *n.*, 247
Ficino, Marsilio, 297
Fitzgerald, Elizabeth, 305
Folquet, 111, 113, 114
Forli, Raniero da, 12
Francis of Assisi, St., 202
Francis I., 309
Francesco (Petrarca's grandson), 235

G

Gardner, E. G., 236 *n.*, 271 *n.*
Gascoigne, George, 303, 310, 311
Gherardo (Petrarca's brother), 2, 9, 14; ascends Mont Ventoux, 37-41; visits Ste. Baume and Montrieu, 56; is called *Monicus*, 56, 169; becomes a Carthusian monk, 147; letters of Petrarca about him, 147, 148; his heroic conduct during the plague, 147; letter to him from Petrarca, 164, 165; visited by Petrarca, 203
Giotto, 205 *n.*, 243, 282
Giraut de Borneil, 111
Giovanna, Queen of Naples, 78, 222
Giovanni (Petrarca's son), 45, 46, 94, 106, 178, 179, 221
Giovanni da Firenze, 16-18
Giovanni da Ravenna, 214
Gonzago, Luigi, 70
Gualterazzi, Carlo, 126
Guillem de Cabestaing, 115

H

Hallam, Arthur, 122
Harvey, Gabriel, 316
Hauvette, H., 227 *n.*
Henry VII., 2, 328, 329
Homer, 25, 61, 185-187, 212, 227
Horace, 5, 26, 59, 212
Humphrey, Duke of Gloucester, 298

I

Innocent VI., 106, 172, 183, 184
Isabella (daughter of King John of France), 181
Isaure, Clémence, 118

# INDEX

## J

JEROME, St., 185, 186, 208
John of the Cross, St., 28
John XXII., 35
John, King of France, 181
Jonson, Ben, 320

## L

LACTANTIUS, 275
Lælius, *see* Stefano
Latham, R. G., 295 *n.*
Laura, first seen by Petrarca, 19; wife of Hugues de Sade, 19 *n.*, 119, 120, 161, 162; her death, 94, 159-161; alleged discovery of her tomb, 162; her place in Petrarca's life, 151-158; Laura in the *Canzoniere* (first part), 129-146; in the *Secretum*, 152, 153; in the *Africa*, 192; in the Eclogues, 199; in the *Canzoniere* (second part), 249-263; in the *Trionfi*, 270-292; in Boccaccio's sonnet, 247, 248; her portraits, 139; compared with Beatrice, 20, 153, 163, 249, 275, 291; Laura and *Laurea*, 42, 65, 153, 199
Lionel, Duke of Clarence, 241
Livy, 18, 37, 77, 194, 195, 208, 211, 212
Lollius, 294, 295
Lo Parco, F., 13 *n.*, 278 *n.*
Lorenzetti, 285 *n.*
Louis, King of Hungary, 223
Louis XII., 309
Lounsbury, J. R., 294, 295
Lucretius, 26

## M

MAIANO, Dante da, 124
Malatesta, Carlo, 214
Malatesta, Pandolfo, 124, 182
Malpaghini, *see* Giovanni da Ravenna
Mandello, Giovanni di, 205
Mannelli, Girolamo, 162
Marot, Clément, 310, 315, 316
Marsili, Luigi, 34, 237, 297
Marsuppini, Carlo, 297
Martini, Simone, 138, 139
Mary Magdalen, St., 56, 201
Mestica, G., 126, 248, 273 *n.*, 274
Milton, John, 321, 322
Molza, F., 298
Monaldesco, 67
Monet, Raimond, 51, 57, 58, 107
Monicus, 56, 169
Mussato, 65

## N

NELLI, Francesco (Simonides), 105, 168, 169, 173, 179, 183, 184, 217, 225, 233 *n.*
Niccoli, Niccolò, 297
Niccolò da Prato, 5 *n.*
Nolhac, P. de, 7 *n.*, 233
Noodt, John van der, 315

## O

OLIMPIO, *see* Accursio
Orsini, House of, 34, 43, 93
Orsini, Fulvio, 125
Ovid, 59, 224

## P

PALGRAVE, F. T., 308
Parker, Henry, Baron Morley, 308
Pastrengo, Guglielmo di, 183
Pattison, Mark, 321
Peire d'Alvernhe, 111
Pellegrini, Flamini, 272
Petrarca, Francesco, his birth at Arezzo, 1; taken to Incisa and Pisa, 2; moved to Avignon, 3; goes to school at Carpentras, 4; his master Convenevole, 4-7, 65, 277, 278; loss of his books, 6; his love of Cicero, 7, 9, 35, 48, 58, 86, 102, 103, 211, 333; of Virgil, 9, 48, 107, 208, 211, 226, 333; expedition to the Sorgue, 8; goes to Montpellier, 9; is deprived of his books, 9; goes to Bologna, 10; his masters, 10-13; death of his parents, 13; epitaph on his mother, 13, 14; state of his affairs, 14; his personal appearance, 15; taste for study, 15; friendship with Giovanni da Firenze, 16-18; with Raimondo Soranzio, 18; with Giacomo Colonna, 19; goes to Lombez, 21; friendship with Socrates and Lælius, 22; enters the service of Cardinal Colonna, 23; meets Richard de Bury, 24; his love of nature, 29; his first travels, 30-33; friendship with Padre Dionisio, 31; obtains canonry of Lombez, 35; other benefices held by him, 238; pleads Azzo's cause, 36; ascends Mont Ventoux, 36-41; his love of St. Augustine, 31, 34, 40, 41, 60, 149, 227, 237, 242; his Italian journey, 42-45; birth of his son, 45; life at Vaucluse, 47-58; visits Ste. Baume, 56; his library, 59; begins

to learn Greek, 61; receives a Homer, 61; his desire for the laurel, 63, 64; offers of the laurel, 65; goes to Naples, 66; his examination by King Robert, 67; coronation in Rome, 67-69; goes to Parma, 70; receives the blind man of Pontremoli, 71, 72; vision of Giacomo Colonna, 74; returns to Avignon, 76; addresses letter to Clement VI., 76; obtains request touching the Jubilee, 77; friendship with Rienzi, 77-78; letter to him, 87-89; letters about him, 103-105; sent to Naples, 78-81; returns to Parma, 82; flies from Parma, 85; Papal secretaryship offered to him, 86, 106, 183; his attitude to the great Roman Houses, 92, 93, 103; parts from Cardinal Colonna, 93; his wanderings, 94, 95; his son, Giovanni, 94, 106, 178, 179, 183, 221; death of Cardinal Colonna, 94; friendship with Giacomo da Carrara, 95, 96; letters to Charles IV., 96, 106, 175, 182; goes to Florence, 99; sees Boccaccio, 54, 99-101, 183, 184-186; friendship with Boccaccio, 226, 227; letter to him about his residence at Milan, 169, 170; about renouncing study, 231, 232; legacy to him, 243; goes to Rome for the Jubilee, 99-101; invited to return to Florence, 101; letter to Andrea Dandolo, 102, 174; writes epitaph for Giacomo da Carrara, 102; travels, and returns to Avignon, 102, 103; accused of being a magician, 106, 107; goes to Cavaillon, 107; death of his steward, 107; leaves Vaucluse, 108; letters about his vernacular poems, 124; letters about Gherardo, 147, 148; hears of Gherardo's heroism, 148; gives Gherardo St. Augustine's *Confessions*, 149; his conversion, 154, 163; letter to Gherardo, 163-165; sojourn in Milan, 166-184; answers his friends' remonstrances, 169, 171; receives Cardinal Albornoz, 172, 173; letters to the Doges of Venice and Genoa, 173, 174; is godfather to Bernabò's son, 174; harangues the people and is interrupted, 175; goes to Charles IV. at Mantua, 176; is created Count Palatine, 177; his residences in Milan, 177, 178; his daughter Francesca, 154 *n*., 179, 234, 244; his illness, 179; writes to Fra G. Bussolari, 180; goes to Pavia, 181; sent to King John of France, 181; receives golden cup from Charles IV., 182; visitors in Milan, 182, 183; the plague induces him to move to Venice, 184; has translation of Homer made, 185-187; letters to Urban V., 187-190; starts for Rome and falls ill at Ferrara, 189; his mistrust of doctors, 202, 206-208, 236; controversy with the Averroists, 208, 209; with the Cistercian monks, 210; his imaginary letters, 211-213; his copyists, 214-216; his obligations to his friends, 217, 218; dedicates his prose letters to Socrates, and his metrical ones to Barbato, 218; reconciles Lælius and Socrates, 219-220; his various friendships, 221-227; reads the *Decameron*, 230; wishes to leave his library to Venice, 232, 233; his breviary, 233 *n*.; his grandchildren, 235; links with St. Catherine of Siena, 35, 236, 237, 287; his poet friends, 237, 238; change in his studies, 238; repeated reports of his death, 239; the Euganean hills, 239, 240; assists at fête in Venice, 240, 241; goes to Pavia to treat with Cardinal Anglico, 241; goes to Bologna for requiem for Urban V., 241; moves into Padua, 241; mission to Venice, 241; dies and is buried at Arquà, 242; his will, 243 *n*.; his possible meeting with Chaucer, 294, 295; pioneer of classicism, 297; influence in Italy, France, and England, 298-323; Petrarca a pioneer, 324; "the first modern man," 324, 334; his character and taste, 325-327; scholar, humanist, and poet, 334

Petrarca and Dante, 20, 49, 92, 123, 183, 195, 201, 226-229, 270, 274, 275, 327-332

Petrarca and Laura, he first sees her, 19; Laura not *Laurea*, 42; he will win the laurel for her, 64, 65; her death, 94, 159-161 *n*.; Laura in his works, *see* Laura

Petrarca's works, his early vernacular poems, 15, 21, 23, 124, 228; *Epist. ad Post.*, 10, 15, 19, 23, 42, 56, 60, 66, 67, 73, 95, 190, 213, 214; *Epistolæ de Rebus Familiaribus et Variæ*, 218, *passim*; *Rerum Senilium*, 184, *passim*; *Epistolæ sine titulo*, 98, 105, 330; the *Africa*, 59, 60, 66, 73, 191, 192, 195-198, 246; *Epist. metr.*, 50, 53, 77, 97, 199, 200; *Eclogæ*, 93, 98, 198, 199; the *De Vita Solitaria*, 56, 59, 200-203, 236; the *De Otio Religiosorum*, 59, 200, 201, 203; the *De Viris Illustribus*, 58, 59, 176, 178,

#  INDEX 349

192-194; the *Compendium* and the *De Rebus Memorandis*, 193-195; the *Secretum*, 147-154; the *Psalmi Pœnitentiales*, 203; the *De Remediis Fortunæ*, 82, 178, 204; the *De Vera Sapientia*, 205; the *Itinerarium Syriacum*, 205; the *Invectivæ contra Medicum*, 206; the *De sui ipsius et multorum Ignorantia*, 209, 210; the *Apologia contra Gallum*, 210, 211; the political Canzoni, 75, 82-84, 89-91; the *Canzoniere* (first part), 109-146; the *Canzoniere* (second part), 155-160, 248-268; the *Trionfi*, 272-292
Petracco, 1, 13
Petroni, Pietro, 231
Phanette de Romanin, 119, 120
Piccarda, 282
Pilatus, Leonzio, 61, 185, 186
Plato, 60, 210, 288, 332, 333
Poliziano, 211
Pontremoli, blind man of, 71, 72
Propertius, 59
Puttenham, 299

Q

Quintilian, 112
Quirino, Girolamo, 125

R

Raleigh, Sir Walter, 317 *n*.
Ravenna, copyist of, 214-216
Renan, E., 208
Rienzo, Cola di, 76, 77, 86-89, 92, 103-105, 106, 167, 172, 175, 192, 199, 327
Robert, King of Naples, 4, 61 *n*., 62, 63, 66, 67, 70, 72, 78, 99, 195, 226, 242, 272
Rogier, Peire, 113
Ronsard, 118, 310, 311, 313
Rostand, 115 *n*.
Rossetti, Christina, 162, 322
Rossetti, Dante Gabriel, 322
Rossetti, Domenico, 194
Rossi, Marsilio, 36
Rossi, Orlando, 35
Rudel, Jaufré, 111, 114

S

Sacramore, 203, 225
Sade, Abbé de, 10, 12, 19 *n*., 139, 154 *n*.
Sade, Hugues de, 19 *n*., 161
Sallust, 208
Salutati, Coluccio, 214, 233, 237, 297

Salvo-Cozzo, G., 126
Samson, Pons, 56
Sannazaro, J., 298, 316
St. Cyr, Hugues de, 115
Saint Gelais, Melin de, 309
San Severino, Ugo da, 216
Santa Sofia, Daniello da, 125
SS. Apostoli, Francesco de', 51
Savonarola, 180
Scala, Martino della, 35
Scipio, Africanus, 22, 59, 60, 79, 195, 281, 282
Selvaggia (Petrarca's sister), 2
Selvaggia, 280
Seneca, 77, 111, 333
Sennuccio del Bene, 68 *n*., 237, 238, 247, 272, 276
Serico, Lombardo da, 125, 193, 225, 233
Settimo, Guido, 3, 8, 9, 10, 54, 173, 174, 177, 178, 179, 221, 277
Sève, Maurice de, 162 *n*., 315
Shakespeare, 305, 318, 319, 321
Shelley, P. B., 28, 50 *n*., 245 *n*., 323
Sidney, Sir Philip, 311, 313, 320
Sigero, Niccolò, 61, 185
Silius Italicus, 197 *n*.
Silvanus, 56, 168, 244
Simonides, *see* Nelli
Sinibuldi, Cino de', 10-12, 247, 276, 280
Skeat, 297
Skelton, 297
Socrates, *see* Campinia, Lodovico di
Soranzio, Raimondo, 7 *n*., 18
Sordello, 111
Spenser, Edmund, 311, 315, 316, 317, 318
Stampa, Gaspara, 298
Stefano, Lelio di (Lælius), 22, 76, 166, 176, 184, 217, 219, 220, 225, 272
Stella, 313
Strada, Zanobi da, 225
Strozzi, Palla, 297
Surrey, Henry, Earl of, 297, 298, 299, 305-310, 313
Swinburne, A. C., 110, 114
Sylvester, Pope, 43
Symonds, J. A., 49

T

Talenti, Tommaso, 209
Talleyrand, Cardinal, 184
Tano, Giovanni di, 2
Terence, 186
Thyard, Pontus de, 310
Tournes, Jean de, 162 *n*.
Tullia, 234, 244

## U

UBALDINI, 272
Urban V., 184, 187-190, 210, 213, 216, 223, 239, 241

## V

VALERIUS MAXIMUS, 194
Varro, 18, 227
Vaughan, Henry, 289, 290
Vellutello, 89
Vere, Aubrey de, 317
Verme, Luchino dal, 181, 240
Vidal, Arnaut, 117
Vidal, Peire, 112
Villani, G., 1
Villafranca, Rinaldo da, 94
Violante, 235 *n.*
Virgil, 9, 26, 33, 43, 48, 59, 67, 107, 208, 211, 215, 226, 280, 333
Virgil, fly-leaf of Petrarca's, 46, 160, 161 *n.*, 221, 222

Visconti, House of, 82, 175, 177
Visconti, Bernabò, 174, 176
Visconti, Galeazzo, 173, 174, 176, 180, 181, 241
Visconti, Giovan Galeazzo, 181
Visconti, Giovanni, Archbishop of Milan, 170, 172-174, 177
Visconti, Luchino, 70, 94
Visconti, Matteo, 174, 175
Visconti, Violante, 241
Vito, Giovanni di San, 21, 44

## W

WATSON, Thomas, 311, 312, 313
Wyatt, Sir Thomas, 299 - 305, 306, 307, 310

## Z

ZUMBINI, B., 29, 329 *n.*